Technical Editing

Technical Editing
The Practical Guide for Editors and Writers

Judith A. Tarutz

PERSEUS BOOKS
Reading, Massachusetts

Many of the designations used by manufacturers and sellers to distinguish their products are claimed as trademarks. Where those designations appear in this book and Perseus Books was aware of a trademark claim, the designations have been printed in initial capital letters.

UNIX is a registered trademark of UNIX System Laboratories, Inc.

Library of Congress Cataloging-in-Publication Data

Tarutz, Judith A.
    Technical editing : a practical guide for editors and writers/
    Judith A. Tarutz.
       p.   cm. — (Hewlett-Packard Press)
    Includes bibliographical references and index.
    ISBN 0-201-56356-8
    1. Technical editing. 2. Technical writing.
I. Title. II. Series: Hewlett-Packard Press series.
T11.4.T37   1992   92-11644
808'.0666—dc20   CIP

Perseus Books is a member of the Perseus Books Group

9 10 11 12 13 14 15–CRW–0201009998
Ninth printing, July 1998

Find us on the World Wide Web at
http://www.aw.com/gb/

Perseus Books are available at special discounts for bulk purchases in the U.S. by corporations, institutions, and other organizations. For more information, please contact the Special Markets Department at HarperCollins Publishers, 10 East 53rd Street, New York, NY 10022, or call 212-207-7528.

To David

Contents

Part 1. The Editor's Role

Part 2. The Editor's Job

Part 3. The Editor's Career

Chapter 16. Is Editing Becoming Obsolete?   **363**

Appendix A. Case Studies   **369**

Appendix B. Sample Style Guides   **393**

Appendix C. Answers to Exercises   **407**

Glossary   **411**

Bibliography   **431**

Index   **437**

List of Figures

List of Tables

Preface

This book reveals the secrets of technical editing. It shows you the way technical editors *really* work, the shortcuts we take, and the tricks we use to get the job done well and on time. This book is for technical editors, people thinking of becoming editors, technical writers who occasionally edit others' works as well as their own, publications managers, and students of technical communication.

This is *not* another boring book about grammar and spelling. It looks at editing as a job that involves more than reading and marking up manuscripts. This book looks at the tough, day-to-day editorial problems and gives you strategies for solving them. By reading this book, you'll learn how to

- Add value to the product

- Apply editorial principles under absurdly tight deadlines and conditions of constant change

- Develop skills and perspectives that will get you an editing job in the future—when software does the copy editing

- Help technical writers solve knotty problems, such as organizing information so customers can find answers to their questions

- Work with writers, managers, production people, and engineers

- Edit publications for an international audience

- Work with the reluctant writer, the engineer or scientist who has to publish an occasional paper or book

- Make the transition from traditional publishing to a desktop publishing environment

- Make style guidelines—and break them to avoid technical ambiguity

- Make a difference even if you have only an hour to edit a book
- Escape the copy editing dungeon and use editing as a growth path to a management-level job

If you're a writer, this book will help you if you're called on to pinch-hit as an editor or perform peer edits. It will certainly help you edit your own work. You will find that this book tells you things most writers don't have the opportunity to learn but most editors eventually do. This book will also give you insight into an editor's perspective, so you can work with editors to your own best advantage.

If you're a publications manager, this book will help you recognize and hire top-notch editors, train new editors, and understand the editorial function so you can evaluate editors fairly and use them well.

If you're an editor, then you probably already recognize that this book discusses topics no other book has broached. This book will show you how to improve your skills. I hope it will also show you some creative directions in which you can take your career.

My intent is to give you guidelines and strategies for making editing work where you work. I am not going to discuss copy editing rules, such as when to put periods inside parentheses or whether to spell it *online* or *on-line,* but I'll recommend some books whose authors will spell them out for you. I won't tell you how to write, but I will tell you how to decide when a developmental edit is appropriate. I won't give you style rules that duplicate the canonical style guides, but I will tell you how to write a house style guide that writers will want to use.

The computer industry employs half of all technical publications professionals so I've provided many computer examples. You don't need to know a lot about computers to understand the examples. I also provide many noncomputer examples.[1]

This book concentrates on how to edit manuals, but most of the information also applies to other publications, including data sheets (spec sheets), technical reports, and proposals. Where there are differences, such as editing online material, I state so explicitly.

---

[1] Most examples of errors appeared in real publications or manuscripts; product and company names have been changed to avoid embarrassing the perpetrators. I do, however, identify the sources of errors that appeared in national magazines and major city newspapers.

Some words you won't find in this book are *rhetoric, abstraction, theory,* and *methodology.* There are many excellent books on the theoretical basis of editing and writing.

This book takes a pragmatic approach. It tells how to do a good job and still meet deadlines. It also gives you some handy tools:

- Checklists for each type of editorial review you might perform

- Tips and tricks you can use every day to solve problems quickly

- Case studies that analyze problems you might have working with writers and managing projects

- A list of the 100 most common errors you'll find in a manuscript

How to Use This Book

Read chapters 1–5 to learn about the editor's role as a member of the product team. Chapters 6–12 cover the details about how to do the editor's job. Chapters 13–16 look at the editor's career. Skip around and read the topics that appeal to you. The only must-read chapter for everyone is chapter 2, "The Twelve Basic Rules." Every idea, tip, and nugget of advice in this book builds on the philosophy of technical editing described in that chapter.

If you're an editor—or an aspiring editor—you'll want to read the entire book. Begin with Part 1, "The Editor's Role" so you see the big picture. The chapters you'll be using day in and day out are 6, 7, 8, 9, and 11 (also chapter 12 if you work in the computer industry), which cover the nitty gritty of editing. Read the other chapters in the order they interest you or when you need them. For example, read chapter 10 when you're asked to write a style guide. If you edit more than one project at a time, or have any kind of project management responsibility, read chapter 14.

If you're a writer and you edit your own work, read chapters 6, 7, 8, and 11 (if you work in the computer industry, include chapter 12). If you do peer edits, also read chapters 3 and 5. You may find chapters 4, 9, and 13 interesting because they'll show you publishing from a point of view that may be new to you.

If you're a manager, you'll be most interested in chapter 4 (how to convince your boss you need an editor) and chapter 15 (how to hire and manage editors). You may also want to skim chapters 1–3 to ensure that you understand what editors really do. Once you do you can defend your decision to hire them and you will know what to expect from the editors you manage. Chapter 16 can help you plan your department's future.

Three appendixes cover case studies, examples of style guides, and the answers to the exercises that are scattered throughout the book. A hint for doing the exercises: They don't necessarily relate to the context where they appear. When you edit, you have to be prepared to encounter any type of error on every page.

The glossary includes publishing terms and computer jargon used in this book. The bibliography recommends good books about technical writing, editing topics not covered here, and other subjects of interest to technical publishing professionals.

Acknowledgments

Many thanks . . .

To Kathy Ford, who designed the pages, developed Interleaf templates for me to use, fixed my ugly drawings, and created many new illustrations. I'm awed by how often she'd create just the right graphic from my vague verbal description, on the first try. Kathy's wonderful sense of humor also made it a pleasure to work with her on this book.

To Marilyn Kotwal, who edited my manuscript for content and technical accuracy. They say a lawyer who represents herself has a fool for a lawyer. Well, I say an editor who edits her own book has a fool for an editor—especially when Marilyn is available. Marilyn is a wonderful editor—an excellent writer, too—and I'm grateful for her sharp mind, good ear, and keen eye.

To Jonathan Price, whose comments on my manuscripts were intelligent, sensible, and witty. Several of his comments were so worthy of publication that I simply stole his wording.

To Barry Rosenberg, a superb writer, a great teacher, and a very funny guy, who gave me constructive feedback on style and content, and—in retribution for my edits on *his* book, *The KornShell Programming Tutorial*—advice on which jokes to delete.

To John Bowie, a Learning Products manager at Hewlett-Packard, who suggested ways to make this book appeal to writers who do peer edits and self-edits.

To Mary Ann Telatnik, who gave me useful suggestions from the perspective of an experienced editor whose background differs from mine.

To the writers and editors who reviewed the drafts and helped keep me honest: Steve Bertrand, Jean Ort, Betsy Perry, Paul Tucker, Mimi Wellington, and Steve Williams. A bonus to having professional writers and editors as reviewers was that their comments were so well-written I could just pop them in the text.

To the future editors and writers who reviewed the draft, especially my students in the Software Technical Writing Program at Middlesex Community College. To Charlie Matthews at the Hewlett-Packard library (Chelmsford) and to the librarians at the Acton (Massachusetts) Memorial Library for their help with the research. To the editors and writers who contributed to the *Apollo Style Guide,* from which I borrowed some material.

To the people at Addison-Wesley and the HP Press: Editor-in-Chief John Wait, Alan Apt, and the ever-patient Simone Payment, who coordinated its production. To Bob Silvey, for supporting this book as an HP Press title and for reviewing the first draft. Special thanks to Pat Pekary, Director of the HP Press, for her help and support.

To my managers in the Apollo Technical Publishing department, Joe Jaynes and Andrea Morris, who enthusiastically supported me at the start of this book. To Lisa Zahn and Ken Heun, who supported my efforts to finish it.

To my friends and family who had the decency to feign understanding when I spent my weekends, evenings, and vacations at my Apollo workstation with this manuscript instead of with them.

Especially to my husband, David Wolff, who read this manuscript so many times that I may have violated the Geneva convention. David is the one who suffered through months of, "How does this phrase sound? Does it work better this way? Is this funny or just plain stupid?" For a software engineer, he's also a good editor. But his biggest contribution was his moral support.

My thanks to all these folks and to anybody else I may have forgotten. And, of course, they're not responsible for any errors in this book.

Challenge to the Reader

If you've worked in publishing for more than a day, you know about those gremlins that crawl between the pages of manuscripts and plant the seeds of errors that don't sprout until the book appears in print. When you find those errors . . . think of them as exercises for the alert reader.

Let me know what errors—technical, editorial, or typographical—you find in this book. If you're the first person to report the error, I'll acknowledge you in the next edition.

Send your catches and comments to:

Judith Tarutz
c/o Editor-in-Chief, Corporate and Professional Publishing
Addison-Wesley Publishing Company
One Jacob Way
Reading MA 01867
U.S.A.

Part 1
The Editor's Role

Chapter 1
What Is Technical Editing?

In this chapter, you'll see technical editing from several perspectives. It's important to understand that technical editing isn't limited to any one or two topics in this chapter. Technical editing is *everything* in this chapter.

First, I'm going to dissect the term *technical editing* and show you its guts.[1] Just as you might not take kindly to being viewed as a bunch of organs, tissues, and muscles, try not to restrict your view of technical editing to any one of the perspectives in this chapter. In this chapter I pull apart the job of editing; I cover the tasks of editing in later chapters. By the time you finish reading this book you'll have the whole picture of technical editing.

This chapter defines technical editing—both its *technical* and *editing* aspects. It compares and contrasts the technical editor with other editors and with technical writers. This chapter also looks at how "technical" a technical editor needs to be.

A Working Definition

Let's set a working—perhaps imperfect—definition, just so we stand on some common ground.

I plan to use *technical editing* in the most inclusive sense. I want this book to be useful to technical specialists who occasionally edit, editors who occasionally handle technical material, writers who edit their own manuscripts, writers who do peer edits, managers who review writers' manuscripts, students of technical communication, and, of course, the people whose business cards read "Technical Editor."

---

[1] If you come across a term in this book you don't know, see the glossary.

By *technical* I mean any specialized subject that addresses a specific audience, has its own jargon, and whose approach is objective.[1] The computer, electronics, aerospace, and other engineering industries hire most technical editors, so these come to mind first. I also include editing for the research, scientific, and medical communities. Much of the material in this book applies as well to editing publications for a wide range of consumer, industrial, and agricultural products. The principles are the same; you may need to tweak some details here and there as you apply them to other fields.

Editing is a craft. Practicing a craft means recognizing and transcending its constraints. For example, the potter is constrained by the physical limitations of the clay. An editor's constraints are

- Audience needs
- Purpose of document
- English language rules and conventions
- Technical considerations (for technical works)
- Formatting considerations
- Time
- Budget
- House style
- Publishing practices
- Need for consistency within a set of documents

Imagination allows the potter to stretch the limitations of—to mold—the clay. Creativity lets the editor work within constraints yet solve each problem uniquely. As no two potters fashion the same bowl, no two writers write the same book. And no two editors edit a manuscript the same way.

Editing involves these activities:

- Reading critically and objectively
- Reading from the audience's point of view
- Questioning what you read and reacting to it
- Verifying, checking, and testing
- Evaluating usability (whether the product's design and documentation make it easy to learn to use the product)
- Judging appropriateness for intended use and audience

---

[1] This book is *subjective,* drawing on the author's experiences and reflecting her opinions. It is not *technical writing.*

You are editing if you are performing these activities, though your job title might be technical specialist, writer, manager, consultant, usability expert, or something else. What do editors do? They create, plan, edit, design, proof, organize, evaluate, test, check, verify, decide, judge, discuss, teach, explain, negotiate, meet, read, question, react, and critique. (Or, as I tell my hairdresser, "I tell writers when they didn't say what they meant to say and didn't tell me what I needed to know.")

Some editors reading this book may be thinking, "Is she saying that these other people, with no training in editing, are editors?" Think of the distinction between editing and being an editor as analogous to playing tennis and being a professional tennis player. The difference isn't in the activity alone but in the skill of its execution.

Other professionals may edit from time to time, but the editor is the skilled professional who does it all the time and so has a more trained eye.

When Is an Editor Not an Editor?

The word *editing* means different things to different people. This section describes the different job titles the world attaches to editors to show you that the title itself means little. I'm going to make some sweeping generalizations in the interest of covering a lot of material quickly. You can use these descriptions, however, to get a quick sense of the range of editorial jobs.

In the publishing world there have always been many different editorial functions performed by individuals, among them, proofreaders, copy editors, acquisitions editors, and managing editors. At one time an editor's full title told you what that person did and how he or she fit into the organization. Not so anymore. Institutions—primarily industry, government, and nonprofit organizations—formed their own in-house publishing departments and staffed them with people whose jobs, although related to editing, differed from the jobs in the publishing industry. They borrowed some job titles from publishing and modified the job descriptions or invented new titles. In some cases, human resource people unfamiliar with publishing assigned job titles based on what they misunderstood the job to be; in other cases, companies invented interesting titles to lure people into what were for the most part essentially boring jobs.

Among the titles you see these days are these: technical editor, writer/editor, copy editor, production editor, documentation editor, production manager, editorial assistant, communications editor, and editorial specialist. The job descriptions vary as widely as do the titles. As a result, if you're a job-hunting editor, you can't tell what kind of "editor" a company is seeking. Different companies use the same title to describe an $8-an-hour proofreader and a $40,000-a-year technical editor. If you're a hiring manager, you can't assume a particular skill set based solely on the job title "editor" on a resume.

The following are my definitions of the different job titles. These definitions are more or less conventional.

Proofreader

The proofreader compares typeset copy to the original manuscript and marks discrepancies. A skilled proofreader also queries possible mechanical errors (grammar, spelling, punctuation) for the writer and/or editor, who has the authority to approve these corrections. Proofreaders cannot make *any* changes to the manuscript without the editor's approval.

Technology is making this job obsolete in industries other than publishing, such as the computer industry. Many technical writers submit manuscripts to typesetting shops in electronic form, either on disk or via modem. This eliminates the step of reentering the text for the typesetting equipment and the subsequent step of comparing the two versions. Spelling checkers and file-comparison software also make literal proofreading something computers can do faster and more cheaply than people.

Production Editor

The emphasis in this job title is on *production,* not *editor.* The production editor expedites the production of camera-ready copy. This position usually has nothing to do with writing and little to do with editing—at most a production editor proofreads manuscripts and/or camera-ready copy.

Some production editors mark up manuscripts with format codes for typesetting. For electronically submitted manuscripts, they determine what additional formatting is needed and resolve technical incompatibilities and formatting glitches.

A title commonly confused with production *editor* is that of production *coordinator.* A production coordinator tracks and coordinates project schedules with the people who print and distribute the books.

Copy Editor

The copy editor marks a manuscript for errors in spelling, grammar, and punctuation; checks facts, cross-references, and other verifiable details; and ascertains that the manuscript conforms to house style. The copy editor also checks the flow of the writing and smooths style differences among coauthors. The copy editor is sometimes called a *line editor* because she or he performs line-by-line edits on the manuscript.

The copy editor implements guidelines set down by others (such as literary editors and managers), but rarely participates in creating these guidelines. The copy editor interacts with the author (sometimes through a literary editor) and the production editor. The copy editor has the authority to correct blatant errors in the manuscript but must have the approval of the literary editor and/or author for significant wording changes.

Copy editing requires high attention to detail and an ability to apply rules. A good copy editor must also be a creative problem solver, because different manuscripts present different challenges.

Literary Editor

The literary editor reads manuscripts from the point of view of the intended audience and suggests improved wording and reorganization of text through substantive and developmental edits. A literary editor may rewrite and reorganize material or may lead and instruct writers in the rewriting process. Although the literary editor may be authorized to change the manuscript without the writer's permission, he or she normally effects changes through negotiation. Depending on the size of the publishing house or company, this person may also perform the functions of a copy editor.

The literary editor works closely with writers (authors), sets editorial policy regarding house style, and supervises copy editors.

Developmental Editor

The developmental editor, as the title implies, helps individual writers and writing teams develop books and documentation sets. The developmental editor actively participates in the planning and organizing stages of writing and typically has a lot of creative opportunity, particularly in the textbook publishing trade. The developmental editor serves as the writer's mentor and consultant for writing and publishing issues. A developmental editor for technical documentation may also serve as a consultant on usability issues.

Technical Editor

In addition to doing everything the literary editor does, the technical editor edits manuscripts for technical consistency and accuracy, by querying inconsistencies and implausibilities. Like the literary editor, the technical editor edits manuscripts for literary style, but with the added constraint of not changing the technical meaning or connotation.

Other duties of the technical editor depend on the company and its products. Some common functions are testing examples and tutorials, coordinating usability tests, and ensuring documentation quality.

Depending on the company's size, the technical editor may perform the functions of both a literary editor and a copy editor, along with additional responsibilities. Some technical editors perform developmental editing. In fact, the career path for a technical editor may lead through production editor, copy editor, and literary editor to developmental editor. For example, a junior technical editing position may be the functional equivalent of a production editor or copy editor, whereas a senior technical editing position may be comparable to that of a literary editor, with the most senior position that of developmental editor.

The technical editor serves as a resource for writers, helping them with writing skills; interpreting corporate legal, marketing, and editorial policies; and serving as the first objective reader and last quality tester of the documentation before it reaches the customer. Technical editors are sometimes part of the corporate project team. Usually the technical editor also serves as the liaison between writers and production (graphic arts and printing) and ensures that the writing—from outline through printed publication—proceeds smoothly and on schedule and that the final product reflects what the writers (and managers) envisioned.

Help Wanted: Editors

The following examples illustrate the wide range of titles used to describe editors.

EXAMPLES

Developmental Editor, College Computer Science and Data Processing

Works with Managing and Acquisitions Editors and Authors in developing new and revised texts and supplements; commissions and interprets manuscript reviews; works with free-lance personnel. Some travel required. Bachelor's degree in Computer Science or related area, with a minimum 3 years' experience in production editing and/or developmental editing and direct experience in working with word processing, spreadsheets, and databases. Knowledge of programming and programming languages helpful.

Senior Writer/Editor, Computer Software Company

In our Publications Communications Group—write press releases as well as internal and external communications; write and edit announcements of new products, programs, and strategic direction. Requires 5–7 years' public relations writing experience and BA/BS in journalism or English. MS or MA desirable. Familiarity with high-tech industries a plus.

Chief Copy Editor, Computer Newspaper

In addition to establishing and maintaining editorial copy standards, you will supervise and train a staff of 8-10 copy editors. You will also take responsibility for overall quality control, and for ensuring efficient and timely editing, changes and copy fits. As the department manager, your duties will include overseeing the writing of captions and headlines, and resolving issues between writers and editors. A minimum of 3 years' editorial experience is required, including some management experience with an emphasis on newspaper-style copy editing and proofreading. A BA in English or Journalism is preferred.

Regulatory Editor, Biopharmaceutical Company

This position requires an individual with a strong science background and excellent editing skills, plus knowledge of Food & Drug Administration filing requirements.

Senior Editor, Textbook Publisher

Manage a software program through all phases of development to ensure the delivery of quality instructional or career-based informational software products. A minimum of 3 years of software development experience in combination with print-editing experience is required.

Some Peculiarities of Technical Editing

Technical editing differs from editing jobs in trade and academic publishing houses. In technical editing, the jobs of proofreader, copy editor, senior editor, production editor, and possibly managing editor are typically performed by one person. In publishing houses the business is publishing. Specialization is efficient and cost-effective. The business of government, industry, and research is not publishing. Generalization—fewer people wearing many different hats—is cost-effective.

Unlike senior editors at publishing houses, technical editors in industry don't choose what to publish; their products determine their publications.

A technical publication isn't an end unto itself; its job is to help readers do *their* jobs. Moreover, customers usually don't want to read the book; typically, they do so grudgingly. By contrast, readers read novels, biographies, and anthologies for the pleasure of reading itself.

Time-to-market pressure dominates technical publishing. In industry, there's never enough time but there's always another revision. You are always rushing one edition to print so you can start the next edition. (Few publishing experiences are as weird as working on two versions of the same book at one time.) Time-to-market pressure often means sacrificing quality for speed. Sometimes you have to ship even if the documentation is bad, because to not ship would be even worse.

Technical editing means coping with constant change. Technology changes all the time, with corresponding changes in language and style. This change encompasses more than the proliferation of new words. The issues themselves change. For example, the hottest trend in the computer industry today is the movement to standards. Standards affect how we organize our documentation sets, which manuals we write and which we buy from other sources, what information goes in the book, how we name different concepts, and whether we want our books to look like those in the mall bookstore.

Furthermore, the jargon and conventions of technology are sometimes incompatible with or different from the rules of English. How does an editor resolve conflicts? (I'm not going to answer that right now. Turn to chapter 9 if you can't stand the suspense.)

Technical editors typically edit a wide variety of publications and media, including information that appears on computer screens (called *online documentation* as opposed to paper, or *hardcopy documentation*). You may be called on to edit online help, online tutorials, user interfaces, videotapes, slide shows, speeches, and technical marketing brochures. You may even edit the instructions that appear in little windows on machines such as photocopiers and medical equipment.

Editing technical material is different from other editing. Most general fiction and nonfiction books use only a few structures (mostly paragraphs). Technical writing uses many, many structures—tables, illustrations, flowcharts, procedures, and a dozen styles of lists. Selecting and organizing these structures are challenges for the technical writer and editor.

Technical editors constantly strive to balance often-conflicting goals: respect for the English language vs. technical terminology, an appreciation for the art of publishing vs. insufficient time and funding to design attractive books, and the need for complete and accurate documentation vs. the requirement to have it available immediately (even while the product is still being changed).

Finally, the technical editor rarely just edits. Technical editors often have other responsibilities, such as training new writers and editors; reviewing documentation plans; serving as consultant to writers on writing, editorial, and production matters; and representing their department and company on various committees, such as those formed to create style guides or implement government regulations.

Exercise 1   Match the job title and job descriptions. (These descriptions are from actual resumes.)[1]

1. Helped assemble, write, and edit draft operations and maintenance manual for a storage system.

    a. Technical editor

2. Wrote, edited, produced: brochures, hardware and service manuals, help screens, white papers and research journal submissions, data sheets, articles, press releases, signage for trade shows.

    b. Technical editor

3. Edited marketing and MIS in-house newsletters and technical documentation.

    c. Technical editor

4. Responsible for editing several major software publications. Involved in document review, planning, scheduling, quality control, and preparing all manuals for production. Contributed to the development of departmental software editing procedures.

    d. Technical editor

5. Responsible for copyediting and production coordination of all hardware documentation. Edit documents for proper grammar, consistency, clarity, and accuracy, as well as for adherence to company format and style requirements. Interface with programmers and engineers to ensure technical accuracy.

    e. Technical editor

6. Responsible for quality control for a series of easy-to-read manuals, editing and updating illustrated parts breakdown manuals, and preparation and distribution of end-of-month reports.

    f. Technical editor

7. Responsible for reviewing, editing, and producing technical documentation, including concepts manuals, reference manuals, user guides, and workbooks. Position entails constant interface with technical writers, quality control people, documentation supervisors, artists, and composition room formatters.

    g. Technical editor

8. Editor and production coordinator for proposals, reports, and briefings.

    h. Technical editor

9. Worked closely with technical personnel. Compiled information for an FAA study of airline safety and worked on proposal for enhancing the computer system at a Navy shipyard.

    i. Technical editor

---

[1] Exercises are numbered consecutively throughout the book.
Answers to exercises are in appendix C.

Exercise 2   Match the job title and job descriptions. (These descriptions are from actual resumes.) Hint: Don't spend more than one minute on this exercise.

1.	Edit and rewrite manuals, brochures, and reports. Coordinate all phases of production.	a.	Senior software editor
2.	Perform substantive, copy, and production edits on all types of software and hardware documentation.	b.	Senior editor
3.	Prepared series of books for translation. Wrote, edited, formatted, and did the production.	c.	Senior technical editor
4.	Edited series of books. Assisted writers with indexing.	d.	Lead editor
5.	Wrote, edited, and proofread user and technical computer software manuals and online documentation.	e.	Senior editor
6.	Edited and proofread documents for grammar, punctuation, format, spelling, and print quality.	f.	Technical writer/editor
7.	Provided copyediting and substantive, technical editing, rewriting as required, and functioned as writer/editor on some projects.	g.	Proofreader

Technical Editing Contrasted to Technical Writing

Many people don't distinguish between technical writing and technical editing. In fact, many companies combine these two functions into a single job (*writer/editor*). Even people who have worked just as writers or just as editors don't appreciate the fine line between these jobs. If you're considering specializing in either technical writing or technical editing and would like to select the one better suited to your personality or skills, this section will give you some insight into the distinctions.

Technical writing and technical editing differ in skill sets, pace, and daily work routine, as shown in Table 1–1.

Table 1-1. Contrast Between Jobs of Technical Writer and Technical Editor

A writer . . .	An editor . . .
is an expert in the product	is an expert in the publishing process
has detailed product knowledge	has an overview of many products
is usually a specialist	is usually a generalist
works on one major project at a time	juggles many concurrent projects
works with technical professionals (engineers, scientists)	works with professional writers[1]
writes and creates	reads, reacts, responds, sometimes rewrites
makes revisions	suggests changes
works on a long project cycle	works on a short project cycle
has long periods of concentration	has many interruptions
has a narrow focus (on one book)	has a broad perspective (on a documentation set)

[1] Some technical editors (for example, those working for professional-book and textbook publishers) work with both professional writers and technical professionals.

Skills Common to Writers and Editors

People often ask if technical writing and technical editing are interchangeable jobs. They're not, although writers and editors certainly share several skills:

- Excellent writing skills

- Ability to grasp technical concepts *and* see the product from the user's point of view

- Concern for quality

- Ability to cope with deadline pressure

- Excellent interpersonal and communication skills

- Project management skills

- Expertise in using publishing tools

Skills (Usually) Specific to Writers

Some skills are more common among writers than editors:

- Interviewing skills (to get information from technical experts)
- Research and information-gathering skills
- Ability to sift through vast amounts of data and select what the readers really want or need to know
- Ability to cajole reviewers into reading drafts and giving useful comments—before it's too late

Skills (Usually) Specific to Editors

Some skills are more common among editors than writers:

- Time management skills (editors typically juggle several different projects at the same time)
- Good judgment and decision-making skills (editors field numerous questions needing immediate answers or decisions)
- Ability to weigh the importance of editorial changes when the writer's time is limited
- Good eye for page design and layout
- Attention to detail without losing sight of the big picture
- Ability to give constructive criticism diplomatically
- Ability to understand the writer's point of view when making editorial comments
- Ability to understand technical issues in several projects with limited time available for each
- Ability to deal with frequent interruptions
- Ability to refrain from imposing the editor's own style on someone else's creation
- Familiarity with book production (processes and costs)

Writers who have worked with both professional editors and peer editors have told me that these special skills and abilities are what set apart professional editors. Furthermore, writers say that peer editors don't approach the task with the same attitude as a professional editor. As one writer told me, "When you edit my book, I know that's your job and you will give it your full attention. When I have to do a peer edit, it's a secondary responsibility. My own book always has a higher priority."

People who don't work in technical publishing think that editors and English teachers are cut from the same cloth and perform similar jobs. The preceding list of skills demonstrates how an editor views a piece of writing differently from an English teacher. The editor doesn't count spelling errors and judge the writer accordingly; the editor is a reader, user advocate, and writing consultant.

Editor's vs. Writer's Perspective

An editor and a writer will view the same project differently. The writer views the project up close and the editor views it from a few steps back. The result is that the editor brings an objectivity to the task that the writer cannot.

The editor has a broader perspective than the writer. The editor faces certain questions, issues, and problems routinely that may be once-in-a-career items for the writer. (For this reason professional editors can usually solve problems faster than writers doing peer edits.)

Table 1–2 recaps the editor's role.

Table 1–2. Technical Editor: Fact vs. Fiction

An editor is . . .	An editor is not . . .
a first reader	a second writer
a user advocate	an English teacher
a consultant and advisor	a dictator
An editor does . . .	**An editor does not . . .**
make suggestions for improvements	demand changes for the sake of change
maintain the writer's style	alter the writer's style without good cause
advise where rewriting is needed	rewrite on a grand scale
suggest changes for specific, valid reasons	make arbitrary changes

Being an Editor: What's Good About It

There are many advantages to editing:

- Editors view publications from a wide perspective and work on many documents, many different kinds of publications, and many different subjects.

- Editors have lots of variety; an editor's projects change daily or weekly.

- Editors work with professional writers (usually).

- Editors have opportunities to teach.

- Editors are not very likely to be bored; an editor is off the project by the time it gets tedious.

- Editors provide general direction instead of rewriting (usually).

- Editors contribute to the overall quality of the product.

- Editors can expand their responsibilities as their skills develop; an editor's job is often what he or she makes of it.

- Editors can acquire good management skills and a more global perspective of a project.

Being an Editor: What's Bad About It

Editing also has some disadvantages:

- Editors rarely get a chance to be product experts because they have too many active projects.

- Editors are faced with short deadlines; there's never enough time.

- Editors have little chance to use their writing skills.

- Some writers are difficult to work with (believe it or not!).

- Editors are often blamed for what they missed rather than praised for what they contributed.

- Editors may be excluded from the project team or they may be on too many project teams.

- Editors must constantly shift gears and juggle schedules that aren't their own.

- The project is never theirs alone.

- Editors' contributions may be only as good as their ability to convince writers to accept their suggestions and the ability of the writers to implement them. Editors can put their hearts and souls into a book and the book can still turn out bad.

Specialist or Generalist?

There is a controversy among managers who hire editors over whether editors should be specialists in the field or generalists. (A comparable argument has raged for decades about technical writers.)

One view maintains that you can't edit what you don't understand, that you need to be an authority or expert on the subject. That's true, to some extent. But an experienced editor can perform a good copy edit and a decent developmental edit on technical material that exceeds her or his knowledge. As Lewis Carroll's *Jabberwocky* demonstrates, you can follow English syntax even if you don't know the words. An experienced editor can find technical inconsistencies without understanding the material and can sometimes find careless technical errors with only a rudimentary knowledge of the subject. You'll see examples throughout this book dealing with technical subjects you may not know, but you'll understand the editorial issues they demonstrate.

An editor who knows a good deal about the subject can do a better job finding technical errors and discrepancies than an editor who knows very little. Although you need not be an expert, you need to know more than the buzzwords. It's not enough to learn the subject "by osmosis" or by passively reading the manuscripts. You need to study the material—read, take courses, perform hands-on work in the field. For example, if you edit computer language manuals, you should be able to write a simple ten-line program that works. You don't have to be able to write a complete application, and you don't have to write elegant code. An experienced programmer may be able to write the same program in two lines that you wrote in ten, and that's fine. (After all, the programmer may also describe it in ten sentences, while you can do it in two.)

Another erroneous view maintains that editors who are technical experts make poor user advocates because they don't ask enough questions, they don't recoil at jargon, and they aren't impartial. We are apt not to question what's familiar to us and to forget that some readers are less knowledgeable, but this is an overblown concern. Experienced editors are trained questioners and won't lose their objectivity as they gain technical understanding. You can understand what a term means and at the same time recognize that it's jargon. You can understand a technical concept and recognize that others may not. If technical experts make poor user advocates, by the same logic good teachers should be as ignorant as their students.

Specialist and generalist are not mutually exclusive. If you're a subject matter expert isolated from your readers, you may make a top-notch technical reviewer but an ineffective editor. If you're a powerful user advocate but a novice in the subject, you may make a strong literary editor but a weak technical editor.

The ideal technical editor has at least some knowledge of the subject—but even more empathy with the reader.

Here I'd like to inject a dose of reality: It's unrealistic to expect to find an editor who is an expert in all the projects she or he supports. Any editor with technical expertise that strong would be working in a higher-paying engineering job.

What are the performance differences between an editor who is a technical specialist and one who is a generalist?

The technical editor who does both content and copy editing is less productive (in terms of pages edited per day) than the editor who does one or the other, but more valuable. A single catch by an editor who knows the company's product line or who understands the technical subject matter could justify that editor's salary for a year. Good editors prevent costly errors—those that require addenda or revisions to correct, invite litigation, or increase costs for customer support.

Large companies with many, diverse products usually prefer generalists because it's impractical to train editors in all their products. (Their writers are usually generalists, too.) These companies usually have central editing departments which support dozens—sometimes hundreds—of products. Large companies typically process documentation like any other machine part. They view technical publishing as just another manufacturing process. These companies see only the short-term costs of training writers or editors, not the long-term benefits to the company in its relationship with its customers.

Small companies with smaller, more manageable product lines usually prefer specialists. These companies expect all their employees to be familiar with their products. In small companies, writers and editors specialize in one or two products.

Even though the generalist often edits more pages a day, the specialist makes a stronger impact. A specialist can prevent expensive problems. Companies do not revise a manual just because a comma is missing. Companies do, however, revise manuals if the information leads customers to complain about technical errors.

Whether the generalist or the specialist is more desirable in your organization, therefore, depends on how your department measures its success—by the number of pages published or by customer satisfaction. If your department measures success by quantity, expect the editorial function to be extinct there within the decade.

Summary

- Most editors do not spend their days sequestered in dark, quiet rooms making cryptic scrawls on manuscripts. Editing encompasses a wide range of tasks and responsibilities, most of which require frequent interactions with many different people.

- There are nearly as many different job titles for editors as there are editors.

- Technical editing differs from other types of editing in several respects.

- Technical writing and technical editing have many common characteristics, but the jobs are not interchangeable.

- A professional editor can bring experience and perspective to a project that a writer performing a peer edit cannot.

- Some editors are technical experts and some aren't. Editors who understand the technical information edit differently from editors who don't know the subject.

Chapter 2
The Twelve Basic Rules

Technical writing isn't literature. Of course, technical books should be attractive and well-written, but that's not enough. There are few coffee-table technical manuals. A technical book has to help someone do a job.

Here are a dozen rules for both full-time and occasional editors to work by, grouped into three categories: rules affecting relationships with readers, with employers, and with writers.

Rules Governing Your Contract with Your Readers

The editor and writer collaborate to ensure that the manual serves its intended audience. You have an implied contract with that reader. When you read the manuscript, it's your responsibility to review it from the customer's point of view. The customer does not care if the project had a tight schedule and an even tighter budget. As a member of the team producing the book, you do care about the deadline and costs, but you must also advocate the customer's needs. One of the most creative aspects of the editor's job is satisfying the obligation to the readers within the constraints of the project. Some pointers for meeting this challenge are presented in chapters 8 and 9.

Rule 1. Customers should never be hurt by errors you should have caught.

"Be careful about reading health books. You may die of a misprint." Mark Twain

As humans, we're going to make mistakes. Let's accept the fact that you can review a manual dozens of times and some errors will slip past you. Let's keep these errors minor. Most customers will forgive a typo, but none will forgive a manual with serious technical errors.

Incomplete or inaccurate installation instructions are inexcusable. Overly alliterative or assonant examples (like the previous sentence) are merely annoying. If you have time, fix both types of problems; if not, fix the more important ones.

Text can be accurate yet still harmful. For example, you can give perfectly accurate instructions on how to format a disk, but if you neglect to tell the user that formatting destroys data already on the disk you've hurt the customer.

You can protect the customer by having potential users test the documentation with the product and by putting warnings and cautions in the manual and on the equipment.

You'll see many examples of the types of errors you can catch in chapters 6 and 7.

◇ ——————————————————————————————————— ◇

Accuracy Isn't Enough

"Where am I?" shouted the lost balloonist.

"You're in a hot air balloon," the fellow on the ground replied.

"You must be a lawyer," the balloonist bellowed. "What you've told me is perfectly accurate—and totally useless."

◇ ——————————————————————————————————— ◇

Rule 2. Satisfy the customers' informational needs.

Technical writing explains technical concepts, describes processes, defines technical terminology, gives diagnostic information, instructs how to use a product, tells how to perform a task, and provides reference information.

Few people are so devoid of a real life that they read technical manuals, reports, and proposals for amusement. Your readers need to read your book to do their jobs. Tell them what they need to know. Period. You don't need to entertain them or impress them with your vast knowledge.[1]

Take the following paragraph, for instance:

EXAMPLE

This book isn't meant to be read, just dipped into, when you've got those clearly visible and immediate problems that don't lend themselves to neat organization or to someone else's ideas of taxonomy or phrasing. We present relevant commands in quick-reference format and procedures in skeletal form. We'll tell you what to do, how to do it, but probably not why (though there will be appropriate notes). We've organized this manual in the standard, rather boring manner . . .

Suppose the system just crashed, you have to fix it before your 250 users fix you, and this book is your primary source for the solution. Now does the writer's light tone amuse you?

Rule 3. The book is written for customers to use, not to admire.

Don't draw unnecessary attention to the book. The reader doesn't care about your trials and tribulations while creating it or your clever solutions to writing and formatting problems. Here are some real examples that illustrate what you *don't* want to see.

This writer is hamming it up for the reader:

EXAMPLE

You probably already know enough to skip this chapter, or you probably want to solve some of your problems, so we've put this introduction here (rather than in an appendix) to let you feel like you're making progress by skipping Chapter 1 and turning to Chapter 2. Also, we've chosen not to "bury" this information in an appendix, because we know you won't look there.

---

[1] It's OK to make the book interesting, but not at the expense of imparting information. By the way, this book has a light tone because, unlike readers of technical manuals, you don't have to read this book.

The following paragraph discusses the book's structure in too much detail:

EXAMPLE

This chapter concentrates on procedures. It describes the most common step-by-step tasks (and subtasks), and it points to fuller discussion/description in other documents.

There's nothing wrong with telling readers how you've organized the book, but don't overdo it. Few readers care to distinguish between tasks and subtasks and between discussions and descriptions.

This next writer could have helped readers more by putting the same effort into organizing the book as he put into being friendly:

EXAMPLE

This material is from Appendix A in the user's guide. Each task item there contains a reference into the text of that manual to tell you how to do the particular task (but we'll give you some brief pointers here).

This manual isn't a catch-all for chapters that should be in other manuals, or for topics that were identified late in the process and felt to be "appropriate" for appendices.

Rule 4. The information should be easy to find.

The book's organization, typography, layout, design, and writing style should work together to enable readers to find the information they need as quickly and as painlessly as possible.

Group information logically and coherently. Provide navigational tools, such as a detailed table of contents with meaningful text heads, a comprehensive index, running heads and feet, and tabs to help readers find the information fast.

Graphic designers, artists, typesetters, and writers all contribute, each from a specialized perspective. The editor views the book from the reader's perspective. The editor alone looks at the whole package—organization, writing style, design, layout, packaging—and assesses whether these elements work together.

Rule 5. The information should be clear.

Once your readers have found the information, they should be able to read and understand it without a magic decoding ring.

It does you little good to finally locate this item in the manual, because its meaning is obtuse:

EXAMPLE

The stickiness of the **Cut** command is even more useful in text than in the component bar because you cannot select multiple text blocks at once as you can select multiple scattered components.

◇ —— ◇

Don't Clog Your Meaning

A plumber wrote to the United States Bureau of Standards to report his discovery that hydrochloric acid was highly effective for opening clogged drain pipes. The Bureau replied, "The efficiency of hydrochloric acid is indisputable, but the corrosive residue is incompatible with metallic permanence."

The plumber thanked the Bureau. It sent him a second warning, "We cannot assume responsibility for the production of toxic and noxious residue with hydrochloric acid and suggest you use an alternative procedure."

The plumber again thanked the Bureau, whereupon it finally replied in plain English: "Don't use hydrochloric acid. It eats hell out of the pipes."[1]

◇ —— ◇

Rule 6. Good editing goes unnoticed by the reader.

The only people who should be able to tell that a book was edited are its author, its editor, and other editors. If the reader notices the editing, it's because the book has errors the editor didn't catch or the writing style is uneven. When a reader comments on the editing, you've got trouble.

I know of one book, written by a technical expert whose native language is not English, in which one paragraph is worded in impeccable, idiomatic English, the next in the stilted, academic style sometimes used by nonnative speakers. Then follow a few paragraphs of stunning prose, and then another choppy one. It was clear to me that a dedicated editor had worked hard to improve the writing, but the author didn't accept all the changes. The two different voices made the book difficult to read.

---

[1] Chernev, Irving, and Fred Reinfeld, *Winning Chess*
(NY: Simon and Schuster, 1948), p. 5.

Rules Governing Your Obligation to Your Employer

Have you ever edited a manual for the sheer pleasure of the experience? As much as I love editing, I wouldn't read most manuals, let alone edit them, if I weren't being paid for my effort.

William E. Unger, Jr., writes:

> I have spent considerable time, for which I was well paid, chopping at manuscripts whose every sentence seemed to contain one or more of the problems I've discussed here. (If I hadn't been well paid, I would have quickly written "unacceptable" on them and gone on to something more entertaining.)[1]

The difference between the editor reading a manual and the customer reading it is that the customer has the freedom to put it down when it fails to meet his or her expectations.

It costs companies money when customers don't read the manuals, because information must still be communicated—but in a more expensive way, such as through customer support or warranty service.

The organization that pays your salary or fee expects you to help the project ship on time and without repercussions. Many companies will fire you if you miss a key deadline or make costly mistakes.

Occasionally you'll perceive conflicts between your contract with the customer and the demands of your employer. We'll look at this problem in the case study "The Manual Doesn't Support the Product" in appendix A.

Rule 7. Ensure that the documentation doesn't hurt the company.

Documentation shouldn't cause the company to lose money, reputation, credibility, or lawsuits.

Flag potentially libelous statements, misrepresentations, leaks about unannounced products under development, violations of truth-in-advertising laws, and errors that could cause personal injury. Be accurate. Tell the truth. Test and verify.

---

[1] *Writer's Digest,* "Prune Your Prose," June 1979.

Rule 8. Don't make costly mistakes.

Inaccurate technical manuals annoy customers and increase costs to your company—the errors need to be fixed by revising or adding publications or adding customer support personnel and programs.

The recipe for Aunt Vertie's Sugar Cookies (*Gourmet*, July 1991, page 88) listed wintergreen oil as an alternative to wintergreen extract. In a letter to the magazine's subscribers, *Gourmet*'s editor-in-chief wrote:

> We have been advised that some persons may be unknowingly allergic to a significant ingredient in wintergreen oil and, further, that wintergreen oil is generally not intended for internal consumption. . . . We urge you to immediately mark the recipe . . . so as to block out the reference to "¼ teaspoon wintergreen oil. . . ." Also, we enclose a sticker containing a revised recipe, without wintergreen oil, which we suggest you place over the recipe in your copy of . . . *Gourmet*.

The tangible costs to *Gourmet* include the printing of the label and the additional mailing to about 800,000 subscribers. There's food for thought, but errors can be even more expensive. The failure of the Adam computer in 1983 almost put Coleco Industries out of business for good. (The Cabbage Patch Kids rescued the company.)

Coleco Industries attributed a $35 million loss on the Adam computer to "manuals which did not offer the first-time user adequate assistance."[1]

> Hundreds of Coleco Industries Inc.'s new Adam home computers are being returned as defective, but the company said the problems stem from instruction manuals for the system. . . . Several computer authorities agreed with the company's position that the problems stem from poorly written manuals for the Adam, and not from defects in the machine . . .
>
> Many of the early problems owners are having are the result of inadequately prepared instruction manuals. Experienced computer users aren't able to program efficiently with the Adam . . . because the manual doesn't explain the machine adequately. Novice buyers aren't warned of problems they may encounter using a computer. Consumers aren't told, for example, that they shouldn't leave software cartridges on top of the printer when it's plugged in or in the tape drive after the machine is turned off. That erases the program stored in the magnetic tape. Coleco said it now is putting labels on its Adam to warn users of this problem and is revising the manuals.[2]

---

[1] *Time,* June 18, 1984.
[2] *The Wall Street Journal,* November 30, 1983.

A Costly Error

FATAL FUNGUS: A deadly mushroom mix-up prompts Larousse, the world's leading publisher of French dictionaries, to recall 180,000 volumes of this year's color edition of its Petit Larousse dictionary. "It's a slight detail that could be fatal to readers, especially when mushroom season starts," says a Larousse spokeswoman. A miscaptioned photograph in the dictionaries, on sale since July in Belgium, Canada, Switzerland, and France, labels a deadly mushroom "harmless" and a harmless mushroom "deadly." Larousse says the recall could cost between FFr20 million and FFr30 million, although it plans to correct the error in existing copies, rather than reprint them. The mistake was spotted by alert readers.[1]

Rule 9. Meet all deadlines and ship on time.

If the information isn't available when the reader needs it, it's worthless. It doesn't help the user to have "the perfect book" too late. You can make trade-offs to balance the schedule and quality. Once you commit to a schedule, follow it.

Rules Governing Your Relationship with Your Writers

The editor's role complements the writer's; it does not duplicate it. The editor is not the second writer, replacement writer, or backup writer. The editor's primary function is to make sure the book works.

Rule 10. Be able to justify every mark you make on the manuscript.

Editing is not about making changes; it's about making necessary improvements and corrections. A sentence hasn't been written that can't be changed by a zealous editor. Expressing an idea differently doesn't make it better, just different. You should ask yourself the following questions before you suggest a change:

- Does the change make it easier for the reader to find information, understand the text, or use the book (or the product)?

- Does the change correct a factual, grammatical, spelling, or usage error?

- Does the change save publishing costs?

---

[1] *The Wall Street Journal,* August 29, 1990.

These guidelines will allow you plenty of latitude for suggesting changes. For example, you can reword an ambiguous sentence, reorganize a chapter's contents, and enforce house style, all on the basis of making it easier for the reader to use the book.

Rule 11. If it's not broken, don't fix it.

This rule supplements Rule 10. Don't change manuscripts for the sake of changing manuscripts. Don't worry that you won't have enough work as an editor if you don't change everything. By the time you've finished this book you'll know so much about editing you'll have your hands full fixing what's *really* broken. You won't have an urge to make gratuitous changes.

Editors are not paid by the number of changes marked in a manuscript. We draw the same salary if we rewrite the text that we do if we pass it back without a mark, as long as we check what we're supposed to check. An editor who *never* finds any errors won't be working for long. Manuscripts typically have plenty of errors. Editors don't need to concoct changes to justify their existence.

Rule 12. It's the writer's book.

It's ironic that editors need superlative writing skills but rarely have the opportunity to write themselves. If you feel a compelling urge to write, become a writer. Or do as I do. Satisfy the writing bug by writing articles, accepting short writing assignments, or—if critically smitten—writing a book about editing.

Writers, refrain from rewriting the books you edit. You'll be tempted to infuse some of your identity into them. Resist that temptation and you will be a better editor.

Summary

Sometimes you'll find yourself concentrating so heavily on a manuscript or on solving a problem that you'll need to step back to see the big picture. The twelve rules in this chapter are the guidelines you can fall back on whenever you need to justify a decision or solve a knotty problem.

Here's a recap of these rules:

Rules Governing Your Contract with Your Readers

- Customers should never be hurt by errors you should have caught.
- Satisfy the customers' informational needs.
- The book is written for customers to use, not to admire.
- The information should be easy to find.
- The information should be clear.
- Good editing goes unnoticed by the reader.

Rules Governing Your Obligation to Your Employer

- Ensure that the documentation doesn't hurt the company.
- Don't make costly mistakes.
- Meet all deadlines and ship on time.

Rules Governing Your Relationship with Your Writers

- Be able to justify every mark you make on the manuscript.
- If it's not broken, don't fix it.
- It's the writer's book.

Chapter 3
Editing As a Mind Set, Not Just a Skill Set

Since you're reading this book you probably have a love of words and more than a passing interest in writing. It wouldn't be farfetched to assume you have a better-than-average writing ability—what people do well and what they enjoy often go hand in hand. However, if someone is holding a gun to your head and making you read this book, direct your assailant's attention to the section called "The Editorial Mind Set." Without the right temperament for editing, you won't be a good—or a happy—editor. No external motivation, whether a paycheck or a pistol, will make you a good editor if you don't also have the right mind set to complement your skill set.

The Editorial Skill Set: What an Editor Can Do

The editorial skill set isn't *all* you need, but it's certainly one thing you can't do without. The editorial skill set includes certain basic skills, knowledge, and abilities—what you should know or be able to do after your first year or two as an editor. You should also be born with a good ear for language, and over many years should have acquired a mastery of grammar and spelling.

An editor should have

- Excellent writing skills
- Facility with language (a good ear)
- An eye for detail

An editor should know

- Grammar, spelling, and punctuation
- Graphic arts and printing terminology and processes, in both traditional and electronic publishing
- Project management techniques
- Time management strategies

An editor should be able to

- Anticipate problems realistically
- Recognize problems quickly
- Solve problems creatively and expeditiously
- Criticize diplomatically
- Organize
- Recognize quality
- Learn quickly
- Adapt to change
- Interpret and apply guidelines
- Understand technical material
- Pay attention to detail without losing sight of the big picture
- Work on multiple projects at different stages of development
- Teach

You see these requirements in editors' job descriptions. You need the complete skill set, though some requirements evolve over time. For example, you need to keep current with the prevailing publishing technology.

Exercise 3   What's wrong here?

A group of private investors, among them the late Armand Hammer, say they will continue to search for oil in Israel.

In addition, your credentials must include a college degree and professional experience. A college degree is an entry-level requirement. However, my observation is that what an editor majored in at college is of little importance. The best editors are those who have diverse knowledge and broad life experience. Watching *Jeopardy!* regularly and reading a variety of fiction and nonfiction will help you more as an editor than English Literature & Composition. Your academic background simply has less relevance to your success as an editor than your raw ability to hear a dissonant phrase or write a clear sentence. So, while your college English courses may not help you solve the mundane problems you'll face as an editor, your other college courses—even that Esperanto seminar—might come in handy some day.

The best experience you can bring to an editing job will include an open mind and some familiarity with the subject you'll be editing.

Exercise 4   What's wrong here?

Response to an interviewer's question in the *Boston Sunday Globe:*

"I've been writing a biography of Harry Truman, and the more I've read about George Marshall, Franklin Roosevelt, Winston Churchill, and some of the other important men of that era, the more I think we were as fortunate then, as we were at the time of the founding fathers. These were exceptional American leaders."

In the real world, you can always look up what you don't know, as long as you *know* what you don't know. Your ear should tell you what sounds wrong and your eyes should tell you what looks wrong. Then you can find the spelling or usage in books written by experts.

The editorial skill set of the future will very likely be different from the editorial skill set of today; the editorial mind set will very likely remain the same.

The Editorial Mind Set: What Makes a Good Editor

How well you perform as an editor depends as much on your attitude as on your background. I've seen editors with terrific experience on paper who fail because they're difficult to work with or lack the proper temperament and personality for the job. It's much easier to build the proper credentials and develop the necessary skill set for editing than it is to adopt the right attitude, what I call the *editorial mind set.*

The editorial mind set refers to how an editor needs to think to be effective, the attitude you bring to the job. The twelve rules in chapter 2 are part of this mind set.

A good editor has these traits:

- Empathy
- Restraint
- Good judgment
- Adaptability
- Flexibility
- Persuasion
- Decisiveness

Try to understand a writer's point of view when making editorial comments. The best way to acquire this empathy is to write. You don't have to change jobs to experience being edited. Simply submit your own writing—even interoffice memos—to others for review, analyze the comments you receive, note your reaction to them, and rewrite the text to resolve the questions and issues.

Refrain from imposing your own style on someone else's creation. You must understand where your input ends and writer's license begins.

If you're a writer performing a peer edit, consider how your abilities and temperament contribute to your writing and how you can apply these to editing. Some, it seems, are getting their revenge on editors and technical reviewers of the past. These writers make gratuitous changes, pen rude comments in the margin, and viciously emulate every perceived wrong ever done to their manuscripts. Doesn't it serve the editor (or reviewer) right? Give your co-worker the constructive criticism you wish those reviewers had given you.

Editors need to adapt to a different work style and pace. Frequent interruptions are the norm. Unless you learn to manage these interruptions, they can overwhelm you. Here's one hint for coping with frequent interruptions: Write "start" or otherwise mark the place you stop reading when you answer the phone or greet a visitor. Then you can easily pick up where you left off. (Chapter 14 gives more tips on managing your time.)

Editors must make decisions quickly and comfortably. Here are some decisions you may be called on to make:

- Should you make this document two books instead of one because it addresses readers with different objectives?

- Should you issue an addendum or revise the book to incorporate the technical changes the engineers made after the book was printed?

- Should you convert this book to the new design even though the content is being changed minimally in this edition?

- Should you use graphics in addition to (or instead of) text to illustrate this procedure?

A good editor spends as much time cultivating working relationships as doing anything else. I don't mean the editor is the social butterfly of the office. The ways you mark a manuscript, discuss changes with writers, and participate in meetings influence the relationships you have with others.

Most of all, you need credibility. You can blanket your wall with diplomas, awards, and certificates, but they're meaningless if the product team, especially the writer, doesn't have confidence in you. You need to inspire confidence, exude competence, and show you're a team player. Otherwise your editorial suggestions will fall on unreceptive ears.

Summary

You can be an expert grammarian, a whizbang writer, and a technical genius—and yet be a terrible editor if you lack the temperament, personality, and attitude for the job. But you can be a terrific editor if you have the right psychological makeup and good interpersonal skills, because you can learn the rest of the job from books and teachers.

A Little Decision . . . a Big Difference

A routine call came into the editing department one afternoon. "Do we hyphenate 'end user'?" asked the advertising manager. Whew, for once an easy question. "No."

Seconds later, the editor's neck tingled, and she called back. "Uh, how were you using 'end user'?" The advertising manager was about to approve a print ad touting how the customer was master over the computer system.

The headline, in type 3 inches high, blared

END USER CONTROL.

Oops. This message was not the one the company wanted to convey. Yes, they changed it to

END-USER CONTROL.

Chapter 4
The Editor As Team Player

Team members can't be very effective if they're unsure of their role; they need to understand where their responsibility begins and ends. And other team members also need to understand their role.

Product teams need editors. Whether you're an editor, a writer, or a manager, someday you will probably have to explain to your manager why your team needs an editor. Many managers think that because writers know grammar, it's redundant to have an editor.

Here are some tactics—traditional and unconventional—you can try.

How to Get an Editor on Your Team (Traditional Approaches)

Justify your need for an editor by showing how editors improve quality and save money.

Talk Quality

If you need to explain the editor's role to a manager who has been a technical writer or who cares about the quality of the writing, describe the contributions an editor can make to the documentation.

Consistency Across a Set of Manuals

It's difficult, if not impossible, for a team of writers to produce a consistent documentation set under deadline pressures. Every writer on the team would have to read every draft of every other writer's book, yet not miss her or his own writing deadlines. Ask the manager to assign one writer the full-time job of reading every book in the documentation set—every review draft of every book—from the point of view of the reader, and to make individual writers aware of discrepancies in technical information or inconsistencies in writing style that a reader might notice. This writer is also in a position to notice if any important information is missing from the documentation set—before customers make that discovery. To distinguish this writer's job from that of the writers who actually compose text, let's call her or him the *editor.*

Objectivity

The editor can find ambiguities that an expert will miss, because the expert knows the subject so well he or she will read each sentence as it should have been written. The editor reads what is actually written, just as your readers—your customers—will. The editor, however, will find the ambiguities *before* the book is published.

Talk Money

If you need to explain the editor's role to a manager who does not have any technical writing experience or who cares more about budgets than about some abstract notion of quality, describe how an editor saves the company money.

Costly Poor Quality

It's more expensive to correct errors and omissions and to provide technical support than it is to do the job right in the first place. "Quality is free," says Philip Crosby, the originator of the Zero-Defect theory of quality—and a former technical editor.[1]

Efficiency and Economy of Scale

An editor who serves as a liaison between writers and production (graphic arts and/or manufacturing) can make the production and distribution process flow faster, more smoothly, and less expensively than can many writers performing the same functions. Also, editors handle more books than writers, so they have a broader perspective and are better able to find ways to save money and improve time-to-market for manuals.

---

[1] Crosby describes his experiences as an editor in *Quality Without Tears: The Art of Hassle-Free Management* (NY: McGraw Hill, 1984), p. 59.

You will need to support these arguments quantitatively. You should produce actual examples—from your own company—of how an editor saved money on a specific project—or how much money an editor, if you had had one, would have saved the company. For example, if you have an experienced editor your department may be able to hire less experienced—and less highly paid—writers. The editor can help train the writers, which will free up some management time. (Managers, you'll need to explain how the time you save will benefit the company.)

How to Pitch Editing (A Nontraditional Approach)

The biggest obstacle you will face when you try to justify hiring an editor is the stereotypical view of editors. Many people (including some who oversee publications departments) mistakenly think editors are merely human spelling checkers. Your biggest task will be to educate managers about the role of an editor.[1] One technique you can try is to ask your manager to read the following article, "The All-Star Editor," which I wrote to educate my managers.[2]

◇ ── ◇

The All-Star Editor

If you were to ask me, "So what do you *do* as a technical editor?" I'd respond with, "Are you a baseball fan?" If you aren't, then you'll get the traditional resume spiel and you'll walk away from the conversation a mite glassy-eyed and moderately informed.

But if you're a baseball junkie, then you'll get a three-word job description packed with more content than a two-page resume or a forty-five minute talk with viewgraphs: I'm the catcher.

Editors and catchers serve similar roles on their teams. Both epitomize the team player, whose individual glory is subordinated for the sake of the team. Both perform highly technical activities that aren't even noticed by the uninitiated. Both are expected to "handle" their peers, train rookies, and serve as defensive experts.

Their jobs sound simple and dull, and look easy on the surface, but have a lot of depth. And the deeper you look, the stronger the analogy between editor and catcher. Let's look at this analogy and see why Hall-of-Fame catcher Yogi Berra—despite how he butchered the English language I'm sworn to defend—is my soulmate.

◇ ──────────────── < *continued* > ──────────────── ◇

---

[1] I assume your editors do play a bigger role than checking spelling, and that their responsibilities correspond to the editing model described in this book.
[2] Judith A. Tarutz, *Technical Communication,* Third Quarter, 1990. Reprinted with permission of *Technical Communication,* published by the Society of Technical Communication.

The Supporting Role

The pitcher is the star or pivotal player. Likewise, the main job in technical publishing is the writer's. There are many other jobs in technical publishing—illustrator, graphic designer, manager, production coordinator—but it's the writer who produces the important element, the manuscript.

Play seemingly begins in baseball when the pitcher throws the ball. Publishing ostensibly begins when the writer delivers a manuscript. In truth, neither event occurs without earlier participation of the catcher or editor, respectively. The catcher and the editor are supporting players. They do not produce "deliverables" in quantifiable terms as do the pitcher and writer; they seem to wait until someone else does the work, they hold the ball or manuscript for a while, and then "throw" it back, usually figuratively for the editor. In fact, both catcher and editor participate much earlier in the process; their roles are just less visible.

The pitcher and catcher form a team within a team, called the battery; the writer and editor also form a team within the department. Yet the division of labor is highly specialized. As the catcher isn't a second, redundant pitcher, neither is the editor the second writer on the project.

(We'll ignore the catcher's offensive role for this discussion because when his team is at bat, it doesn't matter what position he plays. And, for fairness, we'll ignore the fact that the editor occasionally pinch-hits as a writer.)

Knowing Teammates

It's the catcher's job to know the strengths and weaknesses of every member of the pitching staff—from the ace to the third-string relievers. He must know each pitcher's repertoire of pitches, range of speed, and degree of control. And he must apply this knowledge on the field, during each inning, to elicit the best "stuff" his battery mate has to offer.

It's the editor's job to know the strengths and weaknesses of every member of the writing staff—from the veterans to the contractors to the new-hires. The editor must know each writer's repertoire of writing styles, speed at rewriting, and knowledge of the available publishing tools. For example, do a writer's tutorials and reference manuals have the same level of detail and move along at the same pace? Will a particular writer balk at extensive editing?

< continued >

Calling Pitches

The catcher calls for the next pitch, but the pitcher has the right to shake off a pitch he's uncomfortable throwing in that situation or feels is inappropriate for that batter.

Likewise, the editor suggests wording and other changes, which the writer is free to ignore when it changes the meaning or intent or is inappropriate for the product or audience.

On the Defensive

On the field, the catcher is the defensive coordinator, positioning the defense for each batter. As the catcher must know opposing hitters and how well they're hitting this week, so must the editor know what the competitors are doing with their documentation. The editor's defensive role includes staying informed of technical publishing technologies, scouting competitive documentation, and devising guidelines for improving quality.

Seeing the Big Picture

The catcher has the entire diamond in front of him and sees the big picture. It's easy for him to see that the outfield isn't shifted properly for a pull hitter or that the infield is at double-play depth when there are already two outs. The catcher needs to worry about the current game situation—runners on base and how fast they run, number of outs, and whether the next batter is most likely to bunt—so that the pitcher can focus his complete attention on the batter.

The editor, too, has a big-field view, of the publishing process and documentation set.

The editor needs to watch for publishing trends; anticipate production, printing, and distribution problems; and consider the usability of the manual as part of the larger documentation package that the reader receives. The editor has to know what's happening throughout the company. This lets the writer concentrate on all the technical details that belong in a particular manual.

The catcher plays in almost every game; pitchers play in every fourth or fifth game. As a result, the catcher sees more batters and pitches than the pitcher.

The editor's scope is also broader than the writer's. A typical editor reviews more publications in a single year than the typical writer writes in a complete career.

< continued >

Day-to-Day on the Field

During the game, the catcher must observe and adjust to changing conditions, the current opposing batter, the weather, and the condition of the playing field. He must know whether the pitcher is hitting the corners, if his fastball is zipping or crawling, and if his curveball is eluding or hanging.

The editor needs to know the project's position—schedule, goals, constraints—and help keep the writer on track. The editor has to watch if the writer is hitting the target, whether each chapter, paragraph, and sentence is doing its bit to deliver the message appropriately to the target audience. The editor also has to gauge the writer's need for writing assistance, just as the catcher needs to judge when the pitcher is losing his velocity or control.

Working with Other People

Both the catcher and editor work closely with people of varying abilities, temperaments, and ego strengths. Their people-handling instincts have to be finely tuned. When the pitcher is jittery, it's the catcher who runs to the mound to talk to him. When writers face writer's block or problems with engineers, the first person they may turn to is the editor.

Editors and catchers both need to give constructive criticism, diplomatically. A writer may not have his or her "stuff" for a particular book, but the editor should be able to offer pointers or a sympathetic ear to let him or her get back on track. The editor may serve as the writer's teacher, sounding board, devil's advocate, or test user.

Editors must understand and communicate with writers as peers, not as managers. Astute baseball managers assign compatible pitchers and catchers to work together; ditto for wise documentation managers and their writers and editors.

The editor's job is to teach, stroke, encourage, and possibly even defend the writing staff. Editors teach rookie writers tricks of the writing trade and explain the publications process so that the writers can answer questions from their engineers.

Who Is the Player Behind the Mask?

Catchers and editors alike are the most anonymous players on the team, and have the least flashy jobs. The person who says, "What a well-edited book" when reading is probably the same person who watches a ballgame and says, "What a well-caught game."

< continued >

Good catching and good editing often mean the absence of errors. Bad catching is easy to spot—passed balls, batters anticipating the pitch, throwing errors, and stolen bases. Bad editing is also easy to spot—poor organization, choppy or rambling writing, inconsistencies, typos, and other errors. Good catching and good editing are more difficult to judge.

Good editing is transparent to the reader; if you can see the editor's hand in the finished book, it's because there were enough other problems with the writing or editorial fine points to draw your attention to the editing. Good editing means the book reads as it should read; the mechanics that went into the writing should be hidden.

Editors and catchers share anonymity. The catcher's protective mask hides his face. The writer's name appears on the book cover, not the editor's. In the end, the pitcher earns the win or suffers the loss; the writer gets the credit for a well-written book or the blame for a poor one. When the project is completed, the writer, not the editor, gets the recognition and souvenir T-shirt from the engineering team.

You Want to Be a **What?**

In baseball, the top salaries go to pitchers and home run hitters. In technical publishing, top salaries for individual contributors go to writing stars.

As a result, the most talented players don't aspire to catching and the best writers shun editing, a loss to both professions.

The years of being badly treated have exacted a toll on the profession; the top talent seeks out the glamorous jobs, ignoring catching and editing. Major league baseball faces a shortage of quality catchers and technical publishing faces a shortage of good editors.

Can't We Just Do Without Them?

When the bean counters are scrutinizing the bottom line, it's tempting to suggest doing away with "overhead" positions, those that don't produce deliverables on their own. While a major league baseball team would never go without a catcher, many major corporations do go without editors.

Sure, a company can have a department of writers without editors, at least more plausibly than one of editors without writers. A sandlot baseball team can make do without a catcher if it's short on people simply by rotating different players behind the plate. In technical publishing, this is called "peer editing" and the results are predictable.

The stand-in catcher will stop most balls before they roll to the backstop, just as most writers will catch basic misspellings, grammatical oversights, and punctuation errors.

< continued >

But something will be missing.

The baseball team won't have anyone skilled in calling pitches, trained to anticipate a bunt and react quickly to field it, practiced in observing baserunners and knowing when they're faking and when they're about to steal, and then able to execute a perfect throw to second.

The company without editors deprives its writers of a publishing expert, one who can guide them through the early writing stages with developmental edits, lead them to polish their prose through literary edits, and help them prepare their manuscripts so that the production and printing processes will flow error-free.

As the baseball team without a catcher lacks an expert who can go out to the mound and advise a pitcher during the game, the writing department without an editor lacks an expert who can advise the writer on-the-spot, throughout the project. Doing without editors puts a greater demand on the manager's technical, writing, and teaching skills.

Publishing without editors means keeping a valuable resource off the team.

Applying This Analogy

I use this analogy with catching to keep my role in perspective. When I'm tempted to rewrite a manuscript, I ask myself if the catcher would actually deliver the next pitch, or if he'd point out the necessary adjustment to the pitcher. When I'm tempted to force my ideas on a writer, I remind myself that I'm a teammate, not the manager, and carry only the power to suggest. I make myself available to listen to writers, to answer their questions, to hear their writing-related problems and, when necessary, elevate the problem to management. I try to keep my eye on the ball for each play, while watching what's happening out in the field as well—that field includes other publications in my own company, publishing trends and technologies, the marketplace for my company's products, and the technical arena in which our publications fit.

Working with writers is immensely satisfying when the writer and I collaborate to produce the best manuscript possible. The give-and-take stimulates thoughts and lets us jointly produce a manuscript better than either of us would have written alone.

While being an editor isn't the most glamorous job around, it has its rewards. An editor who knows what's happening in the field, "handles" writers to bring out their best "stuff," and executes the technical plays can become a major contributor to the team.

Summary

You need to understand your role on the team, and you must be able to explain your position to your team's members and your manager.

This chapter showed how you can define your role as an editor by

- Ensuring quality
- Reducing costs (quality is free; rework is expensive)
- Improving efficiency and productivity
- Performing a unique function on a team
- Working with other team members

Chapter 5
Working with Writers:
Ten Lessons I Had to Unlearn

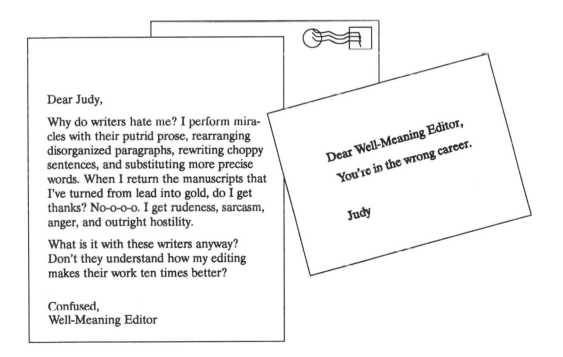

Dear Judy,

Why do writers hate me? I perform miracles with their putrid prose, rearranging disorganized paragraphs, rewriting choppy sentences, and substituting more precise words. When I return the manuscripts that I've turned from lead into gold, do I get thanks? No-o-o-o. I get rudeness, sarcasm, anger, and outright hostility.

What is it with these writers anyway? Don't they understand how my editing makes their work ten times better?

Confused,
Well-Meaning Editor

Dear Well-Meaning Editor,

You're in the wrong career.

Judy

Well-Meaning Editor needs to learn these lessons:

- It's not your book. It doesn't matter how much effort you put into editing it, it's still the writer's book. Unless you can live with that limitation, you will be miserable as an editor.

- Strive for mutual respect, not power. Respect the writers; in turn, they will respect you for your contributions.

- Be able to justify every comment—even if you're not called upon to do so.

- Mark copy diplomatically.

Ten Lessons I Had to Unlearn

I dearly wish I could say that the Well-Meaning Editor is a totally hypothetical character. I've met many of them in my career, and I suspect you have, too.

I'm not a psychologist (and I don't even play one on TV), but I think problems occur more from misunderstanding the editor's role than from evil intent.

The following "lessons" are bits of advice that senior editors imparted to me when I was learning the ropes. I found out the hard way that their advice did not make editing fun. But once I mustered the courage to break away, my relationship with writers improved, and editing became the kind of job I'd always hoped it would be.

◇ ──────────────────────────────────── ◇

Ten Lessons I Had to Unlearn

- Never admit you made a mistake. Writers should think editors are infallible.
- Review every comment and change with writers.
- Be serious. Never write jokes on a manuscript.
- Don't befriend writers. Maintain a professional distance.
- Negotiate changes. Concede some changes so the writer will accept the rest.
- Writers and editors are natural adversaries.
- Be impersonal in your markup.
- Be a generalist. Don't become a subject matter expert or you'll lose objectivity.
- Use red ink to intimidate writers.
- Your role is advisory only. It doesn't matter if the writer ignores all your comments.

◇ ──────────────────────────────────── ◇

1. Never Admit You Made a Mistake

I was taught to encourage writers to think editors are infallible. I was told that if you expect writers to listen to you, you must have a perfect track record.

What I learned:

Writers respect you more when you admit to making a mistake than when you concoct weird reasons and justifications to explain your error. It's OK to admit you misread or misunderstood something.

Of course, you can't make mistakes all the time and expect writers to trust that you know what you're doing. If you slip up now and then, however, admit it. I've never met a writer who wouldn't forgive an honest mistake.

Besides, your job requires you to point out the writer's oversights. Can't you err, too? When editors don't admit to mistakes, writers perceive them, sarcastically, as know-it-all, holier-than-thou prigs. You won't have to fake errors to show you're human—deadlines alone will keep you from being perfect.

2. Review Every Comment and Change with Writers

In the first company where I worked as an editor, the process was for an editor, after reviewing the manuscript, to schedule a conference with the writer to point out each change or correction and explain the reasons for marking it.

These writer–editor conferences were always as tense as guitar strings. They were even worse when the writer's office was 2,000 miles away and you had to dictate your changes over the telephone to a writer you'd never met in person.

Many editing departments still require their editors to hold these discussions.

What I learned:

It's not a pleasant experience for the writer to have somebody point out every missed comma. In some ways it's insulting to have someone call your attention to every minor correction, as if you didn't know any better.

When faced with extensive changes, the writer's natural reaction is often, "The manuscript is fine as is. Thank you very kindly and please help yourself to an arsenic gumdrop."

I've learned to avoid these situations altogether. (I don't care for gumdrops.) I give the writer the manuscript, having marked it so that my comments are as self-explanatory as possible. When I return manuscripts, I remind writers to stop by any time if they want to discuss anything. (Sometimes I mark on the manuscript a passage that I'd rather discuss with the writer than edit to bits.)

This approach returns control to the writers because it lets them review the comments when they're ready and at a pace they set. One writer I know collects all the review copies, spreads them out on her kitchen table, and pours a glass of wine before reading. Then she reads each comment and decides, privately, whether to accept or reject it.[1]

One writer suggests, "Another very good argument against conferences is that they don't give the writer a chance to think about the edits. Overwhelmed with the big and little things all at the same time—and under some time pressure imposed by lengthy meetings—it's very hard to get your mind to the right state, understand the problem, appreciate the edit, and determine whether it's the right solution."

I find that being flexible about writer–editor conferences actually increases the contact I have with writers—we seek each other out to discuss ideas and issues. Our meetings are consultations, not confrontations.

Several writers I've worked with like to write responses to my comments on the manuscript. They don't always show them to me, they say, because in the process of rebutting my changes, they realize I have a point.

One incident that I can laugh about today shook me up at the time. It was my first developmental edit since I joined the company, for a new book about a new product. I'd returned the manuscript to the writer, an experienced writer who was also new to the company. A few days later I found the manuscript on my desk. The writer had written responses throughout, along the lines of "NO!" and "You missed the point!" and "Huh? What are you talking about?" and some considerably ruder remarks. He'd already left for the day, so I couldn't see him until the next morning. I did not sleep well that night. Also, since he was new to the company, there was nobody I could ask about his personality so that I could prepare myself to meet with him. The next day, while I was contemplating how to initiate a constructive dialogue, the writer phoned me. "I've given more thought to your editing comments. It's not your fault you don't know about this product; my draft is the first documentation ever written about it. I realize the writing must not have been clear and your comments give me some direction as to how to proceed. I hope you didn't take my comments personally. I'm used to editors who don't know what they're doing and reacted without thinking." Such was the beginning of a beautiful friendship.

But just imagine how this scenario would have played out in the traditional writer–editor conference.

---

[1] She says, "One significant value of this is that I can see all the edits for each part of the book at once. Some other reviewer might make a comment that solves the whole problem. Besides, it's amazing how many times a paragraph I've agonized over has gone away because the engineer's review tells me the feature has been removed!"

3. Be Serious — Never Write Jokes on a Manuscript

This rule is an artifact from a process where the editor reviews the manuscript just before it's handed off to be typeset, in the days before writers had word processors. Since the physical pages the editor marked up went to the typesetting department, the editor's comments needed to be neutral and prescriptive. The manuscript, with the editor's markup, was typeset verbatim; queries to the writer were written on separate slips of paper.

Another reason for this rule is that unless editors are serious and professional, writers won't respect them.

What I learned:

Once you've established a working relationship with a writer, be yourself. Writers and I have exchanged hilarious comments on manuscripts; doing so has made our jobs fun.

A couple of cautions: I'd never joke around on a manuscript that would find its way into anyone else's hands (especially a typesetter's!) because the risks of misunderstandings or seeing the joke in print aren't worth a few chuckles. I'd also ensure that the writer and I already had a good relationship, so that we wouldn't offend each other inadvertently.

4. Don't Befriend Writers — Maintain a Professional Distance

This rule suggests that you can't edit your friends' writing objectively, and that they'll pressure you into rubberstamping their manuscripts.

What I learned:

This rule is, by far, the dumbest of them all. How can you work with people you don't know? Building a good working relationship with writers is the most important thing an editor can do.

I also do not rubberstamp my friends' drafts. If there's any partiality at all, it's in the other direction: I'm more likely to go a step further in my editing to help a friend build a better portfolio. I'd also have more confidence that any extra work I did would be worth the time, because a friend would respect my opinions more than a stranger and would accept my feedback more readily. Both the writers and I want the books to be good, so the better we work together, the happier we are, and the better the product we deliver to customers.

It's also easier to work out professional disagreements with people you can speak with honestly, openly, and directly.

5. Negotiate Changes

The old rules say that you need to give a little to gain a lot. If the writer keeps arguing, concede on some points as long as you win most.

What I learned:

The game isn't won by how many points the writer and editor each score. The game is won by the satisfaction level of your customers. Assess each item by its impact on the customer—does this change really make the book easier to use? does the writer's tone insult the customer's intelligence?—not by its impact on your ego. Do the right thing. If you're right, fight. If you're wrong, concede and move along.

6. Writers and Editors Are Natural Adversaries

Many companies set up processes that put writers and editors in conflict. They hire too few editors to support too many writers, so that editors don't have time to do developmental or substantive edits. Or they exclude editors from the planning, so that they are inadequately informed or are giving feedback too late to be useful.

Companies often justify poor publications management with, "What do you expect? Writers and editors are just natural enemies."

What I learned:

Yeah. Nah. Sorta. The writer's job is to communicate with the reader; the editor's job is to point out where that communication misses the mark. Some tension is inevitable, but it need never reach hostility.

Writers and editors have more goals in common than goals that conflict. They just need to identify their goals and work toward them. If both are competent, they'll be able to work around personality conflicts.

7. Be Impersonal in Your Markup

This rule is similar to "Never write jokes on manuscripts."

What I learned:

It helps for the writer and editor to think constantly of the person at the other end of the manuscript. I prefer to think of the manuscript as simply a communication device between the writer and myself. The writer uses the manuscript to tell me about a product; I use the manuscript as a way to transmit my reactions back to the writer. If we both had the time and the patience, I wouldn't edit on paper at all—I'd sit with the manuscript as a reader and talk through it, as in a usability test.

I try to simulate a dialogue as much as possible through the manuscript. To do so, I need the writer to perceive my comments as originating from a person representing the intended audience. The best technique for reminding them that a person, not an editing machine, is behind the comments is by interjecting a lighthearted or personal comment, when appropriate. Sometimes I'll preface my remark with "Joe" (this works only for writers named Joe) and sign or initial my comment.

Sometimes I even put in a ☺, although I'd never admit it.

8. Be a Generalist

I was taught that subject matter experts make poor editors because they lack objectivity and perspective, and that they're so enthralled by the material they forget about the readers.

What I learned:

I don't believe there's a cause and effect relationship here, that learning the subject makes you forget the reader. I think that some subject editors just never bother to learn who the readers are or cannot relate to them because they've been out of touch with them for too long. There may be less pressure for an editor who is a technical expert to get out and learn about readers; an editor who doesn't know the subject has to understand the audience or else has nothing to offer.

You can do a copy edit without understanding the subject. You cannot do a developmental edit or evaluate the usability of the manual unless you know the subject at least as well as the least proficient of your readers. The more you know about the subject, the better job you can do, *if* you keep in touch with your customers.

9. Use Red Ink to Intimidate Writers

Here's another absurd rule, based on the false premise that writers and editors are inherently enemies.

What I learned:

Use whatever color you please. I prefer red because it's easier to see, and also it photocopies well. I even prefer that people editing my writing use red ink because it stands out. Some editors avoid red because it reminds writers of school. I don't share that worry. After all, I don't grade manuscripts; I edit them.

10.   Your Job Is Advisory Only

It doesn't matter if the writer ignores all your comments, a former manager used to say, as long as you tried.

What I learned:

If you're not contributing anything worthwhile—or can't show the writer that you are—then why bother to edit at all? Marking the manuscript is only the beginning; you need to follow through to ensure the problems are fixed. Customers see the final book, not your good intentions or ineffectual advice.

Now that we've looked at what *not* to do, let's look at what you *should* do.

Working with Professional Writers

Most writers have had a bad experience with a bad editor or have heard bad things about editors, so they approach editors cautiously and skeptically. When I interview writers, I always ask them to tell me the best and worst experiences they've ever had with editors. Most describe good experiences in a few seconds but require many minutes to recite all the troubles editors have caused them. (I've met a few writers who couldn't tell me anything good about editors but never one who couldn't tell me a horror story. I attribute this phenomenon to the existence of both difficult writers and bad editors. Also, the horror stories are probably more memorable and interesting.)

It doesn't matter if, in fact, the villain is the writer or the editor (or both); what you need to understand is that most writers have a lingering bad taste from previous edits and will expect the worst. This initial perception is the first obstacle you'll need to overcome, whether you're a full-time editor or a writer performing peer edits.

You will need to convey, by your words and your actions, that you have noble purpose, good judgment, and sharp, dependable skills.

How to Show Writers You're Both on the Same Team

Recognize that you and the writers have a common goal: to make the writers' books better. Reread chapters 1 through 4 to make sure you understand your function. Then prepare to explain your role to the writers.

Expect the writers to test you, both subtly and directly.

Use every opportunity to show writers you're a resource, not a barrier, that you make improvements, not just changes. Be open-minded and flexible. Listen to their concerns and respond to their needs. Get to know each writer's weaknesses and skills. It's not enough to promise improvements; you've got to deliver. You can't fake your skills or your sincerity. They have to trust you as a co-worker and have confidence in you as an editor.

A great way to win a writer's respect is to support her or him in some cause, such as effecting a change in the house style or process, if you agree with it—especially if it's unpopular. Nothing will convince a writer you're an ally more than your willingness to stand by her or his side or fight the battle yourself on her or his behalf. You don't even have to win. You do need to be honest in your dealings with the writer—don't pretend to support an idea you disagree with.

Expect to go through a testing process with each writer you face in your career. The testing will diminish as your reputation builds. Once other writers start vouching for your abilities and intentions, you will have to sell yourself less often.

Keep communications open. You will be tempted to hide away to meet deadlines and that's OK from time to time. But the best times I've had as an editor were when my office was close to all the writers I worked with and I had the chance to talk with everyone every day, if only for a minute or two.

Add Value to Writers' Books, Not Steps to the Process

The minute writers perceive you as an obstacle, they'll treat you that way. Obstacles are things you go around and over.

You must have heard writers talk about "Getting the manuscript through editing" in the same way you'd talk about getting through hay fever season.

Conversely, there are writers who talk about "Having my book edited" in the same way you'd talk about remodeling your dream house.

Is the difference the writer or the editor? Actually, it's the combination of a good editor and a writer who has figured out the secret of working with a good editor. The secret that writers learn—some later than others—is that a good editor makes the *writer* look good.

Dos and Don'ts

- Give constructive, not negative, criticism.
- Offer solutions, not problems.
- Say what works, not just what's wrong.
- Be reasonable, not dogmatic.
- Be objective, not subjective.
- Be truthful and tactful, not coy.
- Be flexible, not restrictive.

If you're being subjective, admit it and explain why. You can't delete a word just because *you* don't like it, but you can if *you, as user advocate,* take umbrage at it. Or, if your comment looks arbitrary, explain your reasons. For example, I prefer not to use *a number of* as a synonym for *several* (not only because *several* is shorter). In technical manuals we often say things like, "What you do depends on the number of frobnitzes in the framistam" or "The maximum number of frizzlechips you can have is 64." I think that the word *number* in a technical manual should signal the reader to be ready to receive numerical data, so I reserve *a number of* for those contexts. When I explained this reasoning to a writer who had been thinking, "Here goes another quirky editor," she immediately agreed—and helped spread the word among the other writers that seemingly arbitrary changes weren't necessarily arbitrary. Then she encouraged them to *ask the editor,* a radical idea at the time.

If you're simply enforcing a company policy or adhering to house style, say so. One editor I know marks "Style Guide, page 3-12"; I adopted this technique and learned that not only did it reduce arguments, but it also saved me from writing an explanation, since the style guide already had one.

What Writers Say About Editors and What They Really Mean

Here are some of my observations on writers' most common complaints about editors.

- The editor changed the meaning of my words.
  That stupid editor doesn't know the subject or the product.

- The editor flipflopped on his or her decision.
  I had to redo a lot of work, and it's the editor's fault.

- The editor made arbitrary changes.
  The editor's power trip is cutting into my own.

- The editor knows the arcane rules but won't share them.
  Editors deliberately keep writers in the dark. I have to guess what the rules are supposed to be.

- The editor made too many changes too late in the process.
  I'll never finish the book if I have to make all these changes. I'll look foolish going back to the reviewers now. Why can't that editor leave well enough alone?

- The editor reversed all the decisions the previous editor made.
  I had to undo all the work I did earlier. This proves that editors are just out to make more work for us writers. Or one of them doesn't know what he's doing.

- The editor didn't catch several errors.
  Why bother to have the book edited at all?

How to Deal with Sensitivity (the Writer's and Yours)

Writers, you are not what you write. Editors, you are not what you edit. Neither writer nor editor should take the other's disagreement as a personal affront.

The first time I edit for a writer, I alert him or her to expect a lot of red ink, because that's my style. I also hand over the edited manuscript in person the first time (at least), and let the writer know if the number of comments I've made is typical or not.

When writers swoon at the sight of all the red ink, I point out something few writers know—the time to worry is when the editor hands a manuscript back with no marks, because that means it couldn't be saved.

Another tip: It's less harrowing and more instructive to point out general kinds of errors and suggest ways to prevent them than to mark every instance of every error. For example, here's one comment an editor wrote on a manuscript:

> Use callouts in figures to eliminate wordiness in text. Then you don't need to give explicit directions, such as "in the upper left corner of the screen."

Excerpts from Edited Manuscripts

Here are some examples of constructive, nonthreatening comments from edited manuscripts. Note that it's the *manuscript* that may be wrong; the *writer* isn't. Also, the editor doesn't just tell what needs fixing but suggests how.

EXAMPLES

The editor writes: What this chapter didn't tell me—but should—is what the components of the product are. *"The chapter" is wrong, not the writer.*

The editor writes: Need to give context of what this product is and what it does. This is fuzzy from the marketing hype in Chapter 1. Is this a windowing system plus an editor or are there more tools? Please rewrite Chapter 1 (it's only 4 pages) so that the basic questions of what this product is, what it does, and how it fits into the programming environment are clear. Tell us what you expect us to know, what books we should have available (or have read), what software we need to have installed (and what we could use, optionally, with this product). *Mention specific information the writer can add, instead of saying, "Sketchy" or "Need more info."*

The editor writes: I would expect our users to know basic programming terms—for example, it is inappropriate to define "parse" as "process" on p. 3-4. The Message info in Chapter 2 also seems to "shield" the reader too much from "technical" terminology. It seems as though the audience is perceived to be an end user who is learning programming via this product. Not very likely. *Use of "it" and passive voice emphasize the changes needed, without faulting the writer.*

The editor writes: "Plan on spending about ten minutes" sounds a little bossy. Try something like "It'll take you about ten minutes" instead. *Give reasons for changing words.*

The editor writes: Save this for tutorial. *"Save" instead of "move" because this chapter was edited so heavily. "Save" indicates the paragraph had merit. "Move" would have implied yet another major change. It's the same amount of work, but slightly less demoralizing.*

The editor writes: This is getting redundant. How about . . . *The editor didn't say, "This is redundant," but said, "How about" or "Try" or "Think about changing . . ." Use similar wording to show that you're suggesting possible solutions, not dictating changes.*

The editor writes: This chunk interrupts the flow. I'd prefer to leap right into the stuff in Section 1.2. *Focus on editor as user advocate.*

The editor writes: Thank you. More of these simple examples. I find them good confirmation that I'm following along. *Converse with the writer.*

The editor writes: The section on object orientation was trying too hard to prove that C++ is object-oriented. Is that one of your goals? It seemed a little defensive at times. *Ask, don't assume. Maybe the writer intended to argue and prove a point.*

The editor writes: This sentence confused me . . . I have a problem here. *Like good negotiating strategy, this comment suggests, "Let's work together to solve this problem."*

Special Circumstances

One difficult situation is when the writer didn't compose the draft, yet is responsible for it. For example, a marketing or engineering manager may be the actual author, and the writer's assignment is to shepherd the project through editing and production. This situation puts the writer in an unfamiliar and uncomfortable role. Editors are used to explaining why changes are necessary; writers aren't. If you recognize the writer's position, you can certainly empathize with it—and perhaps give the writer some useful pointers for presenting the changes to the actual author. Or, it may be appropriate for you to meet with the original writer.

Another special case is that of contract (freelance) writers. Contractors are expected to follow the house style. You don't have to be as flexible in your edits with a contractor as with a permanent staffer; you have the right to insist on changes in work-for-hire you might negotiate with a permanent writer. (Still, be nice about it.)

If you're a freelance editor and you have a good working relationship with the client, you may suggest style changes, but do not make any without the client's approval.

Why Not Just Tell Them? (Part One)

A good working relationship between writers and editors depends on cooperation from both sides. Here are some things you can tell writers to help them learn how to work with editors.

Things Writers Should Do

- Recognize that editors are not interchangeable parts. Editors have different backgrounds and styles.

- Ask questions before you write. Ask questions while you write.

- Show your editors preliminary drafts and solicit feedback early on.

- Keep your editor informed early and often of product changes and schedule changes. Changes to your schedule affect the available editing time for other writers' books.

- Keep your editor involved in the project and active on the project team.

- Help the editor learn your product.

- Make changes and corrections as marked or let the editor know why not. Otherwise, the editor will assume you're missing them and will keep marking the same changes.

- Batch up questions when possible (unless you need a quick answer) to reduce the number of interruptions and to give the editor time to remember details of your book from among the many he or she has in process.

- Don't assume the editor's comments are stupid if they're wrong; they may point to a problem in the manuscript.

- Don't lose your temper. Ask for more information or clarification.

- Don't guess. Ask what the editor meant if you don't understand.

- Give feedback. Let your editor know why you think the comments were wrong or not useful—it'll help on future edits. Writers' feedback is a valuable way for editors to learn, just as the editors' feedback helps writers.

- Don't waste the editor's time if you have no intention of making changes. If you don't want editorial feedback, then let the editor give time to writers who do. (I recommend consulting your manager.)

< continued >

Why Not Just Tell Them? (Part Two)

Things Writers Should Know

- The editor's goal is the same as the writer's—make the *writer's* book as good as possible.

- The editor is a resource, not an obstacle.

- The editor's creed is that good editing is not noticed by the reader.

- Editors do not make arbitrary changes, but recommend changes to meet readers' needs.

- The only dumb questions are the unasked ones.

- Editors have heard every excuse: There isn't any time to incorporate editing comments. Grammar is fuddy-duddy. The reader will understand it even if you don't. Nobody's going to read it anyway. (Save your energy for writing, not arguing.)

- Don't worry if your manuscript is covered in red. Worry if you get it back with *no* comments.

- Make sure your schedule leaves adequate time to make changes.

- Don't take comments personally. Editors don't edit writers; they edit manuscripts.

- The editor's comments on your manuscript are private. These comments are to help you, not to condemn you.

- Editors don't keep score or count mistakes. The editor's job is to find problems and errors and help you fix them before they become problems for readers.

- You don't have to implement the editor's changes verbatim if you resolve the problem satisfactorily.

- It takes less time to do it right than to redo it. Ask lots of questions.

- Don't interpret the editor's job too narrowly. If you see an opportunity for the editor to contribute to the project in a new way, suggest it.

- The editor can be the writer's strongest ally.

The Occasional, Reluctant Writer

Sometimes you'll be asked to work with a technical professional (a nonwriter) who has to publish a book or paper on occasion. This person would rather be inventing, engineering, or experimenting in the lab than composing at the word processor. Publishing is a necessary career rite of passage, but not the most pleasant one.

It's rare to find a technical expert who loves to write, has studied writing, and can write well. You're more likely to find experts who think they write well—and don't.

You can expect more defensiveness from occasional writers than from professional writers. The professional writer knows how hard writing is and expects to rewrite routinely. The technical expert is more likely to think, "I'm the expert. Ergo I can write. I can do *anything* and writing is wimpy compared to the *real* work I do." The easier or wimpier they think writing is, the harder it is for them to accept that their first draft might not be a paragon of style.[1]

Read through the article or skim the book before you start to edit. Then meet with the writer. Find out where this article goes next. It makes a difference if it's going to a journal whose own editor will copy edit it or one that will print exactly what you submit. Also find out who will make corrections—the writer, a secretary, a typesetter? Knowing who will enter the revisions will tell you whether or not to use standard editing symbols.

Understand the writers' expectations, but educate them about your role. It's sometimes helpful to give writers a brief description of the levels of edit you use. (This book discusses levels of edit in chapter 8.) Whatever you say, writers will expect you either to proofread or to ghostwrite the article. You will probably be doing something in between; try to convey the scope of what you can or expect to do.

Show samples of printed works, if you have anything that will impress it upon them that you know your stuff.

You must understand which types of editorial changes are acceptable and which aren't; what you do depends on what the document is, who will read it, and under whose name it is being published. If an engineer is writing a manual that will be distributed to customers just like any other manual, then edit it as

---

[1] William Zinsser tells a humorous anecdote comparing writing as a vocation and as an avocation in chapter 1 of *On Writing Well: An Informal Guide to Writing Nonfiction,* Fourth Edition (New York: HarperCollins, 1990).

thoroughly as you would any other manual. (You'll need to explain your changes more carefully, however.) If you're editing a technical paper written by the vice president of R&D, then don't retrofit rules for manuals onto the paper, but focus on ensuring that the vice president comes across as literate and educated.

At the minimum, edit for clarity and make sure the writer is reaching the audience. Do not change the meaning or, more subtly, the connotation of what the writer is saying; the writer is responsible for the content. (Do, however, point out errors or inconsistencies.)

Some factors to consider:

- Is this an ongoing relationship or a one-shot assignment? Is your goal to build a relationship or just to edit the manuscript? This factor affects how much you teach rather than how you edit.

- Will the publication be carrying the author's byline? Everyone wants to sound literate. Appeal to this concern when you explain your changes.

- Is this the publication of a paper or speech that the author has already presented? If so, all you can change is spelling, grammar, and minor inconsistencies. It's intellectually dishonest to change the wording or content retroactively.

- Consider context, audience point of view, and technical details. Technical experts often fail to provide context for others. Bridge the gap between the author, who is an expert, and the audience, which may be experienced but not necessarily expert. It may not take much for an expert to go over the reader's head. It will be a challenge for you to do a developmental edit, but that's also what's fun.

After you've completed your edits, you'll need to present the edited manuscript to the writer. If you've made extensive changes, consider retyping the manuscript. (Editors usually don't retype manuscripts. This is a special case.) Many writers will read it and say, "You hardly changed anything." That's either because they don't see the changes (they think they wrote it that eloquently) or because it's embarrassing for them to admit how much you did change. Whatever, don't make an issue of it. Letting the writer take full credit for the work even after you've turned it completely around is merely a test of the teamwork spirit.

Summary

- Mutual respect and honesty are the first steps toward a positive, productive working relationship between editors and writers.

- Earn the respect of the writers you work with by being a good editor.

- From a writer's point of view, good editors give constructive feedback, not criticism. Good editors do more than tell what's wrong; they suggest solutions.

- Even under the best of circumstances, problems come up and crises do happen. See the case studies in appendix A.

Part 2
The Editor's Job

◇————————————————————————◇

Chapter 6
Types of Editorial Reviews

Writers are often astounded at how many errors editors find. It doesn't happen by magic. We find errors because we've learned how to look for them.

What do you check when you edit? As much as is reasonable in the available time. In this chapter I assume you have the luxury of reviewing a manuscript several times, so I'll show you where to concentrate your attention for each type of review. In chapter 8 I'll show you how to collapse these reviews into one pass.

This chapter looks at the following editorial reviews:

- Developmental edits
- Preliminary edits
- Copy and literary edits (for style, accuracy, and usability)
- Production edits
- Editing for an international audience
- Proofreading
- Blues (salts) and press proofs

This chapter describes the sorts of errors and problems to focus on for each review. Following the descriptions are checklists of what to look for. The chapter concludes with advice for creating your own checklists.

Adapt what you're about to read to suit your job. This chapter describes one way to look at editorial reviews, not the only way. I've divided the tasks into the reviews they generally fit, but some calls were close. I don't follow these checklists religiously and you shouldn't either. Don't be rigid about the number of editorial passes or what you check in each one. For example, don't be surprised to receive a manuscript for a copy edit and find structural problems. Schedule permitting, you may need to perform a developmental edit. You may even have the rare pleasure of getting a manuscript for a developmental edit that is in such fine shape that you need to do only a copy edit.

Finally, on the subject of flexibility, keep in mind there is no single "right" way to edit. Every editor has a unique style; you'll develop your own over time.

The Purpose of Editorial Reviews

Most people have difficulty finding errors in their own work. Take your own writing, for instance. The more familiar you are with the material the more likely you are to read what you expect to read, instead of what's actually on the page. You know what you intended to say; others read what you did say. An editor brings a fresh and objective eye to your work and can tell you if your witticism evoked a grin or a grimace, or if your cliché fell on deaf ears.

The standard advice to writers is to put your manuscript aside for several months so you can read it later with a critical eye. I don't recommend this trick because technical writers who shelve manuscripts for a few months usually lose more than their perspective. At best, if you put the manuscript aside for a few days, you will catch the mechanical errors. If circumstances require you to edit your own manuscript, print out the manuscript and review the hardcopy. You will find many more errors on paper than online, for two reasons: Printers produce better copy than computer screens, and people read text on paper better because that's how we've learned to read. If you edit material designed to be displayed online, however, read it *both* on paper and online because you'll catch different errors.

Most editors usually ask another person to review our writing, even interoffice memos, because we appreciate what another person's perspective and a second pair of eyes can contribute. (Besides, editors have an added burden; nobody ever lets us get away with anything.)

The Editorial Review Process

The number of reviews and when you perform them will vary with the company. To zero in on the nitty-gritty, I'm going to discuss the editorial reviews in the context of the process shown in figure 6–1. Feel free to adapt it to fit the process where you work. If you ever have the opportunity to define the editorial process, I strongly recommend the model described in this chapter.

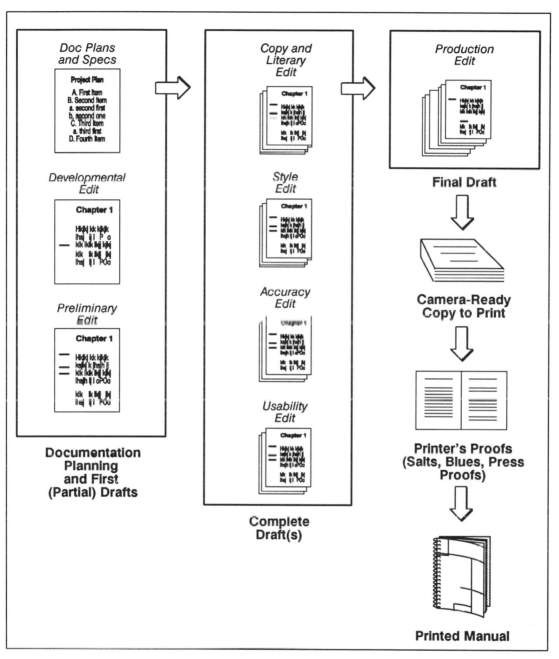

Figure 6–1. Editorial reviews and the publishing process

The model shown in figure 6–1 works as follows. As an editor,

1. You participate in the planning of the documentation and review one or more early, not-necessarily-complete drafts. At this pass, you review the document as a whole. These editorial reviews are called *developmental* and *preliminary edits* in this chapter.

2. You review a more-or-less complete draft. At this pass, you review every word of the document. This review is called the *copy and literary edit* in this chapter. Editorial reviews for style (including internationalization), accuracy, and usability are treated as part of this editorial pass, although some editors handle one or more of these reviews separately.

3. You review a final draft before handing the camera-ready copy to the printer to ensure that the printer receives all the pieces of the book. This final "draft" could be a laser-printed version of the book (especially if the writers prepare the camera-ready copy in your company) or the reproducible mechanicals that the graphic arts specialists prepare after typesetting the manuscript and pasting up the text and art. The review of this draft is called the *production edit* in this chapter.

4. You (or your production department) hand off the book to the printer.

5. You receive proofs, called *salts* or *blues,* from the printer, which you review to ensure that the printer's negatives have been prepared properly. After you approve the proofs, the printer makes the printing plates, and then prints, binds, and delivers the printed book.

Editing Stages and the Product Development Schedule

Figure 6–2 shows one way to plan editing reviews. In this model, the scope of editing tapers off with each successive review. The changes at a developmental edit affect the book as a whole. The copy edit affects the book at the paragraph, sentence, and word level. The production edit deals with the book as a whole, but in the sense of its manufacture. This system avoids duplicated effort and also frees writers to begin their next projects because the editorial changes at the end of the project are minor.

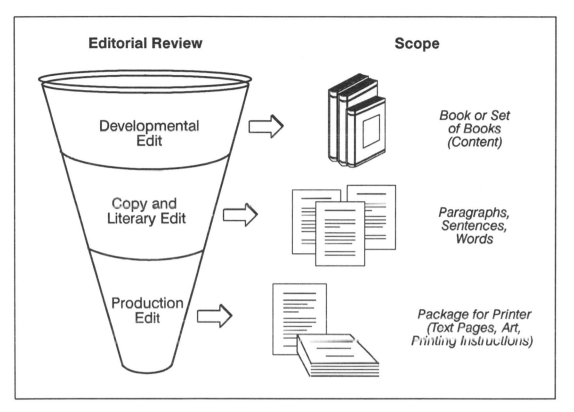

Figure 6-2. The scope of editorial changes narrows at each review

The objective is to make the most extensive changes at the earliest stage possible, because the later the change, the higher the costs and the greater the risk to the schedule. (If a book needs to be reorganized late in the development process, additional resources may be added, driving up costs. Also, there is more flexibility at the beginning of a project than at the end.)

Figure 6-3 shows that the impact of each editorial review decreases as the product development moves from early stages to later stages. (At least that's how it's *supposed* to work.)

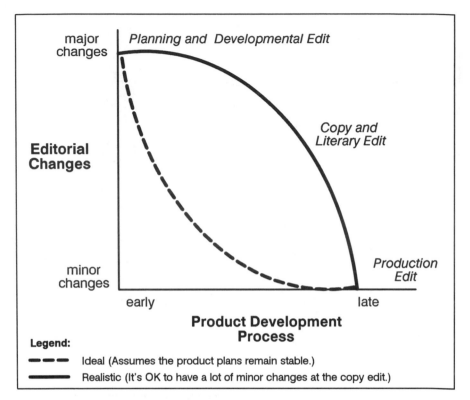

Figure 6–3. The impact of editorial changes should decrease over time

Contrast this system with the common one (figure 6–4) in which the editor doesn't see the manuscript until a few weeks before the scheduled start of production.

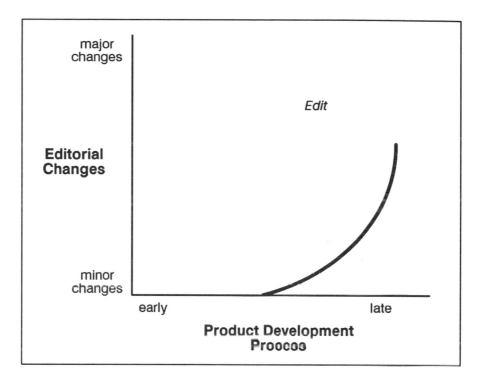

Figure 6–4. Editorial reviews late in the process can necessitate major changes at an inopportune time

Getting Ready to Edit

Maybe some of you can pick up a manuscript and edit away—I can't. Let me rephrase that. I can pounce on a manuscript and do a mechanical edit, but that's only part of my job. To read from the point of view of the intended audience, I need to prepare myself mentally. I review what I know about the reader, including educational background, reading level, experience with similar products, and motivation. Then I adjust how I'll read the manuscript based on what I know about the reader, drawing from the following: any documentation about the book itself, personal experience with customers, and what I've learned from contacts others have had with customers. This exercise helps me get in the frame of mind to read the manuscript from a customer's perspective. For example, a reader of a maintenance and repair manual is impatient and wants to find solutions fast. (She or he is reading the manual because something broke.) Some books have more than one target audience, so you may need to read the manuscript several times, from different points of view.

An interesting aspect of editing is that you read the same manuscript both as a reader and as an editor. Most of this chapter tells you how to read as an editor. You never put your reader hat aside altogether, but you may find it necessary to put aside your editor hat, if you can. (An unfortunate side effect of editing is that you'll find it difficult to simply *read* ever again.) Keep your reader perspective alive and alert at all times, because sometimes that reader will tell you to break an editing rule and you will need to listen. If you don't believe me, go back to chapter 2 and read Rules 1 and 2 again.

Developmental Edits

A *developmental edit*, as its name suggests, takes place while the writer is planning and framing the book. (This review has other names, including *content edit, coordination edit, organizational edit,* and *policy edit*.) Sometimes you'll have a complete first draft of a manuscript to review, but more often you'll review chapters as they're written. (Most writers don't write the chapters in the order they'll be in when published, so you need to be extremely flexible.)

When you perform a developmental edit, you're looking at the book as a whole. You want to make sure the framework will support the individual sentences and words. The writer's intention on the first draft is to get the main ideas on paper. In a developmental edit, you respond to these ideas, less so to their expression. The writer will then revise the draft—craft paragraphs, polish sentences, and carefully select appropriate wording. This second draft will be copy edited—so it's a waste of your time and the writer's to niggle over sentences at this stage when the entire chapter may be drastically reorganized or even deleted.

During a developmental edit, you want to accomplish three goals:

- Help the writer develop a writing plan and outline
- Ensure the book is on track to meet its objectives
- Flag potential troublespots while there's time to fix them

Planning the Book (Documentation Specifications)

The earliest stage of a developmental edit is helping the writer plan the book. The editor participates in the planning by

- Answering questions about your company's processes (for example, who reviews this manual? who signs off?)
- Advising on production requirements and constraints (for example, when is it permissible to print the book in more than one color?)

Often this information is spelled out in a formal proposal for the book that the writer composes and distributes to members of the project team. This proposal may take the form of a documentation specification (or *doc spec,* the term I'll use), a documentation project plan, or a section about documentation in the product's functional specification.

A doc spec typically includes this information:

- Brief description of the product
- Description of the intended users of the product
- Title of the book
- Description of the book's publication history (new book? minor revision? major revision?)
- Description of the target audience(s) of the book
- Type of book (instructional, tutorial, conceptual, comprehensive reference, quick reference, procedural, or any combination of these types)
- Objectives of the book, expressed as observable behaviors; for example:

  By following these assembly instructions, a customer will be able to assemble the tricycle in about an hour

  — A user will be able to find the syntax for any operating system command in this reference manual in less than one minute.

- Plans for testing and reviewing the book
- Names and titles of reviewers
- Schedule
- Distribution plans for the book: Does it ship with the product? Will it be listed in the catalog for customers to order separately? Does it render other titles obsolete?
- Documentation strategy: Is this book part of a set and if so, what's its function relative to the other documents? What's its anticipated life span? Are there other materials that supplement this manual, such as audiotapes, videotapes, labels, or, for computer products, online documents (help, examples, tutorials)?
- Concerns, issues, or risks associated with the book (for example, the writer needs a prototype of the new machine by June 1 or the schedule will slip)
- Production requirements (composition method, illustration needs, trim size, binding method, number of colors, special printing requirements, and similar details)
- Detailed outline of the book's contents

As the editor, you should be on the review list of the doc spec. (If you're not, ask to be.) At the minimum, demand a really good outline before the writing starts, not when the first draft is ready for editing.

As part of the developmental edit you may help the writer develop the doc spec. Under extreme circumstances, you may even write it yourself. This task may require you to interview customers or potential customers, analyze competitors' documentation, study marketing trends, and, of course, learn as much about the product as you can by using it (or a prototype) and reading engineering specifications.

Usually, the writer is responsible for most or all of the planning and research. The developmental editor typically serves in a consulting role, but possibly may dabble in some of these activities to become better acquainted with the project, as his or her workload permits. Sometimes the workload allows you to be more involved in the planning, sometimes less.

Is the Book on Track?

After planning and researching, the writer begins to write the book. You can expect the writer to ask you questions ranging from how to tweak the organization of the book ("I'm thinking about taking those long examples out of chapter 3 and putting them in an appendix. What do you think?") to questions of style ("Should I say *click* the mouse button, *click on* the mouse button, or just *click*?" or "Do equations begin with an uppercase or lowercase letter?").

Write down your answers to these questions. They will be the beginning of the style sheet you will use when you edit the text in detail. (Chapter 10 tells more about style sheets.)

The next phase is reading the first draft of the book. Depending on your department's procedure or what arrangements you and the writer make, you will review either the complete manuscript or one or more of its chapters. You may even review a few chapters and then ask to postpone the rest of the developmental edit until the first draft is done.

Your primary objective on this first editing pass, the developmental edit, is to make sure the book is on the right track, that it will achieve its intended purpose and meet the needs of its target audience.

Here are the main points to check to ensure that the book is meeting its objectives, as stated in the doc spec:

- Audience (is the book appropriate for its intended audience?)
- Organization (is information easily accessible and presented in the right order?)
- Content (is more or less explanation needed, at the major topic level?)

- Overall impression of pace, tone, style, vocabulary (is the writing appropriate for the product and audience?)

- Nomenclature (for example, are references to *lox* permissible, or must the book always spell out *liquid oxygen*?)

- Policy (for example, what disclaimers, cautions, and warnings must be printed in the manual to lessen the risk of liability suits?)

In the developmental edit, review the manuscript according to the ground rules established in the doc spec, not your personal opinion. The appropriate time to discuss the objectives, strategies, and approach is during the planning stage—when you review the doc spec. However, the developmental edit draft might show you that the planned approach doesn't work very well after all. Then the developmental edit is your last chance to suggest major strategic changes.

In summary, the developmental edit asks: Will this book, as planned, do what it's intended to do? What needs to be corrected to keep it on track? Does the doc spec accurately reflect the scope of what's needed and is the schedule realistic? For example, do we need to rethink the documentation set—combine books, divide up books, eliminate titles, or add new titles? Now is the time to alert the project team and management if the book requires more writing than anticipated or if any assumptions made in the doc spec are no longer valid.

Flag Potential Problems

Your other objective during the developmental edit is to identify potential problems. These problems usually have to do with organizational and content matters. For example, you should question manuscripts that devote four pages to the description of a simple task (such as checking the oil) but dismiss more complex tasks (doing a tune-up) in a few paragraphs.

The developmental edit is also a good time to flag potential legal problems. Corporate lawyers typically take a long time to research matters and respond with a decision. (Actually, corporate attorneys say they never make decisions; they only give advice. But just dare to ignore their advice!) If you flag a problem when you see the first draft, you'll be lucky to have a response by the final draft. It's critical to bring legal questions to corporate counsel's attention early if your company requires a legal sign-off before you can send a book to print. Usually lawyers will read a manuscript sooner if someone gives them incentive; otherwise the manuscript may sit until the last minute, where any problems can delay printing. Corporate attorneys are the only people who regularly have larger piles of papers around their offices than do editors, so you need to nudge them to read your book on your schedule.

Some examples of legal issues are mentions of unannounced products, missing or inaccurate trademark or copyright acknowledgments, and potential violations of truth-in-advertising laws.

Scheduling Developmental Edits

For the first edition of a book, you want to see manuscripts as soon as possible, to give you and the writer enough time to find and fix potential problems.

Consider this situation: Let's say the writer finishes a chapter and hands it to you for a developmental edit. The chapter is supposed to be a quick hands-on demonstration of the product, say, a ten-minute exercise to get the user familiar with the product and see a few of its features. But the draft more closely resembles a full-fledged tutorial, taking two hours and explaining many features. How did this happen? Maybe you misunderstood the doc spec or maybe the doc spec just wasn't clear. Maybe the writer started writing a short demonstration and got carried away. Maybe the writer did write a short demonstration but first showed it to the engineer, who screamed so loudly because it omitted many nifty features that the writer rewrote it. Maybe the writer started to write the chapter one way and felt that this approach just wasn't appropriate for this product after all.

Here's another example. A writer you've never worked with before gives you the first draft of a chapter for review. The chapter is replete with inside jokes and obscure literary allusions, and conveys an impression that the reader isn't as well educated as the writer. What's happening? Is the writer pulling your leg? Is the writer ignoring the doc spec or interpreting it more liberally than anyone ever expected? Is there something wrong with the writer's writing or mental competence?

Whatever the reason, the sooner you and the writer identify and start to tackle the problems, the sooner you can fix them.

I prefer to do a developmental edit on a chapter-by-chapter basis for books that are new or are written by a writer I haven't worked with before. I ask writers to give me chapters when they feel they're ready for me to see them. If a book has many short chapters, I prefer to review two or three at a time to reduce my start-up time. Writers may give me incomplete chapters with only topic sentences, partially formed sentences, notes to themselves ("Give example of conservation of energy here") or to reviewers ("The following procedure results in an error—what's wrong?"), and text heads without any following text ("Diagnostic messages to come"). As long as there's enough text for me to get a feel for the chapter, I'll accept the draft in any shape or form. (Remember, I have the doc spec with a detailed outline to refer to.) For example, one writer prefers to write her first drafts in 14-pt type to make it easy to see on the computer monitor. Her first drafts are one ugly piece of work, typographically speaking, but my tired eyes love them.

If I've worked with a writer before and have confidence in her or his ability to stick to the doc spec faithfully, then I'll wait for a complete (or mostly complete) first draft, subject to two other conditions: that the schedule lets me wait, and the book is reasonably straightforward. But if the book presents a particular challenge, say it's about a new and unstable product, it's a new type of book, or we're using a new design, then I prefer to review it by chapters.

How long does a developmental edit take? That varies. I try to return individual chapters within a week, just by fitting them in between other books. I personally find it a nuisance to maintain a schedule at this level of detail, because most books slip a day or two here and there. Sometimes it takes longer to update the schedule for dozens of chapters than to edit the chapters themselves. I prefer to schedule reviews of long chapters (more than 100 pages) and complete drafts, using 100 pages per week as a rule of thumb.

You'll need to consider your own working style and working environment when you schedule developmental edits.

Figure 6–5 shows some excerpts from developmental edits.

If you pull out subsection 1.3.2 and make it a separate section (1.4), you could promote the other subsections. The chapter would be more evenly balanced—the information is as important as the information in other sections, but it's currently buried.

The tone changes abruptly here [in the middle of a chapter]. I can see you're addressing the less experienced segment of readers now, but it's not apparent. Add a transition. If you think you'll need to do this often, we should talk about other strategies.

How about adding a table that summarizes this section?

This section would be good in chapter 4, where you discuss compatibility issues. Or expand it and make it a separate chapter?

The examples don't stand out from the text or each other. It's difficult to tell where one example ends and another begins. Stop by to see samples of how we've handled these examples in other books. Or ask Jill Jacobs to show you her draft.

I don't understand how this subsection relates to the main topic. Is a section head missing? Or are there some concepts that haven't been introduced yet that I (the reader) should know about? Or does this just belong somewhere else?

These examples are great, but you need to spell out what the reader should zoom in on. Also, they sometimes pop out at the reader—a little introduction would help a lot. Do you have plans yet for testing these procedures and examples?

I heard a rumor this morning that technical support won't support this. Can you check this out and let me know—there are a few other books in the doc set that refer readers to *this* book. We may need to take chapter 6 and make it an appendix in the other books.

Figure 6–5. Samples of developmental editing comments

Checklist for Developmental Editing

Inconsistencies with the objectives of the book (as stated in the doc spec):

- [ ] Audience. Are content and level of detail appropriate for the target audience? Are tone and writing style appropriate?

- [ ] Content. Is the product adequately described? For a major revision, does the draft fix known problems or errors and address suggestions and complaints from readers?

- [ ] Organization. Are major topics presented in a logical order? Does each topic lead into the next?

- [ ] Testing. Are the plans still adequate or are there additional areas to test? (For details, see "Editing for Usability" later in this chapter.)

- [ ] Consistency. Does it fit in with other manuals in the documentation set?

- [ ] Examples. Are there enough? Do they demonstrate what they're intended to demonstrate? Where would more examples help? Are any examples extraneous, ambiguous, or confusing?

Content issues:

- [ ] Content. What to take out, what to put in, what to keep, what to change. Does this book fulfill its function in the documentation set? Does the documentation set as a whole achieve its purpose? By far, this item is the most difficult editing—and writing—task of all.

- [ ] What's missing? It's much easier to respond to what's in a manuscript that the writer should remove or change than to identify what isn't there that the writer should add. For example, are any major topics missing? Does the book need more examples? Should the writer add an illustration? Should there be a table to summarize the information?

- [ ] What's superfluous? Is information duplicated from another book? Can we point to that book instead of repeating the information here?

Organization issues:

☐ Is the information organized so that readers can find answers quickly?

☐ Is the information organized appropriately? For example, a handbook that is supposed to show readers how to perform a task (change a flat tire, print a word processing document, wrap a sprained ankle) is probably more effective if the main topics are the tasks (change, print, wrap), rather than the thing (the tire, the **print** command, the ankle or bandage). Are reference pages organized by function or alphabetically? For example, are commands described in the order they appear on the menu or are they listed alphabetically? There are pros and cons for each scheme of organizing information. (See the bibliography for some books that tackle this subject.)

☐ Watch for sentences that point the reader ahead to this chapter and that chapter for preliminary information. For example, a book in which chapter 2 tells you to read chapters 3 and 4 before proceeding to the next step *might* need to be reorganized. These cross-references don't necessarily mean the book is poorly organized. The book may be organized modularly, for example, so that readers of different skill levels or with different needs can skip some topics. Understand the rationale for the organization (the doc spec should tell you) and then, during the developmental edit, evaluate whether the organization works, from a reader's standpoint.

☐ Watch for sentences that seem to say, "Here's something I forgot to tell you earlier." Watch for a lot of parenthetical comments that give background or prerequisite information. For example, in a classic episode of M*A*S*H, Colonel Blake is giving instructions over a bullhorn (from a safe distance) to Hawkeye and Trapper John, who are attempting to defuse a bomb that has landed in the middle of the compound. "Cut the red wire." *Snip*. "But first . . ."

☐ Watch for an abundance of *notes*. Sometimes writers use them for information that doesn't fit smoothly into the text. Make sure that the information warrants it. The underlying problem could be that the book (or chapter) is poorly organized.

☐ Watch for a lot of undefined terms and unexplained concepts in early chapters that are explained in later chapters, a sign that the material needs to be rearranged.

Checklist for Developmental Editing (continued)

☐   Make sure the reader doesn't have to know everything about the subject or product to find information in the manual. For example, if you group plants by genus in the book, also provide an alphabetical listing for readers less fluent in taxonomy. If commands are grouped according to the menu where they appear on the screen, then make sure there is at least one other way a user can find information on a particular command without having to know what menu it's on. Having a detailed index and glossary is a good start. You can make it even easier for the reader. Write a summary that tells where to find information ("How to change a tire—chapter 3" or "Recording one program while watching another . . . page 12"). Print this summary on the inside front cover or, if your budget permits, print the summary on heavier stock or in color.

☐   Bear in mind there is no single correct way to organize all books, although there are good and bad ways to organize individual books. The editor needs to evaluate a book's organization to see if it meets the needs of the reader and conforms to the goals described in the doc spec.

Some ways to organize technical information:

- Most important to least important
- Most often needed to least often needed
- Simple concepts to more complex concepts
- Chronology (step-by-step, such as for procedures)
- Whole and its parts (analytical)
- Subject matter (for example, looking at biology through evolution and then through molecular chemistry)

Style issues:

☐   Conformance to style guide. Note major discrepancies only once, rather than mark every instance of a deviation from the style guide. For example, if the writer consistently uses the wrong font for command syntax, point that out before he or she completes the 200-page reference chapter. If you see isolated instances of the wrong font, make a note to the writer about it and tell what font is correct. Some editors prefer to mark all errors they find, rather than risk overlooking them at the next review. Other editors prefer to wait until the copy edit, because manuscripts can change considerably. What's important is that you don't become distracted by details when you should be looking at the big picture.

☐   Major inconsistencies. Does the writer address the reader as *you* in some sentences and *the reader* or *the user* in others, for no discernible reason? Sometimes it's helpful to recognize and watch for inconsistencies in early drafts.

☐   Major stylistic problems. Is the overall vocabulary level higher (or lower) than the assumed educational level of the target audience? Does the writer overuse the passive voice? Mark the first twenty or so occurrences to show the writer the problem. You want writers to improve their writing skills generally, so give guidance and advice that they can use in the future.

Potential problem areas:

☐   Production. Are there design or production elements that require lead time to prepare? Do we need new photographs? Does the book have foldout pages? Does the artwork have any screens?

☐   Costs. Do the plans blow the budget out of the boardroom? For example, is a special cover design necessary, or is our standard cover acceptable?

☐   Design. Is the writer following the correct specifications or using the right templates for text formatting? Do we need a new page design for this book?

☐   Distribution. Do we need to resolve any issues such as part numbers or pricing? Any distribution restrictions?

☐ Technical. Does the book mention other products that may have been changed? Has the technical scope of this book been changed? (If a software product now runs on a different or additional operating system, how do we need to change the manual? Have probes discovered any new planetary features since the last revision? Does our increased knowledge of how chromosomes work affect the contents of this book?)

☐ Legal. Do we need a trademark search? Are there any potentially libelous statements? Violations of truth-in-advertising laws? Risk that the product will inflict injury or damage? Do we need to print special warnings or disclaimers? Do we need to acknowledge another company's work?

☐ Product nomenclature. Has the product name been approved? Will the product name carry a trademark acknowledgment?

☐ Policy. Are there references to products that have not yet been announced? Is any information company confidential or proprietary? Are references to competitors handled fairly and honestly?

☐ Process. Should anybody else be on the review list?

Preliminary Edits

I perform what I call a *preliminary edit* on the first draft of a manual undergoing a minor revision. Minor revision means we're not going to change the basic approach, structure, and strategy. (If we had reassessed our audience, reorganized the book's contents, modified the documentation set, or made any other critical changes, then this revision would be major, and I'd do a developmental edit.) I check the same points as for a developmental edit, but less scrupulously.

The main purpose of a preliminary edit is to find global problems at an early stage. For example, suppose your department introduced some editorial style changes or minor book design changes since you last revised this book. Would it add significant time to the schedule to implement these changes? If so, are these changes necessary? Should you make an exception for this book?

Sometimes a preliminary edit turns up a big problem that nobody anticipated when reviewing the doc spec. For example, the product strategy shifted (again!) to support the new computer model, the one with a different keyboard. With global political changes and the restructuring of national boundaries, do all the maps in the book need to be redrawn?

Usually, the preliminary edit gives the editor a chance to skim a document for major or recurring problems so that the writer can fix them before the copy edit.

Figure 6–6 shows some excerpts from preliminary edits.

You've used italics to identify new terms throughout—except in chapter 7, where you use bold-face. Also, this draft has a lot of passive voice. I've marked up chapters 1 and 2 to give you an idea. If you have questions or need help, let me know.

The changes are so minor that it doesn't make sense for you to convert this book to the new templates with the PostScript fonts. It would be a lot of work, with little benefit. The fonts are so close that customers won't notice the difference from book to book. We can make the change next revision, if there is one. And if there isn't another revision, we won't need the new fonts anyway.

One change we didn't make at the last revision was to redo all the screen captures. They're ugly, difficult to read, and every one is sized differently. We have better tools for editing these now than we had two years ago, and it would make the book look so much better.

Isn't it time to pull Appendix B? We kept it in last time because there were a few customers still using those old machines, but they were going to drop support at this release. At the last revision, we removed all references to this appendix from the documentation so that it would be trivial to delete it later.

You shouldn't be using the templates for 6x9 books any more. The new trim size for our small books is 7.5x9. We're using up the 6x9 preprinted covers on reprints. All new and revised books are supposed to be the new size.

Here are some words used inconsistently—and our preferred spelling or usage:
on-line, online (no hyphen)
co-processor, coprocessor (no hyphen)
PRISM—must be uppercase, italics for trademark purposes
footnote all trademarked products at first use (see Style Guide, page 3–38 for details)

We changed the titles of the command reference and system administrator's books; the new titles are [. . .]. Give the full title and part number in the preface only and change all those cross-references in the text to more generic references and point the reader to the preface for details.

Figure 6–6. Samples of preliminary editing comments

Copy and Literary Edits

When you do a developmental edit, you view the book's framework. When you *copy edit,* you inspect the book's individual building blocks: its paragraphs, sentences, and words.

Here's where the practice of technical editing clashes with the academics of technical editing. In theory, we'd follow the model of a publishing house, where a literary editor works with the writer to improve the style of the book. The literary editor reviews the book's tone, pace, wording, and sentence structure. This review is generally more subjective than other editing passes. After the writer has polished the prose, the revised manuscript is sent to the publisher's copy editing department. The copy editor generally looks for things that are wrong, namely, those items that break rules. This model may work for fiction, textbooks, and general nonfiction, but not for technical documentation. I've never heard of a technical writer or editor with a schedule generous enough to allow for separate reviews.

In my current job, we call this review a *literary edit* and consider a traditional copy edit a subset of it. Some other names for this review: *integrity edit, language edit, mechanical edit, screening edit,* and *substantive edit.*

Some of these names have special connotations that are important only when you're establishing the level of edit. For example, if you want a shorthand way of saying that you'll ensure that references to other parts of the book (other chapters and the table of contents, for example) are correct but that you won't smooth inelegant sentence structure, you could say you'll perform an *integrity edit,* not a *language edit.*

In this chapter, when I mean just mechanical editing, I use the term *copy edit.* When I refer to the editorial pass that includes a *style edit*, an *accuracy edit,* and a *usability edit,* I use the term *literary edit.* And when I mean you're checking everything possible, I call it a *copy and literary edit.*

The copy and literary edit may be the only time you read the manuscript word for word. You'll be wearing your editor's hat for most of this review (you *do* have a green visor, don't you?), but you need to keep your reader advocacy hat nearby.

When most people hear the word *editing,* they think of the activities that fall under copy editing. Copy editing generally involves fixing the mechanical details—spelling, punctuation, grammar, capitalization, consistency—and checking facts or questioning logical or factual inconsistencies. These tasks are about as glamorous as taking out the trash, but just as important.

During a copy edit, read every word—don't skim. If there's any chance something could be wrong, check it or question it. Check the following:

- [ ] Spelling, grammar, punctuation for correctness and consistency

- [ ] Accuracy (facts and logic)

- [ ] Sentence structure and style

- [ ] Transitions from paragraph to paragraph, section to section

- [ ] Additional explanations and clarifications (at sentence level)

- [ ] Conformance to the style guide your company follows (with respect to compounding, use of en dashes, use of numbers vs. numerals, use of contractions, and similar prosaic details)

- [ ] References to other chapters, sections, figures, tables, and to other documentation

- [ ] Consistency within the manual and within the documentation set

More detailed checklists appear later in this section. Separate explanations of the style, accuracy, and usability reviews, with detailed checklists for each, follow the general discussion about copy and literary edits.

Scheduling Copy and Literary Edits

The most time-consuming edits are those for accuracy, usability, and consistency. There aren't any shortcuts for testing accuracy and usability because every book is unique in these areas. The consistency checking does become faster over time; the more often you do it, the more automatic it becomes.

Your first year or two as an editor, you'll find that you turn pages in a manuscript more times than you had ever imagined possible. You'll read through chapters 1 and 2 and discover inconsistencies in the style of text heads. Back to the beginning. Now you realize that some figure captions have periods at the end. Did the others? You start over. The writer is indenting examples. Better go back and check.

After a while, you will be able to check everything in fewer passes, because you'll learn how to make a really useful style sheet to record your style decisions (see chapter 10) and you'll develop shortcuts and habits.

Don't be discouraged if you need 50 passes to edit your first manuscript. You can simplify the task considerably by checking a few items each time. For example, don't check tables for consistency while you're checking everything else; make that a separate pass. Likewise, check figures and figure captions separately, check all reference pages at one time, and so on, using the checklists in this chapter (and your own) as a guide. Some editors still use this approach after years of editing. Others prefer to check as much as possible in one or two passes. Do what's comfortable for you.

I recommend you read the book first from a reader's point of view to capture your first impression. Let your second reading be with the critical editorial eye. But don't feel restricted by this. If you're reading as a user and find a typo or other error, go ahead and mark it, and continue. (If you come across something you need to look up, I suggest you mark the question so you'll remember it, but keep on reading so you don't lose your train of thought.)

How long should a copy edit take? Over the years I've seen estimates for editing (encompassing all levels, from total rewrites to proofreading) that range from 1 page to 100 pages per day. How long it takes to edit depends on what you're checking (the level of edit) and the condition of the manuscript (for example, writing quality and density of text). I prefer to think of the schedule this way: It will take as long to edit a book as the schedule permits. The more time you have, the more thoroughly you can edit the book. It's most unlikely you'll ever be given a wide open schedule—or have only one book at a time to edit—so understand how to apply the principles of levels of edit and make the most of what you have. (Chapter 8 shows you how to take shortcuts.)

When you perform a copy edit is more important than *how long* you have. You want to do the detailed edit when the content and wording are stable but not frozen.

If you've done a developmental edit and you're comfortable with the direction the manuscript is headed, consider doing the copy edit after the writer has incorporated all the revisions from the final technical review. If you do a copy edit after the technical review, you may be able to check all details just once. Don't delay the copy edit if you know or suspect the writer needs a strong language edit, however, because major rewriting could require another technical review.

If you haven't performed a developmental edit, do the copy edit as early as you can, so you and the writer have more time. Many conflicts between writer and editor arise because the editor's suggestions come later than the writer can deal with them. A good time for the copy edit is concurrently with all technical reviews. The writer expects to revise the manuscript to fix technical errors and can incorporate editing changes at the same time.

If the schedule permits, do one copy edit concurrently with the technical review and another after the writer has made all the revisions.

If you've never seen the manuscript before, or if the developmental edit turned up many problems, the worst time to do a copy edit is after the final technical review. The writer may be predisposed to accept your comments, but the schedule may not permit drastic revision. More likely the writer will resist changes because everyone—the writer's manager, the developers, and the reviewers—considers the book nearly done. The writer would have to justify the additional time spent on the project. Perhaps his or her next project is starting up. The writer may feel the need to fend off criticism or pressure and claim an overeager editor is requesting gratuitous changes. Some writers postpone editing until the last minute so they can claim there's no time to incorporate changes. Some companies that routinely schedule editing at the end of the process are often faced with this problem.

Checklist for Copy and Literary Editing

Mechanical details:

☐ Check spelling for correctness and consistency. For example, is *gray* used in some chapters and *grey* in others?

☐ Check grammar (syntax) for correctness and consistency.

☐ Check for agreement between subject and verb.

☐ Check that sentences don't shift in tense or person.

☐ Check punctuation for correctness and consistency.

☐ Check cross-references to other chapters, sections, and subsections.

☐ Check cross-references to titles of other manuals. If you believe the manual referred to has been revised, make sure the cross-reference is still valid. (You can ask the writer to verify this information if you don't have time.)

☐ Check that part numbers (order numbers) of other manuals are correct.

☐ Check that there are references in text to all figures and tables and that the references are correct.

☐ Check that word usage is appropriate (according to your standard dictionary, style guide, or industry conventions). Technical terms should be used precisely. For example, the term *expression* and the phrase *is a function of* should not be used casually in a book about mathematics.

☐ Check the use of abbreviations and acronyms for consistency of spelling and punctuation and to ensure that their meanings are commonly known or explained.

☐ Check that symbols (such as arithmetic operators and chemical elements) are standard and that they're explained when necessary.

Organization:

During a developmental edit, you check the overall organization of a book (or set of books). At the copy and literary edit, you check the organization at the paragraph and sentence level.

☐ Ensure that terms are defined and concepts explained.

☐ Ensure that steps are presented in the order in which they're performed.

☐ Watch for an overuse of notes, which could signal problems in how the chapter (or book) is organized.

☐ Check the overall flow of text, including the transitions from paragraph to paragraph.

Inconsistencies:

☐ Check for conformance to whichever style guide you're following.

☐ Check for consistent terminology and nomenclature.

☐ Check that product names are spelled and capitalized correctly.

☐ Check for parallel style and construction, where appropriate.

☐ Check for clear antecedents (words to which pronouns refer).

Formatting:

Figure 6–7 identifies elements in a typical technical manual.

☐ Check that the correct template has been used or the correct design specifications have been followed.

☐ Ensure that the design (layout, typography, style of artwork) is appropriate for the information and audience.

☐ Make sure the page looks easy to read and the design is not cluttered.

Checklist for Copy and Literary Editing (continued)

- [ ] Ensure that like information is presented in a like manner.

- [ ] Point out where an illustration or table would present the information better.

- [ ] Check that headers and footers have the correct information.

- [ ] Check that the correct font is used in text (including text heads, tables, and captions).

- [ ] Check that the correct font is used to indicate technical distinctions. For example, in computer manuals, check the fonts for user input and computer output. In calculator manuals, check how keys are represented. Check how constants and variables are handled in equations.

- [ ] Check that the design and formatting details complement the text. For example, don't use silly cartoons in a manual that is written in a sober tone. Highlight important information (for example, heads and warnings) typographically and downplay less important elements (footnotes).

Checklist for Copy and Literary Editing (continued)

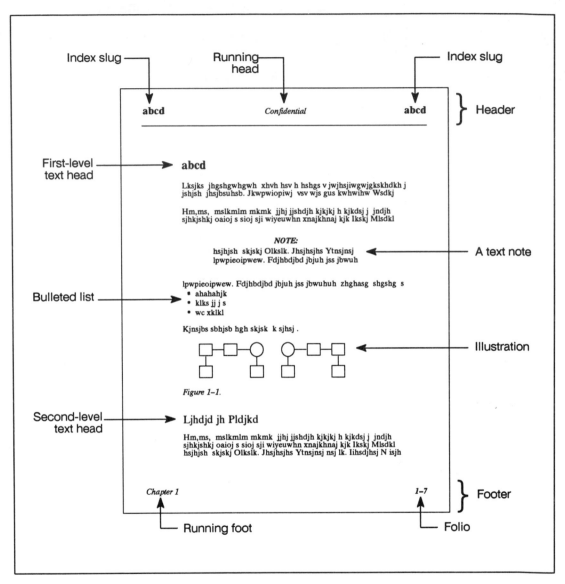

Figure 6–7. Sample page showing formatting elements

Figures and tables:

- [ ] Check that the rules (lines) are the correct weight and intersect cleanly.

- [ ] Check the position of callouts with respect to the images they describe.

- [ ] Check that the correct font is used for the text, including callouts, captions, and titles.

- [ ] Check use of fill patterns (if the artwork is prepared on a computer) for consistency and reproducible quality. (How well or poorly a fill pattern shows up when printed depends on the pattern itself and the equipment used by the print vendor.)

- [ ] Check that the figure clearly represents what it is supposed to.

- [ ] Check that the details are executed neatly.

- [ ] Check that the level of detail in the figure is appropriate for the concept.

- [ ] Check figure captions and table titles for consistency of spelling, style, and punctuation.

- [ ] Check for consistent handling of any continued figures or tables (those that take up more than one page).

- [ ] Check for consistency of table entries (parallel structure, consistent punctuation).

- [ ] Check for parallelism between similar figures or tables.

- [ ] Check for alignment of column heads and entries in tables.

- [ ] Check that column heads clearly and concisely describe the information in the column.

- [ ] Check that there are enough (but not too many) rules to separate information in tables.

- [ ] Check that a table or figure isn't spread across more pages than necessary. (For example, a table that could fit on one page should not be split across two pages.)

- [ ] Check that figures and tables are positioned close to the text that discusses them.

Checklist for Copy and Literary Editing (continued)

Figures 6–8 and 6–9 illustrate these points for figures and tables, respectively.

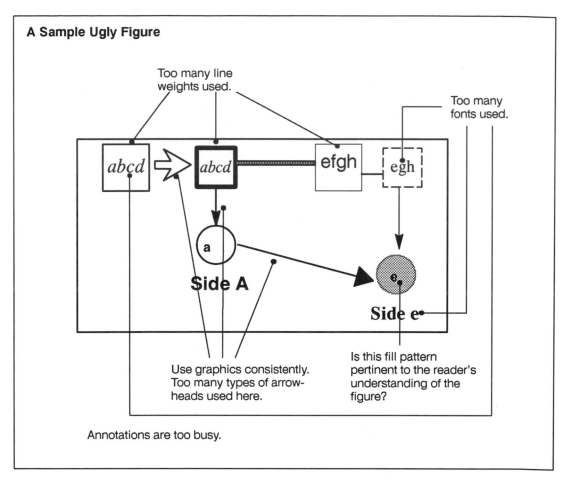

Figure 6–8. What to look for when you edit an illustration

Checklist for Copy and Literary Editing (continued)

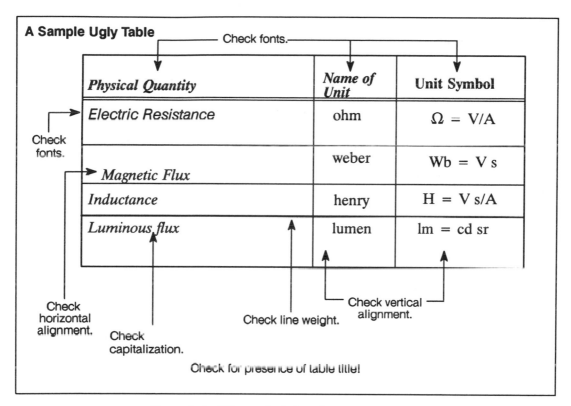

Figure 6–9. What to look for when you edit a table

Miscellaneous:

☐ Check that edits, comments, and questions made at previous reviews have been addressed.

☐ Confirm that the writer has a testing plan for examples, procedures, and tutorials (in addition to whatever testing the editor plans to do).

☐ Verify that the book delivers on its promises (as stated in the doc spec).

☐ Check that required legal notices (trademarks, copyright notices, and disclaimers) are included.

These checklists show only some of the items you may need to check in a copy edit. Chapters 11 and 12 give pointers for editing constructs peculiar to technical writing, such as bulleted lists.

Editing for Style

We've just seen what to look for in the copy edit part of a copy and literary edit. Now let's see what to look for in a literary edit (even if you're doing both concurrently).

Style decisions are subjective. The house style guide should cover topics the company does not want to leave to writer discretion. The rest depends on context. Passive or active voice depends on the point of the particular sentence. Perspective (first, second, or third person) depends on the purpose and audience of the book. Word choice is a writer's decision, unless the word is offensive, ambiguous, misused, or inappropriate (such as dialect in a technical manual). If you can suggest a more precise word, by all means suggest it. But you have no right to insist the writer make the change.

Editing for style does not mean tampering with the writer's style of expression. If you want to impose your own style on a manuscript, then you should be writing, not editing. (Writers who occasionally edit have a difficult time adjusting to this reality because it forces them into a role so different from their usual one.) When you edit, you have to suppress your own style and let the author's style speak. (This caution does not apply if you're editing your own writing.) If a work has two or more writers who are supposed to be speaking in one voice, then you need to smooth the stylistic differences so they don't jar the reader.

What is the limit on the writer's style license in technical writing? Whenever there is a conflict between the writer's style and the rules in chapter 2, the rules win. A style that confuses readers so that they cannot use the book is inappropriate. A style that conflicts with the company's image or marketing goals is inappropriate. Sexist and racist language and remarks in a manual are not style issues; they're policy issues (and a management, not an editorial problem). Aside from these limitations, the writer has considerable license.

Here's a small but instructive example about changing a writer's style. I once undertook a freelance assignment to edit a training manual. When I picked up the manuscript, the client restated what she'd said at the interview, that I was to do only a *light* copy edit, because the writer was highly experienced, knew the company style, and was following an approved outline. (She did elaborate that I was to do a copy edit for grammar and spelling only.) Since the person who gave me these instructions was also an editor, I assumed she and I spoke the same language. I was wrong. A few days after I returned the manuscript, I stopped by the client's office and the editor asked to have a word with me. I expected her to compliment my astuteness because I had spotted some logical inconsistencies that a less experienced editor might have missed. I was wrong again.

"When I said a light edit, I didn't mean quite *that* light," she said in a strained tone of voice.

You could have knocked me over with a Post-It. I knew I had done a solid copy edit.

She picked up the manuscript and turned to the only page she had marked. "Why didn't you change *big* to *large* in this sentence?"

"Why would I?" I asked.

"Because *large* is better."

I don't remember the sentence now, but the document had an informal style and the connotation was physical size. Other than personal preference, there was no reason to substitute one word for another in that context. Word choice at this level is the writer's prerogative. This experience taught me that writers don't always exaggerate when they tell about (some) editors who make arbitrary changes.

◇ —— ◇

Ahem, That's Not What I Meant to Say!

A police cadet said there were more reports than usual of minor traffic accidents yesterday. "The fog is really making it difficult for driving," she said. "Disability is low, but the roads don't seem to be icy."
[From a local newspaper.]

REST ROOM CLOSED EXCEPT FOR SPECIAL EVENTS
[Sign on men's room door. From *The Sunday Oregonian,* via *Parade.*]

Do report any vehicle defects to your Supervisor, however minor.
[We don't care how low your supervisor ranks. From a safety handbook.]

The company will provide head protection in positions where it is required.
[From a safety handbook.]

◇ —— ◇

Checklist for Copy and Literary Editing (continued)

Writing style:

- [ ] Check the overall flow of text, including the transitions from paragraph to paragraph.

- [ ] Check that the text is generally readable, that sentences are clear, and that syntax is simple.

- [ ] Check that the text is concise but complete.

- [ ] Check that the text doesn't overuse jargon or passive voice.

- [ ] Check that instructions use positive and negative statements appropriately.

- [ ] Suggest verbs to replace noun strings and nominalizations. For example, suggest replacing "database maintenance" with "maintain the database" and "the technician's operation of" with "the technician operates."

- [ ] Check that the wording is precise and direct.

- [ ] Check sentence length (no fragments, no run-ons) and variety.

- [ ] Check that the wording isn't convoluted, bloated, ornate, or inappropriate; ensure that the text uses terminology that is correct and standard, not coined or unconventional.

- [ ] Ensure that nothing will offend readers (sexist language, ethnic slurs, libelous statements, derogatory references to competitors, poorly executed humor).

- [ ] Check that the text is appropriate for non-U.S. readers. For details, read "Editing for an International Audience" later in this chapter.

- [ ] Check that things don't happen anthropomorphically or magically (computers don't "think" and software doesn't "understand").

- [ ] Ensure that adequate emphasis is given to what's truly important and not overdone for minor points.

- [ ] Check that the style is consistent throughout the book or at least within each chapter. (For example, if a book has both tutorial and reference sections, each can have a different style, but should be internally consistent.)

Editing for Accuracy

Don't expect to have the luxury of performing a separate review for accuracy. Most editors check for accuracy on the same draft they copy edit.

When you edit for accuracy, check what's reasonable for you to check. Certainly you check all arithmetic and all conversions (binary to decimal, gallons to liters).

You have to give credit to the author for having researched the subject and knowing the information. If the writer is a physicist whose paper challenges some accepted theories, it's not your place to question the data or theories. If, however, one sentence appears to contradict another, then it's not only your place, it's your job to point out the discrepancy. You don't have to know which sentence is correct; it's the writer's job to figure it out. It's sufficient for you to point out contradictions and ask questions.

The more you know about a subject, the better you'll be able to ask intelligent questions. If you also know the answers, that's better still.

Conversions: More Than Simple Arithmetic

When you convert a value from one system to another, you need to think beyond the arithmetic.

Watch for precision in addition to accuracy. The converted value should never be more precise than the original, measured value. For example, when you convert 50 square feet to square meters by multiplying by 0.0929, the arithmetic comes out to 4.645 square meters. In most situations, 4.6 is appropriate, since the 50 square feet may be an approximation. Know the acceptable tolerances in your field and ensure that measurements and conversions are appropriate.

Also bear in mind that simple arithmetic conversions can sometimes give you a number that doesn't have a real-world application.

For example, if you edit an owner's guide for a computer printer, you might have to convert the unit's specifications into metric values. One of the specifications would be the manufacturer's recommended paper weight. In the United States, paper weight is expressed in pounds. If you didn't know any better, you might just multiply the number of pounds by .45 (to convert the pounds to kilograms). The result would be a number, but it wouldn't tell a person in France what paper to buy. Paper weight—*basis weight* in a U.S. printer's lingo—refers to the weight of a ream (500 sheets) of that paper grade in its basic size (set by the paper industry). The basic size for writing paper, which includes bond and duplicator paper, is 17 by 22 inches; the basic size for cover papers is 20 by 26. Outside the United States, basis weight is expressed as *grammage,* or in grams per square meter (g/m^2).

It is possible to convert paper weights from one system to the other, but to do so you need a table of conversion values for each paper size. Your best bet is to use the charts provided by the paper manufacturers. (These charts are often printed in the books of paper samples.) For more information about paper, see the recommended books in the bibliography.

Also watch out when converting sizes for tools, clothing, and other manufactured items. You may need to use charts of equivalent sizes, rather than an arithmetic formula.

Factual and technical accuracy:

☐ Check that all calculations are correct.

☐ Solve all equations. Use the values for constants and variables given in the text and check that the results are the same.

☐ Check that all arithmetic conversions are correct (for example, English to metric, octal to decimal).

☐ Ensure that calculations are made to the appropriate precision.

☐ Check that all numeric sequences are correct (for example, lists, footnotes, table numbers).

☐ Check that all alphabetic sequences are correct.

☐ Check examples for accuracy (for example, run the sample programs, compare the labels on panels and buttons to their spelling in the text, compare the list of parts to the items in the package).

☐ Compare examples and the text that refers to them for consistency.

☐ Ensure that the examples support the text and are at a level appropriate for the audience.

☐ Check command lines by executing them (where appropriate and practical).

☐ Check that names of directories and files (in computer documentation) are correct.

☐ Check procedures by doing them (where appropriate and practical). For example, set the VCR clock using the instructions in the owner's guide.

☐ Test a tutorial by following it (where appropriate and practical).

☐ Check that representations of computer screens, prompts and messages, and command names (including those on menus) are correct.

☐ Flag (question) any technical inconsistencies or discrepancies.

Figure 6-10 shows a page that has been subjected to a thorough copy edit.

Chapter 2. Installing the System

introduces

This chapter ~~provides an introduction to~~ the Dingbat installation pro-

and gives

cess, ~~Its purpose is to provide you with~~ sufficient background infor-

for you

mation to follow the instructions in Installing Optional Software on

the?

(your) Dingbat system.

not defined; say this chapter introduces these concepts

(Partitions and filesets) are presented, since you will need to answer

passive

questions about them during the install.*ation process*

Dingbat

A br~~ief~~ discussion of the differences between versions 1.0 and 2.0 is

will need to refer

presented, since you ~~are referred~~ to version 1.0 manuals to p~~re~~form

passive

the install.*ation*

"your" in first paragraph

Read

~~Finally, you are directed to~~ Installing Optional Software on (the)

Dingbat system. *for detailed instructions...*

This is the overview of the chapter. Tell the main points. Why mention now that the reader will be sent to another book? Is that book a prerequisite? If so, tell them to read it first, then return to this chapter.

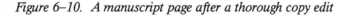

Figure 6–10. A manuscript page after a thorough copy edit

Editing for Usability

A thoughtful developmental edit and a thorough copy edit go a long way toward making a book easy to use.

An editor can contribute to the usability of a book in other ways, too.

Some editors (and writers) work with human factors engineers on formal usability tests, which are usually conducted in special laboratories equipped with one-way mirrors, videocameras, and other instruments that record a session of users working with products and using documentation. For example, a software program might record every character a user types. This data can indicate what types of errors users are most likely to make and can lead to improving the product's design. Other testing can show how often or when a user reaches for the manual, how long it takes to find information, and whether it helps the user perform a specified task. Users complete questionnaires and participate in interviews (debriefings) to supply additional data. (Usability testing is an application of human factors engineering, or ergonomics. The bibliography lists some good books to introduce you to the subject.)

Conducting usability tests to gather data on manuals is a wonderful way to improve documentation—if you work for a company that has laboratories, training programs for writers and editors, and funding for the testing. If your company actively supports usability testing, you probably have testing tools and checklists tailored to your company's products.

This section is for the majority of editors and writers, those who don't have full-fledged usability testing programs where they work. Even without these resources, you have other means for improving the usability of the books you edit and the products they support.

Under ideal circumstances, you would perform different types of usability testing throughout the development cycle and on different drafts of the manuscript. Writing, testing, editing, and rewriting are best done iteratively.

It's more likely time and money will allow you to test only one draft—probably the draft you receive for copy editing. The manuscript you receive for a developmental edit is often incomplete, and the final production edit draft is ready only at the end of the cycle (too late to make major writing changes). The draft you copy edit should be complete and reviewed at least once for technical accuracy. Also, the writer has time to revise the manuscript.

Checklist for Copy and Literary Editing (continued)

Usability:

☐ Read from the point of view of the user, mostly for clarity. (This item covers a lot!) Here's where putting yourself in the user's shoes really comes in handy. Don't just read—read and think. Process the information. Is every sentence clear? What isn't clear? Do you need a small, concrete example to let you know you're following along? Did you stumble over a sentence, maybe because you misread "entrance" as a noun instead of a verb in this context? If so, mark it; chances are somebody else will stumble there, too.

☐ Read and respond the way the target audience would. Your first impression counts. If you sense a condescending tone, the reader will, too. If you have questions about the content, write them down. I often find myself penning a question in the margin, only to have it answered in the next paragraph. That shows the text is flowing logically and that the writer has anticipated the question. By marking my question, I've let the writer know that she or he has successfully led me along.

☐ Be sensitive to the needs of non-American readers. Watch for slang, jargon, idiom, and culture-bound examples. See "Editing for an International Audience" later in this chapter for details.

☐ Check that the writer explains the conventions used in the text (for example, "What the user types is shown in color" or "Terms in italics are defined in the glossary") and that the stated conventions are implemented in the text. When you're writing a 300-page book, it's easy to forget that you meant to use a particular convention. It's even easier to adopt a convention and forget to tell the reader about it. Editors need to be on the alert for these goofs.

☐ Ensure that the navigational aids are accurate and useful (table of contents, index, running heads, page numbers, tabs). Somebody has to check these. It may as well be the editor. An editor's work can't always be spellbinding.

☐ Check the topics in the index to see if any should be added (if a draft of the index is available—probable only for computer-generated indexes).

☐   Ensure that it's clear what the user is supposed to do. Here's where you step into action. Follow every procedure yourself. Follow along on a tutorial or demonstration program step by step. Compare the instructions to the reality: Does the text match the computer screen? Does the gas grill you're assembling look like the illustration?

Mark discrepancies, stumbles, and misinterpretations. You and the writer can always work out how to fix them later, or you can later decide that you were particularly slow-witted that day and that no customer could possibly be as stupid. But you must mark down every error and question no matter how dumb you look. This information is valuable. You'll never be able to reconstruct your first impression later.

If you're editing assembly instructions for a gas grill, build the unit by following the instructions that ship with the product. Follow these instructions exactly as written. Make sure the parts list is complete and correct. Make sure that a list of tools the user needs is at the beginning of the instructions, not buried in step 7c. If you find an instruction ambiguous, make a note of it. Your customers will certainly have the same difficulty—and they won't have access, as you do, to the engineer who designed the grill. They'll return the product for a refund, which will reduce your company's profits—and maybe your raise.

In documenting computer software, execute every command and follow every procedure. Do you get the same results? If not, mark it. You may have misunderstood the text—the text may not have been clear or precise—or you may have discovered a software bug. In either case, it's better that you discover the problem, not the customer.

☐   Check that things don't happen anthropomorphically or magically.

People want computers to compute; they don't want computers to think, understand, have feelings, or be their friends. Watch that the book doesn't attribute human qualities to computer hardware (or other machines) or software. Make sure the text shows that computer programs take orders from people. Ensure that the book doesn't imply that things happen by magic, because that takes control away from the user and gives the impression that the computing environment is illogical and unpredictable.

Over time, editors acquire a sensitivity toward what information readers need, when they need it, and how they need it presented. I'd trust a good editor's gut feeling about a book's usability as readily as I'd trust a detailed statistical analysis of usability testing conducted in a laboratory. If I needed to present a quantitative report to management, I'd choose the usability testing, because managers are impressed by numbers. But if I were a writer who needed only to satisfy my own concerns, and I wanted an immediate, inexpensive, objective assessment, I'd ask an editor to review it.

Exercise 5	Reword for both precision and appropriateness for a television audience. A TV newscaster reports, "One third of the 88 passengers—33 in all—were taken to area hospitals for treatment."

Production Edits

The *production edit* ensures that the camera-ready copy you're handing off to print is complete (sometimes called a *final edit,* because it's your last look at the book, or a *format edit,* because the main items you're checking are format and layout). This review ensures that the book is free of errors so glaring that the first sixth grader who picks up the book could find them.

What you want to do in this review is turn every page as if you were seeing it for the first time (you may be!) and watch for conspicuous errors. Assume you don't have time to read every word, only time to look at the general page layout.

More than the other editorial reviews, much of what you'll be checking at this stage depends on the production method and process where you work. You're mostly checking format (page layout), reading and checking the parts of the book that weren't available at the previous review (table of contents and index), and doing paperwork.

The section "Production Edits for Different Production Processes" in this chapter tells how to tailor this information to your work environment.

If graphic artists prepare the camera-ready copy, the process would be something like what's shown in figure 6-11. The manuscript is typeset. The typesetter produces galleys, long sheets of typeset text. You review the galleys and return them to composition for correction. The corrected galleys are sent to the art department, where they are pasted up. At this stage the remaining elements that make up the page are pasted up—illustrations, headers, and footers, including folios (page numbers). This review is the only time you'll see the final pages, with everything in place, before they're handed off to the printer. The camera-ready copy is sometimes called *repro* (for reproducible masters), *boards*, or *mechanicals*.

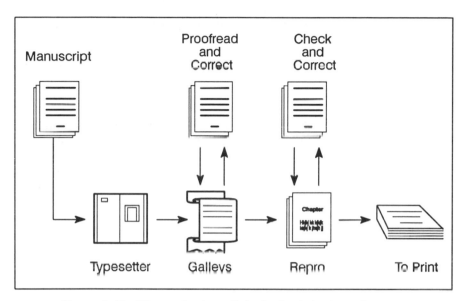

Figure 6–11. The production edit is the final check on the repro (camera-ready copy)

If writers prepare the camera-ready copy on computers, the early drafts probably have all the elements (headers, footers, folios, and illustrations) in place, so you may have checked these details at the copy edit. The production edit is your final look at the book before you hand it off to the printer.

As you read this section, skip details that don't apply to your department's process, or adapt the checklist items to your needs.

Your main concern at a production edit—regardless of the production method—is to ensure that the package is complete. For example, is there a space on the page where a halftone photograph belongs? Is the glossy print in the package? Has it been cropped and scaled? Is there a label on the back indicating the book it belongs to and the page it belongs on? You probably have time to skim the page for typos, but don't be lulled into reading the text unless you have a lot of time to spare.

At some companies, editors get to review the book only once, and that review is the equivalent of a production edit. If that's the case where you work, then you will also need to perform some copy editing during this review.

Scheduling Production Edits

Since the purpose of the production edit is to check the final pages just before they go to the printer, the obvious time to do it is after the writing process is complete. You may have anywhere from a few hours to a few weeks to check the book. If you have a production department, you will only need to check that the package is complete and that the text is correct, because somebody there will prepare the collating sheet (assembly sheet) and instructions for the printer. (See the sample in figure 6–12.) If you have to handle all the production details yourself, you will need more time.

You will probably have little control over the schedule for the production edit, simply because ripples in the writing or production schedule take time away from the production edit. The reason is as obvious as why you always find a lost item in the last place you look (once you find it, you stop looking)—the production edit is at the end of the line, so all schedule slips have their final landing here.

XYZ Computer Collating Sheet   *page 1 of* ___

Title: How to Have Your Cake and Edit, Too

Part #:————————   **Date:** ____/____/____   **Editor:**————————

#	Page	Thumb Bleed	#	Page	Thumb Bleed	#	Page	Thumb Bleed
1	Title		9			17		
2	Disclaimer		10			18		
3			11			19		
4			12			20		
5			13			21		
6			14			22		
7			15			23		
8			16			24		

Manual Title: How to Have Your Cake and Edit, Too

page count: 224   **trim size:** 7.5" x 9"   **number of colors:** 2

text stock: 50# Finoh Opaquo Smooth   **cover stock:** 12 pt Frankote coated

binding: saddle-wire

Figure 6–12. Sample collating sheet and instructions for printer

Checklist for Production Editing

Front and back matter:

☐ Check all pages for accuracy and conformance to your company's policies.

☐ Make sure that no pages or parts of the book are missing.

Text:

☐ Check that the writer has resolved all outstanding issues.

☐ Check that all comments and questions from previous reviews have been addressed.

☐ Check those details that you knowingly deferred from the previous review.

☐ Review your notes about the book, including the doc spec, to ensure that you haven't forgotten to do anything. For example, do you need to remind the purchasing department that the book has special printing requirements?

☐ Turn the pages and skim for typos, but don't read every page unless you're blessed with an abundance of time.

☐ Check chapter titles and text headings for typos.

☐ Read chapters or paragraphs that were changed since your last review.

☐ Check numerical and alphabetical sequences if there is any chance that any items were added or deleted since you last checked them.

☐ If a part of the book has been deleted—a chapter, section, figure, or table—check that all references to it have been deleted.

Page layout:

☐ Check that there are no unsightly line breaks, such as badly hyphenated words.

☐ Check that page breaks occur at sensible locations. For example, don't strand a heading at the bottom of a page.

☐ Check spacing (between paragraphs and before and after tables, figures, and lists).

Checklist for Production Editing (continued)

☐   Are running heads or index slugs correctly positioned? Do they correspond to the text on the page?

☐   Are footers correctly positioned? Do they have the correct information, without typos? Know how the footers are created. Is every one typed separately? If so, you'll need to proofread them on every page. Are the footers on left-hand pages typed once and those on right-hand pages typed once? If so, you'll need to proofread only one left-hand footer and one right-hand footer per chapter. (If the chapter is split among several computer files, however, you may have to proofread the footers more frequently.)

☐   Have all running heads indicating that this is a draft, rather than a final production copy, been removed?

☐   Are all folios (page numbers) where they're supposed to be? Using a nonreproducible blue pencil, number by hand any page that doesn't carry a folio to help the printer keep the pages in the correct order.

Figures and tables:

☐   Check that figures and tables are inserted in the correct place.

☐   Check that rules are neatly drawn.

☐   Check that illustrations to be positioned by the print vendor are properly scaled (and, for photographs, also cropped).

☐   Check that an illustration or photograph to be positioned by the print vendor is labeled for identification (your company's name, book title, page number).

☐   Check that the top is clearly marked on illustrations and photographs to be positioned by the print vendor.

☐   Check that figures and tables aren't split across any more pages than necessary. For example, if a table can fit on one page, don't put part of the table at the bottom of one page and part at the top of the next. Move the table to the next page or start a new page and leave white space.

☐   Check that there are appropriate markers or labels for figures or tables that are continued to the next page.

Checklist for Production Editing (continued)

Table of contents:

☐ Check that all heads are included (except those you intentionally omitted, such as fourth-level heads, perhaps).

☐ Check that there are no typos in the heads.

☐ Check that heads are consistent. (You should have checked these earlier, but you have a last chance to do so here. You also have the advantage of seeing them all in a single listing.)

☐ Check the sequence of numbered heads (Section 1.1, 1.2, etc.).

☐ Check that heads are indented consistently and appropriately.

☐ Check for consistency of wording, punctuation, and typography (especially boldface and italics) in heads.

☐ Check that there are dot leaders for all entries that should have them and that they align properly.

☐ Check that all figures and tables are listed (unless it is your company's style not to list them in the table of contents) and that their captions or titles match the text.

☐ Check that figure captions and table titles are consistent. (Like heads, these should have been checked earlier.)

☐ If the table of contents is generated by computer, make sure that "continued" labels (for example, for continued figures and tables) are not listed.

☐ Verify that the page numbers are correct.

Index:

☐ Check the entries, if you haven't already. Should any entries be combined or split? Check that *See* and *See also* references point to actual entries.

☐ Check that there are no cyclic references. In the following example, each reference merely points to the other—neither has page numbers.

EXAMPLE

artists. *See* illustrators

illustrators. *See* artists

☐ Check the format, including indentations.

☐ Check column breaks to avoid widows. Repeat the main heading if entries are carried over to another column.

☐ Check page numbers.

Final details:

☐ Provide instructions for the print vendor and text for any divider pages or tabs.

☐ Provide instructions for color printing. Supply a duplicate of the camera-ready copy and mark it to show color. (This copy is called a *color dummy.*) Your print vendor may prefer that you mark the color on an overlay attached to the actual camera-ready copy. If your book requires precise registration or more sophisticated color work than two-color offset printing, you will need specialized training or a graphic artist.

☐ Check that all pages are in the correct order.

☐ Check that all materials (pages, artwork, photos) are of good reproducible quality. The definition of good reproducible quality varies. See the bibliography for general books about printing and work with your printer for specific requirements.

☐ Make sure you have all the approvals (sign-offs) your company requires.

Checklist for Production Editing (continued)

☐ Check that the package going to the printer is complete.

☐ Prepare and/or check the instructions for the printer, including the collating or assembly sheet. Make sure these instructions are complete and so clear that anyone could reassemble the camera-ready copy correctly.

☐ Copy and file all paperwork, such as printing instructions and sign-off forms.

Production Edits for Different Production Processes

Here are some tips for adapting the production edit checklists to fit the production process where you work. Find the scenario that most closely matches your production process. Check the details listed there in addition to the items in the production edit checklists.

Scenario 1.
The writer prepares camera-ready copy and hands off physical copy to a print vendor.

☐ Check that the artwork is of acceptable quality.

☐ Ask the writer where there have been changes since you last reviewed the book. Check any affected details, such as cross-references.

Scenario 2.
The writer prepares final text. The final page—with all artwork in place—is transmitted electronically to a print vendor for printing.

☐ Make sure you receive a printed copy of what the printer received. You may need to refer to it if there are questions.

☐ Make sure the printer receives any other information that the writer may not have sent, such as text for tabs and a color dummy.

Scenario 3.
The writer prepares final text, inserting the formatting codes for the typesetter. The files are transmitted electronically (over a network, on floppy disk, or by modem) to an in-house production department or graphic arts vendor for typesetting. The writer and editor proofread the galleys. Corrected galleys are sent to the art department to be pasted up.

- ☐ Proofread the galleys thoroughly for major omissions and formatting glitches only. (You should have already edited the manuscript itself.)

- ☐ Check all formatting: typography, spacing, general page layout.

- ☐ Make sure that nothing is omitted. Check that all paragraphs, heads, figures, tables, headers, footers, and other elements are included. Pay particular attention that paragraphs, figure captions, table titles, and footnotes aren't lost. (With many pages of text, it's possible for a paragraph to be cut off by accident. The smaller elements, such as footnotes and captions, can be overlooked easily.)

TRICK: If you're comparing two versions of the same text, you don't need to proofread every word. Compare the two versions piece-by-piece. For example, check that each head is there, match up paragraphs, count the number of bulleted items in each list. It's a lot faster to compare that both versions have the same number of units than to proofread word-for-word. You'll need to pay attention to the actual words only when you discover missing or garbled text.

Scenario 4.
The writer prepares a manuscript (text only) without formatting. The files are transmitted electronically to an in-house production department or graphic arts vendor. The text is formatted, processed by the phototypesetter into galleys, and mechanicals are pasted up manually.

- ☐ Check all the items in Scenario 3.

- ☐ Check that the formatting matches the design specifications.

Scenario 5.

The writer prepares a typed manuscript only. The manuscript is handed off to an in-house production department or graphic arts vendor. The text is typed in, formatted, and processed by the phototypesetter into galleys. The writer and editor proofread the galleys and return them for corrections. The final, corrected galleys are sent to the art department for pasteup.

☐ Check all the items in Scenarios 3 and 4.

☐ Proofread the galleys character-by-character against the manuscript. Assume that every keystroke could have resulted in an error. Check for typos. Check typography, paragraph indents, line spacing, and everything else. (If you're lucky, a professional proofreader will have checked these details before you see the galleys. You will still need to proofread, but not as closely, and you will need to respond to the proofreader's queries.) See "Proofreading" later in this chapter for some tricks of the trade.

Four Memorable Catches

- The editor sensed something was "off" in the data sheet. He looked at the black and white glossy print and read the specifications. The specs indicated the unit to be about twice as tall as wide; the photo showed a short, squat cabinet. A call to marketing elicited only a gruff, "The numbers are right. The photo is correct. Just send it to print." The editor found out where that model was assembled and then called the factory. He was lucky to reach a cooperative foreman who measured the unit. As it turns out, the specifications were correct; someone had submitted the wrong photograph. (The Marketing Manager was irritated about the delay, but that's another story.)

- While editing a set of software manuals written by her company's French affiliate, an editor came across a term she'd never seen before. It wasn't defined in any of the manuals nor used anywhere else. She asked the Product Marketing Manager, her liaison to the developers and writers in France. He didn't recognize the word but was leery about deleting it in case it conveyed vital technical information. The editor started her research. She checked French and computer dictionaries. Then, guessing it was a typo, she started (mis)typing the word, letting her fingers slip and skid around the keyboard in the hope of reversing the typo. That effort produced a long list of nonsense words. She couldn't contact the writer because the subsidiary hired students to draft these books; the actual writer was long gone. The editor ran out of time and decided not to delete the unknown word, just in case it was important. Several years later, the manager of the writing group in Paris came to Boston for a meeting. On a hunch, the editor showed him the page and asked if he could solve the enigma. He looked at the page and burst into laughter. The mystery word? His secretary's name. What distraction caused her to type it into the manuscript will never be known.

- The year: 1975. The event: the World Series, pitting the Boston Red Sox against the Cincinnati Reds. The setting: game 6, 11th inning. The catch: Dwight Evans's running, over-the-shoulder catch of Joe Morgan's near home run. Evans's throw doubled Ken Griffey off first to end the inning. This catch set the stage for Carlton Fisk's lead-off, game-winning homer in the 12th inning. You've seen this videotape of Fisk jumping and gesturing with his arms. *That* home run. (I never promised this list would include only editing catches.)

- The best catch is always the last one you make.

Editing for an International Audience

If you work for a multinational company or one that sells internationally, chances are the documentation you edit will either be used by foreign nationals or translated into other languages.

If internationalization is important where you work, you may even do a separate editing pass to ensure that the material is suitable for translation or use by a non-American audience.

Editing for an international audience requires a sensitivity to language, cultural, and technical differences.

Language Considerations

Here are some ways you can make manuals easier to read and use for nonnative speakers of English:[1]

- Use simple, clear sentences.
- Use more illustrations.
- Provide an expanded glossary.
- Provide constant confirmation. For example, instructions for a call-forwarding service for a telephone could say, "When you press the # button, you hear a short beep. The beep confirms that the call-forwarding feature is activated."
- Use consistent terminology. Don't use more than one name for the same thing without a valid technical reason.

Here are some ways we inadvertently make manuals more difficult to read for our international audience:

- Changing voice within a paragraph.
- Using slang, idioms, colloquialisms: *stripped down version, jumping to conclusions, stop short, on the other hand.*
- Using industry jargon. (Be aware that readers outside the U.S. may be using the English of ten years ago; their technical dictionaries and glossaries—if they have them—may be out of date. For example, the term *unbundling* was being used in the U.S. to refer to a pricing and distribution practice for hardware and software long before the practice and the term became known in Europe and Asia.)
- Using words that have more than one meaning, particularly verb forms with prepositions; for example, *make up* can mean *to compose* or *to reconcile; exhaust* can mean *to tire* or *to use up.*

---

[1] These are good guidelines for material destined for domestic audiences, too.

- Using noun strings. Even if English is your native language, "logical operator precedence" and "DNA fingerprinting study results" are difficult to parse.

- Using nouns as verbs or using words that can be either nouns or verbs, such as *result* and *order.*

- Splitting infinitives, splitting verbs and adverbs. For example: "put down the telephone" is easier to read than "put the telephone down."

- Using abbreviations (even **Y** for *yes*) and acronyms, which are sometimes impossible to translate.

For an excellent discussion of this topic, see John Kirkman's article, "How 'Friendly' Is Your Writing for Readers Around the World," in *Text, Context, and Hypertext,* listed in the bibliography.

Cultural Considerations

Here are some ways we can be more sensitive to cultural differences:

- Avoid showing human figures, if possible, because of race, gender, and other stereotyping.

- Give metric measurements, followed by U.S. equivalents.

- Give the metric equivalent of the size of U.S.-based tools.

- Use culture-neutral examples, with respect to names, dates, numbers, and monetary systems. Tell what format (for dates and numbers) or system (monetary) you're using.

- Recognize that not all speakers of the same language are culturally the same. For example, there are cultural differences among French speakers in Canada, Switzerland, and France, just as there are cultural differences among English speakers in the United States, England, Australia, and the Philippines.

- Remember that humor doesn't travel easily.

- Use generic terms instead of trademarks, such as *photocopy* instead of *Xerox.* (Besides, you should not be using a trademark as a common noun or verb. A trademark is an adjective, as in Xerox copier.)

- As a matter of courtesy more than correctness, you might include non-Anglo-Saxon names in examples.

- Remember that not everybody knows U.S. geography. For example, the reference, "On the east coast" makes sense to a North American but probably doesn't to anyone else. If you need to refer to such a region, use a more definite reference, like, "On the east coast of North America."

Technical Differences

Here are some production technicalities to consider:

- International paper sizes differ from "standard" American sizes, so you may need to adapt the page design to accommodate the different text image area.

- Many manuals in the U.S. are drilled with three holes. Binders in other countries vary in the number of holes.

- English is a concise language; when translated into other languages, text requires on average 30% more space. Ensure that illustrations have space for translated callouts and labels.

Here are some technical details to consider:

- Ordering is often culture-bound. For example, if the text says, "list the days of the week in order," an American would put Sunday first, but some Europeans would put Monday first. If it matters, make sure you spell out which day should be first.

- Americans would read the date 10/9/88 as October 9, 1988; Europeans would read it as September 10, 1988. The Japanese often format dates in year/month/day order. If you're editing a sample program that uses dates, make sure the text specifies the order expected for input or output.

- Time is culture-bound. Many countries use the 24-hour clock to express written times (although when speaking, people often still use the 12-hour clock). If you're using an American-style time, make sure you include AM or PM to avoid confusion.

- Be careful with time zones. Sometimes documentation refers to the time when daylight savings time begins but doesn't mention the specific date. The date can vary from country to country, and some countries don't go on daylight savings time at all. If the specific date is important, make sure you spell it out, rather than just imply it.

- If you give engineers feedback on the user interface, make sure there is enough room to display translated text in help screens, prompts, error messages, and menus. Editing instructions for a small screen—such as a copier—will be quite a challenge!

- When you organize information—such as reference pages—alphabetically, you may be giving the translator more work.

- Be aware that the American *billion* is 10^9; in the British system it is 10^{12}. The names of other high numbers (such as trillion, quadrillion) are likewise different in the two systems. Instead of using these terms, express the value as a power of 10.

Here are some technical details just for computer manuals:

- Make sure references to the ASCII character set are correct. In some cases, references to ASCII are justified; in others, they're holdovers from the days before companies supported larger character sets.

- Think about when you mean *byte* and when you mean *character.* The two terms are often used synonymously, but in an internationalized system, a character can consist of more than one byte. For example, you may be used to saying that a filename can have up to 256 characters, but that isn't correct if you're using a 16-bit character set.

- Watch for case conventions. Ideographic languages such as Japanese and Chinese have only one case—there are no separate uppercase and lowercase versions of characters. In addition, not all characters in alphabetical languages have uppercase and lowercase versions. Keep these differences in mind if your text includes references to case conversion. The conversion may be impossible to do.

- If your products support European languages, common references such as "Identifiers can include any alphabetical character (A–Z)" may not be correct. Several European languages, Danish for one, have characters that occur *after* Z. Of course, A–Z as an all-inclusive range doesn't even begin to encompass all the possibilities in ideographic languages.

- Check references to sorting order. The text might read, "The utility sorts the names in alphabetical order." But "alphabetical order" differs from language to language—or doesn't exist at all for many Asian languages. For example, the Spanish alphabet begins *a, b, c, ch, d.* The correct wording differs according to what the software you're describing *actually* does. It might sort characters in code-set order, or in language order, or (for ideographic languages) in stroke order, or any number of different ways.

Proofreading

Proofreading isn't strictly an editorial review, but sometimes it's all you'll have time for.

Technically, proofreading means comparing two documents for literal character-for-character integrity. Proofreading historically has been the responsibility of the printer, not the writer or even the editor. Proofreaders compared typeset copy against the manuscript and marked queries about the copy in the margin for the writer and editor.

That type of proofreading is best done today by computers. Software that compares two (or more) text files is available for every computer. Depending on what computer hardware and software you have, a program that compares files may come with the operating system or word processing application or you may have to buy it as a separate application program.

Computers can compare copy and check spelling faster and more cheaply than people, but I still have a nostalgic spot for proofreaders. A staff of patient proofreaders helped me through my rookie year as an editor with marginal queries or an occasional phone call, "Did you really mean a *discreet* system?"

If you have to compare two documents and can't use a computer, your next best bet is to find a partner. One of you reads the original aloud, including all punctuation, and the other follows along on the copy.

The type of proofreading you'll most likely do is the simple check for typos. Typographical errors convey sloppiness and unprofessionalism, so you'd like to find and fix them all. Since this goal is unrealistic, you plan to find as many as you can. One of the most unpleasant experiences you will ever have as an editor will be the occasions (and there will be too many) when someone picks up the book you've edited, opens it to a page at random, and instantly finds a typo. (Your only way to survive this humiliation is to inflict this pain on someone else.)

Even the best editors slip now and then. I recently called a well-known and highly respected publisher to confirm the price of an editing textbook. I dialed the number on the order form but got a "This number is out of service" recording. Then I saw the phone number on the facing page—same digits, different order. I dialed that number. Sure enough—the elite editorial staffers proved they are human. And what a colossal error—two typos in their own phone number, on an order form for a book about copy editing. The incident was surreal, even for a lifelong Red Sox fan.

Certainly typo-hunting is not the editor's most challenging task, but it's one a good editor does easily.

The right way to proofread is to look at every individual *character,* every letter, numeral, and punctuation mark, one line at a time. Don't read for meaning; just look at the physical characters themselves. Once you start reading for meaning, your brain will deceive you and make you see what you expect to see. If you can't stop reading, try this old trick: Read the copy (words, not letters!) backwards. Since you want to look at the physical letters, you may as well look at them out of order. (You'll catch misspellings this way, but miss wrong words, such as *of* for *on,* putting you in the same league as software.)

When you don't have time, here are some tricks you can use.

First, learn to skim. If you don't have time to read every word, scan the page. Let your eyes follow a pattern of the letter *x,* or *s,* or the figure *8,* whichever seems most comfortable to you. The idea is to see all the text on the page in a glance. You've had so many years' reading experience that weird letter combinations should stand out and scream at you. (I call this "gestalt proofreading." It *is* weird, but it works for me.) If your eyes catch something peculiar, then stop and look carefully; you unconsciously spotted an irregular pattern, which is probably a typo.

This technique has a basis in cognitive theory, on a principle known as *closure.* I promised not to get academic, so let me oversimplify this idea. Read the words in figure 6–13.

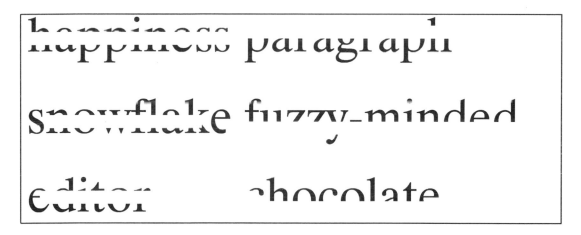

Figure 6–13. You can decipher even partial words

You can read these words because your brain recognizes familiar patterns and fills in details that your eyes can't see. (If you need a hint, the words are, in random order: chocolate, snowflake, editor, paragraph, fuzzy-minded, happiness.)

Just as you can recognize familiar words by their pattern, you can find unfamiliar patterns, namely, typos.

It may take you time to become comfortable with this trick, and some people find it doesn't work at all. Practice it, but don't be discouraged if it doesn't work for you.

It also helps to know where errors are most likely to occur (or to have been missed in other reviews):

- The first line of a page and the last line of a page
- The last paragraph in a chapter
- Heads, chapter titles, captions, and table titles
- Headers and footers
- Text in figures
- Text in all capital letters
- Text in the largest type size on the page (everybody proofreads the tiny type but assumes the giant heading is correct)

Errors tend to cluster. If you find one typo, look for others nearby.

Some letter combinations are difficult to proofread, so they're often missed:

- Words with many skinny letters (*l, t,* and *i*)
- Words with double letters (sometimes end up as triplets)
- Words that end in -ability and -ibility
- Words that have plausible but wrong endings (*producting* for *production*, *extention* for *extension*)

My insurance agency's new stationery advertised, among other products, "homeower's policies." I mentioned the error to my agent when I called to change my auto policy. In the three months they'd been using the stationery, nobody had noticed the typo. I bet more people would have noticed if the typo were less plausible—and less suitable. (If you have a mortgage, you know *homeower* is an accurate description.)

Some words are difficult to spell. There are many published lists of hard-to-spell words. Most of these words are words you know nobody can spell, like *diphtheria* and *inoculate,* so you'd probably look them up in the dictionary anyway.

The words to watch out for are the ones that you'll find all the time. Some words are difficult to spell (*supersede, hexadecimal*), but many are just difficult to type and difficult to see when they're mistyped: *initialization, management, public, administration, accessing, facility, facilitate, different, environment, compatibility,* and *substitute.* Often you're so used to seeing these words that you don't really *see* them.

Watch also for homophones (*they're/their, then/than, it's/its*) and the devious twins and triplets (*that/than, is/in, it/if, if/of, the/that, then/the/they*).

Finally, know which words give you trouble and look them up in the dictionary every time or type them up and hang the list above your desk.

◇ —— ◇

How to Silence Your Critics

Letter to editor:
What in the name of Webster does this subhead signify?:
Seperate Objects, Events
Neither my texts on database organization nor your article . . . defines it.

Datamation's response:
Datamation prints about 100,000 words in each issue. One typo per issue gives an error rate of 0.00001. Can your company equal that?[1]

◇ —— ◇

Blues and Press Proofs

Another review you may perform is checking proof copy from the printer. A common type of proof for offset printing (the printing method most commonly used for manuals) is called *salts, blues,* or *bluelines.* Salts are a proof of the printer's camera work and imposition (ordering of the pages). The salts are direct images of the negatives that will make up the plates, and as such show everything that will be on the printed page: the entire camera-ready page you sent the printer, with color breaks. Also, any dirt marks, scratches, or thumbprints on the negative will be printed unless you mark them. The printer can usually fix these imperfections, unless the flaw is in the camera-ready copy. Printers can photograph only what you give them; if the camera-ready copy has pages with fuzzy type, you will see fuzzy type in your proofs.

The salts also reflect the imposition of the pages, or how they are laid out in the signatures for printing. Many manuals are printed in 16-page signatures, which roll off the press as huge two-sided sheets and are folded in the same operation. All the signatures that belong to the book are then collated (also automatically), bound, and finished. Because the process is mechanized from this point on, this is your last opportunity to correct or change an individual page. Therefore, it is critical to check the salts to be sure that all the pages are there and that the pages are in the correct order. Cover salts are also provided, often separately; check the position of type and artwork carefully.

---

[1] *Datamation,* November 15, 1985, p. 23.

Printers require fast (often 24-hour) turnaround on salt proofs, so check salts immediately.

The review of salts is the last opportunity to make changes to the manual; it's also a time to exercise restraint in what changes to make. Any changes to the book at this stage, particularly adding or removing pages, are very costly and can slip the schedule. (Changes by the writer or editor are called *author's alterations,* or *AA*s, and are charged back to your company. The cost of fixing *printer's errors,* or *PE*s, is absorbed by the printer.) Of course, printer's errors—a page out of order, for example—must be corrected.

This stage is a review of the printing process, not a technical review or a literary edit. Your department probably has a policy on whether technical changes are permitted at this stage. The changes generally considered appropriate are those that affect distribution (such as part numbers, titles), legal notices, and other critical areas, including technical accuracy. (But you should have caught these before the book went to print.)

If you notice that a particular writer or engineer *habitually* waits until the salts stage to correct or review the technical information, elevate the problem to management, because the process may need to be changed.

Another important step in checking salts is verifying that color separations for a second color (if used) and screens (if any) were correctly made.

If the book contains photographs, check that they have been inserted in the correct place. Make sure photographs are not upside down or backwards. Check that the printer has cropped the photographs according to instructions. Check that the quality is acceptable (not grainy or muddy).

Because the salts are made before the pages are actually printed, collated, bound, and trimmed, you can't check every detail at the salt stage. The actual ink color, the intensity of the color, how evenly the ink is spread on the page (particularly for full-page bleeds), and the quality of the binding are some of the details you cannot check at salts. The salts are an excellent way to check what will be on the page, in what color, and what order the pages will be in—before the entire print run is shipped to the warehouse.

Another type of proof is called the *press proof.* To get a press proof, the printer takes a printed, collated book off the production line before the book reaches the bindery. Since the book has already been printed, it's even more expensive to make changes or fix mistakes. Few printers wait until this late in the cycle to get the customer's approval, but if you are asked to check a press proof, understand the consequences of making changes and corrections.

There are many other ways to check printing, especially color printing, that require sophisticated technical knowledge of printing processes, ink chemistry, and paper characteristics. Rarely do technical editors need advanced technical knowledge about printing; if your books require sophisticated printing, your company most likely has an expert—a production manager, graphic designer, or printing consultant—to manage the printing process and oversee the quality.

However, editors and writers should understand the general printing process. Printers gladly give tours to their customers. Visit as many printers as you can to see the different equipment and processes. The more you know about printing, the more printing errors you can prevent. (The bibliography lists some introductory books about printing, but don't just read about printing—see, hear, and smell it. The process is fascinating to watch. The experience will also help you appreciate the relative serenity of editing.)

Exercise 6   What's wrong here?

The question is whether Prozac, unlike other antidepressants, can directly induce violent or suicidal thoughts—thoughts that don't stem from an underlying illness. Dr. Martin Teicher, of Harvard Medical School and McClean Hospital, believes that it can. . . . Teicher hopes that future research will enable doctors to predict how individual patients will react to the drug. But even he has no plans to stop prescribing it in the meantime. Antidepressants are not cough drops. Dr. Joseph Lipinski of Harvard Medical School and McLean Hospital likens them to loaded pistols. They all pose hazards. But until better treatments come along, Prozac remains a vital weapon against a formidable illness.—*Newsweek*, April 1, 1991.

How to Develop Your Own Checklist

You should develop your own set of checklists, tailored to your own needs. Here's a simple strategy:

1. Identify the process for product development and writing where you work.

2. Look at the schedule and the milestones, such as the number of drafts the writer plans to create for review.

3. Determine the number of editing passes that you feel is appropriate.

4. Will the schedule accommodate the number of passes you recommend? If not, determine the number of editing passes you can fit in. (Also read chapter 8.) You will need one checklist for each editing pass. If you have only one editing pass, skip to step 6.

5. Identify the stability of the manuscript at each review. Assume that nothing is stable at the developmental edit. You want to copy edit when the text is mostly frozen. (It's futile to wait until all the changes stop.) You want to do a production edit just before handing off the book to the printer, and you want to find as few corrections as possible. (You want the production edit to cover only what wasn't stable at the copy edit.)

6. Identify the components or elements that need to be checked. Start with the big parts, such as front matter, chapters, and back matter, and then break down each item separately. For example, a chapter has as physical parts a title, number, text heads, paragraphs, figures, tables, lists, headers, and footers.

7. List what kinds of things can go wrong. For example, a running head can be positioned on the wrong side of the page. The text in a paragraph can be worded obscurely. A figure may need a legend.

    Sort these into two groups:

    - Common errors (typos in text headings) or catastrophic errors (wrong title on the title page)

    - Rare errors (missing chapter title) or inconsequential errors (index entries that nobody will ever look up)

8. Save the first group for the basis of your checklist. Put the second group aside; you may want to expand your checklist in the future, or you may have a project where that extra pickiness is important.

9. Divide the items among the different reviews, based on the likelihood that changes in the next draft won't render your review meaningless. You may check the same entry in different ways, depending on the stage.

    For example, at a developmental edit, check the text heads as a means of checking the overall organization of the chapter. Also check that they're in an appropriate and consistent style. At a literary or copy edit, check that the wording of the text heads is appropriate for the material that follows, that capitalization and spelling are correct, that they're in the correct font, and, if the heads are numbered, that the numbering is correct. At the production edit, check any text heads that may have changed or any detail you may have skipped earlier. (For example, if you knew that some sections might be deleted or combined, you might decide to wait until the production edit to check the numbering.) Finally, compare the text heads in the body of the book to their listings in the table of contents.

Exercise 7   What's wrong here?

Brunch is known as a *portmanteau* word, which means that it is a blend of two words—lunch and dinner. (The word *portmanteau* in French means a suitcase that has two compartments.)

◇ ─────────────────────────────────── ◇

A Phew of My Favorite Things

Here are some typos that'll make you cringe . . . and chuckle.

- All first class airfare must be explaned.
  [From an expense report form.]

- According to the *Macintosh Way,* people achieve extraordinary results when they share a dream and are lead by a charismatic high priest like Steve Jobs. Machiavclli's kind of thinking most properly belongs in the anals of history.
  [Did you get *both* typos? From *MacUser,* March 1990.]

- Headline in a four-color special magazine supplement:
  The Wizzards of Wolfsburg
  Continue to go Theh Own Way Saying:
  "It's Not a Car. It's a Volkswagen."
  [Spelling, capitalization, and punctuation, as used in the advertisement.]

- Appendix A. Bigliography
  [It must have been long. From a computer manual.]

- Section V. Interactive Processsing System [From a computer manual.]

- If inexperienced crab-pickers were to attend one of these Middleton crab feasts, Middleton would advise them to use a slower version of the method she uses in contests, and she would demonstrate at a snail's pace. She would advise the would-be pickers to sample crap meat before they eat what they've picked; otherwise, they might be turned off by shells or bones in meat they haven't picked clean.
  [From the *Boston Globe,* Sept. 22, 1982.]

- A New York newspaper's account of Theodore Roosevelt's inauguration:
  "It was a scene never to be forgotten when Roosevelt, before the Chief Justice of the Supreme Court and a few witnesses, took his simple bath."
  [From *2500 Anecdotes for All Occasions,* p. 20.]

- A Washington newspaper, reporting on President Roosevelt's minor bug, ran the front-page headline, "President Kept to Rooms by Coed." Most of that edition's run had been printed and had to be destroyed. The president, however, requested several copies to distribute to his friends.
  [From *2500 Anecdotes for All Occasions,* p. 20.]

◇ ─────────────────────────────────── ◇

Summary

This chapter covered all the basics about marking up a manuscript. You can find the details in style guides and usage handbooks.

If you feel overwhelmed by all the lists of what to check, here are five guidelines to put this chapter in perspective:

- When in doubt, let your judgment as a reader—not an editor—be your guide.

- If it's not broken, don't fix it. What you don't change is as important as what you do change.

- If it's not broken, don't break it. Don't make a bad sentence worse and don't change the writer's meaning or message. (If the writing is so bad you can't decipher the message, ask the writer to explain what she or he is trying to say. Don't guess.)

- After you've checked a fact, cross-reference, or other detail, put a check mark in the manuscript. This mark lets the writer know what you've checked and will help you refresh your own memory in future drafts.

- Finally, don't just tell what's wrong. Tell what works well, too.

Chapter 7

The 100 Most Common Errors

As in fishing, from time to time you'll make a spectacular catch, but most of your editorial expeditions will net you the same old carp. The following lists the 100 types of errors (excluding formatting errors) that will constitute 90% of your haul. These are your bread and butter; the other 10% are your jam. Learn these well.

Fuzzy Thinking

1. logic

From a self-test: When you play athletic or card games with friends, do you play mainly to win or for the fun of it?   yes ❑   no ❑
[From a local newspaper.]

2. factual inconsistency

Due to a typing error, Gov. Dukakis was incorrectly identified in the third paragraph as Mike Tyson.
[From a correction in the Fitchburg-Leominster (Mass.) *Sentinel and Enterprise* via *Newsweek,* April 29, 1991.]

Front cover:
Proceedings of the
ACM SIGSOFT '89
Third Symposium on Software
Testing, Analysis, and Verification (TAV3)
Spine:
Proceedings of the ACM SIGSOFT/SIGPLAN Software Engineering Symposium on Practical Software Development Environments December 13–15, 1989.

3. contradiction

"He slid into second with a stand-up double."
[Sports announcer, Jerry Coleman.]

"Well, we agree different."
[Baseball's eminently quotable Yogi Berra.]

4. unexplained—or incorrectly explained—acronyms

The OSD button on the remote activates an OSD.
[*OSD* is *on-screen display,* but how would you ever know? The VCR manual never defines the acronym.]

Barbara F—, a Boston parent of two public-school students and a member of PACE, or Parents and Students for Education . . .
[No wonder there's a crisis in education! From a local newspaper.]

[Sometimes the explanation isn't obvious. The acronym for Coordinated Universal Time is UTC, because it's derived from the original French term.]

5. terms used without first having been defined

Drop detent spring and ball into hole. Hold ball down and slide shaft on through poppet boss.
[From a repair manual for heavy machinery.]

The magnetostriction constant increased with the increase of annealing time.

6. vagueness

Mode: The act or process of placing the VCR in any of its operating features.
Ex: "Play ▶" mode.
[Is a mode a process? From a VCR manual.]

7. misplaced emphasis

> A clock is an object in which the time of day is detected by use of electricity or batteries.
> [From an exercise in a writing class.]

8. implication that events happen by magic (no agent)

> As the OSD button on the remote is pressed the sequence of overlays shown below will be displayed as long as the arrow appears in the lower right (for about the first 5 seconds). After the arrow disappears, the display will remain on the TV screen until it is removed by the next press of the OSD button.
> [There is no indication that a *person* participates in this action. The passive voice makes it seem as though everything "just happens." From a VCR manual.]

9. overemphasis or unnecessary information

> The twelve hour round clock looks as its name infers, a circular object displaying, sequentially, numbers one (1) through twelve (12). (See Figure 1–1.) Each number subdivides the clock into one hour segments. Each numbered segment represents an hour of the day. . . . Affixed to each clock are a long broad pointer (commonly referred to as the "minute hand"), a short broad pointer (commonly referred to as the "hour hand"), and a narrow long pointer (commonly referred to as the "second hand"). (See Figure 1–2.) These hands operate mechanically in a synchronized manner, moving to the right in a clockwise fashion, to designate the hour, the minute, and the second.
> [Also, *hour, minute, second,* and *clockwise* have not been defined. From an exercise in a writing class.]

10. anthropomorphism

> All file manipulations are at arm's length via the file access protocol.
> [From a computer manual.]

> Commercial applications with their more modest environmental considerations may conclude that the silicone gels can provide all the protection that commercial multichip module packages need.
> [From a journal on components, hybrids, and manufacturing technology.]

Exercise 8   What's wrong here?

From the telephone book (Yellow Pages) of the Concord, Massachusetts area:

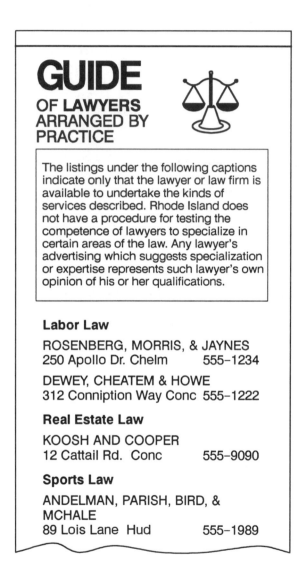

GUIDE
OF **LAWYERS** ARRANGED BY PRACTICE

The listings under the following captions indicate only that the lawyer or law firm is available to undertake the kinds of services described. Rhode Island does not have a procedure for testing the competence of lawyers to specialize in certain areas of the law. Any lawyer's advertising which suggests specialization or expertise represents such lawyer's own opinion of his or her qualifications.

Labor Law

ROSENBERG, MORRIS, & JAYNES
250 Apollo Dr. Chelm   555-1234

DEWEY, CHEATEM & HOWE
312 Conniption Way Conc 555-1222

Real Estate Law

KOOSH AND COOPER
12 Cattail Rd. Conc   555-9090

Sports Law

ANDELMAN, PARISH, BIRD, & MCHALE
89 Lois Lane Hud   555-1989

11. tells too much

This chapter, entitled *Reference Guide,* should be used to look up the syntax, the description, or the examples provided with each command. This guide provides two ways to look up a command: by task, or by command name. The guide begins with a brief summary of all the commands followed by a detailed summary of all the commands. The brief summary of the commands is presented by task; the detailed summary of commands is presented alphabetically.
[From a computer manual.]

Go to Chapter 3. It begins with the section, "Logging In," which explains how to log in.
[From a computer manual.]

[These examples tell too much about the *book.* Also, don't tell more about the subject than the reader wants or needs to know.]

12. tells too little

A man enters an apartment building and asks a boy there where Mr. Cooper lives. The boy leads the man upstairs and points to Cooper's apartment. The man knocks on the door, gets no response, and says, "He's not here."
"I know," the boy answered. "Mr. Cooper was downstairs waiting in the lobby."

Portable or window fans are unexcelled for ventilating purposes, or to circulate the air in a home, office, or apartment. When used for ventilating, the fan will force out the hot and stale air and bring in the cool and fresh outside air. . . . The fan can be installed in almost any window, provided other windows or door openings furnish one or several air currents to or from the fan window. For best results, it is not advisable to have the "IN" and "OUT" windows in the same room.
[This wordy and overly detailed document does not tell which way to face a fan for intake vs. exhaust, even though it shows two illustrations for air flow through the rooms. From the instructions to a household fan.]

If you want to reset the clock, press the Prog button (VCR is in the "VCR" mode) while watching the TV.
[The Prog button isn't on the VCR; it's on the remote control—and the instructions should have given this information. Both the VCR and the remote control have so many buttons it's difficult for the user to remember which buttons are on which component. From a VCR manual.]

TIP: Make sure the documentation tells what the reader needs to know. Ensure that the documentation doesn't answer irrelevant questions at the expense of important ones.

13. faulty organization

Step 3. . . . If you don't get the 3½ to 5 quarts popped corn from the ½ cup kernels, the popcorn may be too dry. To restore moisture . . .
Step 4. Both standard and gourmet/premium grades of popcorn can be used in this hot air popper. . . . One-half cup kernels will yield 3½ to 5 quarts of popped popcorn.
[You might think you're supposed to know about "the 3½ to 5 quarts" but the instructions don't tell you until the next step. Also notice "One-half cup kernels" but "5 quarts *of* popped popcorn." From the instructions for a hot-air popcorn popper.]

14. transition

I'm leaving early today. My dentist has a new office.

15. paucity of examples

TIP: Readers' most common complaint about technical writing is that the documentation doesn't have enough examples.

16. irrelevant or unclear example

Some numbers are prime, such as 1, 2, and 3.
[These examples are useful only if you already know what a prime number is.]

17. omitted steps

Put the filter in the basket of the coffeemaker. Add water. Turn on the unit.
[Don't forget the coffee!]

18. repeated steps or duplicate actions

Turn on the coffeemaker. Put the filter in the basket. Add one bag of coffee. Fill the decanter with water up to the metal band. Pour the water into the coffeemaker. Turn on the coffeemaker.

19. redundant concepts

Letter to the editor:
To the "Goes Without Saying" Department:
IBM Publication GG24-1728-0, *IBM 3090 Processor Complex: Installation and Planning Guide,* advises: "Fig. 2 shows a layout for the model 200. Note that this diagram does not show actual size."
[From *Datamation,* January 15, 1986.]

20. **overly and unnecessarily precise**

> Press the START button. The unit will start in about 50 seconds.
> [Why not just say "about a minute" since you're giving just an approximation? From a computer manual.]

21. **no context**

> ADS is a system documentation tool, not a program documentation tool. It produces reports that respond to user demands for quality documentation, and helps customers meet scheduled commitments, and the handling of competing demands for maintenance programmer time.
> [This description does not tell what the product does. It also fails to distinguish between a system documentation tool and a program documentation tool. This paragraph also shows nonparallel construction. From the newsletter for a technical writing society.]

22. **confusing sequence of steps**

> Placing calls:
> Internal — Dial 4 digit ext. number.
> Local outside — Dial 9 receive low pitched dial tone, dial 7 digit number.
> Long distance — Dial 9 receive low pitched dial tone, dial 1 followed by 7 or 10 digit number.
> [Missing commas and hyphens make this difficult to read. The text is parallel but the actions are not. For example, sometimes the numeral refers to the digit you dial, and sometimes it modifies the number. From the user's guide for an internal telephone system.]

23. **saying "simply" when it's not necessarily so for the uninitiated**

> Simply set syncograph controls to show the distributor firing pattern and to drive the distributor shaft clockwise.
> [From a repair manual for heavy machinery.]

24. **saying "remember" the first time you say it**

> Remember to adjust the color settings to your preference.

25. **not saying what you mean**

> "To be or to be."
> [From a recent edition of *Hamlet.*]

26. use of *etc.* **or** *and so on* **for unspecified or noninfinite set**

> If the measured wavelength is that of hydrogen or carbon emission, the detector serves as a "general" detector for organic compounds. If a sulfur wavelength is monitored, the detector is a sulfur-specific detector, and so on for any element!
> [At least give another example. Also, the exclamation mark is gratuitous. From a spectroscopy manual.]

> Caption: The Electromagnetic Spectrum. Note that electronic transitions are of higher energy than vibrational transitions, which are higher energy than rotational transitions, etc.
> [It is not clear what *etc.* refers to—are vibrational transitions higher than rotational transitions and other, unnamed transitions? Are rotational transitions, in turn, higher than something else? The illustration does not depict vibrational and electronic transitions. From a spectroscopy manual.]

27. ambiguity

> TO CLEAN:
> Press "Clean Opener" button. Complete blade and handle assembly pops out. Wash by hand or in the dishwasher.
> [This false parallelism—*complete* is an adjective, not a verb—can cause the reader to stumble, especially since other procedures in the manual start with imperative verbs. From the operating instructions for an electric can opener.]

> Both diskettes contain the Connection software; we refer to this diskette as the **master** diskette.
> [From a computer manual.]

> Monday night, police arrested Michael H— . . . for open container violations. He was also charged with having a loud exhaust.
> [From a local newspaper.]

> Headline: CANADIAN BANKS HELP LAME DUCKS
> [Watch for words that can be more than one part of speech. From a local newspaper.]

> Headline: DUKAKIS TO DEFY ORDERS TO DROP DISABLED
> [Watch for words that have more than one meaning. From the *Boston Globe*, February 10, 1984.]

> Type shift + zz.
> [This instruction implies that the user should type "s-h-i-f-t" and the "+" character. Better wording: Hold down the SHIFT key and type **zz**. From a computer manual.]

Style and Usage

28. inconsistent terminology (more than one name or spelling for the same concept or thing)

To see the calendar for this month and the next:
1. Press the Program (PROG) button. The menu screen will appear with each feature listed with its selection number.
2. Press the 3 key. This displays the calendar for the current month.
3. Press the 1 key. Screen changes to next month's calendar.
4. Press the Prog button. The menu screen reappears.
The menu:
SELECT MENU NUMBER
1. SET CLOCK
2. SET PROGRAM
3. CALENDAR
4. CHANNEL AUTO SET
TO END PUSH PROGRAM
[Can you find three variations for the Program button? From a VCR manual.]

They sampled the sludge for bioremediation. . . . The town is working to test the bioremediating.
[From a newsletter.]

29. wordiness

A newspaper reporter on his first out-of-town trip got wind of a big story and wired his editor for the go-ahead. The editor wired back, "Write 500 words." The reporter replied, "Story needs 1000 words."
The editor wired back, "Story of creation of world told in 600. Try it."

Within this time frame, take action to prepare the heating environment for throughput by manually setting the oven baking unit by hand to a temperature of 375 degrees Fahrenheit.
[From a parody of government writing.]

Individual General Partners: [names omitted] for so long as they are general partners of the General Partner or the sole general partner of a general partner of the General Partner, and any other individual who may from time to time become a general partner of the General Partner or the sole general partner of a general partner of the General Partner, for so long as such individual remains a general partner of the General Partner or the sole general partner of a general partner of the General Partner. Any general partner of the General Partner of which an Individual General Partner is the sole general partner shall also be deemed to be an Individual General Partner for all purposes of this Agreement.
[From a legal contract.]

Old manual for a refrigerator:
Your refrigerator must have air space. A one inch space is needed between the wall and the coils in the rear of your refrigerator. At least **three inches** of open space is needed directly **above** the refrigerator. Always allow **one half inch** space on **each side** of refrigerator for ease of installation and cleaning. If refrigerator is installed in a corner, additional space is needed to allow doors to be opened.
Revised manual for the same model refrigerator:
Leave at least 3 inches of air space at the top and 1 inch between the wall and the coil on back of the refrigerator.

At the end of any toasting cycle or when the Toast Switch is pressed off, a bell will sound. Toasting may be stopped at any time by depressing the Toast Switch off.
[Can you think of a more complicated way to say "turn off the toaster"? From the owner's guide for a toaster oven.]

30. redundant wording

Be sure you read the following documents, which cover information not covered in this manual: *Release Document,* which discusses . . . and . . . , which are not the subjects of this manual.
[From a computer manual.]

During the diagnostics, an informative message (similar to the one shown below) displays.
[From a computer manual.]

For modem cables, you should connect the pins straight through. The pins should be connected with no crossovers and no pins connected together locally. In other words, the connections are made straight through.
[From a computer manual.]

With the close of this chapter, we conclude . . .
[From a computer manual.]

31. *like* vs. *as*

William Zinsser writes clearly, like a writer should.
[Should be *as.*]

32. *and/or* (or unclear use of slash)

Why don't I try to find you 9/10 o'clock in your office?
[Is that between 9:00 and 10:00? At 9:00 or at 10:00? Make sure writers don't use *and/or* when they mean simply *and* or simply *or; and/or* means Condition A *or* Condition B or both A *and* B. You'll find that 99% of the time the writer means *and* or *or; and/or* nearly always introduces ambiguity into a sentence.]

33. wrong word

A Chase Street resident found a Suzuki 400 dirt bike in the woods near the railroad tracks. Police agreed to leave the bike with the founder until the owner is located.
[From a local newspaper.]

The British were partial to the furlong, a unit of measurement that is used now primarily at horse racetracks. Even before written records of land were kept, British farmers built stone walls to demarcate fields whose length was standardized—the plowmen dug furrows the equivalent of 220 modern yards. *Furlong* was the slurred pronunciation of furrow-long, and the furlong became the designation for 220 years.
[Yards, not years. From David Feldman, *Imponderables: The Solution to the Mysteries of Everyday Life* (NY: William Morrow, 1987), p. 241.]

One or more thieves got into the Department of Public Works building on Forest Road Sunday, and stole an undetermined amount of electronic equipment, according to town officials. . . . the preliminary investigation revealed a "dummy" terminal was taken, one which can only be used when hooked to a larger computer system.
[The term is *dumb*, not *dummy*, terminal. From a local newspaper.]

"My players are frosting at the bit."
[Yogi Berra.]

34. noun strings (noun clusters)

Text heading: System Model Compiler System Model
[Department of Redundancy Department? From a computer manual.]

To reset the clock: Press the 1 key and follow the clock set guide to re-enter the new date and time.
[From a VCR manual.]

Before reinstalling shims, apply a thin even coat of sealer to machined surface of transmission case input shaft quill that contacts shim.
[Five consecutive nouns! From a repair manual for agricultural equipment.]

35. nominalizations

All telephone systems now have the access capability to utilize assigned system speed call numbers for frequently called numbers.
[From the user's guide for an internal telephone system.]

No one company makes all the world's computer hardware, so for some systems you can marriage components from several suppliers to achieve the system objectives.
[Quoted in a letter to the editor of *Technical Communications,* Spring 1983. The writer questions if the components in a dismantled system get divorced.]

36. double (and triple) negatives or information presented negatively

You cannot reconnect without logging in again.
[Sometimes the negatives are subtle. Tell what to *do*: "To reconnect, you must log in again." From a computer manual.]

If you attempt to connect a drive not within the range specified . . .
[Say *outside* instead of *not within.* From a computer manual.]

37. overuse of passive voice

Many times even large applications can be done using shell procedures. Even if the application is initially developed as a prototype system for testing purposes rather than being put into production, much work can be saved. With a prototype for testing, the range of possible user errors can be determined—something that is not always easy to plan out when an application is being designed.
[From a computer manual.]

38. inconsistent use of *you* and *the user;* overuse of *you*

Good physical condition means that we have sufficient physical capacity for the requirements of our everyday life. Your heart and breathing do not become overstrained. . . . In many cases one appreciates good physical condition only after losing it. . . . However, we have every possibility to efficiently take care of our condition.
[*We, you,* and *one* used to refer to the reader. From the owner's guide for an exercycle.]

Connect your PC to your modem using your modem cable.
[Sometimes writers overcompensate to avoid the passive voice and to sound friendly. From a computer manual.]

39. word choice (commonly confused words and homophones)

These are the most common:

affect vs. *effect*

assure vs. *ensure* vs. *insure*

between vs. *among*

compliment vs. *complement*

discrete vs. *discreet*

example vs. *sample*

less vs. *fewer*

may vs. *can*

principle vs. *principal*

should vs. *must*

than vs. *then*

that vs. *which*

use vs. *usage*

This edition of the book has less pages than the last edition.
[Should be fewer.]

First, you should turn on the electricity.
[It's something the user *must* do; you don't want to sound tentative or nagging.
(We don't always do what we *should* do.)]

Bork was hung by the outspokenness of his views and his acerbic assaults on
liberal precedents, feminists, and the press.
[Refer to your dictionary for the difference between *hanged* and *hung.* From
Newsweek, July 30, 1990.]

My mate's prime rib could not have been described as a blue ribbon winner
from a 4-H fair. . . . I feared about equally well with my shrimp and fettucine
Alfredo.
[*Feared* should be *fared.* Also, do they judge steaks—or only cattle—at 4-H
fairs? From a local newspaper.]

The arguments are given to show the order and type of each. Their names are
not mandatory, just suggestive.
[From a computer manual.]

. . . the most populace states
[From a manuscript.]

40. **misuse of** *comprise*

Fifty states comprise the nation.
[The nation comprises fifty states. *Comprise* means *embrace.* Don't be surprised
if you wait ten years to see *comprise* used correctly in technical documentation.]

41. run-on sentences

> CuCr alloys are produced by the powder metallurgy method, their properties depend on the quality of raw materials, for example, on the oxygen content in Cr powder, and on the manufacturing technology.
> [From a journal on components, hybrids, and manufacturing technology.]

42. *may* or *should* instead of *does* or *is*

> When you press the reset button, the copy machine should be ready for use in about 30 seconds.
> [This tentative language makes the reader want to ask, "Don't you know?" or "Is the machine's behavior that unpredictable?"]

43. *different than* instead of *different from*

> An editor's perspective is different than a writer's.
> [Should be *different from.*]

44. bloated (pretentious) wording

> *functionality* for *function* or *feature*

> *facility* for *building*

> *utilize* for *use:* If the unutilized frequency bins have too much energy, we may simply declare the particular block to be unreliable.
> [From a journal on magnetics.]

> Lubricated coupons were horizontally located in a room of Building 4 at Beijing University of Posts and Telecommunications . . .
> [From a journal on components, hybrids, and manufacturing technology.]

45. smothered verbs

> *make a decision* [for *decide*]

> *take into consideration* [for *consider*]

> *take notice of* [for *notice*]

46. capitalizing common nouns for no particular reason

> Insert the floppy disk into the Disk Drive.

47. inappropriate qualifiers

most unique, most superlative

48. mixed metaphors and clichés

I put my foot in my mouth and had to eat crow.

49. unnecessary quotation marks

It's bound to happen at some point "your team runs aground".
[Not to mention putting the period outside the quotation marks. From a newsletter for writers and trainers.]

A team "like a chain" is only as good as its weakest link.
[From a newsletter for writers and trainers.]

Even in team writing projects, that most frequent writer's malady is likely to strike up "procrastination".
[The omission of a dash or colon after *strike up* makes this sentence difficult to read. Again, the quotation marks are unnecessary and the period is misplaced. From a newsletter for writers and trainers.]

Grammar and Syntax

50. misplaced or dangling modifier

Do NOT open more than one file drawer at a time to prevent the cabinet from toppling over.
[Use some other method to prevent the cabinet from toppling over? From a safety handbook.]

By measuring the intensity of emitted light, the concentration of an element can be determined.
[The *concentration* does not do the measuring. From a spectroscopy manual.]

Remove the top cover (item 14) and check the switch operation (item 16) with a V.O.M. (Caution: When removing the switch housing there are three leads that must be disconnected.)
[Also, what's a V.O.M.? From an installation and service manual for a sump pump.]

Headline: With a little help, children can make delightful gifts
[But only to couples wishing to adopt? From a local newspaper.]

In 1930, Philip Wylie wrote a novel, *Gladiator,* about a boy whose mother had been injected with a serum invented by her scientist husband while pregnant with him.
[From a newsletter.]

A longtime fan of the late conductor, the host of 89.7 fm's "MusicAmerica" will journey through the musical world of the Lawrence-born, Harvard-educated composer/conductor who wrote "West Side Story" on Friday, April 26 at 1 PM.
[Mighty fast writing! From a PBS magazine.]

TIP: Watch for the placement of *only, just,* and *even.* Misplacing these can change the meaning or the emphasis of the sentence.

51. nominative case after preposition

just between you and I

52. wrong verb form

He had broke the heads off all the gingerbread men.

53. missing or wrong punctuation

These changes in molecular or atomic properties, called transitions, fall into three categories; vibrations, rotations, or changes in atomic or nuclear structure.
[The semicolon should be a colon. From a spectroscopy manual.]

Other than Broil, it doesn't matter which temperature is selected, because while toasting the Toast Shade Control determines the degree of browning.
[The lack of punctuation makes this difficult to parse—while toasting the control? From the owner's guide for a toaster oven.]

TIP: Watch for missing periods at the end of paragraphs. Sometimes when the writer breaks one paragraph into two, the period gets chopped off.

54. missing or extra comma

With the combination of GC-AES, it is possible to detect *elements* in compounds leaving the column. This happens by exciting the atoms in the chromatographic eluent, and observing the characteristic wavelengths of light that they emit.
[The comma in the second sentence separates the subject and predicate. From a spectroscopy manual.]

Assumptions can be made, that this is the effect of dust particles . . .
[From a journal on components, hybrids, and manufacturing technology.]

55. unclear or incorrect antecedent

WARNING: Lifting the system unit or the monitor requires more than one person because each one weighs more than 40 pounds (18 kilograms).
[From a computer manual.]

Please consult with your doctor or medical authority before undertaking any exercise, especially those who has suffered from prolonged illness, or who has increased risk factors such as Obesity, Hypertension, Cardio-Circulatory problems etc.
[From the owner's manual for an exercycle.]

Usually this connector is a male connector, which determines the sex of the cable you'll need.
[From a computer manual.]

56. missing antecedent

CAUTION: This can destroy the metal finish.
[What does *this* refer to?]

57. convoluted syntax

The Data Base and Transaction Management System provides transaction management as well as data base management and control. It handles concurrent requests, priorities transactions, provides a test made that allows use of live data without permanent change, security features, sharing of data with full integrates, updates capable of being modified, multiple applications operations concurrently against data base, etc. are key features of the system.
[Try parsing or diagramming the second sentence—find the subject(s) and predicate(s). The typos shown here were in the original. From the data sheet for a computer product.]

Using this method we can arrive at the real location if we take the initially approximated location farther than the real one.
[From a journal on magnetics.]

Although not discussing about conclusions, interesting for sponsors of this paper, it is evident that even at loads, many orders of magnitude higher than highest expected CR, the resistance of a whole line of contacts in series can achieve values comparable to load resistance.
[Clearly English is not this scientist's native language. From a journal on components, hybrids, and manufacturing technology.]

58. unclear or incorrect subordination

> Students should have a Macintosh computer available for some follow-up between class sessions. It is suggested that students, who have had no experience with a Macintosh computer, take the INTRODUCTION TO THE MACINTOSH course.
> [From the catalog for an adult education program.]

59. nonparallel structure or idea within a sentence

> A mechanical failure in the disk drive, while rare, can destroy all or part of a diskette. Likewise, power failures or surges, spills, dust, and other substances can get on diskettes and corrupt models.
> [Oops! I spilled another power failure on this diskette! From a computer manual.]

> Whenever a function button (Stop, FF, etc.) is pressed, or when you change channels, a 4 second OSD appears.
> [From a VCR manual.]

> The curved end of the hose has a slip ring to control the vacuum power. Close the hole completely for maximum power; open the hole for cleaning draperies, small rugs, and other light fabrics which require reduced suction power.
> [Other light fabrics? From the owner's manual for a vacuum cleaner.]

60. shift in mood or tense

> First measure twice, then you should cut.
> [Shift in mood.]

> First measure. After you've measured again, cut.
> [Shift in tense.]

61. missing or extra apostrophe

> This procedure improves the batteries capacity.
> [From a manual for a portable vacuum cleaner.]

> *Front page:* Writer's Where Are You.
> *Advertisement on page 3:* Writer's needed for Training & Documentation newsletter. Remember, this is YOUR newsletter. We need your help.
> [From a newsletter for writers and trainers.]

> *it's* and *its*
> [Always check these words because they appear incorrectly so often.]

62. **missing hyphen or inappropriate hyphenation**

> large computer user
> [Which is large—the computer or the user?]
>
> International Air Traffic Organization
> [Is it an organization for people involved in international air traffic or an international organization for people in the air traffic business?]

63. **adverbs in *-ly* with compounding**

> *highly-respected* for *highly respected*

64. **agreement (subject and verb)**

> Neither the writer nor the editor is/are able to attend the 2:00 meeting.
>
> Everyone who worked on the book deserve/deserves praise.
>
> The editor as well as the writer participate/participates in developing the product.
>
> [Test yourself on these. Consult a grammar book for the answers.]

65. **use of *either, neither* with more than two**

> You may either watch television, wash clothes, or water the lawn.
> [Delete *either*.]

66. **nonparallel structure within a paragraph or between paragraphs (or other constructs)**

> You can help save energy if you:
> 1. **Wash full loads**. Running a half-filled dishwasher uses the same amount of electricity and hot water as a fully loaded machine.
> 2. Use the **LOW ENERGY WASH Program** whenever possible . . .
> 3. **Air dry dishes** when you don't need a rapid drying program . . .
> 4. **Load correctly** for best washing results. Incorrect loading . . .
> 5. **Don't pre-rinse normally soiled dishes.** Select the correct program . . .
> 6. **Use your dishwasher** during off-peak hours.
> 7. **Kitchen cleanup** can be done quickly and efficiently through the use of your dishwasher.
> [Boldface is used inconsistently. Not all items follow the introductory phrase, especially item 7. From the owner's guide for a dishwasher.]

Figure 14. Distributions along x direction
Figure 15. Distributions along the z direction
[These two figure captions appeared on the same page of a technical report. Do you see the inconsistency?]

67. pronoun agreement

Each employee is responsible for maintaining their own head protection and for the replacement if lost or stolen.
[Don't lose your head. From a safety handbook.]

68. unclear agent or subject

The countdown can be set from one minute to 11 hours, 59 minutes, and times to an accuracy of one second. Start/stop operation is possible by pressing the **A** button and is confirmed by a signal. A signal sounds at 10-minute intervals. When the display reaches zero, the buzzer will sound for 20 seconds unless the **L** button is pressed. . . . When the display is stopped, the pre-entered time is retrieved by pressing the **L** button.
[From the user's manual for a digital watch.]

According to police, Doherty apparently shot his . . . girlfriend, Hillary B—, with a 12-gauge shotgun Saturday and then turned the gun on himself. . . . Police found a dead cat on the bed in the apartment at the scene. No suicide note or any signs of alcohol or drug use were found . . .
[Did the cat commit suicide upon finding the corpses? From a local newspaper.]

Technical Accuracy

69. miscount

The three dimensions: length, width, depth, and time.

TIP: Get in the habit of counting *every* enumeration—even if you counted the items last time you saw the manuscript. Sometimes when writers incorporate technical changes, they add or delete items from a list and forget to update the corresponding reference ("The following *five* guidelines . . .") in the text.

70. conversion

[See the sidebar, "Conversions: More Than Simple Arithmetic" in chapter 6.]

71. arithmetic (unit or number)

CORRECTION: In the Fun Pages of Aug. 17, the recipe for grapenut custard on page 4 gave the amount of grapenuts required as 12 cups, and the amount of sugar as 2 cups. The amounts should have read ½ cup each.
[From the *Boston Globe.*]

72. precision

"How old are these dinosaur bones?" the tourist asked the guide.
"Exactly one hundred million and three years old."
"How can you be so definite?" asked the tourist.
"A geologist told me they were one hundred million years old," replied the guide, "and that was exactly three years ago."

Student's test scores: 95, 87, 88, 85, 100. Average test score: 91.0.
[The average shows precision to the nearest tenth. It's not wrong; it's overly precise. It would be more appropriate to say 91 because grades are typically expressed as integers. From a computer manual.]

73. numeric inconsistency

Abstract: The development of the first electronic digital computers in the 1940s fulfilled a hypothesis made 300 years earlier by Charles Babbage.
Page 2: It took the eclectic British mathematician and astronomer, Charles Babbage (1791–1871) to marry the concepts of mechanical calculation and the mechanical control of a sequence of operations together in a machine he called the Analytical Engine in 1834.
Page 3: This survey will cover sources that are largely biographical, beginning with Babbage and spanning more than 250 years of progress in computer science.
[If Babbage was born in 1791, a view of 250 years of progress takes us beyond the 1991 publication date of this article. Also, if Babbage made a hypothesis 300 years before 1940, he was quite ahead of his time, literally. From a manuscript.]

74. misrepresentation of data or bad data

Sidebar: Do you believe that because of past discrimination against black people, qualified blacks should receive preference over equally qualified whites in such matters as getting into college or getting jobs?

	Whites	Blacks
Should	19%	48%
Should not	72%	42%

Text: An overwhelming majority of whites in *Newsweek*'s poll say "no" to continued preference; most blacks say "yes." To them, the weight of the past is a daily burden.
[Is 48 percent "most"? From *Newsweek,* May 6, 1991.]

"Two-thirds of the people will come to see me, two-thirds to see Billy [Martin], and two-thirds to see the Yankees."
[The sum of the parts is greater (or less) than the whole. Baseball player Rickey Henderson.]
[Also watch for percents that don't add up to 100.]

75. This space intentionally left blank.

[A little gratuitous humor.]

76. cross-reference to wrong or nonexistent location

See Appendix C.
[. . . which was deleted after technical review. The more changes the writer makes in a hurry, the more likely the cross-references will have errors. This error is also common in minor revisions. A writer may put in the few known changes and corrections, but not check whether these changes affect other chapters.]

77. numeric or alphabetic sequences

Step 1.   Go to jail.

Step 3.   Go directly to jail.

Step 2.   Do not pass Go.

Step 4.   Do not collect $200.

[These errors typically occur in lists (including lists of numbered figures and tables); they're often the result of hasty revisions. (Software that automatically handles numbering can eliminate most of these errors.) You need to pay attention to the information because it could mean that the numbers are wrong or that the steps are out of order. Unless you know the product, you probably can't tell whether the numbers are wrong or the sequence is wrong.]

78. inconsistent information

Page 10: The characters you can use: A–Z, a–z, 0–9, $, %, –, _, @.
Page 74: A–Z, a–z, 0–9, @, _, $, !, # –.
[Not only are the characters different, they're displayed in a different order. From a computer manual.]

Headline of an obituary: Noted actor, Michael Landon, 65
Text of obituary: Actor Michael Landon, who died last week of cancer at the age of 54 . . .
[From a local newspaper.]

79. **wrong number of zeros or the wrong exponent**

> [To catch these errors, you'll have to rely on the context and your knowledge of the subject.]

80. **letter O for zero and letter l for 1, or vice versa**

> computer keystrokes: <ALT> l   <ALT> O
> chemical symbols: A1 for Al
>
> [Sometimes you just can't tell from the typeface (as in the computer examples) and sometimes there's a typo (as in the chemistry example). Watch for this error in mathematical and physical equations.]

81. **factual error**

> Ad in San Antonio newspaper: Powerful Features For Greater Productivity. The Apple Macintosh II comes complete with IBM RAM expandable to 8MB. An 800K floppy disk drive. A hard disk with up to 80MB of storage. A 12" high resolution color monitor . . .
> [IBM RAM should be 1MB RAM. From *MacUser,* July 1988.]
>
> . . . fault-tolerant computers, designed to keep working even if no parts fail.
> [Fault-tolerant computers work *even if* parts fail. From a local newspaper.]

Judgment, Taste, and Sensitivity

82. **inappropriate language: vocabulary, slang, jargon, cuteness**

> Let us pause for the moment and wax mathematical about net present value or NPV as it can be called for short. The mathematical equation for net present value is . . .
> [From a computer manual.]

83. **inappropriate tone**

> [For example, an informal tone in a serious document, like a proposal for a defense contract. Also, a tone that may offend the reader, such as a condescending, flippant, or patronizing tone.]

84. **sexist language**

> If the manager needs more information, hc may . . .
> [Watch that masculine pronouns aren't used exclusively. Ensure that examples don't show only men in positions of authority or success. Watch that references to gender are fair and balanced. Or avoid the problem by using plural pronouns.]

85. North Americanisms (cultural bias)

[If you're editing documents for an international audience, don't assume the reader has heard of the Red Sox. Use examples your audience can be expected to know. If your audience consists of North Americans, baseball or Broadway examples are better than references to cricket or kabuki.]

86. cultural slurs

[Here's a typo that's so appalling it fits this category. When Prince Charles visited the U.S. recently, the graphic on the television newscast referred to him as "The Prince of Whales."]

87. cultural chauvinism

[A speaker once referred to English as being "more advanced" than ideographic languages, because it uses a 26-letter alphabet.]

88. poor taste

Sixth-grader Wayne L—, who should have been a vegetable after fracturing his skull in an auto accident, is learning to walk again with the help of classmate Laurie H—.
[Photo caption. From a local newspaper.]

Typography and Graphics

89. inconsistent use of hyphen, en dash, em dash, and minus sign

Figure 3–2 [en], Figure 3-3 [hyphen]

–2 [en], -2 [hyphen], -2 [minus]

Grace B— [em], Margaret G– [en]

[The distinctions are more noticeable in some typefaces than others.]

90. illustration introduces technical or factual error

Full-color illustration of a hand inserting a floppy disk into a disk drive: The thumb is on the magnetized slot (touching the disk here can cause data loss) and the floppy is being inserted backwards.
[In *Personal Computing,* January 1988.]

Ad for Opus "No Bad Memories" floppy disk: shows a model holding a floppy disk—with her hand on the magnetized slot. A revised ad in the next issue of the magazine shows they'd retouched the photo to move her fingers.
[In a computer magazine.]

91. inconsistency between text and example or figure

If you attempt to connect to a directory named **big,** which is in all uppercase or mixed case, as in //**agent/cooper/ford** . . .
[The example should not be all lowercase. The directory names don't match. From a computer manual.]

For example, we specify that Z is the last drive:
file = 20
lastdrive = z
[The difference between lowercase z and uppercase Z can be significant in a computer program. From a computer manual.]

four-color brochure: Win a Macintosh computer!
[The photo showed a different computer model. From a brochure for American Family Publisher's sweepstakes.]

Caption: Apple has made several changes in the Apple III since its introduction in 1980.
[The photo showed the Commodore CBM 8032 computer. From *InfoWorld,* 1984.]

92. bulleted list, table title, or figure caption inconsistently capitalized

Figure 3–2. A pack of wolves on the hunt

Figure 3–6. A Timber Wolf and His Mate

93. bulleted list, table title, or figure caption inconsistently punctuated

- March: "The year the Sox will go all the way"
- June, "The Sox are out of contention."
- September: What a comeback!
- October— "Wait Till Next Year"

94. heads inconsistently capitalized

Chapter 1. Raising Capybaras for Fun and Profit

Chapter 2. Tricks you can teach your capybara

Chapter 3. If your Capybara Bites, Bite back!

Legal and Ethical Concerns

95. untruths or false claims; inaccurate or untruthful specifications

Swim in our Fountain of Youth and become 20 years younger!

Our software has absolutely no bugs!

96. libel (unsupported disparaging comments)

Our competitor's products stink.

97. preannouncement or promise (warranty)

Full 3D drawing capability will be included in the next release.
[If the company changes its plans and doesn't provide this capability in the next release, a customer might sue, claiming that this promise influenced purchasing or product development decisions.]

At the next release, Version 5.0, we will no longer support **net use** commands. [First, you don't want to say what will be in the next release, because business decisions can change. Second, can you guarantee there will *ever* be a Version 5.0? Third, can you be sure Version 5.0 will be the next release? A Version 4.5 might be slipped in.]

98. insufficient warning of hazard

Cigarette smoking may be hazardous to your health.
[The old warning label.]

Proofreading Oversights

99. double words (especially *the the* and *and and*) and missing words (especially articles)

If we want to improve our physical condition really efficiently, what we need is specific program. One of great advantages of an ergometer is that the exercise loading may be adjust accordingly to be effective and safe for each person. [From the owner's guide for an exercycle.]

100. oh yeah, typos

Sometimes a single letter makes a difference. It made a difference to a man on trial in Nebraska for "possession with intent to deliver" 49 capsules of Ecstasy, a psychoactive drug. The state legislature misspelled the drug's chemical name in the bill that outlawed the drug. He was acquitted because he didn't possess the drug specified in the law.

Incorrect spelling: methylenedioxyethamphetamine
Correct spelling: methylenedioxy*me*thamphetamine

Summary

The examples in this chapter represent the most common errors you'll find in technical documentation. Become familiar with these errors and actively look for them in the manuscripts you edit. For example, every time you see a numbered list, check that the sequence is correct. Every time the text refers to the number of items listed, *count* the items. Check *every* occurrence of *it's* and *its* to make sure the correct one is used.

Don't assume that text is correct just because the manuscript is neatly typed or because the book has been published. Don't assume that it's wrong, either. Do recognize that every statement, word, character, and graphical element in the manuscript *might* be wrong.

Make checking details a habit. You'll know you're on the right track when you catch yourself spotting goofs in the Sunday comics, restaurant menus, and cereal boxes—without consciously trying. You'll know you're hooked on editing when it takes you three times as long to read a novel as it used to, because you can't turn off the "editing monitor" in your head.

Practice finding the errors shown in this chapter in the manuscripts you edit. Become so adept at finding these errors that marking them in manuscripts is almost a reflex. The less brain power you expend finding these errors, the more you can devote to solving unique problems.

Chapter 8
Levels of Edit

Scenario 1.
Writer: "Didn't you test the procedures? I was expecting you to go through each of these procedures step by step, but all you've done is correct formatting inconsistencies. I need to be sure the steps are clear and complete."

Scenario 2.
Writer: "I've only made a handful of minor changes to this book since the last revision. If I incorporate all your editing changes, I'll be rewriting for the next month!"

Scenario 3.
Client: "We specified a light edit because we don't have time to rewrite. You did twice as much as we asked for and now you're billing us for services we don't need."

Scenario 4.
Engineer: "You said you were going to do a heavy edit. I wasn't expecting you to rewrite the whole article! I thought you'd fix up the spelling and make it look nice."

How do you prevent these misunderstandings? This chapter describes two techniques, which you can use in tandem:

- Many editors follow a system known as *levels of edit*. Levels-of-edit systems define how thoroughly you'll edit a particular publication.

- Bridge the gap between the writer's or client's expectations and what you actually have time to do, by performing *triage*.

Using Levels of Edit

Here are some ways to use levels of edit:

- Establish a common language. Instead of vague terms such as "light" or "heavy" edit, levels of edit let you refer to specific tasks you'll do or specific items you'll check. You can ensure that you, the writer, other members of the product team, and your managers are all communicating on the same wavelength.

- Facilitate budgeting and labor tracking. You may charge differently for different services (both as a contract editor and as an in-house editor whose time is charged back to other departments). A levels-of-edit approach lets you quantify the editing process.

- Train new editors and evaluate their progress. A levels-of-edit system lets you distinguish among the different tasks and skill levels objectively. For example, you can have new editors start at the lowest level and gradually work their way up as they master each level.

- Manage your own schedule. You can juggle several projects by applying different levels of edit to each. You can assign a weight to each level, calculate your upcoming workload, and compare it to your previous workloads to gauge whether you can fit in another project or whether you need to reschedule or reassign some work.

The JPL Levels of Edit

Several editing groups have formally classified the levels of edit. The most widely known plan, created for the Jet Propulsion Laboratory (JPL) at the California Institute of Technology, divides editing into nine types of edit, shown in figure 8–1.[1] At JPL, these types of edit have been classified into five levels of edit of decreasing thoroughness.

At a Level 1 edit (the highest level), the editor performs all nine types of edits. Level 2 drops the substantive edit. Level 3 drops the mechanical style, language, and substantive edits. Level 4 drops these and the copy clarification and format edits. At Level 5 (the lowest level), the editor checks only for coordination and policy.

---

[1] Van Buren, Robert, and Mary Fran Buehler, *The Levels of Edit,* Second Edition (Arlington, Virginia: Society for Technical Communication, 1991). Reprinted with permission from the Society for Technical Communication, Arlington, Virginia.

JPL Types of Edit

Coordination edit: planning and coordination

Examples: planning and estimating; maintaining records; scheduling; monitoring and coordinating production processes and interfaces with writer, support groups, and production groups

Policy edit: adherence to company policy

Examples: front matter, logos, credits, disclaimers; hierarchy of heads; use of references, units of measurement; conformance to policy issues (product endorsements, inappropriate comments)

Integrity edit: ensuring that parts of a publication match

Examples: table of contents with text and page numbers; references to figures, tables, footnotes, and appendixes; numeric and lettered sequences; cross-references to other elements of the publication or to other publications

Screening edit: ensuring minimal editorial acceptability

Examples: spelling; subject-verb agreement; use of complete sentences; clarity; suitability of illustrations, graphs, and photographs for publication and reproduction

Copy clarification edit: ensuring that material is clean, clear, and complete for production departments

Examples: clarifying illegible copy, identifying mathematical symbols, indicating crop marks on photographs, coding text for photocomposition

Format edit: ensuring conformance to appropriate format

Examples: type specifications, leading, column width, indentation, layout, placement and display of figures

Mechanical style edit: ensuring conformance to specified style and consistency

Examples: capitalization, spelling, abbreviations, compounding, form and use of symbols (including acronyms, abbreviations, units of measure), nomenclature

Language edit: in-depth review of expression of ideas

Examples: grammar and syntax, usage, fluency (transitions), parallelism, conciseness, correct and consistent terminology

Substantive edit: review content of the publication

Examples: scope, coherence of parts, organization, subordination, eliminating repetition and redundancy, completeness of information

Figure 8–1. The JPL types of edit used to define the levels of edit

At JPL—and at companies that use the JPL approach—editorial policy spells out which level of edit the editor should apply to the different types of publications. For special projects, an editor may perform any combination of edits, independently of the levels, as appropriate for each document.

Here's how the JPL uses the levels of edit:

> It is the position of the Jet Propulsion Laboratory that its publications will receive the most thorough edit possible, and that the only reasons for applying less than a thorough edit are the practical constraints of time and money. The levels-of-edit concept makes it possible to back away from the full treatment in an orderly fashion, so that a publication will still receive the highest level of edit consistent with the time and money constraints imposed upon it.[1]

Before you rush to apply these levels to your projects, consider these points:

- The JPL levels of edit consider the following *extraordinary editorial functions,* outside the scope of these levels:

  - **Providing additional or missing material,** such as research and writing

  - **Working with unusually difficult or time-consuming material,** such as those written in a foreign language or in English by a nonnative speaker

  - **Performing repeated operations,** such as multiple reviews of a manuscript

  - **Editing for technical content,** such as verifying accuracy of technical data, calculating conversions from one system of measurement to another, identifying and correcting inconsistent use of mathematical symbols

  - **Performing time-consuming services,** such as dealing with more than one author or out-of-town authors, traveling

- "The level of edit defines the quality of the end product but not the effort required to achieve it."[2]

I've shown just the surface of the JPL system. You should read the entire 26-page booklet, *The Levels of Edit,* before you implement a levels-of-edit system based on the JPL program.

---

[1] Van Buren and Buehler, *The Levels of Edit,* p. 2.
[2] *Ibid.,* p. 9.

An Informal Approach to Levels of Edit

A formal levels-of-edit system is particularly useful when you have to communicate your intentions to somebody else. If you simply need a system to help you decide how heavily to edit a manuscript, you may want to devise your own hierarchy. Here's the hierarchy I use:

- What you see just by *turning pages:* the superficial look of the text
- What you find by *skimming:* spelling, grammar, punctuation errors
- What you verify by *skimming and comparing:* internal consistency, cross-references
- What you notice by *reading:* writing style, such as wording, transitions, usage
- What you detect by *analyzing:* organizational flaws, missing information, redundancies, technical inconsistencies
- What you find by *testing and using:* technical errors, usability problems

I prefer my informal system because it ties in the levels of edit with the difficulty of the task, the amount of time it takes to perform, and the requisite skill level.

Performing Triage

If you had unlimited time, you'd do everything listed in the editing checklists in chapter 6. The reality is that you'll never have enough time. Sometimes there's next to no time.

Editors need to be flexible and creative. You will be called upon many times to do the best possible job in the least amount of time. In other words, you will need to perform the editorial equivalent of *triage*.

> **triage:** the sorting of and allocation of treatment to patients and esp. battle and disaster victims according to a system of priorities designed to maximize the number of survivors (Webster's *Ninth New Collegiate Dictionary*)

How Do You Decide?

When you determine the level of edit for a document, you need to weigh the project's schedule (which includes the number of editing passes you'll have), scope, audience, budget, objectives, and anticipated life cycle. For each book, you should be able to identify the appropriate level of edit from the information in the doc spec. Then consider what you know about the writer's skills, abilities, and personality. Finally, weigh any special considerations.

Here's a simple way I devised to evaluate any project. Rate on a scale of 1 (low) to 3 (high) the following variables:

- Importance of project (low = 1, average = 2, high = 3) to your company.

- Your rapport with the writer (good = 1, unknown or neutral = 2, problematic = 3). Exception: Assign entry-level writers a 3 rating through their first year to accommodate the extra time you'll spend answering questions, teaching the process, and providing moral support.

- Difficulty of the project (low effort = 1, average = 2, high effort = 3) as stated in the doc spec. High-effort projects include brand new manuals, major revisions, and any "experimental" projects, such as your department's first ventures into online documentation, multimedia, or a new production method. Low-effort projects include minor revisions or updates, low-volume shipments, and documentation for low priority products. Add points for tight schedules.

Add the total points for each book and list them by numerical value. The books with the highest number of points need more editorial support; those with the lowest need less support. You may want to perform three or even more editing passes (developmental, literary, and production edits) on the high priority books, two passes (literary and production edits) on the medium priority ones, and production edits only on the low priority books.

This system lets you compare the relative difficulty of concurrent projects and determine how to budget your time (in other words, triage for your entire workload).

After you see the first draft of the manuscript, you may need to adjust your estimate if the book is in better or worse shape than you'd expected.

Performing triage means you're making two judgment calls:

- Deciding the desired quality of the book
- Determining how much effort needs to be expended by the editor (you), the writer, and the production staff to reach that level of quality

While you're editing, you'll need to make hundreds of decisions about whether each possible change you see is actually worth making. To decide, factor in the following variables:

- *Customers' concerns:* What matters to *my* customers?

- What's *easy* or *feasible* to fix in the available time (editor's, writer's, production staff's).

- What's *important* to fix: How much will the reader notice and care? How much will your employer notice and care?

- What the *client wants* (or your manager or the project team): Sometimes you need to refer to a formal levels-of-edit system.

- How *important* is this document: How important is it to customers? How important to the documentation set? What is the impact on other work of the time you (or others) spend on this document?

Weigh these factors according to their importance; the weight you assign to each variable depends on each project. For example, it may be a lot of work to reorganize a book but nonetheless important if customers have complained of difficulty finding information. Sometimes you'll fix something that's not very important but is so easy to fix that it would be silly not to. And sometimes you need to ignore something that bothers you but it's OK with the customers, it's expensive to change, and it's not important to change. (Just because it bothers you does not make it wrong.)

When you have to decide whether to fix or overlook a "problem," determine what class of problem it is and act accordingly:

- What you can assume every reader will spot instantly. Examples: overall ugliness, such as an abundance of typefaces with a circus-poster effect; missing pages or illustrations.

  Always fix eyesores that advertise unprofessional work. I mean blatant errors, such as a box-rule for an illustration but no illustration inside it. I do *not* mean a footnote rule that is 1-pt instead of .5-pt, if that's what your specifications call for.

EXAMPLE

a footnote with a 1-pt rule

---

a footnote with a .5-pt rule

Unless you're writing a book for publishing experts, your audience won't notice the difference.

- What customers will find and care about. Examples: errors and usability.

  Always fix errors. If you can't ensure accuracy in a technical manual, you shouldn't be publishing it. Accuracy and usability go together, but there are degrees of usability. The must-fix items are those that affect minimum usability. For example, if the reader follows the tutorial as written, everything should work as documented—no missing steps, no extra steps, messages and prompts should be as the reader sees them. The omission of a glossary hurts usability in some books, but it's rarely a showstopper.

- What customers will notice you missed, but not complain about. Example: most copy editing details.

  Fix all you can in the available time. Catch all the typos even if that means not smoothing any transitions between paragraphs. If you have time, you can fix up the wording. Customers will consider a book sloppy and unprofessional if the copy edit was executed poorly or neglected. They'll doubt the accuracy of the information (did *anybody* see this book before it was printed?) and may not even use the book. Unless the errors affect technical accuracy, customers won't go out of their way to tell you the book is bad, but they'll let you know the next time you send them a survey about documentation. Most of these errors you can fix quickly, so just fix them.

- What customers will consider bad, but credit to "typical technical writing." Example: convoluted, passive writing style.

  Fix these if you have time. Most readers of technical manuals can tell when a book is badly written, even if they can't articulate what's wrong with it. Users' expectations of technical manuals are already low, so you can exceed their expectations with turgid writing. (Just kidding.) A book with flawed writing style is difficult to read and difficult to use, but if customers can find the information and it's accurate, they'll tolerate some poor wording. If the writing is so poor that readers can't understand the text or use the product, then you have bigger problems to fix: problems in technical accuracy and usability. Overuse of the passive voice and wordiness are examples of bad, but not fatal, writing.

- What customers will never notice, but only another editor would. Examples: compounding, hyphenation, and use of en dashes.

  Fix these if you have time and the book is a showcase item. It's nice to catch and fix everything, but that'll be a luxury you'll have only occasionally.

Exercise 9   Rank each of the following as a low, medium, or high level of effort:

1. Minor revision, experienced writer you've worked with before

2. Major revision, novice writer

3. Minor revision, novice writer

4. New book, experienced writer you've worked well with before

5. New book, experienced writer you've never worked with before

6. New book, experienced writer you've worked with—and had problems with—before

Triage Tips

Balance your edits. You don't want to rewrite chapters 1–3, find you've run out of time, and limit yourself in chapters 4–9 to fixing typos.

Not all parts of a book are equal; some are more important than others. Edit evenly, more or less, but give more emphasis to the important parts. The first few pages are important because they get the user going. It's cost-effective to spend a little more effort making sure the introduction is clear. Just don't fall into the trap of polishing that prose so that it noticeably outshines the rest of the book or the task consumes all the time you have to edit the whole book.

Some editors time themselves on the first five or ten pages and then extrapolate how long it will take them to edit the rest. The problem with this technique is that some chapters are significantly worse or better than others and some are more important to edit heavily than others.

For example, spend more time on the exposition (smoothness of the writing) for a conceptual guide than for a reference manual. In a reference manual, spend more time on the organization (how easy it is to find information) than on the prose, if you have to budget your time. In a task-oriented book or tutorial, put extra effort into ensuring the accuracy of the content and the flow of the writing; if you have to cut corners anywhere, do so in the formatting. Spend more effort ensuring ease-of-use in books written for novice users and more effort ensuring accuracy in books written for expert users.

Exercise 10   What's wrong here?

Vigorous writing is concise. A sentence should contain no unnecessary words, a paragraph no unnecessary sentences, for the same reason that a drawing should have no unnecessary lines and a machine no unnecessary parts.[1]

Triage Examples

Sometimes the scope of your editing will be determined solely by the available time. Your manager will ask you to do the best you can with an unexpected project. You can decide the quality of the product and the level of edit. The only absolute is the deadline.

What you do depends on how fast you can edit. Your speed, in turn, depends on the condition of the manuscript, your skill level, and your familiarity with the subject.

Let's consider this:

You have before you the manuscript for a 200-page reference manual. This is a new book, and you have only a beginner's knowledge of the subject. You do have two years' editing experience with the company and know its processes and the people on the project, including the writer, with whom you have a good relationship. You've also read *this* book from cover to cover twice, so you know a lot of tricks and shortcuts. Also assume, albeit unrealistically, that you don't have other major assignments competing for your time.

Where do you begin?

First, look at the manuscript and try to assess its condition. Study the table of contents to see the overall organization. Read the preface to see what context it establishes for the reader. Does it identify the target audience? Does it tell what product the book supports? Does it tell how this book relates to other books?

Read the first two pages of each chapter to get a feel for the writing style. Open the book to several pages at random and start reading. Do the paragraphs seem to make sense?

Flip through the book to see how it looks. Do illustrations and tables look professional or amateurish? Are pages cluttered? Does the format look well organized and mostly consistent?

---

[1] Strunk, William Jr., and E. B. White, *The Elements of Style,* Third Edition
(New York: Macmillan Publishers, 1979), p. xiv.

In ten or twenty minutes, you should be able to get enough of a feel for the book to know whether it's in better or worse shape than average. (When you have about two years' editing experience, you'll have a sense of what's "average.") You won't really be able to tell *how much* better or worse than average with a cursory check—you won't know that until you start to edit—but you'll know whether the book will require more or less time than you'd planned.

Exercise 11   What's wrong here?

From a review of Richard Leighton's *Tuva or Bust?*, in which Leighton relates his adventures with Richard Feynman:[1]

This Tuvan odyssey began over dinner in 1977, when the Nobel-prize-winning physicist and all-around unforgettable character Richard Feynman wondered whatever happened to Tannu Tuva, a tiny Central Asian country whose stamps he prized as a kid. When he and his friend Ralph Leighton learned that it had become a Soviet republic with a capital intriguingly named Kyzyl, they set their hearts on visiting.

Let's assume first you have three weeks to edit this manuscript. With such a generous schedule, you probably won't have to perform triage, and you can do a reasonably thorough edit.

If you had one week, what would you check? I'd recommend fixing any cosmetic flaws (physical appearance), consistency problems, and mechanical (spelling, grammar, punctuation) errors, and as many stylistic problems as possible. If the manuscript is in decent shape, you may be able to read for content and do some testing.

If you had one day, what would you check? I'd recommend fixing the easy-to-see and easy-to-fix cosmetic problems throughout the book, the front matter, and the most important chapters (such as chapter 1 and any reference pages).

If you had one hour, what would you check? Think about this as an exercise and then see the following sidebar for some suggestions. This is not as hypothetical a situation as you may think at first. I've faced this situation hundreds (yes, hundreds) of times.

---

[1] *Boston Sunday Globe*, May 26, 1991.

◇ ─── ◇

The Top Ten Things to Check If You Have Only One Hour

- Proofread the distribution information (order number, part number, file number, bar code). Why write a book if you can't get it to the customer?

- Proofread the front cover: Is the title OK? Logo OK?

- Proofread the title page: Is the title OK? Logo OK?

- Skim boilerplate text and proofread unique copy for disclaimers, copyright notices, and other legal or safety notices.

- Read the preface and the first page of text, where the publication makes its first impression on the customer.

- Turn the pages and look for gross errors, such as a blank space where a figure was supposed to have been inserted.

- Scan for obscenities (due to typos), misspellings of your company name, and libelous information. If you see a competitor's name, pause to read the surrounding text as you turn the pages.

- Ensure that instructions to the production staff and/or printer are clear and complete.

- Verify that the package is complete (that no pages are missing).

- Ensure that the process has been followed. Are all sign-off forms attached?

◇ ─── ◇

───

Summary

This chapter showed three systems for adjusting the thoroughness of your edits to fit schedules and budgets:

- A formal system, the JPL levels of edit
- An informal hierarchy of how closely you look at the document
- A system of triage to balance what you *should* do and what you *can* do

You can probably deduce that the better you know the product, the processes, and the publishing tools, the more effectively you can edit when you're squeezed for time.

You can apply triage better if you know the consequences of your decisions. If you know that it takes *x* amount of time to fix *y* or to change *z*, then you can evaluate if the change or correction is worth the effort and expense. For example, if you knew that changing *frob-nitz* to *frobnitz* takes only a few seconds, thanks to the software, you wouldn't hesitate to request the change. But if you knew that changing the margins meant three weeks' work, you'd need to consider other factors. If you knew that changing the typefaces would make the book unreadable in its online version, then you wouldn't ask to change them. And if you knew that the book was going to be a one-shot special project for two customers, you wouldn't expend a lot of effort on tweaking the wording.

Finally, what if the book really needs more editing than the schedule or budget permits?

Let's say you've looked over a manuscript to judge the level of edit you'll perform and realize that the book has serious, deeply embedded problems. Perhaps the book was improperly and inadequately tested and could lead users to make mistakes that would cause injuries. Or perhaps the book's tone could embarrass the company. There is no quick fix that would get to the root of these problems.

If the book is fundamentally wrong, you need to stop its publication. Alert your manager to the problems and be prepared to defend your allegations with examples from the manuscript.

(Yes, you put your reputation on the line every time you shout, "Stop the presses!" But knowing when to shout, and how loudly, is the mark of an experienced and trusted editor. Your managers will long remember the disaster you prevented, because they would have been cleaning up the mess. They'll also remember if you raise a fuss over a few misplaced commas that, to their view, nobody would ever notice.)

You may be tempted to perform triage and fix what you can. Don't. Don't bother to put a splint on a broken finger if the patient is bleeding to death. Apply triage only when you can save the patient. Don't waste time you could use to save another patient's life.

Chapter 9
Following, Breaking, and Making the Rules

"Any fool can make a rule." Henry David Thoreau

"The rights of nations and kings would sink into questions of grammar if grammarians discussed them." Samuel Johnson

"Every editorial guideline exists to be broken." Walter E. Sears, Director, University of Michigan Press

"If all the grammarians in the world were placed end to end, it would be a good thing." Unknown

Following the Rules

We follow several different types of rules:

- Conventions of the English language. In the United States, these conventions include American usage for spelling, grammar, punctuation, and word usage.

- Conventions of the industry you work in, including jargon.

- Conventions of publishing. For example: what front matter comprises, the order we present front-matter pages, and the correspondence of recto (right-hand) pages with odd-numbered folios (page numbers) and verso (left-hand) pages with even-numbered folios.

- Conventions your company publishes in its house style guide. These conventions include design, writing, and editorial guidelines.

The term *rule* is used in this chapter to mean *accepted procedure*, rather than *regulation*. The terms *rule* and *convention* are used interchangeably in this chapter so that you will feel more comfortable breaking them when you must.

Rules Are Our Friends

The rules I'm referring to are our friends. They're the conventions that make it easier for us to write, edit, and produce books and, more important, to make it easier for our readers to use our books. Rules make order out of chaos and books out of random words.

Without rules, our jobs would be immensely more difficult. Imagine trying to invent the equivalent of an English grammar by yourself, for every book you write. (Come to think of it, I know people who do this all the time. But I wouldn't read any books they write.)

Imagine your surprise if your book came back from a printer who practiced an entirely different trade from what you're accustomed to. For example, we would never think to specify to a printer to shoot all pages right side up. Suppose the Print Vendor from Hell prints every third page upside down for variety.

We expect printers to follow certain conventions; likewise, they expect us to follow standard publishing conventions. The surest way to confuse a printer is to use a nonstandard system for pagination.

Conventions organize our working world so we don't have to reinvent it every day. Conventions save us time and money and minimize errors and frustration.

Rules Are Our Customers' Friends, Too

Our readers benefit when we follow normal conventions because they can read faster and with better understanding in a familiar environment.

Think how unfamiliar conventions slow you down when you read. For example, it's hard to read dialogue when characters speak in an unfamiliar dialect. Yet deviation from convention enhances literature, because it sparks the reader's imagination.

Literature thrives on originality. Technical writing, however, isn't literature.

Nonetheless, technical writers sometimes have a legitimate need to break from conventions. Technical editors can help writers break the rules sensibly.

Breaking the Rules

In your professional career, you will meet many editors and managers who slavishly follow all rules. There are many well-meaning purists who believe all rules are made to be followed blindly. (At the other extreme are the anarchists who believe all rules are made to be broken. These people are also known as "marketing writers.") Unfortunately, many purists are drawn to editing and publications management careers, where, ironically, their love for the English language leads them to obstruct good communications.

Before you can either enforce or break the rules, you need to know what the rules are and why they exist. For example, you don't want to be like the editor who firmly—and wrongly—told a writer to spell the name of the Pascal programming language in all caps because she'd heard that all names of computer programming languages were acronyms.

Technospeak

Technical professionals have an endearing habit of butchering the English language. Sometimes a detestable neologism becomes the official technical term, and we Defenders of the English Language have no choice but to concede defeat and vow to slay the next neologism before it permeates the industry.

Some terms we have to live with; some we can avoid. Oceanography has a term *higher high water* which you should not "correct." In contrast, some common programming terms that you should discourage are *comment out* (use *make it a comment*) and *reference* (as a verb).

One usage of *reference* as a verb has become acceptable in programming language manuals: "This program references a FORTRAN routine." The use of *reference* as a verb is so common in this context that *refer to* would sound wrong to the audience. Another reason for condoning its use is that its opposite is *dereference,* for which you could not substitute *derefer,* a term that no programmer would recognize. You may cringe at *dereference,* but it is a valid technical term, and you would no more change it than you would change a person's ugly name. But you can wager at this very moment an editor somewhere is arguing with a writer to change it to "not refer to" or "remove the reference to" or some other grammatically correct, technically inaccurate term.

Punctuation

Back in the ancient days of computerdom before manuals were typeset or even printed out on laser printers, the only way to set apart text was by using the standard characters on a keyboard. For example, where today we can use boldface to say, Start the program by typing **go**, in the old days the books said, Start the program by typing "go". (Actually, in the old days the manual would have said, The program is initiated with "go".)

This use of quotation marks led to all sorts of arguments about whether the punctuation marks go inside the quotes, according to the rules of English grammar. English punctuation is irrelevant in this situation because the purpose of the quotation marks is to set apart the literal user input. For technical accuracy, the period belongs outside the quotation marks.

An even clearer way to show a command line is to display it on a separate line.

EXAMPLE

Start the program by typing:

go

Technical documentation uses punctuation marks and other standard American typewriter characters for a variety of purposes. Here are some technical uses of punctuation marks and other symbols (by no means an exhaustive list):

- . (period) in filenames, as in **.login** or **a.out** (software)
- . (period) in commands, as in troff **.sp** or **.co** (software)
- , (comma) as separator in array (programming and mathematics)
- ! for factorial, as in 5! (mathematics)
- ! for logical NOT in C (programming)
- ^ (caret) to represent CONTROL key as in ^C (software)
- : (colon) to separate directories in some file systems (software)
- : (colon) in Backus-Naur Format (BNF) notation (programming)
- : (colon) for a device name (software)
- : (colon) for unshared pair of electrons or a double bond (chemistry)
- ; (semicolon) comment indicator or statement separator (programming)
- [ ] for an array or a substring (programming and mathematics)
- " " and ´ ´ for literal strings (programming)
- ( ) for a function or an array (programming and mathematics)

- " for inches or seconds of an angle (mathematics)
- * for multiplication (mathematics)
- ** for exponentiation (programming)
- ^ for exponentiation (mathematics)
- " for second derivation (calculus)
- + for positive ion (chemistry)
- + for wild type (biology)

With just a little imagination, you can think of how these characters can wreak havoc with punctuation.

EXAMPLE

The expression 5 x 4 x 3 x 2 x 1 can be written as 5!.
(The exclamation mark is the mathematical factorial operator.)

cp //fred/report/january . (The period is part of the command.)

Sometimes you can avoid ambiguity by distinguishing the symbols typographically, but let's face it—it's rather difficult to tell if a period is in boldface or a different font from the surrounding text. You can avoid the punctuation issue entirely: Put the text containing special characters on a separate line.

EXAMPLE

The expression 5 x 4 x 3 x 2 x 1 can be written as:
    5!

Type
cp //fred/report/january .
at the prompt. (The period indicates the current directory.)

As you can see, there are ways to get around the conflicts. What you need to recognize first is that you can't always follow the rules of English and remain faithful to the technical content.

Case

Technical documentation has different requirements for capitalization. Some terms must appear in all uppercase or all lowercase (or some specific combination of case, such as Na, MiniCOBOL, dBase, Hz, Vac, TermiNet).

Always spell product names and trademarks with the correct (as trademarked) case.

Software commands, calls, and keywords should also be case correct—even in heads, captions, and titles where words are all caps or have initial caps.

EXAMPLE

Here's the correct way to display OmniBack (a product name), **netstat** (a command name), and Hz (an abbreviation) in a head that is specified for all caps:

USING OmniBack

THE netstat COMMAND

INSTALLATION PROCEDURE FOR 50 Hz

Avoid starting a sentence with a term that must be spelled all lowercase. It may confuse your reader.

EXAMPLE

The **error_log** file contains all the error messages. (preferred)

error_log contains all the error messages. (avoid)

If you *must* begin a sentence with a term (command, filename, keyword) that the program requires to be in lowercase, do not capitalize it.

Error_log contains all the error messages. (incorrect)

Reasons for Breaking the Rules

The best justification for breaking a rule in a technical manual is to make sure the technical information is unambiguous and accurate.

Writers often give this excuse for not following the rules. As editor, you should know the subject matter and audience well enough to be able to judge for yourself.

Other reasons for breaking rules are to comply with contractual obligations, to comply with government or industry regulations, or to conform to other sets of standards.

For example, for one of our company's products to receive U.S. Government validation, we had to name the two appendixes in one manual as follows: Appendix A, Appendix F. We originally published our manual with an Appendix A and an Appendix B (following the normal rules for naming appendixes). Appendix B covered our implementation of government guidelines, listed in Appendix F of a Department of Defense document, known as "the RM." The title was

Appendix B. MC680x0 Implementation-Dependent Characteristics
(As Required by Appendix F of the RM.)

This workaround did not satisfy the U.S. Government. We had to update the manual to change the name of the appendix that discussed Appendix F information to Appendix F. We included an explanation to our readers so they wouldn't think they were missing Appendixes B–E.

I break one typographic convention often when editing programming manuals. You have probably noticed that typesetters (and most laser printers) have separate open-quote characters (") and close-quote (") characters.

Computers have a double quotation mark (") and a single quotation mark ('). There is a separate character for a grave accent, also commonly called a tick or backquote (`). Here are some excerpts from a manual I edited recently. Think how confusing this text would be if we used the correct typographic symbols instead of the straight quotes.

EXAMPLES

In the following example, the single quote turns off the special significance of the dollar sign, but the double quote does not.

```
y=50
print $y          The output is:      50
print "$y"        The output is:      50
print '$y'        The output is:      $y
```

Since the single quotes and double quotes themselves have special meaning, you may be wondering how to print them. Consider the following examples:

```
print 'Welcome 'Home''    The output is:      Welcome Home
print 'Welcome "Home"'    The output is:      Welcome "Home"
print "Welcome 'Home'"    The output is:      Welcome 'Home'
print "Welcome "Home""    The output is:      Welcome Home
print "Welcome \"Home\""  The output is:      Welcome "Home"
```

Another instance where symbols interfered with normal conventions occurred in a table that had several explanatory notes. What made this table a problem was that its data included text, figures, and several of the symbols we might have used to indicate a note. For example, one table entry was INTEGER*2. Superscript numbers and letters were difficult to see in the table. We experimented until we found an acceptable symbol, one that was easy to discern without overpowering the data.

Books about indexing advise putting symbols at the beginning of an index. What do you do if you have a term called #include? Some people call it "include" and others say "pound-include." It doesn't matter what *you* call it—readers will look up the term *they* use. The solution? Put it in two places—with the *i* words and with the list of symbols.

Making the Rules

Sometimes rules don't exist because the circumstances don't exist in the conventional publishing world. For example, how would you alphabetize a list of these terms: **#ifdef, %config, –info,** and **__LINE**?

The guidelines you devise for your own documentation form the basis for your house style guide. See chapter 10 for advice on writing a style guide.

How to Change the Rules

If you break a rule, let those affected and involved know. Communicate your decision as well as your reasons. When you explain your reasons your decisions don't appear capricious.

If you need to make a change that affects many people—writers, editors, production people—encourage the others to participate in the decision. Open up the discussion to everyone who would be affected by the change. As a group, identify the issues, the advantages and disadvantages of making the change, the impact of the change, and the consequences of not changing. Together, devise a solution that everyone can work with. (That's not necessarily the same as a solution everyone *likes.*)

If you enforce a rule, let those affected and involved know what the rule is. When you explain the rule and the rationale behind it, your decisions don't appear dictatorial. View the occasion as a teaching opportunity.

Also, let people know what circumstances would have changed your decision, so that if a similar situation arises in the future they'll know whether to apply the rule or the exception.

Murphy's Laws of Technical Publishing

- Editing: When in doubt, delete. When desperate, read the style guide.

- Deadlines: There is never enough time. Everything is due yesterday. Priority jobs come in multiples of ten.

- Corrections: Any line of copy sent back to composition with one error will return with three.

- Proofreading: The chance of missing a typo when proofreading is directly proportional to the size of the type. You will always find the typo in the 7-pt footnote; you will never find the typo in the 30-pt title. The first person to casually glance at the copy you've just finished proofing for the third time will find the typo you missed.

- Revisions: The only portion of an updated document that contains errors is the portion that wasn't updated—and which *you* edited last time. The only detail that you don't check—because it was previously published—is incorrect.

- Figures and tables: If a manual has many figures and tables, they will all have to be renumbered. They will have to be renumbered *again.* You will miss at least one text reference. If you decide to wait until the last minute so you'll only have to number everything once, a new table or figure will be inserted five minutes after you've finished. If a figure is deleted from a manual, the deleted figure will be the first one in the chapter, there will be at least ten figures in the chapter, and the job will already be in production. Furthermore, there will be figure references and cross-references throughout the text and you will miss one. (Technology has repealed this law.)

- Reviews: The last reviewer to return a draft copy has the most changes. Three reviewers will supply three conflicting sets of specifications. The only person guaranteed to have the information you need will be out of town.

- Research: The authorities never agree.

- Standards: The only standards that will be followed diligently are the superseded ones. The day after new standards are printed, the guidelines will have to be changed.

- Schedules: A priority job is any job issued by a shouter. First in, last out. If a deadline has already passed, it can be completed whenever. A job is put on hold only after the maximum effort has already been put into it. Everything is due the same day.

- Features: The feature you work hardest to document is the one that will be omitted from the released product.

- Formatting: The sample you followed to format a document will be obsolete, an exception, or a mistake.

Doing the Right Thing

Meeting customers' needs for clear and accurate documentation overrides all other guidelines. The message is more important than the means of expression; perfect prose is meaningless if customers cannot use the book to do their jobs. If we don't meet the needs of our customers we're not doing *our* jobs.

When the rules get in the way of communicating your message, then breaking them is not only acceptable, it is the right thing to do.

You are editing for readers, not other editors.

Summary

- Follow the rules (grammar, spelling, and punctuation) to convey meaning in an expected manner.
- Break the rules to convey terms that defy ordinary rules of punctuation and capitalization.
- Make the rules when you must, to communicate clearly.

Chapter 10
How to Write a Style Guide Writers Will Want to Use

It's easier to write a house style guide than to get writers to use one.

It's not that writers are opposed to style guides. To the contrary, writers love style guides that save them work. Writers hate style guides that sound like junior high school English teachers: "Never use the passive voice, dummy. Listen when I am talking to you. You must always prepare your outline in exactly this format, with half-inch indentations, or you will never be able to express yourself logically."

Good style guides spare writers from having to make agonizing—and, let's face it, boring—decisions. When you're engrossed in putting thoughts on paper, you don't want to be distracted by minutiae. Most writers don't care whether or not they're supposed to put a colon after the word *NOTE;* they just want to know what to do, and they trust that once they've put that colon in (or left it out), the editor or manager isn't going to make them take it out (or put it in). Good style guides give writers fast answers to easy, routine questions and guidelines for handling more difficult, unusual questions. Table 10-1 contrasts good and bad style guides.

Table 10–1. *Characteristics of Good and Bad Style Guides*

Good style guides . . .	Bad style guides . . .
assume writers know how to write, think, and exercise good judgment	talk down to writers
anticipate that sometimes writers need to bend the rules, so they tell how to bend them	give black-and-white rules in a gray world
stick to style issues	confuse style and process issues
solve real problems	are impractical
save writers and editors time	make work for writers and editors

You can expect to work on a style guide at least once in your career. You may be asked to write a style guide yourself or you may be invited to serve on a committee to publish one. You may even decide to write one when you get tired of answering the same old questions or arguing the same minor points.

Do You Need a House Style Guide?

House style guides—sometimes called publications standards or writing standards—usually pick up where general style guides, such as *The Elements of Style,* leave off.

A house style guide has three functions:

- Stating a preferred style when there is more than one correct way to do something, such as formatting a bibliography or alphabetizing an index

- Setting style for topics too technical for general style and usage guides, such as how to display a nuclear formula, chemical compound, or computer command in text

- Bending other style rules to fit the needs of a specific industry or company

When do you need a style guide? You need a house style guide when

- You have a lot of common style issues that cut across many different books.

- Your company wants all the books it publishes to speak in one voice.

- You want all the books that describe one product to look, sound, and feel as though one person wrote them.

You need a style guide to keep a documentation set consistent when there are different products, writers, and editors.

A consistent style lets your company present a unified image to customers. On a more practical note, a consistent style simplifies cutting and pasting from one document to another. A writer can borrow a chapter from a different book and not have to make extensive style revisions if both books follow the same style guide. For companies that publish many manuals, following standards can save lots of money. As off-the-rack clothing is cheaper than custom-tailored, so are standardized manuals cheaper than custom documentation.

Here's how one company justified its need for standards:

EXAMPLE

Publications standards promote customer satisfaction in three ways. Firstly, <u>design and production standards</u> ensure a consistent appearance in [Information Systems] publications across the product line and throughout the world. This one-company look conveys an image of a large but well-organized computer vendor, a vendor that can organize its considerable resources in a logical way to serve the user's needs.

Secondly, <u>content standards</u> allow us to live up to the image of consistency created by design and production standards. Standardization of the titles, the content, and especially the structure of technical reference publications allows users to familiarize themselves quickly with the document set for any [Information Systems] system. Enforcement of such consistency also simplifies upgrades from one [Information Systems] system to another.

Thirdly, <u>writing and editing standards</u> result in technical documentation that is easy to read and easy to use. This category of standards includes enforcement of uniform product-line nomenclature, use of industry-standard terminology, adherence to generally accepted English usage, strict observance of grammatical rules, use of simple and precise syntax, and the application of efficient publishing techniques.[1]

Creating and Using a Style Sheet

You don't need a full-fledged style guide if your company wants every book to have a one-of-a-kind look and feel. Instead, a style sheet for each book will suffice.

---

[1] Reprinted with permission of Bull HN Information Systems Inc.

A style sheet is nothing more than a written summary of the style decisions that apply to a particular book. It's a handy way to remind yourself that this book uses *database*, not *data base* or *one-celled* instead of *single-celled*. A style sheet ensures that a book is consistent within itself. If the book is part of a documentation set, you might have a style sheet for the documentation set as well. (Style sheets for documentation sets sometimes grow into style guides.)

Even if you have a style guide, you'll find that creating a style sheet for each book you edit will save you time. Every book is unique, even if the writer is following a fixed outline and a predetermined design. The more details you need to track and the less familiar you are with the style, the longer your style sheet will be. You'll have a lengthy, detailed style sheet if you're dealing with a new product or unfamiliar terminology or if the book has many inconsistencies that you need to reconcile. If you have a comprehensive style guide, and the writer has followed it, your style sheet may have only a few items. A style sheet is especially helpful if you're working on several books at the same time (as is the norm for technical editing); the style sheet can remind you what is special about each book.

Figure 10–1 shows a style sheet arranged by topic. Figure 10–2 shows a style sheet organized alphabetically.

Note that one editor's style sheet may be unclear to another editor. Your style sheet is your set of working notes; it must be clear to you. Don't worry if it's not clear to others, unless you expect them to use it.

You might consider a style sheet a subset of a style guide. It covers just those details relevant to the particular book, and it covers only the decisions, not the rationale behind them.

format

page breaks

table formats

capitalization/punctuation bulleted lists

fig. captions centered?

footnotes: size, position

folio: size, placement

fonts

bold for keywords in scripts?

chapter titles (fonts, init. caps)

new terms: italics

syntax examples: serif

reserved variables: bold

single-character operators: bold

misc.

UNIX: adj. throughout?

UNIX: trademarked first use?

KornShell vs. the KornShell
single vs. double quote in serif

use of serif font for comments

compounding

case sensitive

log in (v); log-in (n) (adj)

non-white-space

run time

start-up (adj.); start up (v)

case

right/wrong: lowercase as inline comment

with, within, without: lc in heads

cross-ref. to "Beware": ulc

comments in examples—initial cap? end with period?

full line: treat as sentence

inline: treat as phrase

Figure 10–1. Style sheet arranged by topic

<u>**usage**</u>

appear: when the program shows something on the screen (use sparingly)

application: the use of a program; not for use of model or a built-in function; not to refer to APPLY function

call: call Help or the Editor; don't use "invoke" or "evoke"

character strings: don't use. Say "string of characters" or "symbolic value," if that's what you mean

default: default value; OK to use "default" alone as noun

disable: use for hardware only

display: when the program posts information to the screen

enter: you type letters, numbers, and values; you press special keys (break key, etc.); enter is what you do when you press the enter key; enter means type the command AND press [e]; don't say "enter the editor" or "enter the program"—"using the editor" or "using the program" is preferred

fixed disk: OK for IBM specific doc; otherwise use "hard disk"

function: a mathematical entity; don't say "doing this is a function of doing that" and don't use as a verb

<u>**spelling, capitalizing, compounding**</u>

Built-in function

command: Quit command, Reset command

Display unit

Editor

filename

Help

Option Menu

Status line

subsheet

Figure 10–2. Style sheet organized alphabetically

Planning the Style Guide

If you're developing a house style guide, whether solo or by committee, you'll need to make the same basic decisions you'd make before writing any book: Who is the target audience? What is the objective of this style guide?

Do you expect all or most of your readers to be professional writers and editors? Or do you expect more engineers and scientists to use the book? Does your audience include both professional writers and technical professionals? Will graphic artists, typesetters, illustrators, and printers use the style guide, too?

Do you expect the style guide to serve as a supplement to the body of literature available on writing, editing, and book production? Or do you expect the house style guide to be the only authority for style your readers will use?

Your answers to these questions will help you determine if you need to write a 2,000-page combination writing handbook, style guide, usage guide, abridged dictionary, and production specifications handbook; a 10-page word list for spelling, compounding, and abbreviations; or (most likely) something in between.

Deciding on the Contents

After you've identified your audience and your goals, your next task is to determine what types of information to include and what to exclude.

Most companies don't have the resources to re-create their own versions of *The Chicago Manual of Style* and *The Elements of Style,* a proprietary dictionary, and a company-specific style guide. Yet many style guides start out as the comprehensive guide to everything a writer needs to know. At some point the money, the schedule, or the style guide writer's steam runs out.

The best style guides don't try to duplicate good and readily available books. It's much more practical to designate certain reference books as adjuncts to your house style guide and limit your own style guide to covering additional topics and exceptions.

Many style guides include the most basic information about English grammar and writing:

- Definitions of common and proper nouns
- How to form plurals in English (house-houses, goose-geese, tomato-tomatoes)
- *It's* vs. *its*

Wouldn't you be offended if your style guide assumed you—a professional writer or editor—did not know this stuff? If the style guide's users include engineers and scientists, give them credit for having learned these basics in school, and give them a copy of *The Elements of Style.* (If engineers who don't have basic English writing skills are writing your manuals, then don't expect a style guide to compensate. You'll need to provide additional support, such as heavy copy editing, classes in writing skills, and supplemental books.)

Your style guide must include

- Rulings on style matters that need to be applied consistently throughout a documentation set (for example, how to refer to other publications, when to use *Warning* vs. *Caution*)

- Recommendations for preferred usage when your company permits variation but has a preference (for example, April 10, 1992; 10 April 1992; or 1992 April 10)

- Rulings on subjective style matters (for example, 1960's or 1960s, CPU's or CPUs)

- Details that writers need regularly, but may have difficulty remembering (for example, your company's preferences for spelling and compounding)

- Rulings on style matters where your house style differs from conventional English or industry usage (for example, does your company use a singular verb with data?)

- *Do*s and *don't*s of your industry's jargon

- Information writers and editors need regularly and can't readily find anywhere else (for example, how to display your company's trademarks)

Your style guide may also include

- Answers to *frequently* asked style questions (but don't clutter up the book with answers to every question a writer might ask)

- Reminders of correct usage that writers and editors *frequently* need to look up (for example, *comprise/constitute, assure/ensure/insure, use/usage*)

- Production (format) specifications

Some style guides include a chapter about those writing and style issues that commonly trouble writers at their companies. This chapter can be a great time-saver for writers if it sticks to the most common problems. Resist the temptation to include every possible usage error, or the chapter can become too cumbersome and the project too unwieldy.

Your style guide need not include

- Information that's readily available—and handled more thoroughly—in other books
- Irrelevant information, such as how to punctuate direct quotes in dialogue; some house style guides used in industry actually include this information, though I've yet to see direct discourse in a technical manual
- Style rulings for every possible situation; you don't need a standard way of handling a style matter that occurs once in five years

Selecting Your Core References (Default Style Guides)

Identify the types of reference works you want to supplement your house style guide and select those that most closely suit your company's style. Here are some suggestions:

- English language dictionary, for spelling and compounding
- Usage guide
- Style guide for punctuation
- Technical dictionary for your field
- Your company's corporate standards (for example, standards and policy guides about internationalization, engineering specifications, and display of corporate logo)
- Grammar reference

Interpreting Your Default Style Guides

Review the default style guides and assess where they meet your needs and where they don't.

For example, *The Chicago Manual of Style* doesn't acknowledge that you might want to paginate your book by sections (1-1, 1-2, 1-3 . . . , 2-1, 2-2, 2-3 . . .), because that's not how the University of Chicago Press prefers to paginate its books. Many technical manuals, however, use this pagination style.

I recommend that you establish some policy—at least be clear in your own mind—about how you want to use these other books.

Decide how flexibly you want to interpret the default style guides before making your own conventions. Your policy can range from treating them as authorities to treating them as suggested references, or can fall somewhere in between.

Your policy can be to follow your default style guide strictly. Your house style guide then must carry the burden of explaining how to handle all information not covered in the default style guide. (Most technical information falls in this category.)

You can deputize the books as supplements to the style guide:

EXAMPLE

This standards manual presents only the standards directly applicable to the development of [Information Systems] marketing and [Information Systems] user-support publications. These standards exist within the wider context of English spelling and usage, grammar, editorial style, and data processing terminology. This manual is not and cannot be a substitute for any of the established reference works on these subjects. Because it is desirable to maintain editorial consistency throughout the company, the following works are hereby established as <u>standard</u> supplements to this manual.[1]

Here's a similar approach:

EXAMPLE

This guide does not cover everything you need to know to write manuals at Apollo. We've chosen not to reinvent the wheel and pad this document with information that is readily accessible through other sources. We list at the end of this chapter a bibliography of standard reference works that supplement this guide and that serve as default standards for Apollo Technical Publishing for issues this Style Guide does not cover.

In a few cases we've chosen to duplicate information in the standard reference books. We've done so for areas that require frequent reference, simply as a convenience. In other cases, we've done so to show examples that relate specifically to writing within the computer industry.

You might even add a section to your style guide called "What we do differently."

---

[1] Reprinted with permission of Bull HN Information Systems Inc.

Another approach is to consider these books as references, not authorities. This approach gives writers so much leeway that you may not be able to achieve consistency. Here's a freewheeling policy, in its entirety:

EXAMPLE

Any staff member involved in documentation should have a dictionary and a thesaurus at his/her disposal.

Negotiating the Decisions: Getting Consensus

You can't please everyone and you shouldn't waste your time trying. Your goal is to come up with a decision that everyone can live with.

Some style issues are hotter than others. When you have one that factions disagree about, step back and rethink whether there really is a business reason to have a single convention. Sometimes it's more practical to have different conventions for different situations. For example, you may have conventions that suit software books but not hardware books, or that apply to medical instruments but not scientific measurement devices. The tricky part is determining if there is a business reason for making the exception (to meet customers' needs, to avoid unnecessary expense, to meet government regulations that affect only one segment of a corporation's business) or if the contrary parties are just being stubborn or self-serving. Sometimes the style guide's goals of improving quality and reducing costs override its goal of presenting a standard corporate image.

You can expect some topics to infuse writers and editors with an almost religious fervor. I suspect such zealous opposition is because people resist change and would rather everyone else adopt the conventions *they're* used to. Also, some people like to argue over the little things to avoid tackling the big issues.

Sometimes people argue fervently because they genuinely believe there is only one right way. You'll need to educate them further. For example, many writers and editors have been taught that one should *never* use the passive voice. Instead, tell writers to use the passive voice *appropriately* and refer them to good usage guides for examples of proper and improper use of the passive.

Here are some of these kinds of issues and suggestions for how to deal with them.

Abbreviations

If your standard references disagree on how to handle certain abbreviations, or if they don't list the abbreviations you question, identify the group that uses each most often. For example, hardware writers have to live more closely with decisions about abbreviating units of measurement than software writers. So let the hardware writing group establish these conventions.

A recent trend has been not to put a period after abbreviations, such as *mm, ft, lb*. Many companies make an exception for abbreviations that also spell words (*no., in.*) to avoid confusion.

Typographic Display of Information

Do you show elements in physical equations in italics to distinguish them from symbols for units? Do you use bold or italics for new terms? Do you underline publication titles or put them in italics? Do all groups have the ability to display type in italics and boldface? For online documentation, too?

The difficulty with setting typographic guidelines is that some users of your style guide may be unable to conform due to inadequate equipment. The best guidelines are the most flexible and least dependent on a particular text formatter or process. Establish the broadest guidelines (for example, "Display the information consistently and clearly, so that you don't confuse readers") and let individual groups implement the details within that framework. People will be more likely to comply with conventions that are easy to follow. Also, the broader the guidelines, the less likely technological advances will render them obsolete.

Capitalization and Punctuation of Bulleted Lists

You can't win this one. A compromise that often works is to capitalize and punctuate items that are complete sentences as sentences (capitalize the first word and end with a period) and keep items within a list parallel (good style in any case). Then permit variations as long as each type of list is treated consistently throughout the book.

The Chicago Manual of Style says to put a comma after each item and a period after the last item. Since technical manuals have enough clutter, most companies' house style is to omit the comma and period from short lists (phrases). If your manuals have many different kinds of lists, begin the first word of each item with a capital letter. Then, as lists expand from short phrases to complete sentences with successive revisions, you'll have one less editorial change to think about.

Compounding

Some people care a lot about compounding. Fortunately, this malady can be cured. I was cured by researching a few hundred terms for a word list. That project taught me that you can find a precedent for any spelling and that making a decision is more important than the decision itself. In practice, people get used to spelling a word a particular way and develop a fondness for that spelling. It's certainly easier to stick with the familiar, but when your writers are used to three different familiar spellings, you have to select one.

If your documentation set uses one spelling more often than another, follow the more common one. Everyone who has to change will hate your decision, no matter what it is, so you may as well make the change that affects the fewest books.

Some Relatively Noncontroversial Items

Most of the entries in your style guide will be straightforward tips or reminders and shouldn't generate any controversy. For example:

EXAMPLES

"Can" denotes physical and mental ability or that which is allowable by law or product specifications; "may" denotes permission or merely possibility. Failure to differentiate between these meanings in technical writing produces ambiguous results. Using "may" for "can" is even weaker in the negative than in the affirmative.[1]

Parallel structure puts similar ideas into the same kinds of grammatical constructions. Parallel ideas should be written in parallel form in all respects: voice, mood, number, tense, punctuation, capitalization, and parts of speech.[1]

Do not use commas in binary, octal, or hexadecimal notation: 00110010

You may write dates in the month-day-year format preferred in the United States or in the international day-month-year format. Never use a numbering system for dates:

Use: May 7, 1991 or 7 May, 1991

Do Not Use: 5/7/91 (which means May 7, 1991 in the United States but 5 July 1991 in other parts of the world)

The first time you use an acronym, spell out what it stands for (using initial caps) and enclose the acronym in parentheses.

---

[1] Reprinted with permission of Bull HN Information Systems Inc.

How to Avoid Revisiting the Same Decisions Eternally

You don't want to revisit the same decisions for eternity, or even for the rest of your career. (It'll feel about the same.)

Involve others in decisions. Set up meetings to discuss style issues and invite all groups who will use the style guide to participate. When face-to-face meetings are impractical, send drafts of the style guide to the different groups, give them adequate time to review and respond, and incorporate their feedback. Discuss conflicts with the affected groups; don't just publish a style guide that ignores their feedback and expect them to follow it. It's better to tell them you considered their comments but couldn't make the change (give your reasons) than to imply you didn't care about their needs.

Strive for consensus, where everyone agrees on both the objective and the implementation. Sometimes the best guideline is one with built-in flexibility. State the objective, cite known exceptions, and tell how to handle them. For example:

EXAMPLES

Spell out state names in text, whether they stand alone or follow the name of a city or any other geographic term.

Use: This product is manufactured in California.

Use: This product is manufactured in Cupertino, California.

Do Not Use: This product is manufactured in CA.

Do Not Use: This product is manufactured in Cupertino, Calif.

Do Not Use: This product is manufactured in Cupertino, CA.

For writers who must follow the Associated Press style guidelines, use state abbreviations with periods. (See *The Associated Press Stylebook and Libel Manual* for a complete list of abbreviations for state names.)

Examples: Ala., Ariz., Ark., Calif., Colo., N.D., S.D., W.Va.

Write down the decision and, where appropriate, the reasons for it in the style guide. (Do not write essays about style decisions in the style guide; a simple "for consistency with common industry practice" or "because it makes it easier to translate our books" will suffice.)

Apply the standards evenly. Don't show favoritism. Don't make some writers follow the standards yet allow other writers to ignore them.

Make exceptions only with good justification. Consider the costs of the change: labor, materials, and morale. Make sure you give reasons. Don't give the impression the change is for the sake of change or to jerk people around.

◇ ── ◇

Twelve or 12?

That small but hardy band of dedicated readers who keep track of TIME's practices concerning capitalization, punctuation and other style points will be interested to know that starting with this week's issue, we'll be making some changes. In the past we have spelled out the numbers zero through twelve; now, we'll use figures for 10, 11 and 12. We used to capitalize the word *Government* when it referred to the U.S. governing body; now we will capitalize it only when it appears with the word *Federal. Kidnapping* will be spelled with two *ps.* These modifications are not as trivial as they may seem. They reflect our constant monitoring of a living language and our desire to keep TIME within the mainstream of American usage.[1]

◇ ── ◇

Making a Decision and Moving On

The English language is constantly changing. We're constantly redefining what's "acceptable" usage and what isn't. Those of us interested in the language have much fodder for discussion because authorities seldom agree. Authorities can include professional journals, style guides, usage guides, the comments of the *American Heritage Dictionary*'s Usage Panel, and William Safire's columns.

There are places for these usage discussions: academia, professional journals, lunchrooms. Style must also be kept in its place. You could spend all day arguing style issues and never get the real work done. If you're editing the next edition of Merriam-Webster's *New International Dictionary,* you need to research current usage very carefully. If you're writing a style guide for use by writers in one company (or one department), you don't have to make *the best* style decision; you have to make a practical style decision. If there are two commonly accepted practices, it doesn't matter which one is better. It matters only that you pick one and stick with it. In the corporate world, it isn't cost-effective to argue about which of two good styles is better.

---

[1] *Time*, July 23, 1990, p. 11.

Don't let arguments over style issues interfere with publishing the books. Some writers, if they disagree with a point in the style guide, will take every opportunity to tell you why. I tell writers that I'll discuss these issues on a philosophical basis over lunch, but that since we're facing a deadline, we'll follow the current style guideline, and we can revisit the decision, if necessary, when we revise the style guide.

Sometimes you just need to make an arbitrary decision and move on. If circumstances change, determine whether you need to change the standard. If the change has merit, and if you can change easily, cheaply, and without confusing or annoying everyone, then change it. Otherwise:

When it is not necessary to change, it is necessary not to change.

Don't take it so seriously:

EXAMPLE

The subject of a sentence and the principal verb should not, as a rule, be separated by a phrase or clause that can be transferred to the beginning.[1]

Here's something to take seriously instead:

EXAMPLE

In 1962, during the flight of Mariner I, a computer programmer forgot a hyphen when programming the rocket's course and the Mariner veered off course and was lost. This hyphen-loss cost the NASA program 18.5 million dollars.[2]

---

[1] Strunk, William Jr., and E. B. White, *The Elements of Style,* Third Edition
(New York: Macmillan Publishers, 1979), p. 29.
[2] Smith, Richard, and Edward Decter, *OOPS! The Complete Book of Bloopers*
(New York: The Rutledge Press, 1981), p. 192.

Exercise 12   What's wrong here?

From a newspaper advertisement:

> Winner of ALL 5 MAJOR OSCARS!
> ONE FLEW OVER THE CUCKOO'S NEST
> Best Picture
> Best Actor—Jack Nicholson
> Best Actress—Milos Forman
> Best Director—Louise Fletcher
> Best Adapted Screenplay
> Best Way to spend your evening!

Writing the Book on Style

Organize your style guide so its users can find information quickly, or provide a *great* index. (If writers can't find answers *immediately*, they won't use the style guide at all.)

You can organize the book in several ways:

If you have different groups of users, you might divide the style guide into different parts for each group. For example, Part I can be for managers, writers, and editors who plan documentation. Part II can be for writers and editors who create the manuscripts. Part III can be for typesetters, illustrators, designers, and printers who produce the book. This organization follows the order in which we create manuals: plan, write, produce. (This is how the Bull HN Information Systems style guide is organized. See its table of contents in appendix B.)

You can organize the book hierarchically, to reflect your company's writing and production processes. (These processes tend to change faster than style, however, and may make the style guide more difficult to use in the long term.)

You can organize the book as an encyclopedia, with alphabetical topics. (Chapter 3 of Apollo's style guide and chapter 2 of Hewlett-Packard's are organized this way. The tables of contents for these style guides are in appendix B.)

Distinguish Between What You Recommend and What You Require

Tell if it's the preferred way or the only acceptable way. Use the following words precisely, and make sure your readers know you've chosen them carefully: *do, don't, never, avoid, we recommend, we suggest, we prefer.*

Many style guides label each rule:

EXAMPLES

Don't use command names as verbs.

Don't use: If DIRing doesn't show the files you're looking for . . .

Use: If you list the directory with the DIR command and still don't see the files . . .

Don't refer to specific chapters or sections in other manuals (either by title or by number) because the manuals may change and make your references incorrect. Use generic chapter titles instead. For example,

Don't use: See Chapter 7 in the Owner's Guide.

Use: For more information, see the chapter on diagnostic tests in the Owner's Guide.

Standard: Use numerals in compounds (an 8-bit machine, 5-hole drill).

Exceptions: one's complement, two's complement, one-dimensional

---

Some style guides also note "preferred" usage when more than one is acceptable. (By the way, if you say *preferred* instead of *better,* your style guide will sound less like your junior high school English teacher.)

Some guidelines don't need interpretation or clarification. For example, you don't need to explain why you prefer no apostrophe in *1980s* or why you capitalize *Step* in *Go to Step 3.* You do need to explain, however, when to spell out *zero* and when to use *0.*

Explain What Rule You're Following

If you've arbitrarily picked a convention from among several otherwise "correct" ways, say so. It's not necessary to justify an arbitrary decision as the only way, though some style guide writers do, mistakenly thinking it gives the standard greater authority.

Even if the decision is arbitrary, once you've made it, follow it.

If you know of exceptions to the rules, state them. If you have workarounds for breaking the rules, state those, too.

EXAMPLE

In botany, paleontology, zoology, cap the names of all divisions higher than species, that is, genera, families, orders, classes, and phyla; but not adjectives and English nouns derived from them.

Chiroptera, chiropter	the genus *Hydra;* a hydra
Coelenterata, coelenterate	the tall buttercup (*Ranunculus acris*)
Protozoa, protozoon	the harp seal (*Phoca graenlandica*)[1]

Exercise 13 What's wrong here?

Find a flagrant error—not counting the writing style—in this item from a technical writing society's newsletter:

Our after dinner speaker was Jim Mitchell, Attorney-at-Law. His very interesting talk on "Documentation and Computer Law" was very informative. Jim said that the law, with regard to data processing, is very new and complex due to the remoteness and newness of computer jargon to lawyers, judges, and juries. As of yet, there have been very few cases dealing with data processing issues to set a presidence for future cases.

The Style Guide Must Follow Its Own Rules

Many people will do what you do, not what you say. Be especially careful with production standards. If you show illustrations or examples of type and layout, expect graphic arts people to follow the example as shown; they'd sooner measure the type in the example than read text for the same information.

---

[1] Skillin, Marjorie E., *Words into Type,* Third Edition (Englewood Cliffs, NJ: Prentice-Hall, 1974), p. 169.

Edit it very carefully!

I've seen two style guides with chapters called "Principals of Writing." Another style guide has these contradictory guidelines in one chapter:

EXAMPLES

Do not enclose colloquialisms or slang words or phrases in quotation marks.

Use double quotes to indicate nonstandard terms, doubtful terms, or slang words.

Let People Know the Decision-Making Process

Let everyone know how firm or flexible the decisions are.

EXAMPLES

The conventions the *Apollo Style Guide* documents emerged through a combination of compromise, negotiation, editorial interpretation, managerial fiats, and common sense. We think these conventions are the ones that make the most sense, given our audience, tools, deadlines, and departmental charter. You may think some conventions are arbitrary; in fact, some are. Sometimes, for the sake of consistency, we need to declare one convention or another the Apollo standard. When we have to choose among several approaches of equal merit, we try to lean towards the one that's easier to implement or that's already in common use throughout our publications.

This guide is a living document and will change over time as our documentation evolves. If you have questions about conventions not mentioned in this document, talk to your editor. Your questions may flag the need to decide on a convention or possibly change an existing convention. As a department, we approach changes to the *Apollo Style Guide* with caution because of the impact on writers' schedules and the many books already in print and in use by our customers. We do make changes as needed, but only after weighing the consequences and benefits for our users and for the writers and editors who must implement the changes.

If your guidelines are flexible, you won't have to change them as often.

When you want to give broad guidelines without writing an essay on the topic, state that the decision is left with the individual writer and editor. For example, you can write a book about writing fundamentals or you can give some general advice and let the editor make the individual judgment calls:

EXAMPLE

In general, keep paragraphs short, and use direct, concise, and simple sentences. Your editor can help you decide if the paragraphs and sentences sound too simplistic.

In the following example, the style guide could have listed factors to weigh when making this decision. Instead, it gives some simple advice:

EXAMPLE

A chapter table of contents is particularly useful in command and call reference manuals, where you may want to list the starting page for every command or call description. Decide with your editor whether having chapter TOCs will add value to your manual.

Some style guides err on the side of explaining everything. They're as comprehensive as government and military regulations, and describe all rules and exceptions in excruciating detail. They're about as well received by writers as are IRS forms by taxpayers.

Let people know when you're making an exception for one book or one documentation set. Make sure you have a business reason for making exceptions. Apply and break the rules impartially if you expect people to respect them.

Sometimes you'll make an exception that will work out so well you'll want to change the standard; that's the best way to identify when to change. The time to change is when you must change—to save time, money, or effort.

Set up a process for change and communicate the information to your readers. Let everyone know where to send comments for suggestions and improvements. When people send you comments, acknowledge that you've received their suggestions and have filed them for the next update to the style guide. Let people know how often you plan to update the style guide (monthly? annually? when there are enough changes to justify the revision?). When you do revise the style guide, let people know that you're including feedback you've received since the last revision, and give examples of some changes you've made as a result. Sharing this information lets everybody see that the style guide hasn't been created and isn't being maintained in a vacuum.

Don't Confuse a Style Guide with a Process Guide

A *process guide* covers the internal procedures in your company and/or department. Some examples of process information are who reviews the documentation, who signs off, and how are schedules determined. Other process information includes how to complete forms for the copy center, how to set up the cover page for drafts going to technical review, and how to release a manual to manufacturing.

Keep process information out of your style guide. The number one way to ensure that writers will not use a style guide is to bog it down with process information, which makes the book unwieldy. Another reason is that process information changes faster than style. You can control changes to style, but not process. Furthermore, the process that your site follows probably differs from the process at other sites that use your style guide.

Yet many companies intermingle process and style information in one book. If your budget allows you to publish only one handbook for writers, have separate parts for process and style, and state that the process information is more volatile.

You can see that writers following a style guide with both style and process information could be confused if the process details change but the style guidelines remain the same. If writers doubt the accuracy and timeliness of the information in the style guide, they won't use it.

Exercise 14   What's wrong here?

This copyright notice from a health care brochure is unusual in two ways.

© 1989½, 1989, 1988½, 1988, 1987, 1986½, 1986, 1985, 1984, 1982, 1981, JAT Co.

Summary

Make your style guide a handy reference to solve writers' common and immediate problems. Don't overload writers with nonessential rules and don't invent rules for the sake of having rules—it's unrealistic to expect writers to memorize a tome. If writers don't use your style guide, you may as well not have one.

If you write a style guide that saves work, writers will not only use it, they'll thank you for publishing it.

Am®az™ing!

From Papa Gino's takeout menu:

M&M's and the letter "M" are registered trademarks of Mars, Inc.

From an advertisement in a computer magazine:

Zilog, Z80, and the letter "Z" are trademarks of Zilog Corporation.

Think of the royalties!

Chapter 11
Tips and Tricks of the Trade

This chapter is a grab bag of hints, tricks, and shortcuts for editing technical manuals.

This chapter's purpose is to supplement, but not duplicate, the many good books about technical writing, usage, and style with tricks and guidelines peculiar to editing technical documents. For example, I assume you've read or have access to books about how to *prepare* an index, so this chapter covers only what you need to know to *edit* an index. In some cases there is little or no literature on a topic, or the information that has been published doesn't fit technical writing, so this chapter looks at these topics in more depth. After all, an editor needs to know a lot about technical writing to be able to answer writers' questions.

I've written this chapter so that each major section is independent of the others because each of you will be interested in different topics. Feel free to skip sections that don't apply to your field or that your house style guide covers in greater detail.

If you edit computer manuals, read chapter 12, too.

Knotty Points of Grammar and Usage

If you're editing your own or another's work, you really should know English grammar. Now that I've gone on record with my official position, here are some ways to handle the oddball cases.

From time to time, you'll come across a sentence that just sounds wrong. Some very simple examples include *like* vs. *as* or *which* vs. *that* in certain contexts and agreement of subject and verb in less common usages.

Make your first step toward your bookshelf. The bibliography lists some books on grammar and usage that will help you figure out the right (or the preferred) usage. Don't stop at one book; look up your question in three or four. If your reference books all give you pretty much the same answer or interpretation, then amend the manuscript accordingly and commit your new knowledge to memory.

If the experts don't agree, or if you have to sift through a slew of examples and nested conditional sentences, you'll need to investigate further.

You could call a grammar hotline.[1] Really. Several college English departments around the U.S. have hotlines you can call to discuss grammar with an equally befuddled graduate student. You may get a definitive answer. If not, you'll at least have shared the experience with someone who understands your confusion.

The point is to educate yourself, so that you see that English grammar and usage cannot always be reduced to absolute rules. You'll also learn some nuances of the English language.

TIP: The more knowledge you have in your own head, the faster you'll be able to copy edit, and the more time you'll have for higher-level (developmental) editing. Research takes time, the one resource an editor needs to hoard.

Put down the phone or walk away from your bookshelf and return to your manuscript. Now tackle that sentence so that it communicates. Your first step is to recast the sentence to avoid the awkward construction. If you and a panel of experts can't decide on the correct usage and if the sentence sounds wrong however you phrase it, fix the sentence. You want to avoid drawing your reader's attention to the writing mechanics; you want the reader to concentrate on your message, not the grammar.

When you have an unusual construction, your readers may still wonder if there's an error, even if you've made the sentence grammatically correct. Unless you're writing or editing for other editors or English teachers who will be impressed with your command of the grammar, avoid weirdly complex constructions.

A good litmus test is this: If you and the writer start discussing the fine points of grammar to resolve a sticky issue, then you can be sure your readers will also be confused or distracted.

TRICK: When in doubt, reword.

---

[1] The *Grammar Hotline Directory* is published annually by Tidewater Community College Writing Center. For each free copy of the directory, send a stamped (first-class postage), self-addressed business-letter-size envelope to Grammar Hotline Directory, Tidewater Community College Writing Center, 1700 College Crescent, Virginia Beach, VA 23456.

Compounding

Strange but true: New editors and writers ask more questions about compounding than any other subject. You'd think there were dire consequences for putting in an extra hyphen (*form-feed* instead of *formfeed*) or closing up a compound (*datatype* instead of *data type*), like loss of chocolate-eating privileges. (Or is that chocolate eating privileges?)

Look in the dictionary and your style guide. If these sources don't give you an answer, make a decision, *any decision,* and apply it consistently. Consistency in compounding can depend on how the term is used. For example, your company's usage may include *login* (verb), *log-in* (adjective), and *login* (noun). If so, apply the same principles to *log out* and *start up*. Likewise, treat *online, offline,* and *inline* consistently and hyphenate *high-carbon steel* the same as *low-carbon steel.*

TIP: Don't sweat the trivial details. You'll add more value to a manuscript if you can make quick decisions on the small points and put your energies into the tough problems. Record your decisions on the style sheet so you have them handy as you edit later chapters.

When Jargon Is Not a Dirty Word

When you're writing for a technically proficient audience, use the familiar, common terminology—the jargon. Jargon is absolutely appropriate if your audience knows it. Don't sidestep jargon when you need its precision. For example, it's inadequate to refer to *scratches* and *cuts* in a medical journal when you mean *abrasions* and *lacerations.*

Jargon is a dirty word if you're writing about a technical subject for a nontechnical audience. Teach the new terminology when the reader needs to know it, but not "because it is there." For example, a pamphlet for home first aid may refer to *scratches* and *cuts* instead of *abrasions* and *lacerations.*

It's inappropriate to use jargon unfamiliar to some of your readers. For example, every field has a slang vocabulary in addition to the technical jargon. Replace the slang terms—*zap* for *delete,* for example—with standard technical terms. Keep abreast of what is familiar and common by referring to professional journals, trade association publications, and the standards documents of the discipline you edit for.

If your company's products are innovative, you'll introduce new terms and new concepts in the manuals. New jargon is also acceptable, if you explain the term when it's introduced in text and provide a glossary for later reference.

Jargon is also a dirty word when it isn't legitimate jargon. Some writers coin words to help them explain concepts. Sometimes writers use words coined by engineers in their company and intended only as a shorthand among themselves. While it makes the writer's job marginally easier, the new vocabulary does a disservice to readers, giving them the impression they're learning standard terminology. Here's an area where an editor who knows the subject matter, terminology, and conventions can play an important user advocacy role.

Writing and Organizing Your Thoughts

If you're a professional editor or writer, you already know how to write and organize thoughts logically. But sometimes you get stuck.

Do you ever find yourself deep in a sentence, groping for a way out? Do you find yourself struggling for a word or a phrase, but with every word you add you get more entangled in the sentence?

Do you ever find that you're plunging deeper and deeper, increasing the layers of information? For example, do you need fourth- or fifth-level heads more often than you've been told you should? Do your lists need sublists and do those sublists need sublists? Do your procedures have subprocedures with yet more subprocedures?

Here are a couple of tricks that unravel all these knots.

TRICK: Broaden your focus. You've entangled yourself in a sentence and can't get out. You've been struggling to ferret out the perfect word. But you may be trying to solve the problem at too low a level. If changing a word or two doesn't improve the sentence, look at the whole sentence. If recasting the sentence doesn't seem to fix the problem, look at the paragraph. Keep moving up. You may find that the chapter (or book) has organizational problems. That one word you were fishing for was a symptom of a major organizational disease. Changing that word or sentence would never have fixed the problem because the problem was much larger. The trick is to step back and analyze what's really wrong. Is the sentence trying to cover too much information? If so, how can you break that information into more manageable chunks? Perhaps you need two chapters instead of one. Perhaps you should lift a section and promote it to a separate chapter. Or perhaps you should delete the sentence because the *real* problem is that it's unnecessary.

TRICK: Promote from the bottom. Consider the cases where you're diving deeper into the bowels of the book, adding subheads and sub-subheads and sub-sub-subheads. What's a writer to do? Identify the lowest level of information. Set that to match the lowest level your style guide or design specs allow. For example, if you have chapters, sections, and subsections, make the lowest level of information a subsection. The level above that becomes a section, and above that a chapter. You can always move up—parts are higher than chapters, books higher than parts. If the subject is so complex that you need so many layers, then expand at the high levels—add more volumes—instead of burrowing so deeply your readers won't find their way out.

Speed Editing

As chapter 8 showed, you can always take shortcuts.

There is no rule that says you have to edit a book in order. This is especially true of reference manuals. Your readers will not be reading the reference manual from cover to cover like a novel, so you shouldn't feel obliged to edit it in order. In fact, skipping around is a good way to catch usability problems, such as unexplained terms or acronyms.

If you think it's adequate to explain an acronym only the first time it's used in a reference manual, try picking up the book yourself, selecting an index item at random, and reading the corresponding text. That's how your readers use that manual. Are there terms that aren't explained? If so, is there a glossary? How about a pointer to the chapter that introduces the topic? How quickly can you find a particular topic?

TIP: Edit in sequence material readers need to read in sequence, such as introductory guides and tutorials. If continuity matters to the reader, edit the book sequentially. (If reading the book in sequence is important, make sure the book gives adequate warning to readers who skip around that they might miss something. And then put pointers in the text to help those who ignore your warning to find their way.) If you expect readers to access information randomly from the book, then it's fine to edit the information in a more flexible order.

TRICK: Rhythm helps you pace yourself and zip through that checklist of items you're watching for. Listen to music, chew gum, or tap your foot; you'll get through those pages twice as fast. And you'll probably get a private office, because your office mate will move out.

One Way to Tackle a Big Reference Manual

Here's how I tackle reference manuals: I read (yes, *read,* not skim) the table of contents and the preface to review the overall organization of the book. (Remember, I've seen the plans and reviewed the outline earlier in the development cycle. Reading the table of contents and preface refreshes my memory.) Then I read chapter 1 to introduce me, as the user, to the product or concept. I'll read another small chapter or two before I set the manuscript aside for the morning or day.

When I'm tired—say over the first cup of coffee or in the late afternoon—I'll tackle the appendixes. They're usually easy since they typically contain lists, tables, and other repetitive stuff. There's no point wasting my alert times for the mechanical tasks.

I'll devote a major chunk of time—a morning or a full day—to the reference pages. (Some of the manuals I edit have more than 200 reference pages.) Editing reference pages is one of the most soothing activities an editor can perform at the office. Reference pages rarely contain so much text that you can't sweep through the sentences in a single pass. Mostly, you just turn page after page and make sure that everything is consistent. What could be more hypnotic? Why, *of course* it's boring. *That's* what makes it easy. You're not reading and thinking about the content. (Thinking is hard. Turning pages and comparing items for consistency is so easy even computers can do it.) You're just checking and marking and marking and checking.

I edit the remaining chapters over as many sittings as necessary. When possible, I edit a chapter straight through, without major mental breaks, so I can keep track of the content. (I have to remember to take short physical breaks, stretches and walks, to prevent muscle and eye strain.) I don't know about you, but my short-term memory isn't reliable enough for me to put down a chapter for a few hours and later remember all the details I was checking, even with the help of a style sheet. If a visitor or phone call interrupts me, I have to mark my stopping place in the manuscript, or I may not recognize it ten minutes later.

I'm reading with a pen in my hand and a computer at my side. As I read, I mark my comments on the manuscript pages. When it seems that trying something out on the computer will help me understand the text better or check the accuracy of the text, to the computer I go. What I call *reading* you might call *editing and testing.*

Book Design for Writers and Editors

If you work for a small company, you may be expected to design the documentation, even if you don't have any training in graphic design. If you work for a large company, you will probably work with graphic designers. In either situation, knowing some principles of graphic design, typography, and layout will serve you well. Editors are expected to know about graphic design, if only to communicate effectively with designers. In companies that can afford editors, writers can afford not to learn about design. Writers typically are given fewer opportunities to learn about design and will rely on your expertise—however much or little you have—to resolve problems.

Whenever you have the opportunity to take some courses in graphic design, sign up. You don't need the hands-on skills so much as an understanding of the concepts and a familiarity with the language.

Read books on graphic design and the graphic arts. The bibliography lists some good books to get you started. Subscribe to publications about design, desktop and electronic publishing, and typography to keep current with new technology and techniques.

TIP: Here's the one rule about manual design to follow above all: Keep it simple.

Writers sometimes get carried away with clever and intricate formats. For example, sometimes writers indent different types of examples slightly differently. These minor distinctions are apparent when you're constructing the book but are far too subtle for a reader to discern. As the editor, you need to evaluate how well the design and text work together, from a reader's point of view. In many cases, the less complex the formatting, the easier the book is to edit for consistency and, more important, to read.

Good design

- Is appropriate for the function ("form follows function") (example: use a small typeface for a footnote and a large typeface for a major head)

- Accommodates the best and worst cases (example: make sure very short and very long examples look good, not just examples of average size)

- Helps readers find information (example: headers and footers are easy to see)

Bad design

- Is cluttered, confusing, and chaotic (example: too many different typefaces on a page)
- Is inconsistent from chapter to chapter (or from book to book in a documentation set)
- Hinders the reader from finding and interpreting information

Lists

Technical writing uses many different kinds of lists, as shown in figure 11–1.

As the editor, you'll need to ensure that the correct type of list is being used. You'll also need to check that the lists are parallel in style and form.

It's much easier to scan a vertical list of items than to scan a horizontal list. Compare the following two lists (for two different products), a bulleted list and a simple horizontal enumeration.

EXAMPLES

- Two-board CPU
- I/O board (peripheral, LAN, and async support)
- Graphics board
- Color monitor
- Memory board
- Power supply

Included are: HF rejection, add and subtract, and full auto setup for vertical sensitivity, sweep speed, vertical position, and trigger level.

When it's important for the reader to scan a list quickly to retrieve an item (as in a reference manual) or to remember each item (as in a tutorial), use a vertical list. When you're simply giving examples, enumerate them in text.

Types of Lists

Simple lists, when you just want to enumerate items:

The primary colors are
> red
> yellow
> green

Bulleted lists, when you want the items to stand out:

Ways wolves display affection:

- Pushing noses
- Wrestling jaws
- Rubbing cheeks
- Licking faces

You can achieve the same effect with symbols other than a solid bullet:

- o   Use an open bullet.
- ▪   Use a solid quad.

Checklists, when you want readers to check off items, literally or figuratively. For example, in an installation guide, readers can check that they've received all the parts:

- ✔ one way to show a checklist
- ❏ another example

Numbered lists, generally used only where the order follows a prescribed sequence or hierarchy, in contrast to all other lists, where the order may be arbitrary:

1. Tell what you're going to talk about.
2. Tell.
3. Tell what you told.

Figure 11–1. Types of lists

Here's another example of a list enumerated in text:

EXAMPLE

Less costly scientific superdeep drilling requires long-life hard-rock drill and core bits, increased penetration rates, special core drilling technology, the use of hollow shaft down-hole drilling and coring motors, improved methods for borehole trajectory control, and more sensitive monitors for early deviation detection.

Exercise 15 What detail should you verify in the following list?

Identifiers, also called names, can consist of the following:

- Letters (ASCII decimal values 65–90 and 97–122)
- Digits
- Dollar sign ($)
- Underscore (_)

Parallelism of Style and Form

Parallelism in style means all items in a list have the same grammatical construction. As a general rule, all items should be either phrases (or words) or complete sentences, not mixed. Every item should begin with the same part of speech and be in the same form.

Many style guides give simple rules for editing lists. Often, however, the simple rules they give work only if the document has only one type of list. For example, a typical guideline says to capitalize the first word of each item in the list if the entry is a complete sentence; otherwise use lowercase. A good rule, perhaps, but in technical writing it's common to have several different types of lists on a single page.

Most style guides would accept the following lists as shown, because the former has phrases, the latter complete sentences. Each list, viewed independently, is internally consistent and correct, but the overall impression of the page is inconsistency:

EXAMPLES

Sight flow indicators feature

- single-piece cast bodies
- flanged or threaded connections
- plain, flapper, drip tube, or rotor connection styles

Our magnetic level indicators are widely recognized for these characteristics:

- Externally mounted gauges offer visual level indication.
- Glass does not come in contact with the process.
- Indicators operate in harsh or extreme conditions.
- Many mounting styles and options are available.

Your eye catches the beginning of the line and picks out the inconsistency (even though it's intentional). Sometimes it's less jarring to capitalize the first word of both lists, as in the following example of a list with a sublist:

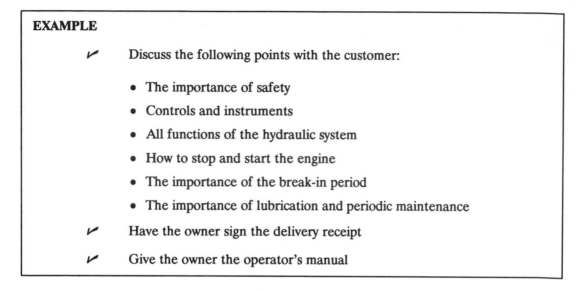

EXAMPLE

✔ Discuss the following points with the customer:

- The importance of safety
- Controls and instruments
- All functions of the hydraulic system
- How to stop and start the engine
- The importance of the break-in period
- The importance of lubrication and periodic maintenance

✔ Have the owner sign the delivery receipt

✔ Give the owner the operator's manual

What to check when you check lists:

- Parallel construction and syntax
- Initial caps or not to start each item
- Punctuation at end or not

Here's an example of a nonparallel list:

EXAMPLE

From the owner's guide for a refrigerator:

Read this manual carefully!

It contains:

- Start/adjust control
- Food storage times and tips
- Use and care information
- Cleaning your refrigerator
- Before calling for service
- Keep this manual for future use

The manufacturer revised this manual. Here's the new version, improved greatly in part simply by changing *It contains* to *Contents*:

EXAMPLE

Carefully read this book!
It tells you how to start, adjust and care for your refrigerator. Also see the permanent use and care information inside the refrigerator door.
Contents:

- Start/adjust controls
- Food storage times and tips
- Energy tips
- Features
- Cleaning
- Before calling for service
- Warranty

In technical writing things change all the time. As the product changes, writers have to add, delete, or change entries in lists. Sometimes short lists are merged and sometimes long lists are broken into two or more shorter lists. These kinds of changes are routine. Whenever possible, format lists so you don't have to rewrite or reformat them when changes occur. The editor should watch for problems caused by frequent changes, such as a lone bulleted item.

Suppose, for a first draft, a writer elects to use a bulleted list with short phrases. After all of the product changes and technical review corrections have been made, some items on the list require more elaboration. If the style guide requires different styles and formats for different types of lists, a small text change means a lot of rework just to make the list items parallel.

Unless house style specifically forbids it, edit all lists in a manual the same way. Usually style guides say to capitalize entries that are complete sentences. But if you may also capitalize phrases, then rework is minimized if one or two entries change.

TRICK: If, at a late stage, one entry needs more explanation than the others, you can use a semicolon or parentheses, instead of recasting all other entries as complete sentences. For example:

EXAMPLE

Advanced micropositioning systems require:

- Different materials; most frequently from aluminum to stainless steel
- Use of precision crossed-roller bearings
- Positioning stages or actuators that use a glass linear encoder

---

Here's another example:

EXAMPLE

Testing services:

- Shock (military approved)
- Vibration
- Temperature/humidity
- Mobility (military approved)
- Stress screening
- Noise
- Vacuum altitude

Product Specifications

Editing product specifications mostly entails editing for consistency in text and format. For example, like items should be treated alike. If the design specifications call for first-level heads to be 12-pt Helvetica bold, all capital letters, then all first-level heads should reflect these specifications.

Check that conversions have been calculated accurately and to an appropriate precision. For example, 15 pounds is equivalent to 7 (not 6.80388) kilograms.

A rule of thumb for precision when you convert from one system (such as the U.S. Customary System) to another (such as the SI): A conversion is accurate to $\pm$ ½ the last digit of its original value.[1] If you're converting a value expressed to the nearest tenth of an inch (say 5.4 inches) to centimeters (5.4 x 2.54), the math may read 13.716 cm, but you need to round that value to the appropriate significant digit, 13.7.

---

[1] The U.S. Customary System is derived from the British Imperial System. The International System of Units (abbreviated SI, from Système International D'Unités), based on an international agreement, is also a metric system, but not the one you learned in school. (The two are similar in many ways—but for editing technical documents you can't casually substitute one name for the other.) One major difference is how the metric and SI systems derive base units. The meter of the traditional metric system is the distance between two marks on a specific metal bar. The base units of the SI system are derived from scientific formulas or natural constants.

TIP: The first measurement should reflect the measurement system used to design the item, followed by the converted value. The specifications for a machine designed in the United States by an engineer working in the U.S. Customary System should give U.S. measurements first (inches, pounds) with metric values in parentheses to show the metric values are converted values and inherently less precise.

Also ensure that all units of measurement are expressed in standard units and that abbreviations conform to "standard" guidelines, namely, those sanctioned by standards bodies (such as ANSI, the American National Standards Institute, or ISO, the International Organization for Standardization), professional societies (such as the IEEE, Institute of Electrical and Electronics Engineers), or your own company's standards.

EXAMPLE

Video Recording System	Rotary four-head helical scan system
Video Signal	EIA standards; NTSC color
Antenna	VHF/UHF–75 ohm external antenna terminal
VHF Output Signal	Channel 3 or 4 (switchable) 75 ohms unbalanced
Power Requirement	120V AC/60 Hz
Power Consumption	18 W
Operating Temperature	5°C (41°F) to 40°C (104°F)
Relative Humidity	10% to 75%
Weight	7.9 lbs. (3.6 kg)
Dimensions	3-3/8″ (86mm) x 12-5/8″ (320mm) x 11-5/8″ (259mm) (H/W/D)

Exercise 16   Checking specifications for consistency

Do you see any nonstandard abbreviations in the preceding example? What inconsistencies do you notice?

TIP: Know the standard units of measurement and tolerances for your field. A difference of a gram may not matter much in civil engineering (if you're giving the weight of a bridge) but in pharmacology an error of that magnitude can kill.

EXAMPLE

Printer Physical Characteristics

Height:	7.5 in. (19.0 cm)
Width:	23 in. (58.4 cm)
Depth:	20.5 in. (52.1 cm)
Weight:	64 lb (29 kg)

Keyboard Physical Characteristics

Height:	2.5 in. (6.4 cm)
Width:	22.5 in. (57.1 cm)
Depth:	9.5 in. (24.1 cm)
Weight:	5 lb (2.3 kg)

PRINTER AND KEYBOARD COMBINATION

Depth:	26 in. (66 cm)
Weight:	69 lb (31 kg)

Electrical Characteristics

Power:	117 Vac + 10%, -15% UL approved
Power Consumption:	0.27 kVA
Heat Dissipation:	500 Btu/hr (126 kcal/hr)
Frequency:	60 Hz $\pm$ ½ Hz

Environmental Characteristics

Operating Temperature:	50°F to 100°F (10°C to 38°C)
Relative Humidity:	10% to 90% (noncondensing)

Cables

Power cord:	6 ft (1.8M)
Interconnecting cable:	50 ft (15.2 m) standard, 100 ft (30.5 m) alternate

---

Exercise 17   Checking specifications for consistency

Do you see any nonstandard abbreviations in the preceding example? What inconsistencies do you notice?

```
┌─────────────────────────────────────────────────────────────────────┐
│  EXAMPLE                                                             │
│                                                                     │
│  Floppy Discs                                                       │
│                                                                     │
│  Capacity (KB):                                                     │
│                                                                     │
│              Unformatted:                                           │
│                                                                     │
│              Per disc:                 1000                         │
│                                                                     │
│              Per surface:              500                          │
│                                                                     │
│              Per track:                  6.25                       │
│                                                                     │
│              Formatted:                                             │
│                                                                     │
│              Per disc:                 737.28                       │
│                                                                     │
│              Per surface:                5.52                       │
│                                                                     │
│              Per track:                  4.608                      │
│                                                                     │
│  Transfer rate:                        250 Kbits/second             │
│                                                                     │
│  Motor on/off time:                    one second maximum           │
│                                                                     │
│  Access time (ms):                                                  │
│                                                                     │
│               Track to track:            3                          │
│                                                                     │
│               Settling time:            15                          │
│                                                                     │
│               Head load time:           50                          │
│                                                                     │
│               Head switching time:       3                          │
│                                                                     │
│               Average seek:            100                          │
└─────────────────────────────────────────────────────────────────────┘
```

Exercise 18   What's wrong here?

I copied these specs from a very old data sheet. I have proofread my typing against the original. Do you see anything in these numbers worth questioning if you were editing these specs?

Tasks

Technical writing includes a lot of tasks or procedures. Tasks are the how-to information, in contrast to the conceptual information (descriptive prose about a subject) and reference information (details to look up when you need them).

Some task-oriented books are instructional, or tutorial. They teach you about a subject and how to do certain activities. For example, a tutorial for a word processing program would teach how to create, edit, and print a document. You would get enough explanation about each task to perform it whenever you wanted, on any document you wrote.

Other task-oriented documents lead you through a process but don't explain what you're doing or why. For example, the assembly instructions for a television stand tell how to put all the pieces together (and have fewer than three screws left over) but not why you're using hex nuts instead of anchor bolts.

TIP: When you edit tasks, make sure steps the reader performs are separated from incidental explanation. Make sure there are adequate cross-references to books (or other chapters) where the reader can find supplementary information. Then make sure those cross-references point the reader to information that is useful and relevant to the task at hand.

When you edit task-oriented documentation, you are most concerned with the order, clarity, and presentation of the information.

Order: Ensure that steps are in the correct sequence. Prerequisite information or prerequisite tasks—having the correct tools handy, formatting the floppy disk, shutting off the electricity—must be stated at the beginning of the procedure, not buried somewhere in step 7.

Clarity: Question ambiguities, inconsistencies, and oddities as you read the text and—when possible—perform the procedure yourself. Clarity also means providing reinforcement—telling users what message they should be seeing after executing this command, showing customers what the partially assembled bicycle should look like after that step, showing the back panel with the cables inserted correctly. Clarity also means not keeping the reader in the dark. Anticipate what may go wrong and tell corrective actions.

Presentation: Check that the visuals (illustrations, tables, photographs) support the text and that the overall design makes the procedure easy to follow. Make sure that it's easy to spot the beginning and end of each step, that the sequence of steps is clear, and that cautions and warnings leap off the page. Check that the reader sees the important details in illustrations and photographs and is not distracted by unnecessary details.

In the following example, the actions the user should perform are in boldface:

EXAMPLE

The following steps will erase all Events programmed into the thermostat's memory:

1. **Slide FUNCTION Switch to CLEAR position.**

2. **Press ENTER button.** All Events in the thermostat's memory will be erased, but the thermostat's clock will not be affected.

The following are instructions for changing the code on an electronic door alarm from two different manufacturers. Compare the two sets of instructions. Observe how the formatting makes the task seem easier in the second example:

EXAMPLES

Manufacturer A:
Remove Door Alarm/Entry Chime from Bottom Cover by removing the two bottom screws, then tilt and lift off. Locate the Orange, Yellow, Green, and White wires with connectors on the end. Decide on your own 3-digit secret code and insert the Orange wire in the position corresponding to your first digit, the Yellow wire in the second digit, and the Green wire in the third digit. The White wire can be inserted into any of the remaining positions; this will be your Panic code.

Manufacturer B:
To change the Factory Code to your own personal code, follow these simple rewiring instructions:

1. Choose 3 easily remembered numbers between 1 and 5 without using the same number twice. (You may want to write it down on a slip of paper and place it in your wallet or purse.)

2. Loosen the 5 screws; remove wire terminals from screws.

3. Reconnect code wires to the code numbers of your choice as follows; tighten screw as each wire is connected.

    ★**RED** wire to your **first** code number.
    ★**WHITE** wire to your **second** code number.
    ★**BLUE** wire to your **third** code number.
    ★TWO **BLACK** wires to remaining screws.
    ★Tuck wire loops into wiring section.

    Example: **5 3 1**
    If your code choice is 5–3–1. (See illustration H.)
    Connect **RED** wire to **5.**
    WHITE wire to **3.**
    BLUE wire to **1.**
    BLACK wire to **2** and **4.**

TIP: If a procedure seems too complicated, try making a flowchart out of it to help you and the writer see where you might break it down into two or more tasks and whether the start and end points are clearly defined. You might think about making the following example into a flowchart. Would you break up any steps into two or more steps? (There is no "right" answer, just something to ponder.)

EXAMPLE

1. Inspect boss O-ring seat. It must be free of dirt and defects. Some raised defects can be removed with a slip stone.

2. Lubricate O-ring using petroleum jelly. Put a thimble over the threads to protect O-ring from nicks. Slide O-ring over the thimble and into the turned down section of fitting.

3. Turn fitting into the boss by hand until special washer or washer face (straight fitting) contacts boss face and O-ring is squeezed into its seat.

4. To position angle fittings, turn the fitting counterclockwise a maximum of one turn.

5. Tighten fittings.

For information about editing tutorials in computer manuals, see chapter 12.

Tables

Tables let us organize lots of data compactly in a logical, structured fashion. For example:

Diamond Bonds			
Bond	**Characteristics**	**Advantages**	**Comments**
Resin	easy to true and dress moderately free cut	readily available easy to learn to use	applicable for a range of operations
Vitrified	free cutting easy to true needs no dressing	longer wheel life than resin excellent coolant	suitable for deep grinding and high-conformity grinding
Metal	difficult to true and dress high stiffness	very durable good form holding good thermal conductivity	requires high power for grinding excellent for slot and groove grinding
Electroplated	highly free cutting not truable	form wheels are easily produced	surface finish poorer than bonded abrasive wheels

A table is an array of information, not just a picture of data. (An exception is a genealogical table, which is rare in technical books.)

Here are some data represented as both an illustration and as a table:

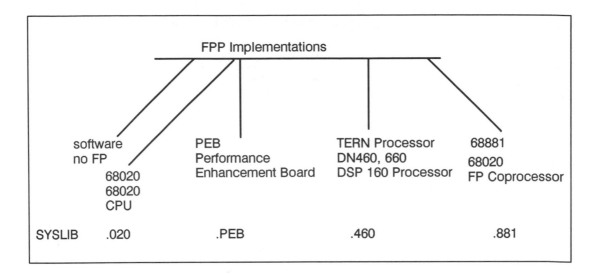

Floating-Point Preprocessor Implementation	SYSLIB Extension Name
Software, no floating-point	??? (none??? not applicable???)
68020 CPU (See original figure. Why is 68020 repeated? Is text missing???)	.020
PEB (Performance Enhancement Board)	.PEB
TERN Processor	.460
68881, 68020 Floating-Point Coprocessor (68881 *with* a 68020 FP Coprocessor???)	.881
NOTE: Because the original illustration is not clear, I've had to mark some table entries with ??? for the writer and engineer to resolve.	

Which do you find easier to read at a glance? The table at least makes it clear where the problems are.

Tables have at least two columns, and every column has a descriptive head. We read tables from left to right and from the top down, so the leftmost column is our guide for how the information is organized. This left column has a special name: the *stub*.

Table titles typically appear above the table. Check that they're always above or always below, whichever is your company's style. It's customary to number tables to simplify referring to them in text. Assign meaningful titles to all tables so that readers browsing through a table of contents can find the appropriate table quickly.

The design specifications will cover what typeface, spacing, and rules to use in tables. As the editor, you'll need to ensure that these are followed consistently for all tables in the manual.

Organizing Information in Tables

Writers sometimes think of tables as places to put data. So editors need to view tables from the reader's point of view, as structures from which to retrieve data. If you cannot tell how the table is organized, ask the writer. Chances are the writer formatted the information into the table in the same order it appeared in the source material.

TIP: Tables that follow a clear hierarchy or sequence are easier to use. For example, check that commands and their descriptions are listed in the sequence in which the commands will be executed (if the order is prescribed and predictable); otherwise they should be listed in alphabetical order.

The options in the following table appear to be listed randomly.

Option	Meaning	Default
–L	Generates assembly listing	✔
–NL	Suppresses assembly listing	
–B	Generates object module	✔
–NB	Suppresses binary file	
–XREF	Generates cross-reference listing	
–NXREF	Suppresses cross-reference listing	✔

A strict alphabetical order would separate some related options, such as –L and –NL, but here's one—by no means the only—way to organize the table:

Option	Meaning	Default
–B	Generates object module	✔
–NB	Suppresses binary file	
–L	Generates assembly listing	✔
–NL	Suppresses assembly listing	
–XREF	Generates cross-reference listing	
–NXREF	Suppresses cross-reference listing	✔

Be aware that different users may need to retrieve the same piece of information in different ways. For example, let's look at several ways to organize operating system commands in a table. (Assume this table summarizes the commands for users who already understand the concepts.)

Suppose the computer system now supports both the DOS and UNIX operating systems. Some users don't know either the DOS or UNIX system—but they're familiar with another operating system—and need to learn one or both from scratch. These users want to find the tasks easily in the table. (They know what they want to do, but don't know the command to enter.) Suggest that the writer organize the table for these users by task, with the tasks grouped logically. One way to organize these commands is to group those that operate on directories together, in alphabetical order, and to group those that operate on files together, also in alphabetical order:

	DOS Command	UNIX Command
Operations on Directories		
Change directory	CHDIR or CD	cd
Create new directory	MKDIR or MD	mkdir
Delete directory	RMDIR or RD	rmdir
List directory	DIR	ls
Operations on Files		
Copy file	COPY	cp
Delete file	ERASE or DEL	rm
Rename file	RENAME or REN	mv

If users are changing over from one operating system to another, a table that shows the command in the old (familiar) operating system and its equivalent in the new operating system is a helpful tool. Let's say your users already know DOS but are learning the UNIX operating system. Recommend that the writer organize the table with the DOS commands on the left, and list them alphabetically.

Now let's assume half your users know DOS and half know UNIX commands, but both groups occasionally need to use the other operating system. Ask the writer to create two tables, one that goes from DOS commands to UNIX commands, and one that goes from UNIX commands to DOS commands.

DOS Command	UNIX Command	Description
CHDIR or CD	cd	Change directory
COPY	cp	Copy file
DIR	ls	List directory
ERASE or DEL	rm	Delete file
MKDIR or MD	mkdir	Create new directory
RENAME or REN	mv	Rename file
RMDIR or RD	rmdir	Delete directory

UNIX Command	DOS Command	Description
cd	CHDIR or CD	Change directory
cp	COPY	Copy file
ls	DIR	List directory
mkdir	MKDIR or MD	Create new directory
mv	RENAME or REN	Rename file
rm	ERASE or DEL	Delete file
rmdir	RMDIR or RD	Delete directory

As another example, you might provide a table of mortgage payments by loan amount, for people who know how much they plan to borrow:

Payments on 30-Year Mortgage at 10%	
Loan Amount	Monthly Payment
$25,000	$219.39
$50,000	$438.79
$100,000	$877.57

You might also provide a table organized by monthly payment, for those who want to work the figures a different way:

Payments on 30-Year Mortgage at 10%	
Monthly Payment	Loan Amount
$219.39	$25,000
$438.79	$50,000
$877.57	$100,000

Fitting Tables on a Page

Another problem you'll face is fitting the table on the page. You may suggest swapping the contents of the columns and rows to fit a table across a page; it's easier to read a table when you can see all the column headings at once.

For example, if you want to display some information about each of the states, you could arrange the columns by state, but you'd run out of room very quickly:

	Alabama	Alaska	Arizona	Arkansas	California
Bird	yellow-hammer	willow ptarmigan	cactus wren	mockingbird	California valley quail
Flower	camellia	forget-me-not	blossom of Saguaro cactus	apple blossom	golden poppy
Tree	southern pine	sitka spruce	paloverde	pine	California redwood

A better arrangement is to put the categories in the column heads, and have the states in the stub:

	Bird	Flower	Tree
Alabama	yellowhammer	camellia	southern pine
Alaska	willow ptarmigan	forget-me-not	sitka sprucc
Arizona	cactus wren	blossom of Saguaro cactus	paloverde
Arkansas	mockingbird	apple blossom	pine

Sometimes you'll see one complex table that would be clearer as two. The following table, from an installation and service manual for a sump pump, is confusing because of the way the numbering is handled. (This example shows only an excerpt from the table.)

Problem	Cause	Correction
Pump cycles too frequently,	0. Check valve not installed, or leaking. 1. Improper wiring or power supply. 4. Discharge head less than manufacturer's minimum. 8. Impeller jammed or rubbing. 10. Excessive water temperature.	1. Check all electrical connections for security. Have electrician check power supply and all wiring for correct voltage, phase and current as indicated on pump nameplate. 2a. Reposition pump or clean basin as required to provide adequate clearance for float. 2b & c. Return for service or see service section. 3. Make sure liquid level is at least 9I from sump floor. 4. Recheck all sizing calculations to determine proper pump size. . . . [11 corrections are listed]
Pump vibrates noisily or vibrates excessively.	2c. Worn bearings. 8. Debris in impeller cavity or broken impeller. 11. Piping attachments to building structure too rigid or too loose.	

In the table, the numbers in the "Cause" column correspond to those in the "Correction" column—but the format suggests something else. The numbers precede the cause, appear in the same typeface and size, and are followed by a period. This format suggests a numbered list—albeit a jumbled one.

There is still another problem with the table, namely, the numbering for correction 2. The writer probably didn't plan the table this way. Chances are that correction 2 was subdivided at a revision. The other corrections weren't renumbered because that would have involved renumbering the causes, too, and there probably wasn't time to retype the table.

Here's how to break up the information into two tables:

Table 1. Troubleshooting		
Problem	**Cause**	**Correction (See Table 2)**
Pump cycles too frequently.	Check valve not installed, or leaking.	**6**
	Improper wiring or power supply.	**1**
	Discharge head less than manufacturer's minimum.	**4**
	Impeller jammed or rubbing.	**8**
	Excessive water temperature.	**10**
Pump vibrates noisily or vibrates excessively.	Worn bearings.	**2c***
	Debris in impeller cavity or broken impeller.	**8**
	Piping attachments to building structure too rigid or too loose.	**11**
* It would be better to renumber these.		

Table 2. Key to Corrections	
Number	**Correction**
1	Check all electrical connections for security. Have electrician check power supply and all wiring for correct voltage, phase and current as indicated on pump nameplate.
2a*	Reposition pump or clean basin as required to provide adequate clearance for float.
2b* & c*	Return for service or see service section.
3	Make sure liquid level is at lcast 9I from sump floor.
4	Rccheck all sizing calculations to determine proper pump size.
5	Check discharge line for restriction, including ice if line passes through or into cold areas.
* It would be better to renumber these.	

Occasionally you'll scc two tables that are easier to read as one.

For example:

Supplied as Part of the Product		
Supplied Hardware or Software	**PC Connection**	**Ring Connection**
Connection software	✓	✓
Ring board	N/A	✓

Required at Your Site		
Required Hardware or Software	**PC Connection**	**Ring Connection**
Operating system	✓	✓
Personal computer	✓	✓
Network cable	N/A	✓
RS-232 cable	✓	N/A

Here's the same information in one table:

Supplied and Prerequisite Components		
	PC Connection	**Ring Connection**
Supplied with product		
Connection software	✔	✔
Ring board	N/A	✔
Prerequisites		
Operating system	✔	✔
Personal computer	✔	✔
Network cable	N/A	✔
RS-232 cable	✔	N/A

Notes and Footnotes in Tables

Tables should be self-contained. Check that everything about the table, including notes about the table itself (legends) or about any of its entries, is enclosed within the boundaries of the table.

The symbol you use to flag a note depends on the content of the table. Some tables contain mostly numerals, others mostly text. It's helpful to use symbols that are not easily confused with the information. If the table contains mostly numerals, it's better to use an asterisk or other such symbol than a superscript numeral (as shown in the following table). If the table contains mostly text, however, superscript numerals are easier to read.

Common Unit Prefixes			
Symbol	Prefix	Multiple (power of 10)	Example
G	giga-	10^9	GHz (gigahertz)
M	mega-	10^6	MV (megavolt)
k *	kilo-	10^3	kV (kilovolt)
c	centi-	10^{-2}	cm (centimeter)
m	milli-	10^{-3}	mV (millivolt)
µ	micro-	10^{-6}	µV (microvolt)
n	nano-	10^{-9}	ns (nanosecond)
* Kilobytes is abbreviated as KB, as in 256 KB of RAM. (K = 1024)			
NOTE: Superscript numerals would be a confusing way to denote footnotes in this table.			

If you have many notes, the table will be easier to read if you use superscript numerals rather than a hodgepodge of symbols. Some style guides (such as *The Chicago Manual of Style)* even recommend hierarchies of symbols.

If a table continues onto two or more pages and there are several notes that apply to more than one page, repeat all the notes at the bottom of every page of the table. Don't expect the reader to turn back three pages to find out what note[3] means.

Column Heads and Table Titles

Column heads identify how the data is organized; ensure that the heads are descriptive.

Don't assume the reader will read the paragraphs before and after the table, where the writer explains that dollar figures are in thousands of dollars. Expect readers to skim the table to pick out the one entry they're seeking—this quick, selective access is precisely the purpose of a table.

Include the unit in the column head or table title for prominent display and to save space in the table: "In thousands" or "Weight (kg)."

Table 11–1. Selected Quarterly Financial Information (in thousands)

	First Quarter	Second Quarter	Third Quarter	Fourth Quarter
Net sales	$82,021	$88,382	$100,408	$120,874
Gross profit	36,101	41,108	47,230	57,257
Net income	539	1,041	2,476	5,275

When a table is split across several pages, give the reader cues about the table. Flag that the rest of the table is on the previous (or following) pages. For example, add the word *continued* (or *cont.*) to the bottom of the first and successive pages of the table and to the table title on the second and successive pages of the table. Repeat the table title and column heads on successive pages, so the reader doesn't have to flip back and forth.

Simply stated, make tables easy for readers to use.

Common Errors in Tables

The most common problem with tables is inconsistency in the presentation of data: capitalization, punctuation, wording. Edit tables by reading across and then down. Also edit all the tables in a book in a single session to ensure consistency throughout the book. You'll be astonished by the number of different elements in tables and the dozens of little inconsistencies that can emerge.

TIP: Tables are also breeding grounds for typos, so pay very close attention when you proofread them.

Tables vs. Tabular Lists

Sometimes information lends itself to a two-column display and doesn't need the formal presentation of a table. For example, a table is overkill for this information:

Chapter 1. Planning
Chapter 2. Installation
Chapter 3. Operation
Chapter 4. Troubleshooting

Don't hesitate to let the writer use a simpler format if it serves the purpose.

Figures (Illustrations)

Illustrations in technical manuals are rarely decorative; they're devices for conveying information. Above all, illustrations need to be clear.

There are many different types of illustrations commonly used in technical manuals. Here are a few examples:

- Schematic diagrams
- Blueprints
- Logic diagrams
- Wiring diagrams
- Three-dimensional drawings, such as exploded parts illustrations and perspective drawings
- Block diagrams, such as flowcharts
- Graphs
- Line illustrations, such as how to connect system units and cables
- Photographs
- Screen captures (actual representations of what's on the computer screen)

Illustrations can supplement or replace text. Suggest that the writer use illustrations whenever you need to *show* something.[1]

TIP: The choice of fill patterns (such as cross-hatching and dots) may be constrained by conventions in your technology area. For example, many engineering specialties use predefined patterns for different materials (such as plastics, steel, and wood).

---

[1] Strictly speaking, a *figure* is an illustration with text, but this distinction is rarely made in technical publishing.

*Do*s and *Don't*s

- Do ensure that the illustration relates to the text. Check that the writer has numbered the illustration (if necessary), referred to it in text *(See Figure 2)*, and written a descriptive caption. There are three good reasons to number figures:

  — If the art isn't close to the text, numbering the figures lets readers match the appropriate text and illustrations.

  — Your production department may require figures to be numbered so the artists can determine where to insert them when they paste up the mechanicals.

  — The figures can be listed in the table of contents, if these are figures that a reader may want to look up.

  If these reasons don't apply, then you don't need to number the figures.

- Do ensure that the illustration supports the text. It should be relevant to the text and should not contradict it.

- Do focus the illustration. The purpose of figure 11–2 (on the following page) is to show the location of the ESCAPE key on the keyboard. A drawing of the relevant portion of the keyboard would have worked.

- Do provide legends if you use symbols or shading.

- Do check that the callouts are clear and consistent.

- Do make sure that the illustration is not too complex for readers to decipher.

- Don't assume the connection between the illustration and the text is obvious. Make sure the text tells the reader what to see in the illustration.

Figure 11-2. An illustration with much extraneous detail

Big Figures

When a figure is too big, you have three strategies to suggest to the writer or artist:

- Make it a *turn page* or *broadside* (rotate it 90°). As shown in figure 11–3, the top of the illustration should be at the left, so the reader always turns the book the same way. The caption has the same orientation as the illustration, so the reader can see both together. Do not rotate the page footer (including the folio); the footers keep a steady position regardless of the orientation of the text on the page. (Your house style may prohibit any text—even a caption and footer—on a turn page.)

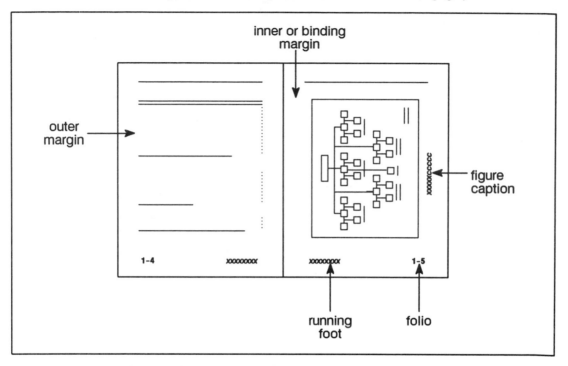

Figure 11–3. Placement of figure on a turn page (broadside)

- Continue the illustration onto several pages, with flags (such as numbers in balloons) to indicate how to connect up the illustrations. (See figure 11–4.) These illustrations are difficult to read, but a practical solution when you have no other recourse.

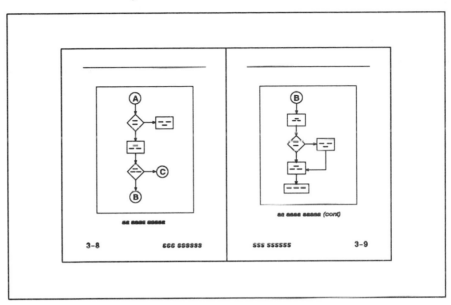

Figure 11–4. A flowchart continued onto a second page

- Make the illustration into two or more illustrations if the information lends itself to division. For example, you could take a complex flowchart and break it into several smaller flowcharts. The first flowchart in the series would be a high-level overview of the entire process.

  Other examples include a map or other illustration with a detailed inset (figures 11–5 and 11–6) or an exploded parts drawing. Sometimes it's good to break up complex illustrations, not only for space and aesthetic reasons—an illustration that is complex to draw (because of intersecting or overlapping rules or text) is probably difficult to decipher and use.

TIP: You might also ask the writer to consider the complexity of the material. If a flowchart cannot fit onto one page, ask the writer if it really is an efficient mechanism for communication.

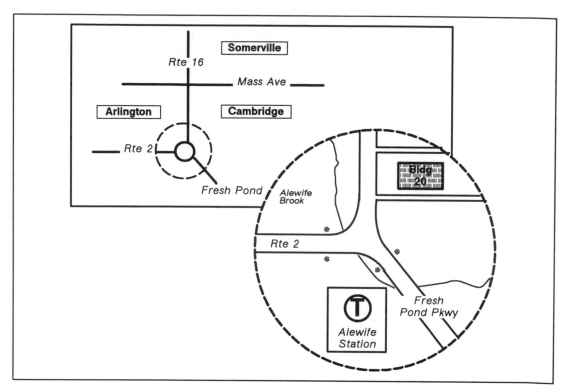

Figure 11–5. Map with inset

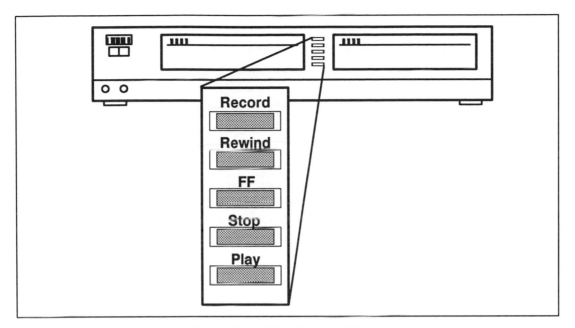

Figure 11-6. Line drawing with inset

Examples

Check that examples match the text. Under deadline pressures, writers may incorporate technical changes to the text but miss a corresponding change in an example.

Type in commands to see if they yield the results the manual says they will. Solve the equations. Conduct the experiment. Check that the file is actually in the directory cited.

When you can't test the examples yourself because you lack time, skills, or equipment, make sure they will be tested by a qualified person, an expert, a novice, or someone in between, depending on the subject and the intended audience. For example, you may want a novice user to test a tutorial for a word processing program, but you'd certainly want an experienced chemist to run lab tests. Your company may have a Quality Assurance department that tests the documentation along with the product or you may be responsible for lining up test subjects and implementing usability tests yourself. You may collaborate with the writer or others to ensure the content is adequately tested. For example, you may cook the salami and salmon casserole, but have the writer taste it.

TIP: The most common errors you'll find in examples are inconsistencies between the examples and the text. For example, a programming example may refer to the **sqr()** function but the text refers to it as **sqrt()**. Other common errors are spelling discrepancies between the panels and manuals. For example, the "HI" button on the blender might be called "High" in the owner's guide.

Strategies for Updating Manuals

Technical manuals aren't just written and printed: They're revised, updated, and revised again. And again.

Revisions

A *revision* is a new edition of the manual. All or parts of a book are rewritten, and the entire book is reissued, usually under the same title and possibly under the same part number. (Every company has its own policy about part numbers, which depends on its manufacturing and distribution system.) The revision may make the old version obsolete or it may coexist with the previous edition, depending on your company's policy for supporting earlier products.

There's nothing special about editing a revision, except that you may be asked to gloss over it if there have been only a few changes. You should review the complete book and let the project team and your manager know if the book is in worse shape than they may have thought when they said "gloss." You may get the green light to edit the book more thoroughly—if you can show the benefits will outweigh the cost in writer, editor, and production time.

TRICK: You can remind the project team that it's expensive to print and distribute a revised book. Making the book better may be only a small incremental cost, but may reap huge returns in customer satisfaction and reduced costs for product support.

In addition to whatever light or heavy editing you do, it's worth your time to ensure that the changes haven't introduced errors or major inconsistencies in the book.

In some manuals, technical changes are denoted by *change bars* (also called *revision bars*) in the margin. Change bars are placed in the outer margin of the page (as shown here). A rule of thumb is not to use change bars if more than 30% of the pages have been changed because, at that rate, users of the previous edition might as well read the whole book.

Addenda and Supplements

Some manuals are updated so frequently that it's more convenient and cheaper to send users replacement pages than to revise the complete manual. These update pages are sometimes known as *addenda* (singular *addendum*), *updates,* or *insert pages.*

You can issue replacement pages only for books that are not "permanently" bound; manuals that are designed to be updated in the field are typically drilled and shrinkwrapped.

To update a bound manual without revising the entire book, you would issue a separately bound volume, commonly called a *supplement* or *update.* (Yes, technical publishing uses the term *update* ambiguously.) Since a supplement is merely another volume that accompanies the original, the only extra work for the editor (besides the editing itself) is to ensure that the front matter clearly identifies the book it goes with.

Addenda can add, change, and delete information; supplements can only add information. On the other hand, addenda require users to physically remove and insert pages, which is a chore. At best, supplements can list changes or deletions for users to mark in their manuals themselves, a chore even more cumbersome than dealing with replacement pages.

Some users love insert pages; they like the knowledge (or the delusion) that they have the most recent information, and they don't mind replacing the pages. Other users despise insert pages; they feel that, having paid so much money for the manual, they're entitled to a free revision. Your users will be passionate on this subject—and they'll represent both camps.

Editing Addenda (Insert Pages)

Addenda create more work for an editor than a supplement does, mainly because editors are expected to be experts in the mechanics of putting together addenda.

Editing an addendum is straightforward: Edit the text of the addendum as you'd edit the text for the rest of the manual. Make the text consistent with the original manual, even if that means not incorporating recent changes in house style or design. (An exception: Do incorporate new legal notices and disclaimers, unless advised otherwise by counsel.)

Make sure the user knows what the pages are updates to—that the original document is correctly and clearly identified by title, part number, revision level, and date of publication. The user will not be served well by inserting the update pages into the wrong edition of the book.

Your company probably has some way to indicate the part number and/or date of the addendum pages themselves so that users can tell which pages were part of the original printing and which were replacement pages. You must check that these pages are correctly labeled.

One challenge of editing addenda is to ensure that users can insert the new pages without losing information. In particular, you must make sure the pagination works. Verify that the update pages themselves can be physically inserted into the book.

TIP: An embarrassing mistake new editors make is to start a chunk of replacement pages on an even-numbered page or end on an odd-numbered page. These chunks cannot be physically inserted into the book. For example, if you need to replace pages 50–53, you should provide pages 49–54.

If the replacement pages have many changes, additions, or deletions to text, some text may be lost. Check every item—every paragraph, illustration, caption—to ensure that nothing is omitted inadvertently.

Editing replacement pages is relatively easy when you replace a series of pages with the same number of pages. For example, you'll remove pages 4–1 through 4–10 and replace them with pages 4–1 through 4–10. What do you do when you have more pages?

If page 4–10, to continue with this example, is the end of chapter 4, then you can simply insert pages 4–1 through 4–14 (or whatever). If chapter 4 goes through page 4–88, you don't want to repaginate all the remaining pages and reprint them simply to squeeze in a few more pages. In this situation, use a *point page* numbering scheme. The point page scheme lets you number the pages in this example as follows:

4–1, 4–2, 4–3, 4–4, 4–5, 4–6, 4–7, 4–8, 4–9, 4–10 . . .
Here's where you want to insert 4 new pages, so you number the pages after 4–10:
4–10.1, 4–10.2, 4–10.3, 4–10.4
Now you can continue with the rest of the chapter, unchanged: 4–11, 4–12, . . . , 4–88

Some companies letter insert pages (4.10a, 4.10b, 4.10c, etc.).

The point-page numbering scheme lets you add any number of pages between two pages. It's an ugly system, but very practical and economical.

Your final task is to prepare collating instructions that clearly tell the user what pages to remove and insert.

Here's an example:

```
EXAMPLE

Remove                        Insert
iii through xii               iii through xii
1–9, blank                    1–9, blank
2–1 through 2–6               2–1 through 2–6
3–7 through 3–22              3–7 through 3–22
                              3–22.1 through 3–22.6
index (1 through 36)          index (1 through 38)
```

A useful collating sheet tells where there are blank pages and point pages.

A truism of technical writing: When you issue update pages, you should resign yourself to the fact that all users will have "custom" versions of the documentation because they won't insert all the updates (because they don't receive them all or because they don't have the time or inclination) or they won't insert them correctly.

TIP: If you find you're asking the user to replace 20% to 30% of the pages in the manual, consider revising the original book instead.

Reference Pages

A good reference page gives readers *immediate* access to information. A reference page should have no extraneous information or clutter. Consistency of format and style lets the reader zoom in on the information and get back to the task at hand. Inconsistencies distract and delay the reader.

Here are the three most important things to know about editing reference pages in a book (or a reference book itself):

- Make sure it's easy to find information. The reader wants the information *now*. Think of access time in seconds, not minutes.

- Make sure the information, once located, is clearly written, so the reader doesn't waste time deciphering the message.

- Make sure the information is accurate and complete. The purpose of reference material is to give *solutions*. It should not introduce new problems or raise new questions.

When you edit reference pages, first check that all the reference pages themselves have been included. Somewhere you'll have a list of all commands, system calls, programming statements, or functions that apply to the product—whatever information the reference pages summarize. Compare that list to the reference pages. Every item on the list should have a reference page. Conversely, every reference page should reflect a topic on the list.

For example, figure 11-7 shows a page from a C language manual:

The page shown in figure 11-7 summarizes the topics covered in the book's 150 reference pages. The editor needs to compare the items in this summary page to the reference pages themselves, one item at a time.

This tedious exercise turns up more oversights than you'd think. It is *always* worth your time to check the integrity of the list and the reference pages. Sometimes you'll find a reference page that should have been deleted; more often you'll find omissions or inconsistencies (such as a command name spelled differently on the reference page from elsewhere in the manual).

TIP: It's not enough to count the number of items on the reference page and the number of commands. Let's say the writer's first draft has commands A, B, and C. The developers later drop C and add D. The commands are now A, B, and D. The *number of commands* is still three, but they're different commands.

Before you start to edit any reference page, study all the reference pages in the book, chapter, or section. Note the order in which information is presented. (Does there even appear to be a consistent order? You may have a lot of work ahead of you!) Examine the overall format. Pay attention to what items are capitalized, which do or do not have end punctuation, and the spacing between elements. Check for terms that are repeated from page to page and check whether any discrepancies are intentional.

TRICK: Make a photocopy of a representative page from the book and annotate it. Use that copy as your style sheet.

```
                         Keyword Listings

break                                 if
continue                              return
do/while                              sizeof
for                                   switch
goto                                  while
```

```
                  Preprocessor Directive Listings

__DATE__ and __TIME              __LINE__ and __FILE__
#debug                                #line
#define, #undef                       #list
#eject                                #module
#if, #ifdef, #ifndef, #else, #endif   #section
#include                              __STDC__ and __BFMT__COFF
                                      #systype
```

```
                         Other Listings

arithmetic operators                  expressions
array operations                      increment and decrement operators
assignment operators                  logical operators
bit operators                         pointer operations
cast operations                       predefined macros
comma operator                        relational operators
conditional expression operator       structure and union operations
enum operations
```

Figure 11–7. This page lists all the C manual's reference pages

Figure 11–8 shows an example of a reference page, annotated to show what formatting and style decisions have already been made. (This reference page is for a language that isn't case sensitive, so *Odd* and *odd* can be used interchangeably.)

odd ——— *index slug (lowercase) at the outer margin of the page*

Odd   Tests whether the specified integer is an odd number.

function name in bold (with an initial cap), followed by a tab; blurb starts with a verb (with an initial cap), ends in a period

FORMAT ——— *repeating heads are in all caps, left justified*

odd(*i*)   {**odd** is a function.} ——— *comment in { }, ends in a period*

note that these align

ARGUMENT

   i   Any integer expression.

every argument in format line should be listed here and defined

FUNCTION RETURNS

   The **odd** function returns a Boolean value.

——— *note that these align*   *complete sentences*

DESCRIPTION

   Odd returns true if *i* is an odd integer and false if *i* is an even integer.

EXAMPLE

```
PROGRAM odd_example;
{This program demonstrates the use of the odd function.}

VAR
     i : integer;
BEGIN
     write('Enter an integer -- ');
     readln(i);                        code is aligned neatly
     if ODD(i)
          then writeln(i:1, ' is an odd number.')
          else writeln(i:1, ' is an even number.');
END.
```

check that names match

USING THIS EXAMPLE

Following is a sample run of the program named **odd_example.**

```
Enter an integer -- 14 ——— user input in bold; mark for print vendor for
 14 is an even number.     this text to print in color
```

Figure 11–8. Annotated reference page

Here's a brief generic list of what to check on reference pages. You'll need to adapt this list to the book you're editing.

- Consistency: indentations, fonts, punctuation (especially use of colons to introduce items and periods at the end of items), capitalization

- Names of commands and parameters that appear in several places on the page (or elsewhere in the book): consistent spelling and capitalization

- Repeating heads: consistent wording, capitalization, fonts

- Repeating phrases and sentences: consistent wording, capitalization, punctuation

- Line spacing

- Order of elements on the page

- Cross-references

- Completeness: are all items included?

- Placement of examples: do examples consistently precede or follow the text that discusses them?

TIP: Watch for little changes that are made in one place but not another. For example, if the spelling of a command name is changed, make sure that the index slug is changed, too.

Let's look at some sample reference pages and the elements that need to be checked for consistency.

EXAMPLE

COVELLITE

    KEYS: Metallic luster. Can mark paper. Blue color.
Streak: Gray or black. **Cleavage:** 1 direction.
Specific Gravity: 4.6–4.8 (medium weight).

    Illustration of specimen, pointing out salient characteristics. (Example: Indigo blue.
Turns purple when wet. Often iridescent tarnish. Cleaves into thin flexible plates.)
Details about its discovery, where it can be found, origin of its name.

GALENA

    KEYS: Metallic luster. Can mark paper. Gray or black color.
Streak: Lead-gray. **Cleavage:** 3 directions.
Specific Gravity: 7.4–7.6 (heavy).

    Illustration of specimen, pointing out salient characteristics.
Details about its discovery, where it can be found, origin of its name.

This reference guide helps you identify a particular rock or mineral.[1] The author organized the reference pages by the properties of the minerals. For example, he grouped all the minerals with metallic luster together, followed by those with nonmetallic luster. After you've identified the luster, you look at other properties. Can it mark paper? Can it be scratched with a knife? Can it scratch glass?

The properties are in boldface. Every item ends in a period. Specific gravity is given as a range, with the numbers separated by an en dash. Weight is in parentheses, and expressed as light, medium weight, heavy, or very heavy. (I don't know if there is significance to *medium weight* instead of simply *medium*, but if I were editing this book I'd check.) Heads (*Specific Gravity*) are initial capped, but text (*Can mark paper*) isn't. A detail to note on the style sheet is the spelling of *gray.*

---

[1] Pearl, Richard M., *How to Know the Minerals and Rocks*
(NY: Signet, 1955) , pp. 56–57.

A consistent format helps readers move from one subject to the other. Readers don't have to waste time deciphering the organization and adjusting to the style on every page. The following example from a cookbook shows a consistent format.[1] In this book, every vegetable starts with a head in this form:

Name of vegetable
Other names it is known by (if applicable)
Its Latin name (if applicable)

EXAMPLE

OKRA
Gumbo
`Hibiscus esculentus`

The next paragraph or several describes the vegetable: its different varieties, where it is found, how it looks, and how it tastes.

The details — everything you want to know about the vegetable, but not necessarily at once — are included under the following heads:

How to Buy

How to Keep

Nutritive Values

How to Use

The entry concludes with a few recipes using that vegetable.

---

[1] Hazelton, Nika, *The Unabridged Vegetable Cookbook* (NY: Bantam, 1980).

TIP: Don't make readers guess terms. Check that common synonyms are listed in the index. If the topics are brief, then include pointers directly in the text. (See the following example.[1])

EXAMPLE

Graphite. See "Pencil" in "Stains," p. 235.

Grass Stains. See "Grass, Flowers, Foliage" in "Stains," p. 229.

Gravy Stains. See "Stains," p. 229.

Grease Stains. See "Grease and Oil" in "Stains," p. 229. See also "Furniture" and "Wallpaper."

Gum. See "Chewing Gum," p. 226, and "Resins," p. 236, in "Stains."

Gum Arabic. A material obtained from plants, which is used to stiffen laces, veils, etc. For directions, see "Starch and Special Finishes."

Gum Tragacanth. Another material from plants, used instead of starch for finishing certain materials. See "Starch and Special Finishes."

If you were reading this book from cover to cover, you'd probably find these cross-references annoying. In this context, however, the cross-references are quite helpful. If the author had not included all these *See* and *See also* references, readers would have to think of their own synonyms to see where the author hid the information. Or worse, readers would assume the book didn't have the answer and go to another book.

If your readers can't get the information they need from your books, they'll call your company's customer service department.

If you were the writer and had gone to the trouble of writing about a subject, you'd want to make sure readers can find it. As the editor, you help the writer as well as the reader by suggesting alternative listings and cross-references.

Glossaries

A glossary is a list of difficult or specialized words with their definitions. Check that glossaries you edit include all the words that need to be explained. Conversely, check that the glossary isn't padded with extraneous terms.

---

[1] Moore, Alma Chestnut, *How to Clean Everything* (NY: Simon and Schuster, 1977), p. 103.

Alphabetizing the Entries

Check that the writer used a consistent style for alphabetizing the glossary entries. Here are two different styles.

Word-by-word style:
Clock cycle
Clock pulses
Clock rate
Clocked flip-flop
Clocking

Letter-by-letter style ignores the spaces between words:
Clock cycle
Clocked flip-flop
Clocking
Clock pulses
Clock rate

You may follow either style, but whichever you choose, follow it consistently in both the glossary and the index.

Capitalizing the Entries

Some glossaries capitalize each entry. If you're editing software manuals, you may have several terms that must be case correct. For example, many computer terms are always lowercase; it's incorrect to capitalize them, even for a glossary entry.

Defining Acronyms and Abbreviations

Include acronyms and abbreviations according to either their spelled-out form or shortened form, depending on how the term is better known in the field. Put a *See* cross-reference where you list the other form.

For example, BASIC, although an acronym (Beginner's All-purpose Symbolic Instruction Code), should be listed under *BASIC,* as it's commonly known, not *Beginner's.* FORTRAN originated as an abbreviation for Formula Translation, but everybody knows it as *FORTRAN.* Likewise, radar (radio detecting and ranging), scuba (self-contained underwater breathing apparatus), and sima (silica magnesium) are recognized words, no longer mere acronyms, so each should be listed in its acronym form. ECO (engineering change order) is not widely known, so list it under its spelled-out form.

TIP: Another rule of thumb: If you typically pronounce the acronym or abbreviation (*scuzzy* as opposed to *S-C-S-I*), define it under SCSI with a cross-reference to its spelled-out form. Here are some more examples: List ASCII (pronounced *asky*), HUD, and NASA in the glossary under the acronym, with cross-references from their spelled-out forms.

Defining the Terms

Good glossaries describe, define, and give context to the terms:

EXAMPLE

Application program   A program written for or by a user that applies to the user's work. In networking terms, a program used to connect and communicate with stations in a network, enabling users to perform application-oriented activities.

The phrase, "in networking terms" gives context; it distinguishes the term as used in this book from its other meanings.

Here are some more examples:

EXAMPLES

Opaque. *In photoengraving and offset-lithography,* to paint out areas on a negative not wanted on the plate. *In paper,* the property which makes it less transparent.

Page makeup. *In stripping,* assembly of all elements to make up a page. *In phototypesetting,* the electronic assembly of page elements to compose a complete page with all elements in place on a video display terminal and on the phototypesetter.[1]

Making Cross-References

Add synonyms to the glossary if readers may recognize one term but not another. For example:

impulse   Synonym for *pulse.*

---

[1] *Pocket Pal,* Twelfth Edition (NY: International Paper Company, 1979).

Note that *pulse* is in italics because it's a separate entry. Some glossaries use boldface, small caps, or other techniques to denote terms defined elsewhere in the glossary.

spine   See *backbone.*

pasteup   Same as *mechanical.*

Use *See* references for entries that are phrases, to point to the main entry. For example:

Transmission gain   See *gain.*

Use *See also* or *Contrast with* references for terms that have related but not synonymous entries:

artificial intelligence[1]
(1) The capability of a device to perform *functions* that are normally associated with human intelligence, such as reasoning, learning, and self-improvement. (2) See also *machine learning.*

Indexes

This section discusses what to watch for when you *edit* an index. If you need to create an index, you'll need to know much more detail. (I recommend attending a workshop instead of just reading about indexing.)

Test the index to see how useful it is. Look up items as you think a reader would. Think of what concepts, topics, and tasks a reader would look up in the index, and see if the index has entries for them. Check that entries point to significant information, not passing references.

Make sure the index includes every procedure or task a user might want to do. Make sure it covers every part of the product that the user sees. For computer software, these items include all the commands, options, and selections on dialog boxes. For machines of any kind, these include all switches, buttons, cables, dials, levers, gauges, lights, and other parts the user manipulates, reads, or sees.

TIP: Pick a few topics and think of all the ways you might search for them. If there aren't index entries for your test words, there might not be for others.

---

[1] *American National Dictionary for Information Processing, X3/TR-1-77* (Washington, D.C.: Computer and Business Equipment Manufacturers Association, 1977).

Think of synonyms for main entries and ask the writer to include those in the index. For example, the user's guide for one electronic publishing software program does not include *delete* or *remove* as a main entry; you have to know to look under *cut,* the command name. (If users already knew the command, why would they be looking it up in the index?)

Similarly, if readers might look up *carriage return,* a term that doesn't actually appear in the manual, indicate that the writer needs to include the entry:

Carriage return   *See* RETURN key

Check that entries are in alphabetical order, based on the first significant word. "Noise words," such as *and, of,* and *with,* are typically ignored when alphabetizing. Follow a consistent alphabetizing method, either letter-by-letter or word-by-word, but don't intermix the styles in a single index. (See "Glossaries" earlier in this chapter for information on these styles of alphabetizing.)

Ensure that entries are consistently worded and punctuated. Proofread for typos, indentation errors, inconsistencies, and incorrect page sequence. The page numbers should increase, reading from left to right. For example:

      wolf, 9, 12, 56, 82 (correct)
      wolverine, 14, 34, 8, 3 (incorrect)

Make sure columns break between main entries (when possible). Repeat the entry name at the top of the new column.

Check for duplicate entries and similarly worded entries that ought to be listed as one. For example, the following entries should be combined into one:

compiling, 8–8
compiles, 8–8
compile, 8–7
  in C, 8–9

Suggest ways to break long entries into subentries to make it easier for the reader to find a specific reference. For example:

EXAMPLES

Bad example:

wolves, 2, 18, 36, 44, 57, 89, 93–114, 256

Good example:

wolves,
    breeding habits, 36
    danger of extinction, 93–114
    feeding habits, 44, 57, 89
    howling, 2, 18
    sleeping habits, 256

Add *See* and *See also* cross-references, as appropriate. Check that *See* and *See also* references point to actual entries. Also check that *See also* references lead to additional information and not the same information under a different head.

Alphabetical Order

List symbols separately, at the beginning of the index. Also list special characters under their spelled-out name (for example, *ampersand, backslash, asterisk*). If a character is commonly known by more than one name (such as *pound sign* and *number sign* for #), include the synonyms and provide *See* references to the main entry.

Software terms sometimes have symbols as the first character, such as *%include* or *#define*. To help users find the entry, list these terms both under Symbols and as if they were normal words. For example, put *%include* alphabetically where *include* would go if the % weren't there.

Include acronyms under both the acronym form and the spelled-out form. If the acronym is more common than the spelled-out name, make the acronym entry the main entry and also spell out the full term in parentheses.

EXAMPLE

VFR (Visual Flight Rules), 3–2, 3–11 to 3–15

Visual Flight Rules *See* VFR.

Checking Page Numbers

Somebody has to do it.

Checking Computer-Generated Indexes

There are two types of computer-generated indexes. Some computer programs—mostly old ones—list every word used in the manual and the page numbers where each occurs. By "every word," I mean *every* word: prepositions, articles, adjectives, and other words that nobody looks up. That's not what I consider an index.

The computer-generated indexes to which I refer are those in which a real person (usually a writer, sometimes an editor or a professional indexer) decides what entries belong in the index, tags the references in text, annotates the entries, and determines the hierarchy of entries (entries, subentries) according to their context. The computer generates the index only in the mechanical sense: It sorts the entries and subentries alphabetically, prints the correct page references for each, and (sometimes) formats it neatly.

When you edit an index, keep in mind the less-than-ideal circumstances under which the writer may have created it:

- Many writers haven't had any training in preparing an index.

- Most writers don't have much time to do the index. Many schedules don't allocate time specifically for the index; the writer is expected to just "fit it in."

- Many writers leave it to the last minute, because they have more pressing—and more interesting—things to do.

- Many writers put in the tags (sometimes called *flags* or *tokens*) on the fly. (They read the book on the computer screen and add tags as they go along.)

- Many writers don't put in enough tags because there's never enough time.

- Some writers put in tags by strictly following the text. As a result, the index might have entries for all the details but not for the general topic.

- Most indexing software doesn't let the writer see all the entries at once. It's very difficult even for consistency-minded writers to maintain consistency. (Some writers solve this problem by planning their indexes on index cards or with outliner software.)

Don't assume the index is comprehensive or carefully thought out just because the writer used a computer. Edit the content of the index as thoroughly as you would edit one created any other way. The advice given earlier in this section applies to computer-generated indexes, too.

TIP: If writers say they can't edit the entries because the computer generated the index, don't just take their word. Learn how to create an index with the software they're using—maybe they just don't know how. (Teach them if necessary.)

If the index has been generated by computer, you don't have to check every page number, but you should check for gross errors. Usually computer errors are big ones; instead of one or two page numbers being wrong, *all* the page numbers will be wrong. (This kind of error probably indicates that the index is out of date.) The most common error is the omission of entries from an entire chapter. Another common error is that all the page numbers are in only one or two chapters. Check that every chapter and appendix has at least one entry. Spot check the page numbers for each chapter and appendix; I usually check an entry at the beginning, middle, and end of each chapter. If you find *any* errors, assume the entire index is inaccurate and have the writer rerun the indexing program.

TIP: Some indexing programs sort by ASCII value. The ASCII character set lists A–Z separately from a–z. As a result, *Wolf* would precede *weevil* and *wolf* in an index sorted by ASCII value. The program probably has an option to sort in "real" alphabetical order, but the writer may need to specify it.

Text Heads

Make sure the writer has used informative, descriptive, and parallel text heads. Do you have any doubt about what will be discussed under the following heads?

EXAMPLE

Preparing to Unpack and Install
Unpacking the System Unit and Monitor
Installing the System Component Boards
Connecting the System Unit and Monitor
Connecting to the Apollo Token Ring Network
Connecting to the 802.3 Network
Setting Up the Partner Node—Diskless Systems
Booting the Workstation
Booting the Server
Testing Operation

Here's another good example:

EXAMPLE

Seven Keys to Recognizing Minerals
Mineral Key No. 1 Luster
Mineral Key No. 2 Hardness
Mineral Key No. 3 Color
Mineral Key No. 4 Streak
Mineral Key No. 5 Cleavage
Mineral Key No. 6 Fracture
Mineral Key No. 7 Specific Gravity

Exercise 19   Capitalize the following head:

how to change a tire

Here are some examples of nonparallel heads:

EXAMPLE

Brightness
Setting the Time
Setting the Alarms

Tuning the Radio
Radio Volume
Presetting Your Radio Stations
Using Presets
Antenna

Answer Machine ON/OFF
Recording Your Greeting
To Check Your Greeting

Here are some inconsistent heads:

EXAMPLE

The Experiments on the Contact Operations

The Main Results of the Contact Operations

       Contact Resistance

        The light colored specimen

Breaking of the Nickel Oxide Layer

Check that heads aren't absurdly long:

EXAMPLE

Once Your PC Ring Connection Arrives, Do You Have All of These Supplied Parts?

Also check that heads are meaningful. The following example, from the operating instructions for an answering machine, makes you wonder if the manufacturer expects some people to use the device as a toaster:

EXAMPLE

Main head: **Operating the Unit**

Subhead: Operation as an answering machine

In addition to checking for parallelism of form, check for consistency of capitalization.

Many technical manuals have heads that are numbered to reflect the hierarchy of the text. This system is called *decimalization* or *weighted decimal system* and the sequence is: 1.1, 1.1.1, 1.1.2, 1.1.3, 1.2, 1.3, etc. (How you or I feel about this system is irrelevant; your house style will mandate or forbid its use, based on the expectations of your audience.)

Even when the numbering is computer-generated, check the sequence.

TRICK: If you can generate a table of contents on the computer, do so with the first draft. Then you can check all the text heads in a book for consistency at a single glance. It's much easier to skim a single listing than to turn all the pages in the book to review the heads. This trick is especially useful for checking numbered heads (weighted decimal system).

There's a rule, and a good rule at that, governing the balance of heads. The rule says that at least two subheads must follow a head. Whenever possible, follow this guideline for documents with clear organization and hierarchy of information. However, when the book reflects the organization of the product, and the product's design didn't take this balance into account, it's OK to accept some imbalance. You don't need to go through contortions just to make the heads balance.

For example, the book described below is easy to use even though there are at least two sections with single subheads. The writer might have combined the two single subheads under "Finding and Replacing Text," but that would not have made the product easier to use.

EXAMPLE

Editing
        To insert text
        To insert a picture
        To insert blank lines
        To remove with Cut from the Edit menu
        To remove with the Backspace key
        To remove a Return character
        To replace a selection
Finding Text
        To search for characters
Finding and Replacing Text
        To find and replace

Trademarks

Editors are expected to know how to use and denote trademarks. There is more to handling trademarks than putting a ® or ™ in the text.

A trademark is a name, symbol, word (or group of words) that identifies a specific product of a particular company.

It is the obligation of the owner of the trademark to protect it. (It's *your* job to check trademarks in publications you edit.)

To protect a trademark, you must use it properly. Trademarks can be lost through misuse. Misuse occurs when the trademark loses its association with a specific product and becomes a generic name. For example, *kerosene, mimeograph, escalator,* and *cellophane* were once trademarks.

Your company will have a specific policy regarding how to acknowledge its own trademarks and those of other companies. A trademark can be *registered* with the United States Patent and Trademark Office, in which case it is denoted by a ®. A trademark that is claimed but not registered is denoted by a ™. Verify with your company's lawyers which of your products are trademarks and which are registered trademarks. (Don't trust the marketing or engineering departments for information about trademarks.) Also, ask the lawyers which products of other companies you should acknowledge in text and how.

The policies vary immensely from company to company. Some companies use the ® or ™ symbols with their own *and* other companies' products, some use the symbols for their *own* products only, and some don't use the symbols at all. Some use an asterisk or other symbol in the text and footnote the acknowledgment; others list all trademark acknowledgments on the copyright page. Some companies acknowledge trademarks of others only where required to by contract—or when threatened by lawsuits.

You need to check with your company's lawyers for the specifics, but here are some general guidelines:

- Use trademarks as adjectives, not as nouns. A trademark modifies the product category (Vaseline petroleum jelly, Macintosh computer, Crayola crayons). The product category should be in lowercase, so that it doesn't compete with the trademark for prominence. For emphasis, use the word *brand*, as in BAND-AID brand bandages.

- Spell a trademark according to how it's registered. For example, if the product's official name is all caps, spell it in all caps *all the time.* If the trademark is registered in a particular typeface or style (such as italics), take care to display it accordingly.

- Make sure it's clear who owns the trademark—a concern when there are references to your own companies' trademarks and those of other companies in the same document.

Remember, a trademark is an adjective, not a noun, so these additional guidelines apply:

- Don't use a trademark as a possessive. *Wrong:* Crayola's new colors.

- Don't use a trademark as verb. *Wrong:* The kids had fun MacPainting.

- Don't use a trademark as a plural. *Wrong:* Remember to bring the BAND-AIDs.

One Last Trick

You have two nearly identical versions of a page and want to find the difference(s) without reading them character by character. Put one on top of the other and hold them up to a strong light. (If you have an artist's light table, lay them flat on the table, one on top of the other.) Align the type. Watch for irregular areas—where one page has more or fewer characters than the other. You should be able to spot discrepancies very quickly.

How to Improve Your Skimming Powers

The ability to skim a page and zoom in on errors is the greatest magic trick an editor can perform. What's magical is the time it will save you. Some people have an innate ability to spot patterns. If you haven't been so blessed, there are some exercises you can do to train your brain.

- Go on a timed typo hunt. Take a manuscript you haven't edited yet and practice looking only for typos. Impose a time limit of ten seconds per page. Circle all typos you find on a page within the time limit and move on to the next page. Gradually—over a period of months and practicing on different manuscripts—reduce the time until you have only one second per page.

- Circle all occurrences of a common word—such as *the* or *of*—in a magazine or newspaper article under time limits.

- Solve crossword and other word puzzles (on your own time, of course) that depend on recognizing patterns. If you don't think you use pattern-matching skills to solve crosswords, answer this: Where would you find the letters *mtst* in consecutive order?[1]

- Skim lists for names you recognize. When you receive a mailing from a charity or political organization listing sponsors or a membership directory, skim—don't read—the list and see if any familiar names leap out at you. Every year my local newspaper prints the names of runners entered in the Boston Marathon, contributors to Christmas funds, and people who have unclaimed bank accounts. I set a target for myself (such as find 5 familiar names in 30 seconds) to keep in practice.

- Skim your regional telephone directory for numbers with your local exchange.

- Circle all occurrences of items in a particular class. For example, find the names of all countries in a newsmagazine. This exercise requires you to skim and interpret. The skill comes in handy if you need to change all command names to boldface (you'll need to find them and identify them as commands) or if you need to capitalize all first-level heads—all without reading the text.

- Solve the kinds of visual puzzles you did as a child. (These puzzles were intended to prepare you to learn to read.) For example, a popular series of children's books hides a character named Waldo in an intricate illustration, such as a beach scene with hundreds of other people and their beach accoutrements. Solve other puzzles that let you practice your observational skills, such as "What's wrong with this picture?" or "How are these two pictures different?"

---

[1] Answer: Mt. St. Helens.

Summary

This chapter showed some editing tricks you can use. Refer to the books listed in the bibliography for more information about technical writing and general (nontechnical) editing.

If you edit computer manuals, read chapter 12 for more tips.

Chapter 12
Editing Computer Manuals

This chapter tells you what you need to know to edit a computer manual without making a fool of yourself. It assumes you don't know anything about programming. Read this chapter so you can make intelligent decisions.

This chapter looks at the following topics:

- Terminology
- Syntax
- Typographic conventions
- Programming examples (source code and pseudocode)
- System prompts and output
- Input
- Error, informational, and warning messages
- Editing for different kinds of computer users
- Reference pages
- Online documentation
- User interfaces

Because the computer industry comprises many subspecialties, and the technology in all areas is constantly evolving, we look only at the basics. This chapter gives you a foundation you can build on as you learn the terms and specific conventions of your technology—operating systems, networks and communications, database, graphics, languages, software engineering tools, hardware, or whatever your area.

Common Software Terms for the Nontechnical Technical Editor

Most editors don't consider the task of marking a manuscript to show what terms should be in boldface and what should be in italics to be especially challenging intellectually.

Exercise 20 illustrates that what appears to be a simple, low-level task requires you to know more about computers than you might expect. You at least need a solid grasp of the terminology. Try doing this exercise after you've read this section.

If you edit software manuals you'll need to understand the meaning of some common terms such as *command, option, argument,* and *variable.*

Even if you edit documentation for end users of computer applications, instead of programmers, you should understand the concepts and be conversant in the jargon. You may not use some of these terms on the projects you're working on today, but you may need to know them for later. You certainly need to know them to communicate with the programmers who develop the product. At the minimum, you need to keep pace with your users, who are becoming more sophisticated in computing every year.

Here's a mini-lesson for editors who have had only limited experience with computers. It assumes you have a basic knowledge of how to use a computer, but not much more. For example, it assumes you understand that a file or document holds data, that you can organize files into directories, and that you can manipulate files and directories in different ways; for example, you can copy, move, name, and rename them. (If these terms and concepts are new to you, take an introductory computer course or read a book for new computer users.)

The terms defined in this section are those you need to know regardless of your computer specialty; you'll have to supplement your education with the specialized terms for your particular field. For example, if you edit manuals for networking products, you should know what a command is; you'll also have to learn other terms, such as *protocol, transfer,* and *bandwidth.*

Command

A *command* is an instruction to the computer. The syntax of a command specifies how to enter the command: exactly what information to type and in what order, if order matters.

Exercise 20 The house style guide you've been given says to put keywords, commands, options, literals, and pathnames in bold, and to put user-supplied arguments in italics. Applying these guidelines, mark the following examples for bold and italics. (Hint: Read the next few pages before trying this exercise.)

1. mv old_file new_file[1]

2. ln –s //node/domain_examples/pascal_examples/getpas dir/getpas where node is the name of the disk where the examples are stored and dir is the name of a directory in your path.

3. Use the in operator to determine if exp is an element in setexp.

4. Compile a Domain Pascal source code file by entering the following command:
   pas source_pathname [option1 . . . optionN]
   where:
   source_pathname is the pathname of the source file you want to compile. We recommend that source_pathname end with a .pas suffix.

5. For example, the following commands compile source code file circles.pas:
   pas circles
   pas circles –l
   pas circles –map –exp –cond –cpu 3000[1]

6. The reserved words begin and end establish the limits of a sequence of Pascal statements. You must use a begin/end pair to indicate a compound statement.

Option

Sometimes you can give even more explicit instructions with a command; you do that by specifying *options.* Options let you modify or fine-tune a command. Although it may sound like an oxymoron, there are indeed *required options* for some commands in some programs (on some operating systems). Specifying a required option is like buying an ice cream cone. You can't just ask for "ice cream" at Baskin Robbins; you must specify a flavor. Likewise, you can't always tell a computer to execute a particular command; sometimes you have to specify which variation you want. Not all commands have options—just as some places (like the company cafeteria) don't give you a choice of flavors.

---

[1] There isn't a period at the end of this line because it's a command line, not a grammatical sentence. A period would change the technical meaning.

Default

A *default* option is what a program does if you don't specify anything else.

Argument and Required Option

Sometimes it's not even enough to tell the computer what *to do*; you also have to tell it what thing to *do it to* or *with*. For example, you can't just tell a computer to copy a file. The machine can't read your mind; you have to tell it what file to copy. You may even have to tell it where to copy it to or what name to give the new file. The name of the file to copy, the place to copy it to, and the name for the new file are all *arguments* you supply when you give the command.

Argument and *required option* are nearly synonymous. *Argument* usually refers to data supplied by the user (such as a name, number, filename), while a *required option* usually refers to something that has already been defined and that you could look up in the manual, such as the **–all** option to the **disk_copy** command. Arguments that the user supplies are called *user-supplied arguments*. Examples of user-supplied arguments are *old_file* and *new_file* in item 1 of exercise 20.

Value

A *value* is a specific number, letter, or string that a variable or argument represents.

String

A *string* is a collection of letters, numbers, or symbols treated as a single unit, such as *abcd* or *wolf* or *3 Dog Night* or *w!#34Gx%*.

Program

A *program* is a set of instructions to the computer. A computer solves problems by manipulating the contents of its memory. Here's a simplified example. A computer adds two numbers by taking the value in one memory location and adding it to the value in another memory location. It's easier to write and read programs using symbolic values for memory locations instead of specifying the locations themselves. (Memory locations have easy-to-remember names like 40F7A734.)

Variable

If you were writing a program that took the test scores of all the students in a class and divided the total score by the number of students in the class to get the class average, you would find it easier to use symbolic names, such as *test_score*, and to write something like this

(*test_score* + *test_score* + . . . + *test_score*) divided by *number_of_students*
than to write its equivalent in the computer's machine language.

In this example, *test_score* and *number_of_students* are names you've assigned to the locations in memory that store that information. (This definition is oversimplified, but true.) The technical term for this symbolic name is a *variable*. It's called a variable because its content varies; the value of *test_score* changes for each student.

This use of *variable* mirrors how you used it in high school algebra. For example, to solve the equation *distance* = *rate* x *time,* you would substitute different values (numbers) for *rate* and *time* and solve for *distance.* The values of *rate* and *time* varied with each homework problem. In a computer program, the value of a variable may differ each time someone runs the program or even when the program is being run. For example, we would run the program once to calculate the average test score for the class. But even during that one time that we run the program, the value of *test_score* changes for each student.

Literal

A *literal* is a *constant* (unchanging) value, such as text within quotation marks (`"Enter your password-"`) or a number.

Keyword

A *keyword* has a predefined meaning, and often cannot be used in a program or command line in any other way. An example of a keyword common to many programming languages is **while**; in those languages a programmer could not use **while** as a name for a variable.

Parameter

Another useful—but fuzzier—term is *parameter.* Depending on the circumstances, a parameter can be an option, an argument, or—its original meaning—a limit. Here are some ways the term is used: "If you use the **delete** command without any parameters, it will default to . . . " or "The C language passes parameters to subroutines by value, not reference" or "The *value* parameter specified a bad address." You can also refer to "environmental parameters."

Now that we've covered these basic concepts and terms, let's tackle the difficult situations in the next section.

Syntax

English language syntax has conventions that govern the way we order parts of speech. For example, "She to me the book gave" is faulty English syntax, although appropriate in some other languages.

Computer programs expect to receive commands that follow a particular syntax. Computer languages also have detailed syntactic rules.

See figure 12–1 for an example of what syntax looks like—for an operating system command and for a programming language statement. (Don't bother to decipher these examples.)

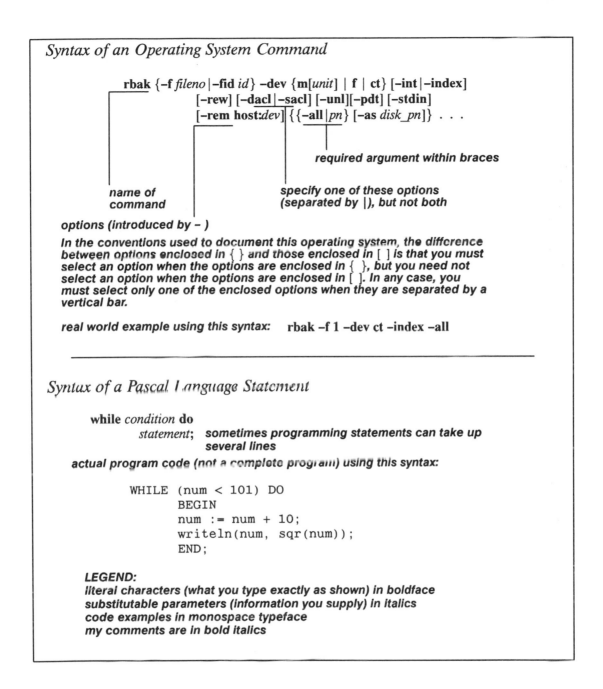

Syntax of an Operating System Command

rbak {**-f** *fileno* | **-fid** *id*} **-dev** {**m**[*unit*] | **f** | **ct**} [**-int** | **-index**]
[**-rew**] [**-dacl** | **-sacl**] [**-unl**][**-pdt**] [**-stdin**]
[**-rem host**:*dev*] {{**-all** | *pn*} [**-as** *disk_pn*]} . . .

required argument within braces

**name of
command**

**specify one of these options
(separated by |), but not both**

options (introduced by –)

**In the conventions used to document this operating system, the difference
between options enclosed in { } and those enclosed in [ ] is that you must
select an option when the options are enclosed in { }, but you need not
select an option when the options are enclosed in [ ]. In any case, you
must select only one of the enclosed options when they are separated by a
vertical bar.**

real world example using this syntax: rbak **-f** 1 **-dev** ct **-index** **-all**

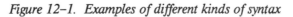

Syntax of a Pascal Language Statement

while *condition* **do**
  statement; **sometimes programming statements can take up
        several lines**

actual program code (not a complete program) using this syntax:

```
WHILE (num < 101) DO
      BEGIN
      num := num + 10;
      writeln(num, sqr(num));
      END;
```

LEGEND:
literal characters (what you type exactly as shown) in boldface
substitutable parameters (information you supply) in italics
code examples in monospace typeface
my comments are in bold italics

Figure 12–1. Examples of different kinds of syntax

Here are some examples of syntax from the C, Pascal, and KornShell computer languages, with boldface used for literal keywords and italics used for symbolic values. (For example, the programmer would substitute some actual code where *statement1* appears in the syntax definition.)

EXAMPLES

C Language:

      if (*expression*)
      statement1;
      else
      statement2;

Pascal Language:
if *condition* **then** *statement*;

KornShell Language:
if *condition*
then
      command1
      . . .
      [*commandN*]
else
      command1
      . . .
      [*commandN*]
fi

Exercise 21   Break the rules!

What typographical rule is broken in the preceding example—intentionally and correctly—to avoid technical ambiguity?

Common Typographic Conventions

Back in the ancient days before writers could distinguish words typographically (different typefaces, boldface, italics)—the same old days when programmers had only line printers for output—computer documentation used symbols available on every keyboard to show commands, options, required options, and the like. The symbols available included the various punctuation marks and other characters, such as \, |, <, >, {, }, [, and].

Technical writing today isn't as constrained as it used to be. Most manuals use typographic variety to convey information. Some manuals use color to highlight special items, such as commands, user input, or system output.

Many of the old conventions are still used for online documentation (since not all computers can display different fonts) and are even still in some companies' printed manuals.

The conventions your company uses will probably differ, but let's look at some examples. Browse through this section to see the diversity of conventions, but don't try to learn them all.

TIP: You should conclude from the diversity of these examples that there is no single correct way in the computer industry to express syntax. Even common symbols such as { } and [ ] can have many different meanings. Follow the conventions for your company's products. Tell your readers what conventions you're using. Tell them at the beginning of the book (in the front matter or in chapter 1) and, if necessary, where you apply the convention.

Command Names

Here are some ways command names have been displayed:

EXAMPLES

Distinguished by case (uppercase or lowercase):
```
QUIT date
```

Distinguished typographically:
quit <u>login:</u> **SAVE** *print* `bye`

User-Supplied Parameters

Here are some ways user-supplied parameters have been displayed:

EXAMPLES

In angle brackets:
```
cpf <old_file> <new_file>
```

Following the command, with no special notation:
```
EDLIN filespec
```

In italics:
cpf *old_file new_file*

Optional Parameters

Use when users *may* specify one parameter (or maybe more), but don't have to specify any. Here are some examples:

EXAMPLES

In braces or square brackets (depending on the program):
```
[-pdt ] [-conv ]
{ -date }  { -size }  { -blocks }
```

Required Parameters

Use when users *must* specify one parameter. Here are some examples:

EXAMPLES

In brackets:

[disk | cartape | magtape]

In this example, the default option is underlined. The default option is what the system uses if no option is specified.

Some systems do the same thing, using braces instead of brackets:

{disk | ctape | mtape}

In this example, the default option is underlined.

Grouping

When choices are grouped together inside braces, brackets, or parentheses, that usually means the choices are mutually exclusive. Here are some examples:

EXAMPLES

In the following example, the user can specify –date or –size or –blocks or none of these parameters:

ld [–date | –size | –blocks]

If you wanted to show that the user could specify any number or combination of these options, here is how you'd group the options:

ld [–date] [–size] [–blocks]

Sometimes the selections are displayed vertically:

$$\begin{Bmatrix} \text{–STATUS} \\ \text{–DISPLAY} \end{Bmatrix}$$

In angle brackets, with parameters separated by a vertical bar:

MODE LPT<1:|2:|3:>=COM<1|2>

In parentheses:

ASSIGN device MT(0-7)

Literal Text

There are different ways to show literal text—exactly what the user types, what the programmer writes into the code, or what the system displays as a prompt or as output. The editor has to understand which are syntax requirements and which are documentation conventions, and must ensure that the distinction is clear to users.

Here are some examples:

EXAMPLES

In single quotation marks:

```
The program prompts, 'Enter your next move.'
```

In double quotation marks:

```
The program responds, "Checkmate."
```

In a different typeface:

```
The program responds: Checkmate.
```

TIP: Do not edit literal text, no matter how "wrong" it looks. Do not change the spelling, capitalization, or punctuation of literal text.

Let's say a manual you're editing has a programming example that refers to these programming calls:

- **db_$SET_Type_identifier**
- **db_$Field_Type_identifier**
- **db_$Record_type_identifier**

You may be tempted to make the capitalization consistent (put *$SET* in initial caps only and capitalize *type* in the third item). These items *are* inconsistent—but that's how they appear in the software code and that's how other programs recognize them, so that's how they should appear in the manual.

Work with the programmers to ensure consistency in parts of the program that users see. If the programmers don't change the code in the program, however, don't change the spelling in the manual. The manual and the program *must* match.

Some Other Conventions

Here are some other conventions that have been used in computer documentation:

EXAMPLES

Underlining prompts:

```
SEQUENCE DATA ON -- DEPT-CODE
MORE? LAST-NAME
```

Change of typeface to indicate instructions for the user to follow:

The following instructions typically apply to most terminal types. First **turn on the power** for the terminal. **Pick up the handset** of the telephone for your terminal and listen for a dial tone. Then **dial one of the computer's time sharing telephone numbers.**

Change of typeface to indicate commands:

Type `cat chapter1` to display the contents of the file.

(If you find the two typefaces in this example too similar to entrust with the important task of distinguishing technical information, I'm on your side. Yet many technical manuals use cues this subtle.)

Apostrophe to indicate symbolic (nonliteral, substitutable) value:

```
'abc 'value1
```

Apostrophe to indicate base or radix (as in binary, octal, or hexadecimal):

```
'11414 (octal)
```

Parentheses to enclose function arguments (nearly a standard, from mathematical origins):

$\cosh(x)$ $\log(x)$ $\mathrm{mod}(x1, x2)$ $\mathrm{pi}()$

TIP: There are many, many conventions. The way they taught you in your last job isn't the only way. What's best for your documentation depends on your products, your users, and your equipment.

Challenges in Command Line Syntax

Commands for personal computer applications are relatively short and simple. Commands for system software, particularly for programs developed for software engineers, are typically more exotic.

Writing and editing documentation for commands becomes a special challenge when

- The commands contain a potpourri of special characters. The challenge is to distinguish unambiguously which symbols are literal values (those a user actually types) and which are symbolic values.

- The commands allow numerous permutations of options and arguments. The challenge is to reduce the complexity of the software.

Commands with Special Characters

Technical clarity is a particular concern when programs use periods, quotation marks, colons, and other punctuation marks as part of the commands themselves. Some writers treat the punctuation marks as embarrassing relatives—if they don't call attention to them, maybe nobody will notice. Granted, these characters can make commands look downright ugly, but you can save the reader considerable hassle by pointing them out.

When introducing a command that includes punctuation marks or other symbols, mention this use in the text. In the following examples, the use of double quotes is explicitly called out, even though the programmers for whom the documentation is written would probably understand that the quotation marks are significant. (You can never be too clear.)

EXAMPLES

find *pathname* **–name** **"*.old"** **–print**
This command finds pathnames that have the suffix "**.old**." Double quotes are needed so the **find** command evaluates the metacharacter and doesn't pass it to the shell.

---

grep –i "perfect binding" printing_info
This command finds occurrences of the phrase "perfect binding" in a file called **printing_info**. The double quotes are required because the search string includes a blank space.

TIP: Some programs interpret single quotes and double quotes the same way, but many treat items in single quotes differently from items in double quotes. For clarity, say whether you mean single quotes or double quotes. Don't use the ambiguous term *quotes* or worse, the verb *quoted.* Don't say, "Special terms must be quoted"; say, "Enclose special terms in single (or double) quotation marks."

TIP: The following example emphasizes the period because users may overlook it, given its tiny size and placement at the end of the command.

EXAMPLE

cp *pathname* .
This command copies a file to the current directory, represented by a period (.).

Commands with Many Options

You need a large grammar to describe complex software programs and languages. Earlier in this chapter you saw some conventions for indicating what options are available and, of those, which are required. These conventions let you compress scads of data in a small space. Sometimes this shorthand is too condensed.

TRICK: Mitigate the complexity of a command by giving an overview of its syntax.

For example, here's another way to show the syntax for the moderately complex command shown in figure 12–1. In the following example, nearly twenty options have been replaced with the symbolic name, *options,* in the main description. The detailed list of options then follows.

EXAMPLE

rbak {**–f** *fileno* | **–fid** *id*} **–dev** {**m**[*unit*] | **f** | **ct**} [*options*] {{**–all** | *pn*} [**–as** *disk_pn*]} . . .

where *options* are

–dacl	**–sacl**	*(brackets may sometimes be omitted with a vertical list)*
–int	**–index**	*(description of these options in this column)*
–rew	
–stdin	

. . . [*and so on for the rest of the options*]

When you edit descriptions of command syntax, ask the writer if the order is significant; if not, you may want to suggest that the writer list them alphabetically or put related commands together.

Conflicts Between Software and Documentation Conventions

The documentation conventions must not conflict with the software conventions.

Sometimes quotation marks, parentheses, ellipses, braces, and brackets (among other characters) have special meaning in the software. If so, ensure that the meaning is preserved. For example, some programming languages use brackets to indicate arrays, as in **students[11]**. This use of brackets preempts any other use of brackets as a documentation convention in a book with examples in that programming language. You could use *very* different-looking brackets for different purposes, however. For example, you could use 10-pt brackets to show an array and 24-pt brackets for grouping.

students[11] (brackets for an array)

command $\left[\text{ source\_file1 source\_file2 source\_file3}\right]$ (brackets for grouping)

Remember to tell your readers what conventions you're using in the manual

---

Programming Examples

You may need to edit examples of *source code*—the actual lines of code a programmer writes—that appear in manuals. You won't be expected to correct the program itself, but you should check for inconsistencies between the program and the text that discusses it, as discussed in "Examples" in chapter 11. Also check for spelling and grammatical errors in the *comments,* the programmer's documentation about the program. If you know enough about the source code to judge, suggest ways to improve any cryptic comments.

The example should begin with the name of the program and a brief description of what it does. The program may have its own copyright notice and acknowledgments. Know your company's policy for printing these notices in the book that contains the sample programs and ensure that the policy is carried out. (If you're responsible for online documentation, learn the policy for online notices, too.)

Source code examples are usually typeset in a monospace (sometimes called *single-width* or *fixed-width*) typeface, sometimes for historical reasons (at one time computer displays and printers could only print monospace characters) and sometimes—for a few programming languages—because it's important to see how the code lines up in each column.

You can tell how many spaces there are between characters in a monospace typeface, but not in a proportional typeface. For example:

EXAMPLES

It's easy to line up text in a monospace typeface.

```
You can tell that there are four spaces
here:    and only two spaces here:  .
```

It's not as easy to line up text in a proportional typeface.

Can you tell that there are four spaces
here: and only two spaces here: ?

Comments in Programs

The comments programmers add to their code are part of the original computer documentation. A comment tells what each portion of code does. (A portion of code here can be a single line or dozens of lines.) Programmers write comments for themselves and other programmers. The comments tend to be terse, jargon-ridden, and cryptic.

In most cases, you won't be able to change anything other than spelling errors, because the listing shows the code itself. Unless some programmer is revising the code to ship with the manual, you won't have the opportunity to change the comment. (After all, you want the manual to match the product.)

If the writer or programmer wrote the examples for the manual itself, then you can probably influence him or her to make some changes in the comments. Keep in mind that the comments are for programmers, not end users, so they don't have to be user-cuddly. But they should be clear so that another programmer looking at the code can understand what each part of the program does.

How can you tell the code from the comments? Every programming language has at least one way to indicate a comment; some languages indicate comments different ways on different machines. (The reason comments are preceded by or enclosed within special characters is to tell the computer to ignore the comment and not execute it as an instruction.)

Here are some examples:

```
EXAMPLES

# This is a comment in UNIX shell scripting languages

/* A comment in the C programming language */

{ This is a comment in Pascal }

(* Another way to show a comment in Pascal *)

C A comment in FORTRAN; the C would be in column 1

REM This short form of "remark" indicates a comment in BASIC

** A comment in Macintosh BASIC **

NOTE This word starts a comment in COBOL; a period ends it.
```

How can you tell what the comment symbols are for a particular language? Read the manual. There are at least as many ways to indicate comments as there are programming languages. Sometimes it matters whether the comment is on the same line as the code (called an *inline comment*) or on a separate line. Some languages allow comments to continue over several lines (with or without repeating the comment indicator). Become familiar with the conventions for the language used in the manual you're editing. You may even catch a significant typo, such as a forgotten */ after a comment in a C program.

Exercise 22   Editing source code

Figure 12–2 shows an example of a correct Pascal source code listing. Using your powers of observation, find the errors I introduced into a similar example, figure 12–3. (Hint: There are ten inconsistencies—not necessarily errors—you should question. Finding four is good.) You do not need to know anything about programming to find these errors; you need only look for inconsistencies within the program itself. Answers are given in figure 12–4.

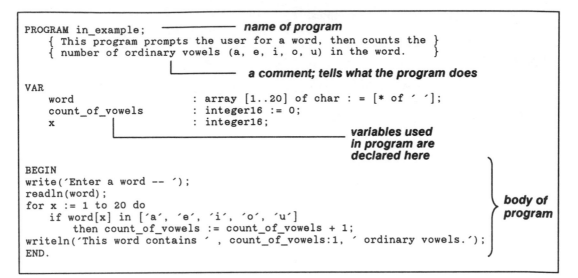

```
PROGRAM in_example;                         name of program
    { This program prompts the user for a word, then counts the }
    { number of ordinary vowels (a, e, i, o, u) in the word.    }

                                  a comment; tells what the program does
VAR
    word                         : array [1..20] of char : = [* of ´ ´];
    count_of_vowels              : integer16 := 0;
    x                            : integer16;
                                                 variables used
                                                 in program are
                                                 declared here
BEGIN
write('Enter a word -- ');
readln(word);
for x := 1 to 20 do
    if word[x] in ['a', 'e', 'i', 'o', 'u']
        then count_of_vowels := count_of_vowels + 1;
writeln('This word contains ' , count_of_vowels:1, ' ordinary vowels.');
END.
```

body of
program

Figure 12–2. A correct example in Pascal

```
PROGARM sqr_example;
   { This program demonstrates the use of the sqr function, }
   { which calculates the square of a specified number.     }


VAR
   i_short            : integer16;
   i_long             : integer32;
   r1, r2    : real;



BEGIN
   write('Enter an interger -- ');
   readln(i_short);
   i_long := sqr(i_short);
   Writeln('The square of ' , i_short:1, ' is ', i_long:1);

   write('Enter a real number -- ')
   readln r1);
   n2 := sqr(r1);
   writeln('The square of ', r1:1; ' is ', r2:1);
END
```

Figure 12–3. A Pascal example with many errors[1]

---

[1] Note to alert editors: Yes, this example is in a larger typeface, so you can read
it more easily when you do the exercise. The larger typeface is *not* one of the
errors.

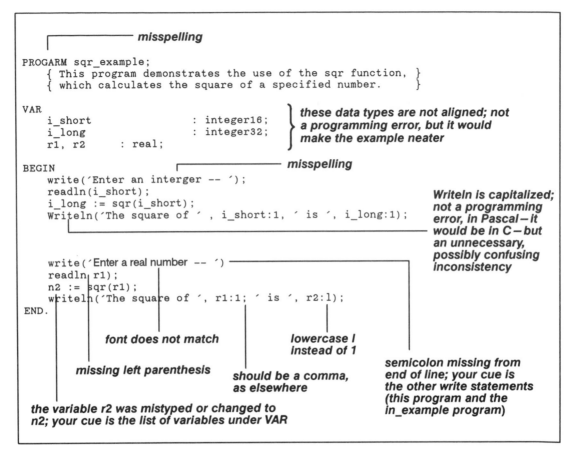

```
                     ┌──────── misspelling
PROGARM sqr_example;
    { This program demonstrates the use of the sqr function, }
    { which calculates the square of a specified number.     }

VAR
    i_short              : integer16;
    i_long               : integer32;
    r1, r2      : real;

BEGIN                            ┌──────────── misspelling
    write('Enter an interger -- ');
    readln(i_short);
    i_long := sqr(i_short);
    Writeln('The square of ' , i_short:1, ' is ', i_long:1);


    write('Enter a real number -- ')
    readln( r1);
    n2 := sqr(r1);
    writeln('The square of ', r1:1; ' is ', r2:1);
END.
```

misspelling (two labels)

these data types are not aligned; not a programming error, but it would make the example neater

Writeln is capitalized; not a programming error, in Pascal—it would be in C—but an unnecessary, possibly confusing inconsistency

font does not match

lowercase l instead of 1

missing left parenthesis

should be a comma, as elsewhere

semicolon missing from end of line; your cue is the other write statements (this program and the in_example program)

the variable r2 was mistyped or changed to n2; your cue is the list of variables under VAR

Figure 12–4. The Pascal program, annotated to show the errors the editor should catch

TIP: Sometimes when the text of source code examples is formatted, the reformatted text develops bad line breaks, such that program code that should be on one line is on two lines. Another result of bad line breaks is that the program's comments may need to have additional comment indicators. A tip-off that the text formatter may have changed the line breaks is a line of text that extends to the right margin (especially those followed by short lines of text). If you spot any such irregularities, let the writer know.

TIP: If the type specifications call for a sans serif typeface for examples in a computer book, look at a sample of the typeface to ensure that you can distinguish between 1 (one) and l (el) and between 0 (zero) and O (oh). These distinctions are important. If the typeface does not distinguish these characters clearly, flag the issue with the production department or designer. Lobby to have the type specs changed to ensure technical clarity.

When you edit examples of source code, in addition to checking the details shown in figure 12–4, make sure that any annotations or callouts that describe the code can be readily distinguished from the code itself. Use an obviously different typeface and, if your budget permits, print the callouts in color. Ensure that callouts are brief enough to fit without being cryptic.

Pseudocode

You may sometimes have to edit examples of *pseudocode.* As its name implies, pseudocode is not actual programming code, although it may look like it to a nonprogrammer. Let me tell you what pseudocode is and then I'll give you some clues to recognize it.

When you sit down to write a program in a procedural language like BASIC, C, COBOL, FORTRAN, or Pascal, the next-to-last step is writing the actual code. (The last step is spending the rest of your life debugging and tweaking it.) You first determine what problem the program will solve, devise a strategy (an *algorithm*) for solving it, and sketch out some pseudocode—an English-like equivalent for the steps the program will follow. Then you translate the pseudocode into a real programming language. (You may be familiar with a flowchart, which is a graphical form of pseudocode.)

Here's an example of pseudocode:

```
EXAMPLE

Ask the user to enter two numbers.

Check that what the user types is really two numbers.

If not, repeat directions.

Read those numbers.

Add the numbers.

Print the result.
```

You can recognize pseudocode because it looks a lot like English. It is English, in fact, although probably a shorthand form. You can tell it's not real code because it doesn't have any of the charming peculiarities of authentic code, such as punctuation marks strewn everywhere.

Why do you need to recognize pseudocode at all? If the manual you're editing has real code and pseudocode, you may need to check for inconsistencies in the real code (such as semicolons at the ends of programming statements) that you won't need to check in the pseudocode. You will have to check the pseudocode for spelling and other simple errors.

System Prompts and Output

The computer communicates with the user through prompts and messages. A *prompt* is the computer's way of saying, "It's your turn to talk." If the computer needs more information, it will prompt the user for it.

EXAMPLE

The dollar sign is one of several symbols that UNIX operating systems use to indicate a prompt. When you see the $, you know the system is ready for your command.

For example, if you type the **date** command at the $ prompt, the UNIX system will respond with the current date and time:

```
$ date
Sun Jun 23 19:29:24 EDT 1991
```

It's clearer to distinguish user input typographically:

```
$ date
Sun Jun 23 19:29:24 EDT 1991
```

Generally, you'll want to show the prompt and the system output in the same typeface, because the prompt is just a specific kind of system output. This may not be noticeable if the prompt is a single character—like $—but would be for a longer prompt.

Input

User input is any command or information the user gives the computer. There are many ways a user can give instructions to the computer, depending on the particular computer hardware and software.

User Input via the Keyboard

The most common way to give instructions to the computer is by typing on a keyboard.

You can distinguish between user input and system output in several ways: different typefaces; bold, italics, underlining; second color; screens; callouts; or parenthetical text. Your choice depends on your house style, resources, and conflicting needs. For example, the budget will determine whether you can use second color or screens. If the book uses boldface for other purposes, such as to indicate new terms, then you may want to indicate user input with some other method.

TIP: Consider all your options and needs before settling on any convention that affects the entire book. You don't want to mark all user input for boldface in the first five chapters and then discover you absolutely need to preempt boldface for other purposes in chapters 6 and 7.

User Input via Pointing Devices

Other ways to give instructions to the computer are by pointing and clicking with a device such as a mouse, joystick, or trackball; pointing to a menu on a screen with your finger; and speaking to the computer.

For these types of user input, you need a different style of documentation.

The writer and editor need to meet before the writer starts writing. (If the writer and editor are the same person, the meeting should go quickly.) Together, list the different elements of the interface that you'll need to refer to, such as names of menus, names of commands on menus, and names of dialog boxes, stickups, or forms (or whatever these components are called in that program). Decide how you'll refer to these—all capitals, in quotation marks, in boldface? Will you say, "The SAVE command on the FILE menu" or "**SAVE** on the **FILE** menu" or "FILE———▶SAVE" or something else?

Also list the actions a user will perform, such as clicking, pointing, double-clicking, and dragging. Decide how you'll use each term, and then tell the user what conventions you're following in chapter 1 or the preface. Make sure the glossary includes these terms.

TIP: Look at existing documentation from your company and others to see if you're reinventing the wheel by trying to make these decisions. If a convention has emerged, use it. If there are several variations, go through the books to see which conventions in each book work well and which work poorly.

Exercise 23   What's wrong here? (Remember, when you edit, don't just check the words; also check the illustrations.)

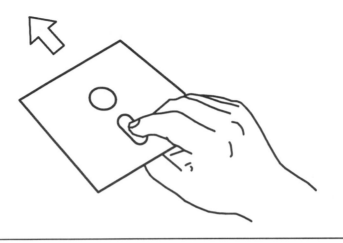

Error, Informational, and Warning Messages

Messages are a form of system output. Messages can indicate errors, give information, or give warnings. Although some writers refer to all messages as error messages, it's considered poor documentation etiquette. Users make errors, but not all messages are a result of the user's mistakes.

Here are some examples of different kinds of messages:

EXAMPLES

This error message notifies me that the workstation named **//wolf** could not be found on the network:

```
?(ld) "//wolf" - object not found (OS/file server)
```

This informational message confirms that the file I asked the system to delete was indeed deleted:
```
(file) "todo.bak" deleted.
```

This warning tells me I've run out of space:

```
DISK FULL
```

At times, you may have the opportunity to edit the actual system messages to ensure that they're in English and not computerese. (The editor cannot unilaterally decide to edit system messages. Make sure the programmers can and will use your editing comments before you start. Otherwise you're wasting your time.)

More often, you'll have the thrill of editing a chapter containing listings of messages and their meanings.

When you edit a listing of messages (in a chapter, appendix, reference card—whatever), check that the messages are in a sensible order and that the explanations are clear.

TIP: Users look up messages when something has gone wrong. Don't aggravate them further by making them hunt through twenty pages to find a particular message. And then, when they finally find the message, don't infuriate them with cryptic wording.

A sensible order for messages is any order that makes it easy for the reader to find the message without already having to know what the message means. Some messages begin with a numeric code:

```
49          Too many include files.
```

This is good. The user doesn't have to know anything more than how to find number 49 in a numerical listing to locate this message in the chapter.

If the messages are unnumbered, consider listing them alphabetically.

Exercise 24

How would you handle this?

What would you do if the first word of a message varies, depending on the circumstances? For example,

Sample "generic" message:	**How the message may actually appear:**
<number> is too low.	1 is too low.
<file> is an invalid name.	make$ is an invalid name.

(In these examples, the system substitutes the appropriate value when it displays the message.)

Many lists of error messages appear to be in random order. In fact, they usually are in order—if you're the programmer who has access to the internal, non-user-visible coding sequence. As the user advocate, you need to impress upon the programmer or writer to sort these into an order *readily apparent* to a user. You may have to ask programmers to prefix messages with a number.

Sometimes well-meaning writers sort the messages into categories, such as networking messages, operating system messages, and window manager messages. It's nice to have the information sorted this way—if you know what category to look under—because the message itself tells you. For example,

---

EXAMPLES

```
Object not found (OS)

Transmit failure (Network)
```

Many times the users won't know where to look, so they'll need to skim five or ten different listings.

TIP: When you edit documentation about error messages, visualize the user as someone who is cranky and in a hurry. The documentation—depending on how easy it is to find, how clearly it is worded, and how specific its content—will either solve the problem or further irritate that user.

Exercise 25   Let's say you're a customer and you see this description and explanation of an error:

Description	Explanation
If an STDC controller is in the top backplane of a P3570 system, and the system is booted using the BOOT, BOOTP, or BOOTT commands, the controller will not be recognized by the operating system when the I/O chassis is logically split and mapped to two CPUs.	Self-explanatory.

Compose a letter to the writer of the document where this appeared. Express yourself freely.

Editing Computer Books for Ordinary People (End Users)

Most of the information in this chapter—and in this book—applies also to manuals written for the ordinary people who use computers. (In computer jargon, these people are *end users.*) This section gives some pointers for editing books for this special audience.

Know Your Audience

TIP: End users are not all alike.

The idea that there is a typical computer user is a common misunderstanding among novice editors. There are many different types of computer users, with a wide range of background, skills, and learning habits.

Not all users have the same needs. A systems software engineer may lose patience with a book that spends three pages defining files, directories, and pathnames. Conversely, start at the beginning if you're documenting a drafting program for mechanical designers who have previously used only a drafting table and T-square.

If you were to judge from the patronizing tone of some technical writing, you might think end users are uneducated, unsophisticated, and incompetent. (Maybe some computer users fit these descriptions, but most don't.) These folks use computers as tools to do a job. (Even if that "job" is only playing a computer game.)

Many end users are no more interested in the computer itself than most homeowners are interested in the inner workings of their power tools. Other end users are curious about the computer, but only to a point; they're much more interested in their own work. There are also end users who are eager to learn all they can about computers.

Your audience might very well include all these types of users, and more. Also recognize that users' needs change over time. Last year's novice may now be interested in tips, shortcuts, and nifty tricks.

Then there are the computer experts and programmers who also use ordinary programs—spreadsheets, word processors, and games. But these people don't need your *special* attention; they just need good technical writing.

Here are some pointers on identifying your audience:

- If you don't know who your specific customers are, but you know they're professional or business types, edit the manuscript from the point of view of the small-business person. This person may need to use the computer, but every minute she or he spends learning how to do something costs money. The small-business person is a more demanding user than the laid-back, underworked employee who can devote a week to the tutorial. Make sure the documentation gets to the point quickly.

- If you don't know who your specific customers are, but you know they're people who use the computer in service to others—data-entry people (including cashiers) and clerical workers, for example—assume they may be less enthusiastic about computers than their bosses are. Make sure the documentation motivates them.

TIP: Know *your* users, not some hypothetical user you read about or somebody taught you about in school. Meet your users. Visit them in their workplace, go to user group meetings, or telephone them to ask their opinions of your documentation and the company's products. Do the kinds of tasks that your users do. Empathize with the reader.

Ensure that the writer has tailored the books to your readers with

- The topics covered and those skipped
- The segregation of certain types of material (or layering of information) to accommodate users with different levels of experience
- The level of detail provided
- The pace at which information is presented
- The chosen vocabulary
- The design of the printed and bound book

TIP: Always read the doc spec to remind yourself who the audience is before you pick up a book and start editing.

Writing Style

Style depends on your audience. You can't go wrong with clear, direct, and friendly (but not cloying).

End-user documentation generally avoids computer jargon, unless it's useful for the user to learn the term. For example, refer to *getting help* (what the user wants to do), not *using the help facility.*

Make sure there are lots of examples. Most users really want books with examples of what *they* want to do. They don't care what *other users* want to do; they want to know how to get the computer to do exactly what *they're* thinking, right now.

Make sure the user is in control. Don't say the user is *in the program*; say the *program is running.* Don't say *to get out of the program;* say *to stop the program.* Use language that doesn't imply the reader is being manipulated physically. For many people, using a computer is scary enough; don't compound their fears with imagery from sci-fi movies.

Make sure new terms and concepts are explained clearly and used consistently. For example, if the book defines the term *enter* to mean "type something and then press the ENTER (or RETURN) key," make sure the book doesn't also say at times, "Type your name and then ENTER it" or "Type your name. <RETURN>."

Computer Reference Pages

Read chapter 11 for general advice about editing reference pages. Here are a few pointers specific to computer manuals.

Check the syntax definitions very, very carefully. Make sure that every element that appears in the syntax line is defined or explained. Make sure that these elements have the same name in both the syntax definition and the description.

Check that heads are consistent in capitalization, typeface, and punctuation.

Check that index slugs (the heads that run across the top of the page with the command name) match the text, are correct typographically, and are correctly positioned. (Usually index slugs are positioned on the outer margin, on the right of odd-numbered pages and on the left of even-numbered pages. Check that left and right slugs are equidistant from the top of the page.)

Exercise 26   Find the inconsistencies in the command description shown in figure 12–5. Don't bother rewriting for clarity or style; just observe the types of inconsistencies.

```
fpat (find_pattern) — Find a text pattern in an ASCII file.
usage: fpat [-a | -x] [-c][-l] [-m n] [-lf] [-lm] [-rm n] [-rmf n] [pathname . . . -p] reg_expr. . . [-out pathname]
```

DESCRIPTION

fpat searches its input file(s) for lines matching the specified regular expressions and writes them to standard output or the file specified.

ARGUMENTS

reg_expr . . . (required)   One or more regular expression patterns. By default, a line that contains any of these expressions matches and is written to standard output. For a description of regular expressions used for pattern matching, type **help patterns**. Patterns containing embedded spaces or shell special characters must be enclosed in quotation marks.

pathname **-p** (optional)   Specify name of file to be searched. If you specify a pathname with this argument, you must follow it with **-p** to separate the pathname(s) from the search patterns on the command line. Multiple pathnames and wildcarding are permitted. Default if omitted: read standard input.

OPTIONS

If no options are specified, any line that matches any of the regular expressions is considered a matching line.

-out *path*   Write output to specified file. If input filenames are specified, the output filename can be derived. If this option is not specified, matching lines are written to standard output.

-a   Select only lines that match all regular expressions, in any order.

-x   Selects only lines containing none of the regular expressions

-c   Write only a count of matching lines, not the lines themselves.

-i   Ignore cases for search (that is, become case insensitive).

-l   Writes line number with each line that matches the regular expression.

-m *n*   Set the maximum number of search lines to *n* (a decimal value). **fpat** terminates after searching n lines.

-lm   Similar to **-lf**, but display the name(s) of only those file(s) that contain matches for the regular expression

-rm *n*   Sets the maximum number of matches to be reported for this execution of **fpat**.

-rmf   Set the maximum number of matches to be reported for each file being searched.

Figure 12–5. A command reference page with many inconsistencies

Online Documentation

Online documentation can be as simple as displaying on a computer screen the same kind of text we put on paper. It can also be a little fancier, such as online tutorials, demo programs, and examples. Online documentation can also be as sophisticated as expert systems or hypertext systems that use a variety of media (such as soundtracks and video) and allow high levels of interaction between users and the system.

The technology for making sophisticated online documentation gets better, cheaper, and faster every year. The current revolution in technical publishing is in multimedia, hypertext, and interactive systems. These systems will let users explore: read a little text, execute a programming example, view a video segment, listen to sounds and music, and much, much more.

Most editors have not had specialized training in editing video, film, and sound, but these are areas you may want to start studying to be prepared for the next generation of documentation.

This section gives some pointers for editing the more common types of online documentation: tutorials and demonstration programs, help files, and UNIX man (manual) pages.

An excellent book about online documentation is William Horton's *Designing and Writing Online Documentation*. He covers all topics, including how to decide what information should go online, how to display information online, how to write online documentation, how to make information accessible, and how to organize online information.

Online Tutorials and Demos

A tutorial teaches someone how to use a program. A demo (demonstration program) shows the program in action. Generally a demo is a sales tool or a quick overview of the product. A tutorial instructs and explains.

When you edit online tutorials and demos, do a basic copy edit—spelling, grammar, punctuation—for starters. Then address the additional challenges that online documentation presents.

TIP: Review the documentation in hardcopy *and* online form. You'll find different errors and problems.

Evaluate the visual effect—the screen display. Is the text easy to read? Is there too much text? (It's harder to read on a computer screen than on paper, so online documentation should have fewer words.) Are there visual devices to help you navigate or find your way around the program? Does every screen look the same? Can you tell what part of the program you're looking at, or do you feel lost? Conversely, does every screen look so different that there is no coherence to the program? Can you distinguish between when the program is ready for you to give a command or enter text and when the computer is busy? Are the visual transitions—such as zoom and pan—used effectively and consistently? Does too much information depend on color? (Color blindness affects 8% of men and 0.4% of women.) Do moving objects move too fast or too abruptly?

Pay attention to speed and time. How long does it take to run the demo? Is there enough time between screens to see what's going on but not so much time that you get bored? Can you adjust the speed? How long does it take to go through the exercises in the tutorial? Do you sit and watch for unreasonably long stretches? Do you spend all your time typing and little time exploring the program? Do you spend an uncomfortable amount of time waiting for the computer to do something? Does the computer react quickly and obnoxiously (with a loud noise or annoying flashes) before you've even had a chance to get your bearings?

Do you have to type large blocks of text? (Not all users type quickly.) If you make a mistake in the tutorial, can you recover? Are sound effects used consistently? Can you adjust the volume or turn off the sound?

Here are some pointers for editing computer tutorials:

- Do the tutorial in whatever forms users will do it (online, hardcopy, audiotape, videotape, or a combination of media).

- Ensure that users have some control. For example, if the tutorial asks users to enter some text or a number, let them choose what to enter. (The tutorial must be able to accommodate their choices and handle errors.)

- Make sure the lesson isn't just a typing exercise. ("Type this. Now type this. Now type something else.") People don't like to have computers or manuals push them around.

- If the tutorial requires a lot of typing just in preparation for something else, suggest other ways to have that text available. (Have the user or software read it in from a text file.)

- Make sure the instructions tell users how to recover from mistakes. When you test the tutorial, make different errors yourself and check how the software and the manual guide the user.

- Check that the tutorial appeals both to users who want to understand what they're doing and to those who just want to know what to do. Make sure there's enough explanation for the inquisitive users, but not too much for the impatient or apathetic users. (Give pointers to where users can find more information instead of overwhelming them with details in the tutorial.)

- Check that the tutorial teaches the correct way. Teachers say that if you tell students how *not* to do something, that's what they'll remember.

- Make sure the tutorial sticks to explaining the rules and doesn't confuse the student with exceptions.

- Make sure there are exit and re-entry points. Break the exercises into small chunks. Give a rough estimate of how long it might take to do each exercise so users can set aside enough time. (Estimate high so people don't feel dumb if it takes them an hour to do a so-called 20-minute exercise. Most users don't have the time—or patience—to work on a tutorial for an hour or more at a stretch.) Tell users how to stop at any point and restart later. If the exercise can't be interrupted and restarted conveniently, make sure the good stopping places are marked.

- Check that the tutorial lets users make mistakes and recover gracefully. If the exercises build one upon the other, don't penalize the user for making a mistake early. For example, if a user enters a bad value in exercise 2, have exercise 2 check the number and ask the user to enter a different number. Otherwise, a later exercise might go wrong, and the user might never know why.

- Check that there are some exercises that let users practice what they've learned.

- Make sure the exercises appeal to users with different careers, interests, and computer experience.

TIP: Make sure the tutorial has an interesting story line. The story, however, shouldn't overpower the subject the tutorial is intended to teach. Read *How to Write a Computer Manual* by Jonathan Price to learn more.

Editing online tutorials and demos means putting yourself in the user's seat and going for a test drive. Far better for you to complain that the program is slow, the screens cluttered, the command names ambiguous, and the type tiny than for the customers to complain.

Online Help

Online help is a way for users to get information about a program without reading the manual. Many programs use exactly the same text for help as the manual. It saves a lot of development time to put the manual online. If your company's support of online help is limited to converting the reference manual to an online form, then just edit the manual and don't bother with the online help. At most, check general readability—screen size, type size, and minimal conformance to human factors standards. Don't spend a lot of time unless there's an engineering commitment to fix the problems you find.

If you're editing a more sophisticated system of online help, you need to do more than just edit the words. Evaluate how easy it is to navigate the system—to find a particular topic, to move from topic to topic, to find the way back to a previous topic, to find the way back to the program. Check whether you can find information when you have a general question but you don't know the name of the command. Offer suggestions for additional keywords and cross-references. Check whether the "context-sensitive" help really answers the questions a user might have. If you don't feel competent to judge, make sure that someone who is qualified is testing the help system.

Manual Pages (UNIX Man Pages)

Read this section only if you expect to edit documentation for UNIX systems.

UNIX manual pages, commonly called *man pages,* are online versions of the UNIX manuals. (They're called man pages because the command to read them is named **man.**)

The first time you see UNIX documentation, you'll be stunned by how badly it's written and amazed that anyone can find anything, because the order seems haphazard.

It really is written badly, but there is some order. You just need to have the secret decoding key. Here it is: Each section of the original UNIX documentation covered a specific topic. References to **chmod(1)** and **find(1),** for example, mean the **chmod** command and the **find** command are in section 1 of the documentation. In the printed books, you'd turn to section 1 and find these commands, in alphabetical order within the section. In addition to commands, man pages cover subroutines, utilities, and file formats.

The sections are structured differently for different UNIX systems.

Before you make any changes to man pages, you should know two things:

- What is your company's policy about making changes to man pages? The policy may be "hands off" for a variety of reasons, such as licensing agreements, availability of resources to make the changes, or user preference for "familiar" man pages.

- What conventions already exist for man pages?

Man pages have the following heads and conventions:

NAME gives the name of the command, subroutine, utility, or file format and an alternative name (if any) with a brief (short phrase) description.

SYNOPSIS tells how the command is used (syntax), lists possible options (sometimes these are in a separate OPTIONS section), and tells what type of argument(s) the command expects. It gives a comparable summary for subroutines, utilities, and file formats.

Under the SYNOPSIS head, words in boldface are considered to be literal and typed exactly as shown. The command, subroutine, or utility name is always shown as a literal. Options are usually literal.

Square brackets around an argument indicate the argument is optional and does not always have to be specified with the command.

The word *file* always means a filename.

Ellipsis points (. . .) following an argument indicate that the argument may be repeated any number of times.

DESCRIPTION gives the details of the command, subroutine, utility, or file format. It lists all options, and explains how each option modifies the command.

FILES lists the names of any files important to that command.

SEE ALSO refers to related topics or other useful documentation, no doubt written just as badly.

DIAGNOSTICS explains error messages.

BUGS lists known errors and their workarounds. This section often contains irrelevant jokes.

All man pages have NAME, SYNOPSIS, and DESCRIPTION heads. The other heads appear only when applicable. Some other heads you may see are ERRORS, NOTES, and OPTIONS. The sections vary somewhat with different UNIX implementations.

Strictly—and historically—speaking, the term *man pages* applies to UNIX operating systems only. Reference pages for some companies' products use formats similar to UNIX man pages, and some companies call all online reference pages *man pages*. Don't let the terminology restrict you: Online reference pages for products other than UNIX operating systems can follow whatever page format and use whatever heads that the writer, editor, and graphic artist agree to use.

User Interfaces

The user interface is the part of the program that the user sees and interacts with. To most users, the interface *is* the program: The interface is the commands users type, the menus we select from, the forms we enter text into, the messages we see, and the beeps and prompts and flashes and pictures that tell us the computer is computing or acknowledging our existence. To the software engineer who designed the program, the interface is stuff you throw together at the end so people can do nifty things with the elegant code you wrote.

It's important for an editor to understand the differences in perspective, because you're right in the middle.

If you're fortunate enough to have the opportunity to edit the user interface, you'll be in a position to contribute directly to customer satisfaction in using the program. Besides, every unpleasantness in the interface means an extra page of explanation in the manual.

How much you contribute to improving the user interface depends on how effectively you can convince the software engineers that the interface is not a minor piece to be grafted onto the program but an integral component of the user documentation and product.

You can limit your editing of user interfaces to proofreading the screens for typos, suggesting alternative names for commands (is *save* better than *file*?), and advising on general layout (overcrowded screens, type sizes).

You may also participate in the design of the user interface. A good interface is intuitive; it should work the way a user would expect from its design. See the bibliography for some suggested titles on ergonomics (human factors engineering).[1]

The ultimate contribution you can make to the user interface is to use the product yourself and provide feedback on what aspects of the interface make it easy to use the program and where the interface is complex, confusing, or irritating. Make this part of your job—participate in the project early, use the software, and raise usability problems with the development team.

TIP: Any time you come across text in a manuscript that reads something like, "If you do thus-and-so, the result may be different from what you expect," you are seeing a documented flaw in the product design. It's good to alert users to potential pitfalls. It's even better if the writer and editor can influence the development team to improve the design.

---

[1] As Jonathan Price reminds me, "Books have a user interface. We call it design. In an application, you should be able to get access to facts or commands, move around within the software, and get out quickly, just as you dip into a book."

Summary

You don't have to be a computer wizard to edit computer documentation competently, but at the very least you should understand the terms used in this chapter and be able to apply them to the publications you edit.

The more you know about computers, the better your editing will be—and the greater your enjoyment of your job. It's far more interesting to evaluate user interfaces and run programs than to check formatting and spelling.

Part 3
The Editor's Career

Chapter 13
Editing in a Desktop Publishing Environment

The publishing world has focused a lot of attention on the writer's evolving role in desktop publishing environments. This chapter turns the spotlight on editors. It explores how editors can adapt their skills to a workplace using desktop publishing, and emphasizes how writers and editors work together in this different environment.

I'm addressing editors specifically in this chapter, in part to correct for their omission from the literature on desktop publishing. Writers will probably be most interested in the section on the writer–editor relationship.

In *desktop publishing*—as the term is used in this chapter—writers prepare camera-ready copy with little or no support from graphic arts professionals. In desktop publishing environments, every writer has access to a workstation or personal computer and electronic publishing software.

Here are the areas in which desktop publishing differs from traditional publishing:

- The publication process (from manuscript to camera-ready copy)
- Interaction with other people and departments
- Marking up the manuscript
- The relationship between writers and editors
- The tools that help you do your job
- The editor's responsibilities
- The editor's job description

317

This chapter shows how desktop publishing presents editors with a ticket to a more creative, more challenging career. No, you don't have to move to writing or management to find this new career—desktop publishing actually frees editors to edit.

Traditional Publishing vs. Desktop Publishing

The main difference between traditional and desktop publishing is what drives the process:

Production drives traditional publishing.
Writing drives desktop publishing.

This chapter looks at only one segment of the publishing process, from the writer's manuscript until the camera-ready copy is ready for printing.

The Traditional Publishing Process

Figure 13–1 shows an example of the workflow in a traditional publishing model. This flowchart packs a lot of information, but you don't need to understand every item in it to follow the discussion; I'll explain the important steps as we go along. If you're curious, you can find these terms in the glossary and recommended books about production in the bibliography.

The process flows something like this: After reviews and revisions, writers hand off manuscripts to editors, who mark them up and hand them off to a graphic arts department for typesetting and pasteup. The text goes to composition and the illustrations go to the art department.

Sometimes developmental editing reviews fit into this model—and sometimes not. Sometimes writers revise manuscripts based on the final editing review, sometimes not. (I've been told—curiously, always by writers—that in some companies writers don't even see, let alone have the opportunity to approve or reject, the editor's changes.)

In the traditional model, the schedule and process are driven by production considerations. From the editor's perspective, the milestones are production-oriented. In this model, the editor's job is more closely aligned with production. In fact, a major responsibility for the editor is to keep production costs down.

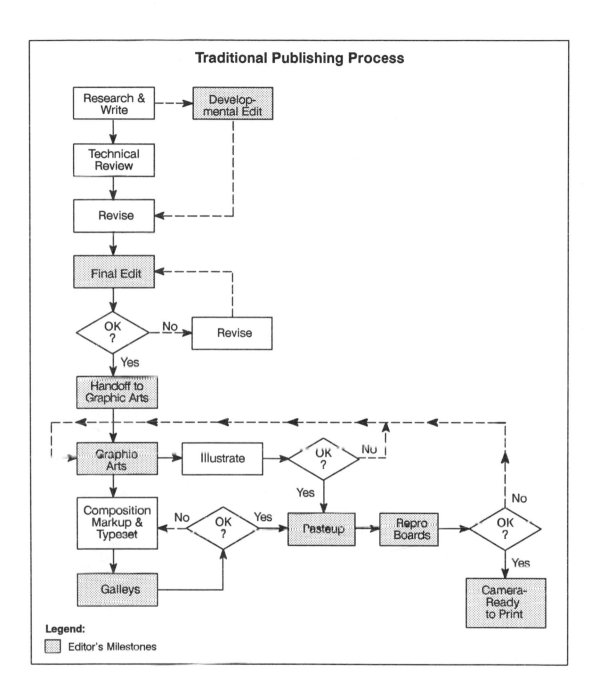

Figure 13–1. Workflow in a traditional publishing process

Here's a summary of the key points to note in figure 13–1:

- The editor's milestones are *production* milestones.
- A critical milestone is *handoff to graphic arts*, because that's when writing stops.
- The writing drafts themselves are not prominent.
- The process is linear—it's expensive to back up one step in the cycle.

Note that the writing drafts are not prominent in this illustration. Writers, don't take offense. This chapter takes the editor's point of view, and in the traditional publishing environment, production milestones are more important to editors than the writing drafts. In fact, writers and editors both take note: The opposite is true in desktop publishing. But I'm getting ahead of myself. Read on.

If you were an editor in the 1970s you would have learned all about the production stages shown on this flowchart your first week on the job. You can be an editor in the 1990s and never learn this process. (But you'd be the poorer for it. As a knowledge of world history often sheds light on current events, a familiarity with publishing history helps you better understand current practices.)

By the way, a company that has desktop publishing hardware and software used by graphic arts specialists instead of writers is following a traditional model, in terms of process.

Desktop Publishing

Figure 13–2 shows an example of the desktop publishing model. Here's what's important to note:

- The editor's milestones are *writing* milestones.
- The technical writer drives the process.
- The process is iterative. It's easy to add another editing or review cycle.
- The writing and formatting happen concurrently.

In the desktop publishing model, the writer produces camera-ready copy, with or without support from graphic arts professionals. From the editor's perspective, the milestones are writing drafts. Writing considerations drive the schedule and process. In the desktop model, the editor's job is more closely aligned with writing.

It's not accidental that the writer is depicted in the desktop publishing illustration and not in the traditional publishing illustration. Of course writers are important in both contexts. They write the drafts that are produced under either model. There would be no publication without the writer, regardless of who produces the camera-ready copy. But writing is more important than production in desktop publishing.

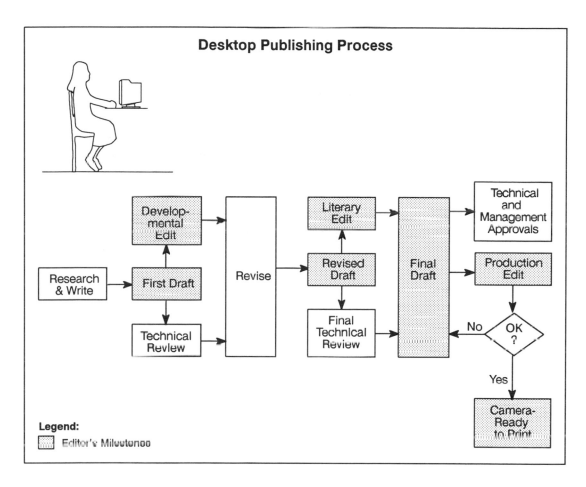

Figure 13–2. Workflow in a desktop publishing environment

How the Process Changes

Traditional publishing required a lot of time for the production of camera-ready copy after the writing was done, generally three to four months, plus another month for printing. If the entire project schedule allowed eight months to a year to write, edit, typeset, paste up, and print a product manual, how much time do you think would be spared for editing and the subsequent revisions? Because so much of the project schedule was consumed by production, editors would have one short pass at a manuscript, maybe two for a high-visibility document.

With desktop publishing, there isn't a "handoff to production"—most graphic arts activities are part of the writing process itself. For example, writers generate their own tables, create figures, and handle the formatting while writing the text. This technology gives writers a lot more control over their books, and also enables them to use more tables and illustrations. (It's cheaper to create tables and illustrations electronically. Most typesetting houses charge extra, a so-called penalty fee, for tables.)

Since desktop publishing makes it easy to revise and issue new review drafts, writers are more likely to keep feeding (force feeding?) revised manuscripts to the editor.

The benefit to editors is having greater opportunity to contribute to better written, better looking, and more consistent documents. The editor also will see these manuscripts earlier, not at the end of the process. As a result, the editor has more time to influence writing, anticipate potential problems, and resolve them.

Desktop publishing lets writers and editors see how the page will look—in terms of both typography and layout—so you can fine-tune early. As a result, editors and writers can make formatting decisions based on the content—not just for looks, but for best presentation of information.

Automatic index generators let editors see a draft of the index early enough to suggest additional keywords. A bonus of having an index while you copy edit is that you don't have to remember where you saw every reference to a topic; you have an index (albeit an imperfect one) to give your memory a boost.

In desktop publishing, text and graphics usually follow the same path, so you can review both and see how they work together. Although it's true that most writers don't have the skills to design books, select appropriate typefaces, and create good illustrations, there are techniques for handling this problem. For example, some companies have artists who design page-layout templates for writers to use.

When I worked in a traditional environment, I felt I never had enough editing passes. Now I sometimes feel I have too many; writers sometimes churn out more drafts than I have time to read. If I had my choice, however, I wouldn't go back. The editing does go quickly if you've seen the manuscript two or three times already, and you have the luxury of catching errors you might have missed earlier. Most writers mark the passages they've changed since I last saw the manuscript, and that's a great time-saver. (Here's a piece of nostalgia: We used to be able to feel changes. When we had to find changes in a hurry, we'd slide our fingertips over the mechanicals to feel where corrections were cut in.) It's not perfect, but I give the edge to desktop publishing.

Table 13–1 gives a summary of how traditional and desktop publishing environments differ.

Table 13–1. How the Process Changes

What Changes	Traditional Publishing Environment	Desktop Publishing Environment
who prepares camera-ready copy	graphic arts professionals	writers
where edited draft goes	to writer or production	to writer
number of editing passes	usually 1 or 2	several possible
when editing occurs	late (pre-production)	early
when book is formatted	after writing	concurrent with writing
text and art	separate	together
writing freeze	at handoff to production	independent of production
workflow	linear, rigid	iterative, flexible
schedule	production-driven	writing-driven
editor's milestones	production stages: handoff, galleys, mechanicals	writing drafts
editor's function	reduce production costs; production-based	improve writing; writing-based
feasibility of late changes	usually need to justify	usually can do
turnaround for small text change	hours or days (beginning of pipeline)	minutes or hours (redo affected pages)
cost of text change	impact on all other projects in production	writer's time
number of drafts	"never enough"	"sometimes too many"

Just One Tiny Change

What happens when a writer makes a change after the mechanicals have been prepared?

For the sake of simplicity, let's assume that the writer has rewritten just one paragraph. What happens in the traditional environment? First, the job has to be logged back into production and routed to the appropriate people. A simple text change would not need to go through the format editor again, but something more complicated, such as a table, would. The new copy is typeset—a typesetter types in the text and sends the file to the phototypesetter to be output. The film is developed. Then the correction is proofread and, if there are no further corrections, handed over for pasteup. With luck and foresight, the new text is about the same length as the old, so the rest of the chapter doesn't need to be laid out again. That's a relief, because the table of contents is being proofread and the index being created. Meanwhile, someone has been scheduling and tracking this correction as it moves through the graphic arts department. At each stage, there are official hand-offs and sign-offs to ensure safe passage (no repercussions) to the next stage of production.

Making this simple change means going back to the beginning of the pipeline, where it will have a ripple effect on other projects. After all, production groups, by definition, have many projects in process at the same time.

Now let's look at the same change in a desktop publishing environment. The writer makes the change, prints out the new page, and hands it to the editor. If the corrected paragraph is longer than the previous one, the writer prints out the entire chapter, along with a newly generated table of contents and index.

Corrections that would have been too costly to make at galleys or later in traditional publishing can be made in desktop publishing. The linear process of traditional publishing meant going back and redoing several stages, interrupting production workflow.

What can take a day in the traditional environment—say, changing one paragraph—can take ten minutes if the writer is doing it. I recall rush jobs where I would walk the final corrections through graphic arts. Even with everyone stopping all other work to accommodate me, it would still take an hour because of the number of steps and the number of people involved. And we'd still have to wait for the phototypesetter to churn out the film, and for the film to be developed and dry.

Desktop publishing lets us make that last-minute change. The result is a higher quality document. (OK, not all last-minute changes are improvements, and sometimes these late changes introduce new errors—but these same disadvantages existed in the traditional model, where the costs of making those errors were much, much greater.)

How Interactions Change

Editors, if you make a transition from a traditional publishing environment to desktop publishing, be prepared to interact differently and with different players. In fact, interactions are very likely to be more complex because you'll be interacting with more groups and people. Because the production cycle is more flexible, the interactions among team members are also very likely to be more fluid. Your respective roles may be less rigidly defined. You'll find your job requires you to be more flexible and more creative. You've moved from the production world to the writing world. Your role is closer to creating the documents than manufacturing them.

You may work with engineers, graphic arts specialists, quality assurance people, and many others, depending on how your company is organized. Figure 13–3 shows one possible scenario. In this example, the editor and writer interact frequently, as do the writer and engineer. The editor and the engineer work together from time to time. If there is a production department, the editor interacts with its members directly, the writer occasionally. The editor or the production department works with the printer.

What is most important about figure 13–3 is that it shows that in traditional publishing you could predict where in the process these interactions would occur. For example, the engineer is involved early in the process, but is out of the loop by the time the manuscript reaches editing. The linear production process meant that all players could anticipate when they'd be expected to contribute to the project. The desktop process is iterative; most players are in action or on call throughout. As a result, by the time the project has been completed, members of the desktop publishing team will have worked together more closely and more frequently than members of the traditional team. Don't underestimate the payoff when it comes to pulling the team together for another project.

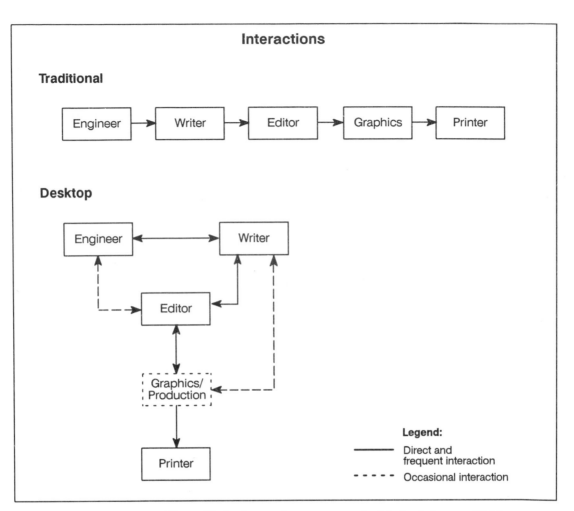

Figure 13–3. Interactions are more flexible in desktop publishing

How Manuscript Markup Changes

When I started editing in workplaces that used desktop publishing, one of the biggest adjustments I had to make was one I hadn't anticipated at all—how to mark up a manuscript. I was used to marking up a manuscript to reflect how I thought the copy should read and look, discussing the changes with the writer, and handing those same pages over to graphic arts. One aspect of markup was to indicate typographic features, such as bold or italic, that we wanted in print but couldn't show in a typewritten manuscript. Another aspect of markup would be changes to the text itself. For example, I'd recast sentences, change words, or draw lines to show how to reorder paragraphs. I'd mark queries (editing jargon for *questions*) on separate flags and affix them to the manuscript; after the writer and I had resolved the issues, we'd discard these flags.

Today, the manuscripts I edit may still be covered with ink and have some editing symbols here and there, but the words and markings are mostly my original questions and comments for the writer. Very few are actual changes.

If you're making a change to desktop publishing, take note. The manuscript goes back to the writer, so what you mark on the manuscript will differ from what you used to mark on the copy that went into typesetting. Why? Because typesetters used to enter comments verbatim; writers interpret them. What you marked on the copy got typeset; you were giving instructions. What you now mark on the manuscript is feedback for the writer; you are giving advice. The advice you give the writer may be firm, but it is not an order.

Here are some ways the manuscript markup is different:

- The major difference is that the manuscript is now *private*. When we look at the writer–editor relationship later on, you'll see how crucial this difference is.

- Your comments can be friendlier and more personalized. You can say what's not clear, give alternatives and examples, explain the reasons behind your comments, and ask questions.

- In the days before word processing, extensive changes meant the writer had to retype the manuscript. Writers and editors commonly negotiated changes based on the amount of retyping.

- You may find yourself using few standard editing symbols, because most writers are unfamiliar with them. Be prepared to teach them to your writers or get unusual results. When I'm working with a writer for the first time, I often indicate italics by drawing a circle around the word and writing *italics* beside it.

- I can't remember the last time I wrote *stet* except in a comment to myself. (I usually write *Never mind* or *Oops* or *OK as is*.)

- Because the writer makes the changes and corrections, your comments can be broader; you can suggest what rewriting is needed instead of rewriting the material yourself. You can focus on writing issues, not instructions to the typesetter. You also have room on the page to write substantive comments.

Figure 13–4 shows how desktop publishing allows you to gauge the amount of detail or guidance you put in your edits according to the writer's style and needs.

Traditional Environment

For example, ~~now~~ you can simply mark a paragraph as *passive* and let the writer
~~determine the best rewrite~~ *fix it* ; in the "old days" we'd have to edit each sentence *or rewrite* ~~so that~~
~~the compositor would know what to enter~~. In the old days, the editor changed the
writer's copy. Now, the writer controls *the* wording, ~~under the guidance of the editor~~.
The result is often a better rewrite because the writer knows the subject better. ~~My~~
~~experience has shown that both editors and writers overwhelmingly prefer the new~~
~~method.~~

This manuscript goes to composition for typesetting.

Desktop Environment *Will the old days seem like ancient history by 1998? Cut.*

For example, now you can simply mark a paragraph as *passive* and let the writer
determine the best rewrite; in the "old days" we'd have to edit each sentence so that
the compositor would know what to enter. In the (old days) the editor changed the
writer's copy. Now, the writer controls wording, under the guidance of the editor.
The result is often a better rewrite because the writer knows the subject better. My
experience has shown that both editors and writers overwhelmingly prefer the new
method. *Wordy — Be more direct. You can cut qualifiers and some explanation.*

This manuscript goes to the writer for revisions.

Figure 13–4. Sample edited manuscript in traditional and desktop environments

How Manuscript Preparation Changes

Go to your library and pick up any book about editing or writing for publication. Look at how many pages are devoted to preparing the physical manuscript. For example, one author gives as many pages (six) to manuscript preparation as to how to create an index.

In the old days, I used to spend a lot of time on manuscript preparation. It was the editor's job to ensure that the copy that went into graphic arts was clean and clear, because that saved money. We had to follow very detailed instructions.

Figure 13–5 shows an example of one company's manuscript preparation guidelines.

Manuscript Preparation Guidelines

A clean, clear, and complete manuscript will prevent costly rework and delays.
The following guidelines are recommended.

Text

- Type new material double-spaced on 8-1/2 x 11" white paper, one side only. Hand-written editing marks are acceptable; however, handwritten manuscript is not acceptable. Typed text should be uppercase/lowercase as desired in final text.

- Cut old work into a single column and paste up on 8-1/2 x 11" white paper with inserts in place.

- Add extra space between paragraphs.

- Indicate heading levels by means of a circled numeral in the left margin.

- Make all editing marks as neatly and as consistently as possible.

- Number all pages by section (1-1, 1-2, 1-3, etc.).

- Number all pages sequentially in the upper right-hand corner.

Figures and Illustrations

- Prepare a separate art package by copying all pages that contain illustrations.

- Use the following code for unnumbered or non-captioned figures:
  1x1 (Section 1, first unnumbered figure)
  1x2 (Section 1, second unnumbered figure)
  1x3 (Section 1, third unnumbered figure)
  2x1 (Section 2, first unnumbered figure)

- When using illustrations from an existing manual, note on each illustration the order number of the manual from which it was taken and indicate any changes.

- Submit glossy prints when photos are needed since they cannot be borrowed from other repro packages.

Figure 13–5. Manuscripts submitted to production must conform to strict requirements

Figure 13–6 shows how manuscripts used to look. We used to call these *roughs,* and for good reason!

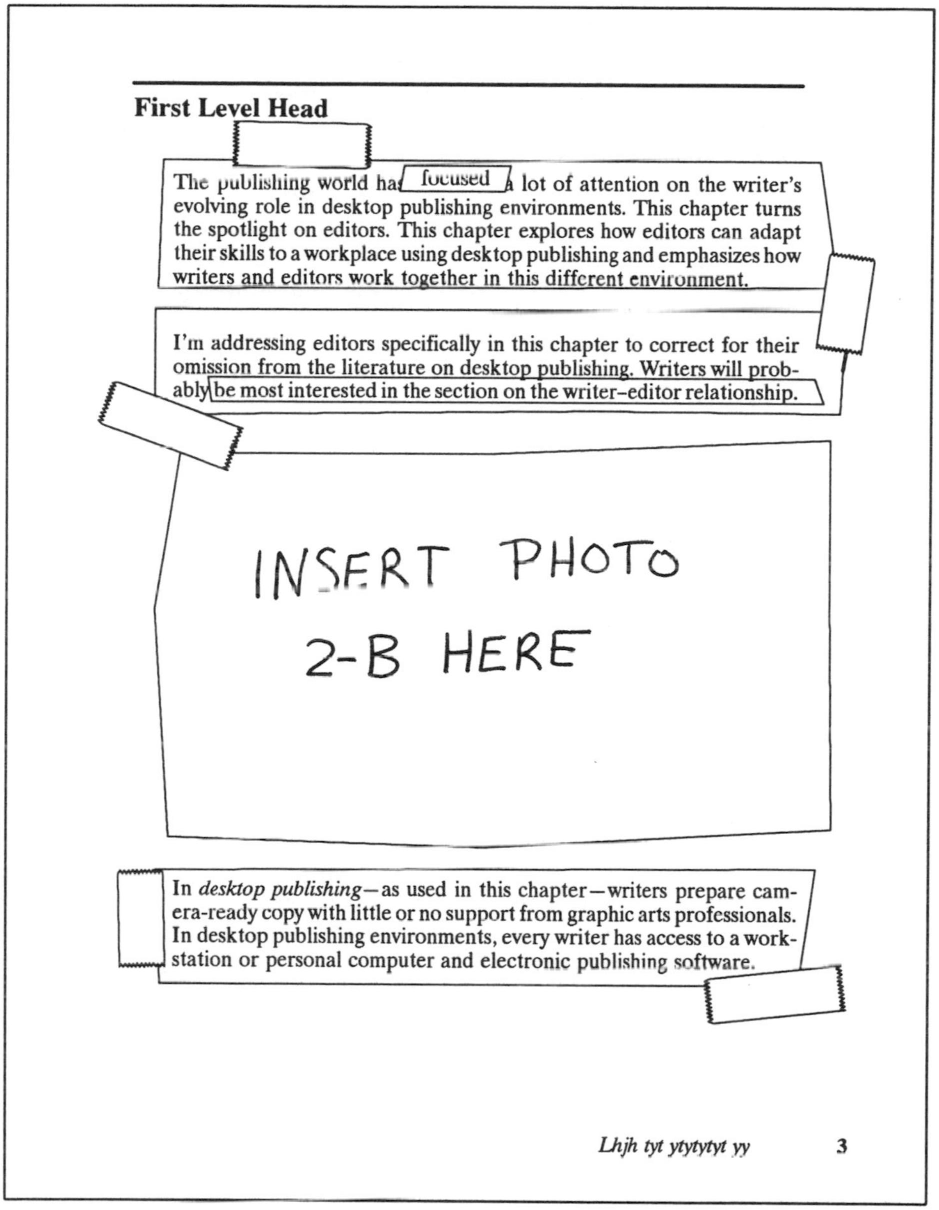

First Level Head

The publishing world has [focused] a lot of attention on the writer's evolving role in desktop publishing environments. This chapter turns the spotlight on editors. This chapter explores how editors can adapt their skills to a workplace using desktop publishing and emphasizes how writers and editors work together in this different environment.

I'm addressing editors specifically in this chapter to correct for their omission from the literature on desktop publishing. Writers will probably be most interested in the section on the writer–editor relationship.

INSERT PHOTO
2-B HERE

In *desktop publishing*—as used in this chapter—writers prepare camera-ready copy with little or no support from graphic arts professionals. In desktop publishing environments, every writer has access to a workstation or personal computer and electronic publishing software.

Lhjh tyt ytytytyt yy   3

Figure 13–6. Editors used to get some messy manuscripts

Now I get manuscripts that are complete and clean. The manuscripts have a table of contents and an index, all the pages are numbered, the artwork is already in position, and the text looks very close to a finished book. I don't have to visualize how italics or boldface would look; I can see it. I can see how the text and artwork complement each other. I can concentrate on the words. Best of all, I don't have to spend an hour adding the part number and page number to each manuscript page.

How the Writer–Editor Relationship Changes

The biggest difference in desktop publishing is in how writers and editors work together. The key to the new relationship is now privacy, teamwork, and cooperation.

Since your comments go directly to the writers, you're not inviting all 30 people in graphic arts to peek at your corrections. Writers don't have to feel that everyone who handles their manuscripts down the line will see they didn't write perfect prose the first time. Writers can take your comments and improve their work instead of feeling defensive. You'll find that writers are less likely to argue about editing comments, since there is no longer an audience.

What does this mean for you?

- The interaction between the writer and editor is characterized by teamwork. The editor is the writer's ally; you're on the same team so you're no longer fighting each other.

- Since the writer makes the final corrections, you can make those late changes that would have disrupted production or been too costly in traditional publishing. When writers have more control over their own work, they're usually more receptive to editorial feedback.

- The editor can return a friendlier manuscript. You can personalize your comments—refer to a previous project, a conversation you had last week. You can give a fuller explanation of what you mean. You even have the liberty to add jokes, which in traditional publishing is taboo lest they appear by accident in print.

"Never Put Anything in a Manuscript That You Don't Want Printed"

"Never put anything in a manuscript that you wouldn't want to see in print" is advice handed down from one generation of editors to the next. It's good advice—when the manuscript is going into production.

In what has become a classic example of what can go wrong, an editor at the *Boston Globe* flagged a placeholder for the text of a Jimmy Carter speech as "Mush From The Wimp." This label became the headline in one edition. (It was corrected in the later editions.)

◇ ◇ ◇ ◇ ◇ ◇ ◇ ◇ ◇ ◇ ◇

The short story writer Bret Harte, working as a small-town newspaper editor, flagged a typo (*chastity* for *charity*) in the proofs with a question mark, expecting the printer to check the original manuscript and see the "obvious" error. The corrected obituary read:

She was distinguished for chastity (?) above all other ladies in the town.

◇ ◇ ◇ ◇ ◇ ◇ ◇ ◇ ◇ ◇ ◇

A software catalog I edited required such extensive keyboarding that the typesetting house sent it to its Bombay subsidiary, where the labor was cheaper. The people who typeset the book did not speak English (I learned when the galleys came back) and faithfully transcribed every character on the page, including the handwritten and circled annotations to the typesetters and artists. Yes, every *Stet, Insert A here,* and *Italics instead of underscore* showed up (without a typo!) in the galleys. For example, the typeset version was intended to read:

Master Production Schedule—COBOL-68

The markup symbol for an em dash is $\frac{1}{m}$ Here's what the galleys showed:

Master Production Schedule $\frac{1}{m}$ COBOL-68

Yes, we fixed them all in time. That experience taught me that if I needed to express myself on the manuscript more elaborately than editing symbols alone permitted, then I also needed to follow through and learn where the production would actually be done. The next time our graphic arts department knew of a manuscript that was to be typeset outside the United States, they let me know in time to double check its markup.

The lesson is that manuscripts that go into production departments are produced, not read. The Indian typesetters were supposed to type, not read and interpret, so they did their job well. Writers, however, do indeed read the comments on their manuscripts, and they also have a personal stake in ensuring that remarks such as *Ambiguous antecedent* or *Need an example* don't appear in print in their books.

How the Editor's Responsibilities Change

If you're a typical overworked editor, you've been able to justify your existence only by expediting production. Desktop publishing has been the catalyst for changing industry's overworked copy editors into overworked literary editors. The workload may still be burdensome, but the job is more interesting.

When companies give writers desktop publishing tools, editors sometimes acquire new responsibilities. This is especially true in small companies where graphic design and illustration work is contracted out; there may be no other in-house "expert" to turn to with on-the-fly questions.

Most writers have had little or no training in graphic design, typography, layout, or illustration. Editors may need to train writers or provide some basic quality guidelines, such as, "Don't use the heaviest rules to outline illustrations."

Editors may be even more closely involved than before in anticipating potential printing problems, especially those related to binding and use of color. The editor's role is especially critical if writers also design the books. Editors may not be experts in design or typography, but they often have more experience with these matters than writers. At the minimum, editors can communicate better with outside designers because they've had more opportunity to learn the language than most writers.

Editors who are familiar with typesetting and graphic arts terminology can help writers better understand their desktop publishing tools and the manuals that come with them. For example, there may be a menu selection in your electronic publishing software for kerning, but if you don't know what kerning is, it's not going to be a useful feature for you. Some terms that commonly need explanation are *leading, index slugs,* and *dingbat.*

How Changes in Tools Help Editors

Electronic publishing tools free you from some tedious chores, at least at the first pass. Many operations we used to do manually we can now do with computers. More sophisticated publishing tools are being developed all the time.

Do you remember "the good old days" of searching manuscripts for *every* occurrence of a particular word to ensure consistent spelling? I do, and I don't miss those days of circling all references to *I-D-S/II* or *floating-point* or *high-level* (and other terms on our standard spelling list) throughout a 350-page manual. This operation was slow, tedious, and time-consuming. This used to be the most difficult change to make, because it was a manual operation for editor and composition; now it's the easiest. Writers can change all occurrences of *accursed Red Sox* to *World-Champion Boston Red Sox* throughout a book in seconds. Editors need only mark the change once, making for a less busy manuscript. Both writers and editors can concentrate on higher-level issues because they're not turning pages looking for the same old correction.

Spelling checkers are far from perfect. Most can't (yet) distinguish between *they're* and *their* or between *it's* and *its*, but they will someday. They also can't tell if *that* should be *the* or *of* should be *on*, but they will someday. Some editors write off spelling checkers altogether. I don't. I wouldn't trust them completely, but I'd much rather edit a manuscript that has been run through the spelling checker than one that hasn't. The more low-level problems that get fixed in the manuscript before I see it, the more I can concentrate on the more interesting problems.

Likewise, programs that automatically generate tables of contents and indexes aren't as good today as they'll be someday, but they take some of the drudgery out of the editor's job. I still check the page references, but find fewer errors than in the contents and indexes generated by hand.

Tools that automatically number sections, lists, figures, and tables, and renumber them as the writer adds and deletes entries, are also time-savers. I still find errors, but not as many as I used to, and I certainly do not miss numbering all the figures and tables and renumbering them and renumbering them. (An old editing saying goes something like this: Any set of figures and tables worth numbering once is worth numbering a dozen times.)

Most electronic publishing programs let you set up a template or style sheet to maintain a consistent format. For example, the software I'm using to create this book (Interleaf TPS 4.0) lets me define the properties of a paragraph once: They include margins, spacing before and after, typeface, type size, indentations, and dozens of other properties. I merely select the paragraph component and type; all the formatting is handled automatically. I have other components to define a bulleted list (the component includes the bullet character, the tab, and handles the wrapping and indentation of each line of text), one for notes to myself (so I can select and delete them all before sending the manuscript to the publisher), and many others. Unless I deliberately change individual items, the book's formatting will be consistent with very little effort. That's certainly an improvement over the days of checking for consistent spacing before and after text heads, consistent type size in chapter titles, and so on.

How the Editor's Job Changes

We could say, "Hmm . . . Editors don't do manuscript preparation, don't have to check for consistency as much, don't have to check spelling, and spend less time rewriting. Let's have fewer editors." We could say that. But we won't.

Instead, let's have editors use the time formerly spent on these routine chores in activities that produce a better product. Let's redefine the editor's job. Instead of being a person who facilitates *production,* let the editor be a person who contributes to a better *product.*

Some editors resist the changes brought about by the new technology. I don't understand what they're fighting to preserve: the opportunity to number figures by hand or the privilege of changing *on-line* to *online* two thousand times in a manuscript? Editors, use the changes in the technology to your advantage. Let the computer do the boring stuff and give you time to do better things:

- Do more developmental editing
- Serve as a writing consultant
- Be a publishing resource
- Be a user advocate
- Perform usability testing
- Become an expert in your company's products
- Be the team member with the broadest overview
- Serve as project leader for a nonpublications project (marketing, R&D)
- Be a troubleshooter for problems with electronic publishing tools
- Be a documentation architect
- Write a book

Summary

Technology has changed what many editors now do (process, manuscript markup) and how they do it (relationships with others, tools). This chapter looked at these changes, brought about by new ways to prepare camera-ready copy.

What can we look forward to as the technology improves? What changes will occur when we no longer produce camera-ready copy and instead send books to printers electronically? How about when we also distribute the books electronically to customers? (This technology is already in use; most of us don't have enough experience with it to analyze its effect on editors.) What changes can we expect when we can edit online without sacrificing any of the advantages of editing on paper?

Chapter 16 looks at the future of editing and the new skills editors must acquire to succeed in that future.

Chapter 14
Managing Projects and Time

Any time you're responsible for a set of books, or whenever you work with more than one writer, you are, in effect, managing a project, even if all you're managing is your own time.

For example, if you're the editor for a new product release, you need to think about the entire documentation set. In one capacity, you ensure consistency of style and synergy of content; in another capacity you ensure that the books stay on schedule.

Projects you may be called upon to manage include

- New product releases, with many documents going to print over a short period of time
- Continuing product support, with ongoing revision of a major documentation set
- Product releases with several writers contributing to the overall effort (sometimes called *collaborative writing*)
- Joint projects with other departments, divisions, or companies

Chapters 6–12 discussed how to edit the books for consistency and integrity. This chapter shows you how to manage the overall project.

Working with Others

There is only one word you need to know to successfully manage a project of any size:

Communicate!

Failure to communicate effectively and often will harm the project faster and more devastatingly than any other error.

Defining the Project

Know the scope of the project and your specific area of responsibility. For example, you should at least know the marketing objectives, engineering deliverables, and overall project schedule for every product you're working on. (You may need to know a lot more for some projects.) You should know whether the documentation set your group is supplying is the only documentation for the project; if not, learn what other groups are contributing to the documentation effort. For example, is training planned for field engineers? How do training plans and materials mesh with the user manuals?

To organize your work, you must understand the project as a whole and know how your contribution helps meet the project's goals.

Setting Goals

After you've identified how your work fits into the big picture, establish your own goals for the project. Your objective may be simply to meet the deadlines. (Sometimes known as *dread*lines. The reason they're called *dead*lines is if you miss them, you die.) You may have specific quality goals or broad goals, such as making the books easier to use than the previous release. Try to set your goals at the beginning of the project, because once the project is underway, you'll be so busy you won't have time to evaluate what you're doing and why; you'll be concentrating on implementing those goals. If you have a clear focus on what your objective is—say, to make it easier to find information in the user's guides—you can make individual decisions on the fly and be consistent with the overall objectives.

Here's an example. One of the engineering objectives for a recent project was to make the product easy to maintain and update. The company's long-term strategy is to revise the product as often as necessary to satisfy customers' insatiable thirst for the newest technology. In a competitive marketplace, businesses need to adapt products to new demands quickly. To implement the business strategy, the engineers try to design and build the current product so that there aren't any obstacles to revising it.

On the documentation side of the business, we need to keep pace with the engineering effort. Our manuals are critical components of the product, since our customers cannot use our products without the documentation. We need to plan and "build" our documentation so that we can revise it as quickly as the engineers add new features.

On a day-to-day basis, that means we write and edit the books so that we don't have to make gratuitous changes when we revise them. When possible, we structure books so that they won't become obsolete when other products and books are changed. This planning saves us work and money and saves our customers the expense of buying new manuals, or worse, the agony of using an old manual with a new product.

Knowing this objective makes it very easy to answer the questions that arise on a daily basis: Which formatter do I use to write release notes? Certainly not the one we're phasing out next year. Do we weave information throughout the text for both user interfaces or do we put that information in an appendix? Integrate the information for the new default interface, which we expect to use for a long time, but put the information for the old, soon-to-be-retired interface in an appendix where we can drop it easily when necessary.

You can make decisions a lot faster when you have clearly stated goals.

Specifying Milestones and Deliverables

You should know what the milestones and deliverables are for the overall project or the parts of the project that affect you. A *milestone* is an event, such as "software freeze" or "eight prototype units available for internal use" or "first draft ready for technical review." A *deliverable* is the physical object you're producing: approved mechanicals for a new cover design, a complete manuscript, a printed manual, or a magnetic tape containing the software.

Know what the pieces are that you'll be shipping to customers as "documentation"—books, labels, binders, stickers, diskettes. Know when to expect each piece, from whom, and in what form. You also need to know what you're expected to do with it, when to hand it off, in what form, and to whom.

As an editor, the milestones that concern you the most are those that specify when you receive manuscripts and when you return them to writers or hand off material to production or printers. You should keep an eye on the schedule for the overall project, however, so you can take advantage of schedule slips.

Ensuring You're All Speaking the Same Language

The first time you work with a group of people, it's worth the extra time at the beginning to explain your process, expectations, and terminology. It may seem silly to spell out to the manager of another writing group what you mean by "camera-ready copy," but it won't seem silly if, the day before you're supposed to send the book to print, you receive "camera-ready copy" that needs a week's worth of pasteup, illustration, photo cropping, and other work before it meets your expectations of camera-ready copy. Write up a list and a description of what you expect.

If you think it's a waste of time to define your terms, consider this situation. In a planning meeting between two divisions of one company, everyone referred to the deliverables as "books." Later in the meeting—and fortunately not on the hand-off day—it became evident that to one group "book" meant completed manuscript ready for typesetting and to the other "book" meant printed manual.

Until all members of a group have had experience working together, don't assume that you're all speaking the same language. Even if you're all professional communicators and think you're using publishing jargon precisely, it's worth spending a few minutes on show-and-tell: "Here's a package typical of what we send to print" or "This book shows the binding method and the covers we plan to use."

Here's another example. If the schedule says, "manuscript to edit May 11," does that mean it's on the editor's desk at 8:00 on the morning of May 11 or does it mean the writer has it ready to hand off to edit by 5:00 that evening? When schedules are tight, this difference is critical. If you've worked late to finish editing one book because you're expecting another in the morning, you won't be happy to learn the writer had been planning to deliver the manuscript at the end of the day. The minute it takes for the writer and editor to verify that they're speaking the same language can prevent misunderstandings and ill will.

Keeping Everyone on Track

You will be on the receiving end of some deliverables and the sending end of others. Keep frequent tabs on both ends. Remind writers to let you know about changes to their schedules that affect you. I ask writers to let me know when there are rumors of schedule slips, so that I don't plan other projects around soft schedules.

A week or so before you're due to receive a manuscript, check with the writer to make sure the schedule is still valid. Likewise, let the people who will handle the book next know what to expect and when. Confirm schedules with production regularly. A week or so before you're handing off a book, remind the production group that the book will be ready. Also remind production of any special requirements the book has (that you all agreed to earlier in the process, of course).

If you maintain frequent and open communications on schedules, deliverables, and expectations with all groups, you'll avoid unnecessary rework, expense, and delay.

How to Manage Your Time in Normal Times

Effective time management means spending your time wisely. Completing a dozen trivial tasks is not good time management if you've done this work at the expense of an important project.

The first step in managing your time is to have clear goals and priorities.

Your managers will establish the relative priorities of the projects you're assigned to. Beyond that, you need to think about which discrete tasks you perform and how important and urgent each is. You can categorize tasks as follows, in order of priority:

- Urgent and important
- Urgent but not important
- Important but not urgent
- Not urgent and not important

As an exercise, look at your "to-do" list and sort each task into one of these four categories. Here's a partial list of tasks and how I rate each:

- Complete the paperwork to borrow a workstation for home. Important because I need it, but not urgent because a delay won't slip any schedules.

- Fill out and return survey about library. Urgent because it's due today, but not important to me.

- Check the print specifications and cover artwork for *Framistam Development System Reference.* Urgent because I'm handing off the book to print. Important because it's a revenue-producing product.

- Call the writer of *Printing User's Guide* and confirm the schedule change I requested last week. Important because I'm trying to accommodate this new book into an already tight schedule. Urgent because the first draft of the book is due soon.

- Rewrite boilerplate for preface for the next operating system release. Important because it affects all the books we publish for this product. Not urgent because we're not going to print for five months. (Four months from now it will be urgent.)

- Read the articles, newsletters, and memos that are piling up. Not important because they don't help me meet my project deadlines or reach my performance goals. Not urgent because they have no time value.

As these examples show, the urgency and importance of tasks change over time. A task that wasn't urgent yesterday may become urgent tomorrow.

You must take care of everything that is urgent and important. When you're swamped, you do the urgent and important first, then the urgent and unimportant because you can't put them off. (By definition they're time critical. You have to decide whether to do the task or skip it because it's unimportant.) Next, do the important but not urgent tasks. All the manuscripts you edit for revenue-generating products are important. Likewise, all proposals that solicit work are important. Your other responsibilities—usability testing, meeting with customers, and keeping abreast of industry trends—are also important. How urgent each of these tasks is depends on how short the deadline is.

Don't set aside time for tasks that aren't important and aren't urgent; by definition these are throwaway projects—ones you can safely ignore without penalty. Tasks that are unimportant and not urgent can sit around until you find yourself at your desk with nothing to do, or until your boss or client asks about them. (Once the boss reminds you about a task, you'd be wise to elevate it to "urgent.") Any task that you're assigned as a "backburner" or "filler" project falls into the unimportant and not urgent category until the person who asked for it remembers it. (Often they forget it themselves.)

A simple way to set priorities of projects you're editing is this: The further along the book is, the higher a priority it has. The reason is simple: Schedules are always shorter at the end of the line. Your editing projects, then, have this order of priority (barring extenuating circumstances):

- Checking salts (highest priority because the book is at the printer's)
- Production edits
- Literary or copy edits
- Developmental or preliminary edits
- Reviewing doc plans and project plans (lowest priority because the project can probably make up the time if you're a day or two late returning comments)

All the above tasks are important; their priority ranking depends on their urgency. A delay at the end of the schedule has more serious consequences than one at the beginning.

Get in the habit of keeping good records. Make a to-do list and keep it up-to-date. I keep my to-do list roughly in the order of priority discussed above, but I mark what needs to be done that week and especially that day. I update it throughout the day, check it before I leave at night, and look at it first thing in the morning. It's not enough to write a list—you must keep it up-to-date and use it.

How to Survive a Major Crunch

Editors are always busy, so you need good time-management skills just to get through the routine days. Sometimes, when you think you can't handle another piece of paper, the crunch sets in: It's finally time to send *all* the books to print.

When you have 20 books going to print in 3 weeks, you had better be in control. Here are some tips for getting through a major crunch without losing any pages or your sanity:

☐   Set a routine that's easy to follow. For example, I prefer to edit manuscripts in the morning and early afternoon, when I have fewer interruptions and my eyes are still fresh. I return phone calls, attend meetings (if possible), and schedule conferences with writers mid-to-late afternoon when my eyes can no longer focus on manuscripts. Monday mornings, I plan my upcoming week and remind writers if I'm expecting anything from them, and I confirm with production what books I'm handing off during the week. I save "housekeeping" tasks—updating schedules, reviewing the weekly database report, reviewing plans and specs—for Friday, a day I like to leave for wrapping up loose ends.

☐   Manage interruptions. I encourage afternoon interruptions and discourage those in the morning, when I'm most productive. When I need a block of uninterrupted time, I forward my calls to voicemail and close my door. Electronic mail keeps me in touch with the world outside my office, and I frequently check the light on my phone that tells me if I have a voicemail message. I return calls and electronic mail messages reasonably promptly—often within ten minutes—but the difference is that I can pause at the end of a chapter or train of thought, as suits my working pace.

☐   Prepare as much as possible before the books start coming in. Write checklists of what you need to do, have copies of all the forms you need, and complete as much of the forms as possible ahead of time. For example, if you have to prepare collating sheets for the books, make copies of the collating sheet form and fill in the titles and part numbers. I keep an extra supply of the business reply mailers, approval forms, and sign-off forms that make up part of the to-print package, too. It's inconvenient to interrupt a production edit to find and copy a form. Besides, laser printers and copy machines always know when you have a deadline and will break down then.

☐ Have adequate supplies on hand. Stockpile envelopes or boxes for shipping the camera-ready copy to your production department or printer. Replenish your stationery supplies—correction fluid, pens, whatever you depend on—before the books arrive. I hoard a few reams of paper for the laser printer so that we don't find ourselves unable to meet a deadline because the stockroom ran out of paper. (It's even better to let the people who order paper and maintain the printers know when you're going to have a heavier demand than usual, so they can order extra paper and toner in advance.)

☐ Make sure your office has room for all the manuscripts you'll be getting. Clean it up as much as possible; file papers or throw them out. Clear off the surface of your desk. You may want to borrow an extra table just to have a place to hold manuscripts. Keep your workspace organized so you don't misplace pages of books—or entire books.

☐ Make daily to-do lists. Every evening before you leave, update the list to show what needs to be done for each book. Follow that list the next morning, checking off items as you complete them.

☐ Micromanage the schedule. The closer the deadline is, the closer you need to manage the schedule. (Project management software can help.) Hours count. I prepare a daily checklist for myself and also for writers (who prepare their own camera-ready copy) to let them know what tasks we each need to complete that day. (For example: final corrections to chapters 1–10 today, check table of contents and index tomorrow.)

☐ Ask for clerical help for your peak days. Student interns and administrative assistants have saved me hours on major crunches by handling photocopying; shuttling manuscripts among writers, production, and me; proofreading tables of contents; and doing other time-consuming tasks.

☐ Avoid duplicating your effort. Constant revision is a fact of life in technical publishing, but you can minimize the amount of rework by careful planning. For example, check the contents of an index at the literary edit, but don't bother checking its format until the production edit. Check cross-references and running heads at the latest stage possible so you need to check them only once.

☐ Enjoy the adrenaline rush, but also relax. Never let writers see you panic over their books; they're trusting you to be in control. Express your panic when you're alone or with other editors, who will enjoy watching.

☐ Never forget your prime directive—serving the customer's needs. Everything else is trivial by comparison.

See appendix A for a case study ("Sending 20 Books to Print in 5 Days") that shows how to enlist the support of the writers in a crunch situation.

Meeting the demands of a tight and inflexible deadline and completing all your books and other projects on time, without fatal errors, is the most exhilarating experience you'll ever have as an editor. It's hard work, but it's fun—if you're prepared.

Summary

The key to successful project management is good communication. The key to successful time management is spending your time wisely, on important activities. Successful editors have both keys on their key chains.

◇ ──────────────── ──────────────── ◇

How to Survive a Major Crunch

- Set a routine that's easy to follow.
- Manage interruptions.
- Prepare as much as possible before the books start coming in.
- Have adequate supplies on hand.
- Make sure your office has room for all the manuscripts that you'll be getting.
- Make daily to-do lists.
- Micromanage the schedule.
- Ask for clerical help for your peak days.
- Avoid duplicating your effort.
- Enjoy the adrenaline rush, but also relax.
- Never forget your prime directive—serving the customer's needs.

◇ ──────────────── ──────────────── ◇

Chapter 15

How to Get Hired
As a Technical Editor and
How to Hire Technical Editors

This chapter is for editors (and people who want to be editors) and hiring managers.

The first part of this chapter is for people who want to be hired as technical editors. This chapter omits general job-hunting information such as how to find a job, write a resume, and dress for an interview. You can find that information in many other books. This chapter discusses only the aspects that relate specifically to technical editing. It suggests some questions you can ask to size up the job and some ways you can sell yourself.

The second part of this chapter is for hiring managers. It suggests interview questions and gives you some pointers for evaluating editing samples.

How to Get Yourself Hired As a Technical Editor

You have three aids to selling yourself: your resume, your portfolio, and your performance on an interview.

Your Resume

Resumes help hiring managers to screen out candidates. The purpose of your resume is to convince the hiring manager you're worth the time to interview. Your resume should tell enough to show you meet or exceed the minimum requirements. It should show the depth, as well as the breadth, of your experience.

Tell more than just the job title. As you saw in chapter 1, job titles don't adequately describe most editing jobs. Describe the position, briefly. Don't just copy your job description. The job description tells what is expected of *everybody* who ever holds that job (you and possibly dozens of other people); it doesn't tell what *you* actually accomplished. List your achievements; be specific about your contributions. Here are some examples:

EXAMPLES

Edited proposals for air traffic control project. Generated and produced 22 volumes of material in 6 weeks (6500 pages), including foldouts and detailed line art.

Edited nine seminar proceedings (150–200 pages each), which consisted of faculty papers, schematics, charts, and diagrams. Wrote foreword for two proceedings. Wrote biographical sketches of seminar faculty.

Responsible for editorial development of line of 15 trade books a year. Moved company into health and business line.

Responsible for all hardware and software technical manuals. Established the standards for this documentation and coordinated its generation with all levels of management.

Edited 21 new manuals and 30 revisions.

Developed indexing workshop to train writers and editors.

Directed the editing and production of a 12-volume documentation set.

Trained more than 20 new writers and editors.

Managers usually get resumes by the dozen. They sort them into two piles: *no* and *maybe*. Then they look through the maybes to see who is worth interviewing. For you to survive the first cut, your resume needs to show that you meet the minimum requirements and that you don't have any disqualifiers. For you to advance from a maybe to an interview, your resume should show you have good (or better) experience relative to the other candidates. You have no control over who else is applying for the job, but you have complete control over how you present yourself.

First and foremost, don't do anything to disqualify yourself. The simplest way to disqualify yourself for an editing job is to have a sloppy resume. Proofread your resume carefully. Then proofread it five more times. Many resumes end up in the trash because of typos. I recall one candidate who seemed promising, until I tried to call her and found that she'd given the wrong telephone number. The florist whose number she gave had never heard of her. I guess it was a typo, but of course I never bothered to track her down.

We recently received a letter from an editor inquiring about editing opportunities at "Hewlitt Packard." If this editor couldn't be bothered to check the spelling of "Hewlett-Packard" when she wanted to impress us, could we trust her to ensure accuracy in our manuals?

Typos in writers' resumes are disconcerting, but a hiring manager might overlook one or two, unless the candidate makes a point of his or her excellent spelling or proofreading skills. A typo in an editor's resume nearly always means doom. (I once did recommend hiring an editor who had a typo in her resume; her experience dwarfed the other candidates, and the typo was the only obvious reason to reject her. We brought her in for an interview, and one of her first comments was an apology for a typo in her resume. We hired her, and she was good.)

Always remember that your resume and your cover letter are samples of your writing and editing abilities. Use them to show that you can organize your thoughts, express yourself clearly, and format a page attractively.

Your Portfolio

The best way to show what you know about editing is to show what you've done. The best way to show what you've done is with samples of your editing.

Choose samples that show what you've contributed to the book. It's nice to show a printed book, but let it be in addition to—not instead of—an edited manuscript. The finished book simply doesn't show the manager what *you* did. You need to have samples of marked up manuscripts. The marked up manuscript and the printed book together can make an effective presentation, because the manuscript shows what you suggested and the printed book shows whether your suggestions were incorporated and how. It reflects on your credibility with the author of that book.

You don't have to show manuscripts from a complete book if a chapter or two is representative of your work on the book. You also don't need to present the original manuscript, so don't worry if the writers you work with like to keep the manuscripts. A photocopy is just fine. When you have finished an edit that you are proud of, photocopy the manuscript before returning it to the writer. If you get in the habit of copying manuscripts, you'll always have a supply of samples to choose from.

Your samples should show as much variety as possible. Show manuscripts that reflect different levels of edit. Show different types of publications. Show that you've edited different subject matter. Show that you've edited publications for beginners and experts. Provide as much perspective on your experience as you can.

By the way, you don't need a leather portfolio case.[1] A manila envelope stuffed with substantive samples will impress more managers than a fancy portfolio case with weak samples.

Keep your portfolio current. Add at least one good sample every year and weed out the poorer samples. I'd be leery of anyone who couldn't show me a good example of work done in the last year. But if you did a spectacular job five years ago, don't hesitate to keep that sample in your portfolio. Good editing never goes out of style.

If you have a lot of samples, you can tailor your selection for each interview. When possible, show manuscripts similar to the books the people interviewing you produce. For example, if you're interviewing for a job editing software manuals, bring a sample of an edited software manual.

If you don't have an appropriate sample, here's a neat ploy. Get a copy of a book published by the company where you want to work and edit it. If your editing is on target and diplomatically worded, the employer won't be offended.

You might want to include some samples of your own writing to demonstrate your versatility and willingness to take on a writing assignment in a pinch.

---

[1] Not that I recommend doing this, but I know an editor who carries his samples in a plastic milk crate.

Annotate your samples. Attach a note to each manuscript telling what you did. You might want to describe the circumstances and challenges of the project. Were you instructed to keep costs to a minimum? Was the writer particularly difficult to work with? (Pray that writer doesn't work where you're interviewing.) Was the subject matter especially difficult? Was the schedule unusually tight? This kind of information gives people reviewing your samples a much better insight into what you can do.

Your annotations serve a few purposes. Making them shows that you've taken the time and care to prepare your samples for an audience. During the interview, the hiring manager may review your samples. If you have annotated your samples, then the interviewer can read the annotations, too, while you enjoy a brief mental rest.

The Interview

The interview lets you tell the hiring manager how well you can fill the position and gives you the opportunity to determine if the job is right for you.

The manager will be trying to ferret out your experience and judge if you have the necessary skills. The manager will also be trying to see if you fit the job in temperament and style. Be prepared to answer the questions in the latter part of this chapter (the manager's section).

Here are some questions you can ask to judge the position:

- What is the ratio of editors to writers today? What do you see as a desirable ratio? (A writer-to-editor ratio of 4:1 is considered average, where the editor performs substantive and developmental editing. A higher writer-to-editor ratio translates to a lower level of editing.)

- What is the history of editors in this department (at this company)? How long have you had editors?

- What backgrounds do your editors have?

- How long do editors typically stay as editors here?

- When editors leave, do they take editing jobs elsewhere or do they change jobs in the company?

- What happened to the last person who held this job? (Why is there a vacancy?)

- What kind of growth path do you offer someone who wants to stay an editor?

- What kind of career path is there for editors beyond editing?

- What value do editors add to your department and company, in your view? Does your manager share this view?

- How are disputes between writers and editors resolved?

- Who sets the project schedule? Who sets the editing schedule? What kind of input would I have into the scheduling process?

- Who determines how many editing passes a manuscript will have and how much time there is for each pass? What kind of input would I have?

- Who determines the level of edit? What kind of input would I have?

- What backgrounds do your writers have?

- How do your writers feel about having their work edited? What kinds of problems have arisen?

- How many developmental, copy, and production edits would I be expected to do?

- How much rewriting do editors do here? How much is desirable?

- Who puts the editing changes into the manuscript? (This question is a more subtle way of asking, "Are you looking for an editor or a production assistant?")

- What is the production process here? Who does what?

- What is the writing process? How many drafts do writers produce? When do technical reviews occur? Where does editing fit in?

- What would you say to a writer who came to you and said his or her work didn't need to be edited?

- Who signs off on the manuscript before production and on the camera-ready copy before it goes to print?

One last bit of advice: Don't ask all these questions of one interviewer. Chances are you'll meet with several people, and they'll impart some of this information in the normal course of telling you about the position and department. Ask different people different questions. You may want to ask the same question of a few people and compare answers. Also, save some questions for the second interview. Just be sure you know the answers to these questions before you accept the job offer, so you aren't surprised to learn after you've started work that the so-called developmental editor position is really an opportunity to exercise your proofreading skills.

Ask About the Working Environment Before You Take the Job

At *Success,* the magazine he runs, Mr. DeGarmo recently began fining senior editors for approving articles containing typographical and grammatical mistakes. . . . Most typos . . . cost $25, but the price for misspelling the name of the main person in a story is $500—minimum. . . . The fines are deducted from next year's pay raises for the six affected staffers, Mr. DeGarmo says. He adds that he tried "all the nice, positive things"—gently citing mistakes and lauding perfect copy—but simply tired of editors saying they couldn't spell. "Believe me," Mr. DeGarmo says, "if they're motivated, they'll learn."[1]

◇ ◇ ◇ ◇ ◇ ◇ ◇ ◇ ◇ ◇ ◇ ◇

[Under the ownership of Condé Nast, 1909–1957, *Vogue*] was so status-conscious that only editors were permitted to wear hats. When a young woman asked Nast for a promotion, he consented. She didn't get a raise, but she could come to work in a hat.[2]

Hiring Technical Editors

Many publications managers are experienced at interviewing and hiring writers but have little experience with editors. Their standard interview questions for writers aren't necessarily appropriate for screening editors.

This section gives some advice and suggests some interview questions that will help you evaluate the depth of a candidate's editing experience and assess whether her or his style fits your needs.

Evaluating Resumes

Take the job title with a grain of salt. Look at the specific duties, responsibilities, and achievements the candidate lists and use your own good judgment to determine the nature of the job.

Put more stock in variety and types of experience than simply years of experience. Some editing jobs are so demanding that an editor with only a year's experience will have faced many difficult challenges and will have acquired many skills. In contrast, some editing jobs don't offer many learning opportunities, so five years' experience doesn't mean much.

---

[1] *The Wall Street Journal,* December 19, 1990.

[2] *Newsweek,* April 8, 1991.

Review the resume and cover letter carefully. It is absolutely fair to consider these samples of the candidate's writing and editing skills. You have every right to judge an editor more harshly than a writer on the mechanics (spelling, grammar, punctuation) because you'd expect the editor you hire to help your writers on these points.

Assume an editor who can't be bothered to proofread his or her own resume won't bother paying attention to details in your manuals.

If you find a typo (or grammatical error that could be a typo), find out if the candidate or the agency typed the resume. If an agency typed the resume, the candidate probably didn't have the opportunity to proofread it (but ask the agent; sometimes candidates do check).

If the candidate typed the resume, then you need to decide if you still want to consider that person for an editing job. If the candidate's qualifications otherwise merit an interview, and if you don't have other good candidates, you may still want to pursue this person. Be sure to point out the typo (or ask the candidate if he or she knows about the typo) and gauge his or her reaction. Conduct this test face-to-face rather than in a telephone interview so that you have the additional input from body language and eye contact.

Even if the agency typed the resume with the error, ask the candidate about the typo. Some candidates are mortified, others annoyed. Others have reactions you may not expect.

One candidate, who had typed her resume herself, had this response when I pointed out that one word was misspelled three times in her resume, "It's probably *liaison*. I never can spell that word." She couldn't be bothered to pick up a dictionary while writing her resume? I'm supposed to recommend hiring her to edit? I couldn't resist a follow-up question, "How do you feel about it?" She shrugged and replied—I am not making this up—"It's no big deal. So what?"

Evaluating Editing Samples

When you schedule the interview, ask the candidate to bring samples of his or her work. Emphasize that you would like to see marked up manuscripts, not printed books.

Expect some people to balk: "I don't have samples because writers keep the manuscripts"; "I only have samples of editing I did for marketing writing, not technical writing"; "I only have printed manuals." Impress upon the candidate that you need samples to evaluate her or his qualifications. Many candidates will suddenly remember where they can scrounge up manuscripts.

Sometimes candidates just lack confidence about showing their work; their reluctance to show samples doesn't necessarily mean their work isn't good. Some good editors just never think they'll need to look for another job and don't save samples. Editors who started in an entry-level position, where they didn't need to show editing samples, may not be aware that managers hiring senior editors want to see manuscripts.

A candidate may want to bring a printed book along with the manuscript to show you the before and after versions. By all means agree; you'll get a good idea of how many of the editor's comments were incorporated into the final version, and that will give you some indication of how effective the editor was.

Some candidates will have only partial manuscripts. For example, I may save only one or two chapters from an enormous manual if I think those chapters demonstrate what I've done. I'd rather lug many short samples from a variety of documents than one big book.

If the candidate doesn't have editing samples, or if the samples don't give you enough information, you may want to administer an editing test. You will need to work closely with your personnel department to ensure that any test you design and administer is handled fairly, within federal equal opportunity guidelines.

When you review the samples, look at the types of comments the editor has made. Using the descriptions in chapters 6 and 8, determine what type and level of edit the candidate applied. If the candidate has described a sample as a heavy edit, but you see only a few commas added or deleted and a handful of spelling corrections, you should question the depth of the candidate's experience. It would also help to know how much time the editor had to spend on the manuscript.

Read the manuscript and see if you spot errors—actual errors and not simply matters of style—the editor didn't mark. Are there inconsistencies? Did the editor catch most or all nits?

Read and evaluate the manuscript from the point of view of the intended audience. Do you notice any glaring anomalies? Recognize that the writing style may be more or less formal than what you use, but that might reflect policy at the candidate's company. Ask the candidate about any style differences that trouble you.

Look at the table of contents to get an overview of the organization of the book. Does anything seem amiss?

Be careful not to judge the editor because you don't like the wording (if what's written is otherwise acceptable) or for other subjective reasons.

Don't hold following a different style guide against the editor, as long as the candidate has followed it consistently. For example, if you prefer items—including simple phrases—in a bulleted list to end in a period, but the editor's sample shows only complete sentences ending in a period, don't fault the editor. But if similarly constructed lists are handled in different ways, then the editor has goofed.

If you're reviewing a sample of a developmental edit, be aware that the editor may have intentionally ignored literary and copy editing details, expecting to deal with these matters at a later draft, when the content was more stable.

Pay close attention to how the editor addresses the writer. Are the comments tactful? If you were the writer, would you find the tone and style helpful? Insulting? Constructive? Offensive? Informative? If you have doubts about a comment, ask the editor. A comment may seem inappropriate to you, but perhaps it was appropriate in the context.

Has the editor rewritten large blocks of text? If so, ascertain whether that was expected and desired for that particular manuscript or in that position. Some editors simply like to rewrite; sometimes that's a plus and sometimes not.

Look at the manuscript as if you were the editor to see if anything was overlooked. Also look at the manuscript as if you were the writer to see if you'd like to work with this editor.

Questions to Ask the Candidate

As with any interview, you want to ask questions that will elicit descriptive answers. Here are some questions that will give a candidate the opportunity to tell you what experience really accompanies the job titles on the resume:

- What are some contributions you've made to a project that another editor might not have made?
- What's the biggest mistake you've ever made that found its way into print?
- What's the biggest mistake (yours or someone else's) you caught before it got to print?
- What do you consider a significant catch?
- What do you look for in a developmental edit? In a literary or copy edit?
- Define substantive editing.
- Do you follow any system of levels of edit? Describe.
- Describe a difficult writer you've worked with. What made that writer difficult? What were the circumstances? How did you handle the situation? Would you handle it the same way again?

- Have you helped to interview writers? What do you look for?
- Do you think it's appropriate for an editor to let a manager know if a writer can't do the job or isn't pulling his or her weight?
- How do you handle disagreements with writers?
- How do you return an edited manuscript to a writer? Do you make an appointment to discuss changes? Do you send it via interoffice mail? Why do you do it this way? (The important part is *why*.)

An editor who has never made a mistake or who has never had a problem with a writer probably has very limited experience. If you're filling an entry-level position, that's OK ; if you're filling a senior-level position, it's not.

For most of these questions, there are no right or wrong answers. What's important is whether the editor's working style and problem-solving methods suit your organization's style.

Information to Give the Candidate

The candidate may not ask enough questions about the job, particularly if she or he is an entry-level candidate. It's in your interest to let the candidate know enough about the position so that you're not faced with a dissatisfied employee after a month on the job. Be sure to impart the following information to any candidate you're seriously considering:

- Number of writers and books (and what the typical workload is)
- What your expectations are of the number of pages edited per week (if you care)
- How involved the editor will be with the project team, production staff, and writers (or what your expectations are)
- How proactive you expect the editor to be in working relationships with the project team, production staff, and writers
- Reporting relationships of writers, editors, production staff (show an organization chart)
- How work is assigned (are editors assigned to individual writing groups, or does work come into the editing department and then get assigned?)
- How editorial and writing issues and conflicts are resolved and who resolves them
- What types of editorial and writing issues and conflicts have arisen in the last year and whether you expect these to recur
- How you (and the rest of the department or company) position the editing function (a dead-end job, a steppingstone to a better job, an exciting career opportunity?)

- How much grunt work the editor should expect to do and how much planning, project management, and editing
- How much rewriting is desirable
- Your standards for quality
- Your (department's) relative priorities (schedule, quality, quantity)

Keeping Your Investment

If you've ever tried to hire an editor, you know that good editors are very hard to find. There are fewer editors than writers to start with, and editors burn out at a faster rate than writers. Unfortunately, many of the best editors are the first to burn out and leave editing.

In many companies, editing is a stopover en route to other careers. Why? Because in these companies editing is an entry-level position with no advancement opportunities. The best editors in these companies have no incentive to remain editors. If you care about nurturing good senior editors, make sure there are real opportunities for them.

Keeping editors happy doesn't require different management magic from keeping other employees happy: interesting work, new challenges, opportunity to learn and develop new skills, balanced workload, supportive environment, feedback, career path, professional growth, and good wages. Just don't forget that editors need the same care and feeding as everyone else.

Also recognize that an editor's workload is invariably heavier than that of any writer, so you will need to manage that situation. Ensure that the editor has some control over the schedule or deliverables, such as determining the level of edit. Give your editor time to learn new tools and become familiar with your products. Managers typically build learning time into writers' schedules; do the same for your editors. When possible, provide backup support for the editor, especially to relieve some of the grunt work. Help writers understand the volume of work and pace the editor lives with, and make sure the writers cooperate by allowing adequate time in the schedule for editing (including making revisions the editor suggests) and by honoring their schedule commitments. Make sure there are calms amid the crises.

Let editors work on projects that give them a change of pace from time to time, such as an occasional writing assignment.

As long as editors find the job interesting and challenging, they'll grow with it. Read chapter 16 to see some new directions for editing and ways to prepare your editors for them.

Summary

This chapter showed the hiring process from both sides of the desk, and it suggested questions you can use on your next interview. Table 15–1 reviews the main points.

Table 15–1. Summary of Tips for Hiring Editors and Being Hired

	Interviewee	Interviewer
Resume	give details of your accomplishments	look for specific achievements
	don't copy your job description	ignore the job title; check the responsibilities and duties
	demonstrate good writing and editing	watch for errors; the resume is a writing sample
	show depth and breadth	look for a variety of experience
Portfolio	show variety and relevant samples	look for variety, depth
	bring marked up manuscripts	ask to see marked up manuscripts; evaluate how the editor communicates with writers
	annotate your samples so people can evaluate your work	judge the editor's work; don't judge the writer, the designer, or the style guide
Interview	ask questions to find out if the job is right for you and if you're really right for the job	ask questions to find out if the candidate has the experience and the attitude you need
Job	find out what it's like to work at the company before you take the job	if you're lucky enough to find and hire good editors, keep them happy

Chapter 16

Is Editing Becoming Obsolete?

"The editor hanged himself a few minutes ago."

"Have they cut him down?"

"Not yet. He isn't dead."

Is technical editing dead? Not yet. But it's hanging by a thread.

Editing: Past and Present

Editors have always had it tough in industry. Editors are the last hired and first fired, under the justification that you can't edit a manuscript that hasn't been written.

Managers perceive editing as a frill. To them, editors nitpick over details that cost time and money to fix. Besides, if writers didn't make mistakes, we wouldn't need editors. (*We* know this description of editing is wrong. Does *your* manager know?)

Technical writers haven't had it much better. Many companies do not value technical writing. Some managers can't even distinguish between writing and typing. For decades books and journals about technical communications have lamented the professional problems of technical writers: job insecurity, lack of respect, job insecurity, lack of respect, job insecurity, and lack of respect. Not to mention low wages.

It has always been much worse for editors.

You don't find very many senior editors. Do you know why? Most editors burn out or wise up before they acquire many years of seniority. Many good editors transfer to writing jobs because writing has fewer deadline pressures, a lighter workload, and slightly better job security.

There have always been fewer editing jobs than writing jobs, even in economic booms. After all, one editor can support many writers, so a company needs fewer editors. Many companies combine the writing and editing functions into a single position, and many others don't use editors at all.

Even managers who want to hire editors face difficulties getting the funding. Managers can fund writers more easily than editors. In many companies, the writer's salary can be charged to a specific project. Budgeting is more complicated for editors, because editors generally support many projects. As a result, editors are usually carried in the budget as overhead—the most dangerous place to be when budgets are being slashed.

We start with the dismal fact that editing jobs are scarce and always have been. Now look at what most editors are doing in the jobs they have. Most technical editors are still performing copy edits, format edits, and production edits. A few perform true technical edits, usability testing, and developmental edits.

I hope that this book has shown you that there's more to editing than checking spelling and filling out collating sheets. I hope you've learned for two reasons:

- The more managers, writers, and editors who recognize the potential contributions technical editors can make, the more opportunities editors will have to make these contributions.

- The higher level of edit you perform, the less likely software will replace you. Any aspect of editing that can be reduced to a set of rules is fodder for artificial intelligence (more specifically, expert system software).

Software Can Replace You

What will you do when software can do your job—or when your manager thinks it can? How will your manager justify your salary plus overhead to senior management when a $50 software package can do the same tasks—or managers think it can?

Don't say it can't happen. Publishing software keeps getting better and cheaper. Managers will put two and two together and get three, close enough to justify replacing an editor with a spelling and syntax checker.

If all you're doing is adding some commas and fixing spelling, you will be replaced by software.

You and I know that software today can make some horrendous errors. It simply isn't good enough to replace the sharp editorial eye. Moreover, grammar and style checkers on the market today are poor substitutes for a person with a good ear for language and the ability to understand what she or he is reading.

We also know that a developmental editor solves knotty writing and usability problems that computers won't be capable of solving for another 30–50 years.

But we're not the people who will make the decision to replace editors with software. The managers who make this decision don't know the fine points of our job and don't care to. Besides, the software that will be available in five or ten years will do as good a job as the average copy editor in checking mechanics. That's all many companies need. If that's all you do, it's not enough.

When good editing software is available, I'll be the first to buy it. The more mechanical tasks I can delegate to software, the more time I'll have for the challenging and fun parts of the job: developmental editing, usability testing, and serving as a mentor to writers.

For example, here are some tasks that I've dropped over the years, mostly thanks to technology:

- Photocopying manuscripts before starting to mark them up. Before word processing, I was given the only physical manuscript that existed. Now that the books are on disk and we can print out a clean manuscript any time, this precaution is no longer necessary.

- Marking heads to indicate their relative hierarchy for formatting. Many word processor and text editors can generate different fonts, so even the first drafts distinguish heads typographically.

- Turning the pages in the book to make sure heads are numbered correctly (when the book follows the weighted decimal system). The computer-generated table of contents lists all heads; I can check these at a glance to ensure there were no glitches in the computer-generated numbering. Likewise, I can check figure and table numbering.

- Numbering manuscript pages by hand (or worse, with an awful stamping machine). The publishing software does this, too.

- Sizing illustrations. Writers insert the artwork electronically in the books.

- Worrying about whether to treat something as an open, closed, or hyphenated compound. I make quick decisions on these and worry about more important issues. If necessary, my decision can be reversed with a few keystrokes.

- Preparing an art package or redrawing sketches after editing the callouts so the artist can have a clean draft to work from. The writers create most of the art themselves and get help from illustrators—all electronically.

- Proofreading galleys and checking repro. I edit writers' formatted drafts, instead.

- Marking all occurrences of spelling changes. I mark the change once.

- Preparing manuscripts to meet submission requirements of the production department.

How to Survive

To survive as an editor, you need to add value, acquire new skills, and educate your managers.

Add Value

If you've been following the editing model described in this book, you know how to add more value. Add value by making the product easier to use, by training junior writers, and by improving the manuals.

Add value by improving how documentation is organized (documentation sets as well as individual books), so that customers can find information quickly. Work with writers to ensure that the documentation covers the appropriate topics and discusses each to an appropriate level of detail. Ensure that the documentation is free of technical errors and technical inconsistencies.

It's not enough to mark up a manuscript. If your editing doesn't produce improvements, if the writer ignores your great suggestions, if your ideas don't increase customer satisfaction—then you've just wasted your time. All you've done is a meaningless exercise of putting marks on paper.

Contribute directly to customer satisfaction. Learn what your customers want and find solutions for giving it to them. Suggest ways to streamline the writing, editing, and production processes so that you have more time to build quality into the product. Develop better ways to test the product with the documentation. Ensure that people implement the testing programs and follow through on the results. Give feedback that improves the product's design and usability.

You need to make a difference.

Acquire New Skills

You also need to acquire new skills so that you can adapt to the changes in technical publishing.

Here are some of the trends to monitor.

- Electronic handoff of publications means books can go from the writer directly to the printer over telephone lines or by satellite. Where does editing fit? Investigate the technology and develop new processes.

- Multimedia. Learn how to edit—for content, if not also mechanically—sound, video, and animation. Learn how to use different media to convey technical information. How do your users respond to the new media? How do you distribute the documentation? (Do you even call it *documentation*?)

- New distribution methods. Do you abandon hardcopy manuals altogether? What role do editors play when you distribute electronic books?

- Internationalization. Books must be easily adapted to global markets.

- User interface design. How can you make the product self-documenting?

- Online documentation. Keep current with developments in hypertext. How do you edit a hypertext document, where every reader invents a different book?

Also keep the old skills sharp. Read *The Elements of Style* and *The Chicago Manual of Style* every year, if only to remind yourself how much information these books cover. Good style never goes out of style.

Educate Your Managers and Others

Educate writers, writing managers, engineers, engineering managers—and anybody else who influences your job—about the editing function. You will have to break down the stereotypical image of the green-visored editor hunched over galleys to proofread for missed commas. Shatter this image by showing how you can contribute to customer satisfaction—through a better product and better documentation.

Be active on the project team. Know the product and make suggestions for improving the product. Demonstrate that you're part of the writing team, not a production coordinator.

Actively participate in the evolution of the next stage of editing. Keep abreast of advances in publishing technology, writing issues, and new developments in writing techniques and strategies. For example, recent hot topics have included collaborative writing projects and intelligent online systems.

Don't be caught with outdated twentieth-century skills in the twenty-first century.

Does Editing Have a Future?

Excel, adapt, and educate. The future of technical editing is in *your* hands.

Appendix A
Case Studies

These case studies show typical problems you might face as an editor and suggest some solutions. By the way, most writers are good to work with—but you don't need case studies to learn how to work with them.

These stories and personalities are composites of actual events and people. The names of the people and some of the details have been changed.

Case 1: Writer Ignores Editor's Comments

The Situation

You're an editor at the Fenway Computer Company. Jacob is a writer in your department. Even though you've both worked for the same company for several years, you've never worked together, thanks to the shuffling of people in departmental reorganizations. You know Jacob simply as a quiet, pleasant fellow. When you cross paths, he always flashes a quick smile and a friendly greeting. He also seems to be a hard worker; he always looks busy.

You're the editor for Jacob's next manual, a revision to a user's guide. Throughout the planning process, Jacob consults you. He asks you to review his doc spec before it goes to other reviewers. He calls you twice a week to ask several other questions. For example, he has some ideas that he wants to pass by you about reorganizing the book to make it more task-oriented. You notice that he sometimes asks the same question three or four times in a week, almost as if he's waiting for a particular answer, but you chalk up that suspicion to watching too many TV cop shows.

Jacob hands you the first draft of the manuscript on schedule. So far, working with this writer has been an editor's dream—he keeps you informed of the project's status, he notifies you of schedule changes, he asks your advice before going ahead with major changes, he meets his deadlines, and his easygoing personality makes all your interactions a pleasure.

The manuscript, however, is a mess. The sentences simply don't make sense. Besides, the wording is convoluted, the text is riddled with noun strings, and the sentences seem to be punctuated according to what I call the five-ten rule (put a comma after every fifth word and a period after every tenth). Half the sentences are in the passive voice, the only verb he has used is *to be*, every other sentence is a *note*—and half of them seem irrelevant. The titles of the chapters and sections follow the outline you reviewed, but the paragraphs in those sections don't pertain to the subject. The outline could just as well belong to another book.

Well, you tell yourself, it's a first draft; maybe he has been concentrating on the technical accuracy. You test a few examples. What you see on the computer screen doesn't match what's in the text. The prompts and messages are slightly different, and the commands don't work as the manual says.

You plunge into the manuscript and, since this is the first draft, you focus on the big issues. You suggest ways to reorganize paragraphs and sections, you mark which examples no longer work, and you point out some general stylistic problems, such as the inconsistent use of *user* and *you* to address the reader—sometimes within the same sentence. You also indicate that there are writing problems that you'll address in the next draft. You give a few examples so that Jacob is aware of them and can work on them as he works on the revisions. (After all, Jacob has more than five years' experience as a technical writer; he must know his job.)

You also offer to review the draft chapter by chapter, to save time. Jacob says that ordinarily that would be a good idea, but the engineers are making radical changes to the product so he'll be making wholesale changes throughout the book. It will be too tricky to give you a chapter to edit while he's still revising it.

Meanwhile, he skims through your comments and seems delighted you've spotted flaws. "The last revision of this book was done under incredible circumstances," he explains. "The deadline was just impossible, the engineers kept making changes, and a lot of errors crept in. There was no time to fix anything, and we didn't even have an editor assigned to the project. I'm glad you marked all these problems so we can fix them this time."

You invite Jacob to let you know if he has any questions as he works on the revisions, and then you return to your office to work on one of your other 18 manuals. You have a slightly uneasy feeling about Jacob; if he knew the book had serious writing problems, why didn't he say something to you earlier? Why didn't he ask for a few more weeks on the first draft to fix known problems? Your phone rings. Another writer wants to know if you can come to a presentation and help field questions. You head off to the meeting, putting Jacob and his book out of your mind.

Several weeks pass, during which time you have a few brief conversations with Jacob. Your comments go something like this: "How's it going? Do you have any questions about my edits? Can you read my handwriting? I'd be happy to look at any chapter that you have ready." Jacob's part in the conversations goes something like this: "You wouldn't believe how many changes the developers are making. I'm working 14-hour days to put in all the technical changes. I have to rewrite bits and pieces everywhere. I haven't put in most of your changes yet because the book is changing so much that many of those corrections are no longer relevant. But as soon as I get a stable draft to work from, I'll go through your comments in detail and put in all changes that apply."

A few weeks later, Jacob gives you the next draft. You can't believe it. There are new sentences and paragraphs scattered throughout. Most of the new sentences are labeled as notes so they're easy to find. But most of the old text is still there, with the same problems as in the previous draft. Well, not quite. Jacob did fix the typos (or most of them). But the organizational, syntactic, accuracy, and usability problems still exist.

What do you do? Here are some of your options:

- Confront Jacob. Ask him why he ignored your comments and if you'll be wasting your time editing this draft, too.

- Ask Jacob—nicely—what's going on.

- Go to your manager for advice.

- Go to Jacob's manager to complain.

- Edit the manuscript as if nothing happened.

Analysis

First, don't go to your manager or Jacob's—yet. If you approach a manager, all you've demonstrated is that you lack the confidence or the ability to solve the problem yourself. You may eventually need to elevate this problem to management, but you haven't even begun to look at ways to solve it.

If you edit the manuscript as if nothing had happened, you may find yourself in exactly the same position a month from now, when there's less time to fix it. The manuscript has problems serious enough to prevent users from understanding and using the product. Burying your head in the sand, er, manuscript, doesn't solve the problem. An overly long delay could jeopardize the book and the product.

You and Jacob need to talk. What tone do you want to set for that conversation? (You certainly don't want to be sarcastic—"Will editing this draft be a waste of time?"—because that gains you nothing.) What do you think will happen if you confront Jacob and accuse him of ignoring your comments? His past behavior indicates that he'll do anything to avoid an argument. He'll tell you that he just hasn't had time to fix the writing problems, but he certainly intends to do so. He'll compliment your work. ("You caught some really important problems. It's great having an experienced editor . . . ")

If he'd only come out and say that he's ignoring you on purpose—that your editing changes are inappropriate or that editing is just a nuisance—you could discuss his objections to the editorial process or your specific comments on his manuscript. Or you may have to bring in management to address the breakdown in the departmental processes.

But Jacob isn't directly challenging you; he acts as though he wants to cooperate with you, but circumstances beyond his control are keeping him from implementing your suggestions.

You may be tempted to give Jacob the benefit of the doubt. After all, he was coping with lots of technical changes and a tight schedule. So you replay in your mind the history of this project. Doesn't it seem odd there are so many technical changes but the project schedule itself hasn't slipped? Not necessarily, but you also know that two engineers have left the project, and they haven't hired replacements. Isn't it more likely the project team is cutting rather than adding new features? Isn't it also strange that not one of these so-called drastic changes requires the manual to be reorganized? Wouldn't you expect at least one chapter to be added or eliminated? What about all those notes? Could the technical changes that have Jacob in such a tizzy actually be technical corrections the reviewers are marking? As you found errors in the prompts, messages, and commands—which Jacob still hasn't corrected—the engineers may be finding other technical errors. Are those notes simply Jacob's way of inserting corrections? Why wouldn't he integrate the information into the text? Doesn't he know how to rewrite?

Something else clicks—didn't Jacob say the last revision (which he did) was this chaotic, too? And why was Jacob asking you the same questions over and over? Is it possible he didn't understand what you were saying? Or was he waiting for you to suggest doing what he wanted to do anyway? Did he really want your input on the doc spec—or was some unseen hand (his manager, perhaps)—pushing him your way?

Could Jacob simply need more help than he's willing to admit? You've assumed that he's an experienced writer; perhaps he has been around for five years, but maybe his skills aren't very sharp. He may not be putting in your editing changes because he doesn't know how to.

You've identified two separate issues: Jacob may not be as skilled a writer as you (and maybe others, including his manager) thought. And he hides his incompetence by going through the motions of cooperation.

This behavior does not necessarily mean the writer is incompetent. Sometimes competent writers ignore their editors' comments. And a writer can behave differently yet still be incompetent. The situation with Jacob is the worst case: You have a writer who can't do the job and won't ask for help.

Now that you recognize the problems, you can start to help solve them. Take a more active role in Jacob's project. When you edited the first draft, you gave broad instructions ("overuse of passive voice" and "this section needs to be more procedural and less descriptive"). Perhaps you should have given him very explicit instructions. Perhaps you should have edited—or rewritten—each sentence that had stylistic problems. Ask specific, guiding questions for sentences that had technical ambiguities ("Does the user do this or does the program take care of it?"). Spend more time with Jacob; teach him what he needs to know. Be sensitive to Jacob's feelings, however. He's an experienced writer and doesn't need to be treated like a beginner. When you rewrite a paragraph, add a comment that shows what you were trying to accomplish and why. Let him know that your rewrites are suggestions; if he has a better way to express the idea, he should use it. After all, he is the writer. (Remind him that you understand your role and his and that you don't want to step on his toes.)

Keep copies of the edited manuscripts and your correspondence with Jacob. If the final draft is still inaccurate or unclear, you'll need to alert management. It's the editor's responsibility to go to management—your manager or Jacob's—when the project is at risk. Let management know if the book doesn't meet the minimal standards outlined in the doc spec or if it's so bad that customers can't use it.

It's very likely the engineers have already complained to Jacob's manager about him, if your suspicions about the technical reviews are valid. Jacob's manager may come to you for more information. Jacob may even blame the editor—yeah, you—for introducing errors into the book. Be prepared.

This story may also have a happy ending: Jacob's next draft is acceptable (maybe even good, but settle for adequate and accurate), you've taught him something about writing which he'll be able to apply throughout his career, and you've established a cooperative working relationship.

Case 2: Writer Argues with Editor About *Everything*

The Situation

Two months ago you were reassigned to a new writing group as a result of a departmental reorganization. Most of the writers accepted you quickly. After all, they've all worked with editors before and you've worked in this company long enough to have established a reputation as a knowledgeable, competent, and fair editor.

One writer, however, challenges your every word.

Jamie has a Ph.D. in English and taught English composition and literature at a community college before becoming a technical writer ten years ago. Her speech is sprinkled with words like *metonymy, pathetic fallacy,* and *litotes,* terms you remember from college but don't often come across in technical editing.

You're not sure how Jamie even manages to slip these terms into conversation, but you can guess why. Jamie thinks that she knows much more about writing, technology, and, well, everything, than you do. And she's not going to let you forget it. Any comment you mark on her manuscript—other than the correction of a typo—precipitates a discussion, or, more appropriately, a lecture by the professor. The lecture topic is always the same, "I am right. You are wrong."

If you mark one of her sentences as being unclear or ambiguous, she tells you you're stupid for not understanding it. If you explain how any reader could misread the sentence, she digresses into an explanation of her rhetorical technique.

You wouldn't mind so much if it were a simple matter of right and wrong. After all, you have an open mind and you're willing to learn. What Jamie is always "right" about, however, are those style issues that have no single right answer. For example, do you refer to "chapter 1" or "Chapter 1" in cross-references? You mark the manuscript according to your company's style guide; Jamie appears in your office with *The Chicago Manual of Style* and tells you the company's style guide is wrong. You could counter with another authority to support your point of view and defend the style guide, but you know that Jamie will just come back with yet another authority to support her views.

Jamie clearly misses academe and the joy of lecturing. You, on the other hand, find Jamie's pontification boring and you don't hesitate to show your impatience. You would rather proofread an index than discuss the merits of *on-line* vs. *online*.

Sometimes Jamie's comments pique your curiosity, but your deadlines don't permit you to research every point she raises. You brush Jamie off with a "That's the way we do it here" and brace yourself for her *next* issue.

You know your approach isn't constructive, but you don't know how to get Jamie off your back.

How do you break this stalemate and get your work done?

Analysis

Don't get sucked into academic arguments. Keep the focus on your readers. When Jamie brings up rhetoric, remind her that the readers can only judge whether or not the manual meets their needs. Suggest usability testing if Jamie doesn't trust your judgment as user advocate. Don't argue that "my credentials are bigger than yours." Simply speak confidently—and calmly.

Explain to Jamie that you're her ally, not her adversary, and that arguments about style detract from your mutual goals.

Acknowledge Jamie's interest in style, but point out you both have to follow the style guide so that her book fits in with the documentation set. Add that you'll recommend she participate in the next revision of the style guide.

Address the issue of control. You both want to control the situation. You don't need to be so abrupt ("That's the way we do it here"), but Jamie doesn't need to be such a pest, either. Discuss your jobs: what decisions fall to the editor, which to the writer, and where you both concede to the style guide or other departmental rules. If you have a real difference of opinion, tell Jamie to ask her manager (or yours) to clarify your role. Let Jamie go to management, not you. If your editing comments are appropriate, the manager will support you. Jamie will look like a whiner for going to management because you said to write *online* without a hyphen.

Remind Jamie that, unlike academicians, you don't have the luxury of researching the absolute, best solution. You may be forced to live with a B-decision because the A+ decision is too expensive to implement.

Invite Jamie to discuss subjects of mutual interest on a theoretical basis, in your free time. Make it clear that these academic discussions are for fun and mental stimulation but separate from actual work on the manuscript. Jamie may actually miss academic discussions and may have typecast you, an editor, as a possible soulmate.

Case 3: Editor's Changes Panic Writer

The Situation

Nicole, a junior writer, knocks on your door. Seeing that she's close to tears, you invite her to sit down as you close the door.

"Am I a failure, or is Jill picking on me?" sobs Nicole as she hands you a manuscript covered in red ink.

It's appropriate for Nicole to come to you. As a senior editor, you're serving as mentor to Jill, the entry-level editor assigned to Nicole's manual. You assigned Jill to Nicole's book because Jill and Nicole had worked together well on a small project a few months ago. You wanted to build on that relationship and give Jill the opportunity to do a developmental edit on a new manual. This is a challenging project for a new editor, but Jill seemed ready. She has been learning very quickly, and you've heard nothing but compliments about her from writers.

This isn't the first time you've seen Nicole upset—the engineers have pushed her to tears three times in the last six months—but it's a first for her with an editor.

You quickly assess the situation. You know the quality of Nicole's writing can be inconsistent, but she usually can judge her writing herself. Here's a manuscript she thinks is good, yet it has a lot of red ink—more than you've seen Jill mark on other manuscripts. That red ink could be addressing minor matters, such as inconsistent compounding or incorrect figure references, or it could be noting major organizational and stylistic problems. It's also possible Jill got carried away on her first big project.

What are your concerns and what do you do?

Analysis

Your immediate concern is that you have a very upset writer on your hands. She has a need to be heard; you're the person to listen. You can't solve the problem in this meeting, but you can alleviate the tension by listening.

Your other concern is that you don't want to undermine another editor's effectiveness. Jill may be in a learning period, but you know she'll be an excellent editor. You don't want to weaken her credibility in the department by overruling her judgment or by going behind her back. You will need to involve her in this problem, but not while Nicole is crying in your office.

Your first step is to gather more information. Invite Nicole to tell you more. To put her at ease, explain that the amount of red ink doesn't necessarily mean there are big problems but maybe lots of small problems. Tell her that it's worse to get a manuscript back from an editor with no marks, because that means the editor gave up.

Ask Nicole about the writing and editing process so far on this book and other projects. Have Nicole and Jill been communicating regularly? Have there been any other problems? Have Jill's comments been reasonable to date? How are the other aspects of Nicole's book coming along? Is she overwhelmed with technical changes? Is editing the straw that's about to break her back? You want to learn if the problem is really in this manuscript or if the problem with the manuscript is a symptom of a larger problem, one that may be outside your jurisdiction. Establish that it's your role to help with editorial-related problems only. For example, if Nicole has serious personal problems, refer her to human resources. (If she's just having a bad day, lend her a compassionate ear.) If the engineers are making changes and not telling her, she should talk to the engineering manager and her writing manager.

End the meeting by asking for time to read the manuscript and evaluate it fairly. Also tell Nicole that you will not overrule Jill in any editorial matter, but that you will talk to Jill privately. Say that you will speak to Nicole again, privately, after you've gathered more information.

Now review the manuscript. If Jill botched up, have a private meeting with her, not to reprimand, but to teach. Explain which editing changes are appropriate and which ones aren't. Point out any insensitive wording on the manuscript and suggest better wording.

If the manuscript needs a lot of work, meet privately with Nicole. Don't just explain what needs to be done, but offer solutions to the writing problems. Add the perspective that rewriting is a normal part of writing, and a heavy edit is not a condemnation of her abilities. Also remind her that she won't have to face the chore alone, that she will have editorial guidance. Let her know that Jill is qualified to help. Suggest that Nicole ask Jill to review each chapter as Nicole revises it. Recommend submitting new manuscripts for editing one chapter at a time. (Tell her that many writers do this, so she won't feel singled out.)

Whether Jill got carried away or whether Nicole wrote a sloppy manuscript, wrap up the incident the same way: Meet with each privately, and then back out so they can continue to work together. Let Nicole know that you and Jill have spoken and that you feel that they can resolve the issues between them. Add that you're available if they (speak of them as a team) need your advice, but that you're confident they can work together. Treat the entire incident as a normal disagreement between professionals on the same team, without making either feel as though the other has "had a talking to." To Nicole and Jill, your role must appear to be that of the person who puts the disagreement into perspective, not the judge of who is right.

Case 4: The Casual Review

The Situation

You and Rita are writers in the same writing section. You've spent the last week doing a peer edit of Rita's book. Your manager, Jim, stops you in the hall. "You've been editing Rita's installation manual, haven't you?" Jim asks. "How's it going?"

You mutter something about the thrills of reading someone else's book when you have your own book to write.

"How is Rita's writing, anyway?" Jim asks casually.

How do you respond?

Analysis

This is an awkward situation for both peer editors and full-time editors.

Think before you speak. Since managers don't ask casually about a subordinate's performance, you shouldn't answer casually, either. Tell the truth, but choose your words carefully. Don't make sweeping generalizations—"Her writing is a horror show"—or accusations you cannot support.

This is not the time to spill your guts about everything Rita has ever done wrong—especially if you and she resolved the writing problems through the normal editing process. (That's what you're there for.) If, however, you spend a disproportionate amount of time helping Rita with writing skills that she should have mastered by now, speak up. Tell how Rita can improve her writing. If Rita repeatedly misses deadlines or doesn't keep you informed of schedule changes—even though you've reminded her many times—say so. (But don't bring these problems up to her manager if you've never mentioned them to Rita herself.)

Also tell what she does well—she rewrites so skillfully that her second drafts rarely need more than a light edit, and she gives lots of good, clear examples. Or she gave me a lot of help when I was learning the new text formatter.

You need to grapple with some ethical decisions, such as these:

- To whom do I owe my real loyalty—to my colleagues, my boss, the project, or the reader? Remember the rules in chapter 2. Assess the situation honestly and objectively.

- Is the writer–editor relationship confidential?

- Do I compare one writer to another? No, that's the manager's job. But if you spend a lot more time with Rita than with other writers, say so, because the time you spend with one writer affects the productivity of the department.

- Do I state only the facts and omit the context? For example, do I say that she always meets her deadlines, or do I add that she meets them only by scrambling at the last minute after I repeatedly remind her? Do I say that her work has improved, but only because she's finally responding to my suggestions?

When in doubt remember this: Your manager will be asking Rita and other writers you work with about *your* editing. Evaluate others as you expect them to evaluate you. Be honest, but fair.

Case 5: Writer Goes Shopping for Another Editor

The Situation

Dana hands you the second draft of her user's guide. As you read through it, you notice that she has ignored many of your comments on the previous draft. You walk to her office. "Dana, I thought we'd agreed to show the tutorial with C, Pascal, and FORTRAN examples. What happened to the Pascal and FORTRAN examples?"

"Well, I asked Marilyn, and she said it was OK to drop them."

You telephone Marilyn, another editor in your department. Marilyn says, "That's not exactly what I said. I told Dana that we're not writing any new Pascal examples for the programmer's guide for *my* product and that my product doesn't have much of a FORTRAN market. My product is really for C programmers. I didn't tell Dana what to do in her book."

What do you do?

Analysis

Dana is shopping around for an editor to agree with her. Stop this practice from both ends. Let Dana know that you alone have editorial responsibility for her book and that you're familiar with her product and related products. Explain that the users of Dana's book need the Pascal and FORTRAN examples, something that Marilyn would have no way of knowing.

Also explain that editors are not interchangeable black boxes. If you ask two editors the same question, you won't necessarily get the same answer. That doesn't mean one editor is wrong; it means that editors have different styles.

If Dana still misses the point, ask her how she'd feel if you were to consult another writer about *her* book.

Also talk to the other editors. Share your concern about one editor contradicting another editor. Promise to not interfere in their projects if they don't intervene in yours. Agree that you'll all refer writers to their own editors. You'll find the other editors eager to participate in this pact.

There are two variations on this theme:

- The emergency. A writer waits until you've left for the day and then calls an editor with an "urgent" question in your absence. The editor's sense of responsibility—it's an emergency—overrides the editors' pact. The editor can't tell that the "emergency" could wait for the next day.

- The vacation. You've asked another editor to cover for you. Dana and other writers ask the editor to make decisions that, in effect, overturn your earlier decisions. (The writers don't tell the editor you already made a decision they don't like.)

The solution to both variations is to have the substitute editor keep track of his or her decisions and pass them along to you—and to let the writers know in advance that this is the standard procedure. The writers will suddenly remember that you've already answered the question.

Editors should let each other know about important decisions. Good communication among the editors helps prevent editor-shopping and may save the other editors some work.

Case 6: One Editor and Many Writers Collaborate

The Situation

The writing effort for the SoftSoft project is being handled as a collaborative project. The writing team consists of five writers and you, the editor.

The SoftSoft documentation set has 17 titles: 3 new books, 11 revised books, and 3 short publications—release notes, installation instructions, and a quick reference guide. The documents range from 10 pages to 300 pages. Some books require extensive revisions; others have only minor changes.

Here's how the collaboration works. The writers share the writing for *each* book. Each writer documents a specific piece of the product. For example, Jane is writing the text about networks, her specialty, for eight different books. (For some books, she writes complete chapters; for others she supplies a few paragraphs or sentences.) Likewise, Dave is documenting the programming interface and Matthew, the user interface; the other writers have comparable assignments.

Each writer, in addition to documenting his or her technology for the entire documentation set, also manages one or more books. Managing a book includes making sure each writer delivers her or his pieces of the book on time, coordinating the technical and other reviews, and serving as the focal point for any questions about the book. This system ensures that one writer is ultimately responsible for each book.

The SoftSoft project is the first collaborative project you've worked on. You've worked on projects that have had more than one writer, but each writer worked on a separate book. You've edited a few books with two writers, but each wrote different chapters and edited the other's writing before your editorial review. You once edited an anthology of technical articles, but those writers interacted with you, not with each other. You anticipate this project might pose new challenges.

What concerns do you have about your role on the team? What specific contributions can you make to this project? Where might you need to show resilience?

Analysis

You have a greater responsibility to communicate editorial changes to all members of the team. Changes in one book may affect all five writers, so you must constantly analyze every change to determine whether it affects others.

For example, you need to communicate even minor style decisions to all writers. You don't want every paragraph in a book to look as if a different writer wrote it—even though that may be the case. Expect the copy and literary edit to take more time than usual. (Schedule 50% more than your average turnaround time, if you can.) Even with thoughtful planning, you'll have many inconsistencies to reconcile.

You most certainly will be busy performing conventional editing. Yet, it's even more critical for you to watch for technical changes. You may be the only person to read every book in the documentation set in its entirety. Technical reviewers often read only the chapters or individual pages that relate to their areas of expertise; few read the complete manual. The SoftSoft writers will be busy writing, revising, sending books to review, collecting books from review, and keeping track of the pieces of their books. They won't have time to read anybody else's books. In fact, they'll be lucky to read the ones they're managing.

Pay particular attention to the manuscripts *after* technical review. Watch for technical changes that show up in some books and not others. For example, watch that features that have been added (or removed) are included (or deleted) throughout the documentation set. Let the writers know what inconsistencies you find; they can resolve them if you identify them.

Use your experience in creating style sheets to save time for the writers. Meet with the writers to agree on common terms and documentation conventions before they begin writing. Record the decisions as the SoftSoft Documentation Style Sheet. Distribute the style sheet among the writing team and other interested team members. (Engineers love this stuff.) State that writers should understand and apply the style guidelines in their drafts. Update the style sheet as often as you need to. Put the date on each version so people don't waste time figuring out if they have the most recent version.

Meet with the writers to discuss any tasks that you may be overlooking or duplicating. (If your company has a hands-on, top-down management style, discuss these issues with your manager and let her assign tasks.) You may need to negotiate what you'll do and what each writer will do, based on everyone's unique strengths and experience. It would be wasteful to have three people coordinating with manufacturing to get part numbers, but worse if nobody did it.

Decide how to communicate as a writing team—regular meetings, electronic mail, a file you'll all edit over the network. Don't leave communication to chance. A 6-person team has 15 2-way communications paths; everyone has to cooperate to keep these paths open.

As for resilience, expect to perform tasks that cut across the documentation set, that don't belong to any one writer. For example, you may compose a preface that all writers can use as a basis for their books. Or, you may devise usability tests to ensure that the documentation set works as a set, not just as a collection of titles.

Case 7: Editor *Ruins* Writer's Manuscript

The Situation

You are a writer. You are a furious writer. You just received the galleys for your manual. You didn't even know the book had gone into production. A few weeks ago you submitted a draft to editing and that's the last you heard of it. (You didn't think it needed editing, but every job has to have an editor's signature or production won't send it to print.) Now you have the galleys and you see some editor has changed the words you painstakingly chose.

What do you do?

- Mark up the galleys to restore the original wording.

- Give a copy of your original manuscript to the production manager for the typesetters to type in from scratch. (Or submit the file on diskette.)

- Write a nasty memo to the editing manager and your manager.

- Charge down to the editor's office and demand an explanation and an apology.

- Go to lunch and then go home.

- Ask your manager if you can have a desktop publishing system so you can create your own camera-ready copy from now on.

- Do some relaxation exercises and then carefully read the editing comments.

Analysis

Let's first assume the process has broken down. Your surprise that the manuscript already went into production suggests that the normal process is for the editor and writer to discuss the manuscript before it leaves editing. Do some relaxation exercises and then find out what happened to the process; maybe someone just goofed.

You have a right to be annoyed with a process that allows somebody to change your manuscript and send it to production without your knowledge. If that's the process in your company, ask to have it evaluated. Support your case by showing examples of bad editorial changes that needed to be changed again at a later stage (when it's more expensive).

Next, look over the editing changes. (Do some more relaxation exercises. Or go to the health club during lunch.) Did the editor really make such horrible changes? Do you hate the fact that someone made changes, or do you object to the changes themselves? Does the rewording make you think that maybe the text wasn't as clear as you'd thought? Can you find an even better way to rephrase it than the editor's? Do *any* of the editorial comments improve the manuscript? Is there *any* error you're relieved the editor caught?

If you can't find anything positive about the editing, ask someone else to look at the edited manuscript—the editing manager, your manager, a writer you respect—to give you an objective opinion. (For an honest opinion, ask one of your department's good writers if you're overreacting. Ask a good writer because you want someone competent to judge if the editing improves or diminishes the quality. Ask if you're overreacting because it's easier for someone to say that than to say you're being a jerk.)

It is possible the editor did a poor job. It is also possible the editor did such a good job that you're embarrassed. It's difficult to be impartial about your own writing, but try to think of the manuscript as *words*, not as a piece of yourself.

When you've calmed down enough to listen, talk with the editor. You have the right to know the editor's reason for every change. At some point, because of the time involved, you have to decide if the editor is competent and stop second-guessing every little change. If the editor isn't competent, complain to your manager and demand a *good* editor.

Case 8: Writer Doesn't Need an Editor

The Situation

You've been working at Dilbert Inc. for only two weeks when the thrill begins to wear off. You've spent much of this week meeting individually with the writers in your group to get to know them and their projects a little better. Your meeting with Alex killed the thrill.

Alex told you about the project he's working on and gave you a demo of the product. Then came the surprise: "This is just for your general information. You won't be editing *my* book." A few more questions from you draw out the reason—no, there isn't an alternative plan for editing his book. In Alex's words, "I don't need an editor."

Your first impulse is to argue, "But you have to have an editor. That's what I'm here for." You manage to suppress this urge by squeezing your fists so tightly your fingernails leave imprints on your palms.

Your next thought is to sell yourself, to tell Alex what a great editor you are and how much you can do for him. This approach reminds you of meetings you've attended where people whine about how unappreciated they are. "Scratch that idea," you tell yourself. The word "scratch" makes you think of cats. Then your thoughts drift to something that's always puzzled you: Why does a cat always approach the one person in the room who ignores it? "That's it! Let Alex come to me."

In the few seconds these thoughts flash through your brain, you force out a smile, look at your watch, and excuse yourself for another meeting.

You have a general idea what approach you want to take, so you scramble to your office to work out the details.

How can you make Alex *want* you to edit his book?

Analysis

It won't hurt to do a reality check first. Without mentioning your conversation with Alex, ask your manager if there are any circumstances where documents aren't edited. You should know this policy anyway. Maybe your manager will drop a hint about Alex. ("We're keeping editors away from Alex for their personal safety.") Listen and file away the information, but don't discuss Alex yet.

At this stage, you want to handle the problem without a manager's assistance. Your relationship with Alex won't be very good if the only reason he works with you is because he's been threatened from above. You have an opportunity to build a productive, cooperative working relationship with Alex. Don't throw away that chance for the quick fix of a managerial fiat.

Recognize that Alex is testing you. Every writer you work with in your career will test you. Most writers test you more subtly than Alex, but don't kid yourself; they're all watching. The probation period is generally until the first major product release.

Signs you've passed the test:

- Writers ask you questions, ask your advice, and discuss your comments.
- Writers give you schedules or product information before you nag.
- Writers treat you like a writer. (They invite you to the same meetings and parties.)

Signs you've failed the test:

- Writers ignore you.
- Writers ignore you some more.
- Writers still ignore you.

One good way to pass Alex's test is to wait for word-of-mouth recommendations to reach Alex's ears. Don't solicit these; just edit other writers' projects well. Writers talk about editors, just as editors talk about writers. In time, writers will be singing your praises. Be patient.

Be friendly. Keep in touch with Alex as often as you meet with other writers. If you have mutual interests, use them as a means to build rapport. Ask him how his book is coming along, if you can sound interested without being pushy. Don't discuss editing; if he mentions it, just let him know you're available when he's ready, if he wants your help.

Don't worry about whether or not Alex will let you edit his book. When the time comes, he will. He's bluffing. Alex will give you the manuscript if only to avoid a greater hassle. He'll have a difficult time explaining to his manager why he bypassed editing—especially if the other writers are telling the manager that you're good. He's probably planning to ignore your comments, but he'll give you the manuscript.

Getting the manuscript is only the beginning. It doesn't really count if Alex follows procedure and gives it to you. What counts is getting him to think your work adds value to his book.

Do your usual good editing. Be attentive to how you word your comments; they shouldn't sound bossy, condescending, or tentative. Make your comments professional—but keep them friendly. Be very careful in the use of humor; consider omitting it in this case.

Here's a big tip: In addition to your usual meticulous editing, make a point of finding errors that you know Alex would be grateful you found. Find a mistake that would come back to haunt him—a technical inconsistency or an example that doesn't work.

If you can't find anything wrong, think of some other terrific improvement you could make to his book. Suggest an enhancement that will make it an outstanding portfolio item for him. Be careful to stay within your department's guidelines; you don't want to reinforce the wrong behavior and give a confusing signal to other writers.

The one message you want Alex to get is that you're his ally.

If all else fails—if Alex sends his book along without your review—you have one final recourse. Go to Alex as soon as you find out (preferably when there is still time for him to recall the book) and tell him something like this: "One advantage to having me for your editor is that I stand behind my work. If I edit a book and it has problems later, I will work as hard as necessary to see that the problem is fixed. For example, if the print vendor has trouble following the specifications, I'll work with production to represent *your* interests. If purchasing complains that you shouldn't be using costly foldout pages or a second color, I'll let them yell at me—not at you. Then I'll explain how these features meet customer needs. If there's a problem with manufacturing—a mixed-up part number, for example—I'll take care of it. *But* if I haven't participated in the development of the book, I am not going to bail you out of any trouble later. It will be *your* problem, not mine."

In 15 years, I have only had to use this threat once. It worked.

Case 9: The Manual Doesn't Support the Product

The Situation

Sometimes your role as user advocate conflicts with your responsibility to your company.

Fred, a writer in your group, comes to you for advice. He has been assigned to write a printer operation manual. Andrea, the product manager and Fred's key source, gave him the manual for another printer your company manufactures and told him just to change the model numbers and artwork.

This is Fred's first writing job, so he wants to make a good impression. He found a prototype of the new printer and became familiar with its operation. In the process, he discovered that the new printer was very different from the earlier models. If he made cosmetic changes to the other manual, as instructed, users wouldn't be able to use the printer.

Fred went to Andrea to share his discovery, but she seemed neither surprised nor concerned. Instead, she repeated her earlier instructions, stating that there was neither time nor money to write a completely new manual and besides, nobody reads the manual anyway. (Andrea's background is in marketing, not writing.) Fred's supervisor, Paul, didn't want to listen to the problem and told Fred to play along.

He may be inexperienced, but Fred's no dummy. He knows it's wrong to publish an inaccurate manual, but he also knows he can't write a new manual without approval. At the very least, the product manager and the writing supervisor need to sign off on the book. He would also have a difficult time explaining why this project is taking longer than planned.

Fred has come to you for advice and support. He shows you his notes and explains the differences between the two printers in detail. You believe his analysis that the old manual does not support the new printer.

What do you do?

Analysis

You're pretty good at cutting corners when money is tight. You know that saving money is one part of your job. But you don't believe in saving money by cheating customers. It's not only dishonest to give customers an inaccurate manual, but in the long term it's expensive, too.

After much discussion, Fred and you devise an outline for a new printer manual that wouldn't require much more writing time than already budgeted. The new printer works differently from the old printer, but Fred can use the old manual as a guide. For example, he can follow the same outline. Customers perform the same general operations—load paper, clean the unit, fix paper jams. The procedures themselves are different, and that's what Fred will spend his time writing. The old manual also has several appendixes (character sets, troubleshooting, and general maintenance) that can go in the new manual with minor changes.

Also let Fred know why it's worth fighting to do this project well; it may not be worth it for the next one. For example, if this was a special product for only one customer, a patched-up manual with an errata sheet might be appropriate.

You're confident that you and Fred can sell your proposal, if you can get the decision makers to listen.

Fred and you put together a presentation. Here are your notes:

☐ If we ship an inaccurate manual, here's what will happen:

- Good customers will become angry customers.
- Customers who are already unhappy with us will leave us.
- We demonstrate that as a company we don't care about quality. A grossly inaccurate manual will cause customers to question our engineering quality.
- The product will get bad reviews from the trade press, which counts documentation in the ratings. Bad reviews and bad word-of-mouth comments will hurt sales.
- Customer support can expect many calls about routine problems. It costs us x dollars for each call. (Get the most recent figures before the meeting.) We can produce a new manual for y dollars. (You'll need this figure, too.)

☐ It won't be easy to update the manual in the field. Here's what we've learned from experience:

- We can't guarantee that any revision we ship to a customer will get to the individual who needs it.

- It's expensive to publish one manual and issue a revision or errata pages soon after.

- It's cheaper to build quality into the original.

☐ What it would take to do the book right:

- We can leverage existing material. (Be sure to use *leverage* for this audience.) The old manual is on disk; the new book will use the same design. Fred will follow the same outline and reuse some appendixes.

- Fred will write new procedures, but he won't have to write the entire book from scratch. Some procedures are similar; he can use existing text and reword only as necessary. The book needs new artwork, but Fred was planning to do that anyway.

- Fred will indicate for reviewers what material he took from the old manual to save them time.

- The bottom line is, this book will cost you only x more days of writer time to do it right than to do it wrong.

You have a rough draft of the presentation. Next you need to set up the meeting. Since Andrea and Paul have already made their decision, you're going to need another manager to raise the issue.

Go to your supervisor and explain the situation. Add that you have new information that Paul and Andrea didn't have available when they made their decision. (Don't expect a manager to reverse a decision without new information.)

Emphasize that your proposal satisfies everyone's concerns. Your proposal offers a way to ship an accurate manual and save the company money. The short-term costs of a little writing time will quickly be offset by huge reductions in support costs. (A graph would be a nice visual aid.)

Ask your manager to set up a meeting with Andrea and Paul. Consider inviting the customer service and marketing managers for the product if you expect to need more support. Let your manager decide who will make the presentation.

If your proposal is turned down, update your resume. This company doesn't need writers and editors; it needs typists and spelling checkers.

Case 10: Sending 20 Books to Print in 5 Days

The Situation

Your division has been working on a major product release for 18 months, and next month is the climax for the Technical Publications Department. Your department will be sending a 50-manual documentation set to print within a 5-day span. You're the editor for 20 of those books.

The timing is crucial and inflexible. You can't send any books to print early because the final technical sign-off takes place only one week before the to-print date. That's good timing for having the information up-to-date. It's bad timing because the books don't trickle in; they flood in. As for sending the books to print late, don't even think about it. The to-print date is the latest for the books to get to the warehouse in time to ship with the product.

Here's what you can expect to happen during those five days. (Let's call it production week.) In your department, the writers prepare camera-ready copy. You have already edited all the books at least once; this month the writers are making final revisions, working on their indexes, and testing their examples. The next time you see the books will be for the production edit (during production week).

One big plus is that all the writers you work with on this project are in the same department and have offices in the same building. The writers know each other and interact frequently. How can you use this geographic convenience to help you meet your deadline?

Analysis

One month before a major project, start micromanaging the schedule. Meet with the writers as a group, either in your department's weekly meeting or in a separate meeting. At the meeting, explain that you're in the critical path for documentation on this project. Tell them that your ability to work on each writer's book depends on how well everyone cooperates. (Make your comments personal. "Mimi, if you're late, I may have to take time from Betsy's book to catch up, and that's not fair to Betsy.")

Here is an outline for that meeting:

- Explain how the to-print date was determined by counting back from the date the books are needed in the warehouse.

- Review the process during the final week. Explain what you check at production edit and what preparations you make before you hand off the camera-ready copy. You might want to distribute copies of your production edit checklist (similar to what's in chapter 6). The message is that if you don't have time to do it, the writers will have to do it themselves. Be sure to list the tasks the writers *hate* to do, such as preparing the collating sheet. (You decide whether to express this message aloud or let the writers figure it out.)

- Confirm the schedules with the writers.

- Remind them you'll spend only an hour or so on each book, and therefore you won't be finding typos or other errors they may be assuming they can rely on your eyes to catch.

- Identify any books that are most likely to have their contents frozen earlier. Plan to check these a week or two before production week.

- Ask which writers expect to have books ready at the beginning of production week. Ask who expects to be working up to the last possible moment. (The latter category includes both the procrastinators and the writers whose books are most likely to have late technical changes.)

- Tell the writers that even a half-day makes a difference under your tight schedule. You don't want their sympathy; you want their cooperation. (Take the sympathy, too, if you can get it.)

- Together, draw up a tentative schedule. List what books will come in each morning and each afternoon of production week. Make the first day the busiest to get over the hump fast. Schedule the first four days only. Keep the final day open for work you don't finish. You may need the time to cope with the unusual and unexpected.

- Give everyone time to review the schedule and commit to it. (You can probably get consensus at that same meeting; it's a full month before the books go to print. The writers haven't yet started to panic.)

- Follow up the meeting by publishing and distributing the schedule to everyone.

Setting the schedule is easy. Holding writers to it is more difficult. Many writers will experience some crisis in their own schedules and will be tempted to hand over their books a day late. A day's slip is disastrous for you; don't let it be an option.

Here's what you do when a writer asks if he can give you his book a day later than planned. Agree—on one condition. The writer has to negotiate for your time with another writer. If he can convince another writer to swap deadlines (and let you know about the change), that's fine with you. If not, remind him that collating sheets aren't difficult to fill out, just boring. (Many writers would rather work over the weekend to meet the deadline than do the tedious production edit themselves.)

The week before production week, remind the writers that you're depending on them to meet their committed schedules. Review the main points from last month's meeting. Offer to give refresher lessons in preparing collating sheets and proofreading tables of contents for writers who think they may miss their deadlines.

Now it's production week. First thing Monday morning, check with the writers who have books coming in that day. Second thing, reconfirm the schedules with the writers who have books coming in Tuesday (so they know you're serious). Confirm schedules this way every day this week. If (when) writers ask for more time, don't tell them *you're* swamped. State the effect their delay has on their fellow writers. Remind Steve that his late book affects Kathy's schedule and remind Kathy that you won't be ready for her book if Steve hands his in late. Then remind them that this is why the contingency plan is for late writers to do their own production edits.

(It's more difficult to elicit cooperation when the writers you work with don't know each other because they're geographically dispersed or belong to different departments. Any time you can remind writers that you're all on the same team, your job will be much easier.)

When the books start flowing in Monday morning, dive in. You'll need to zip through each book using every trick you've learned in this book.

You'll have only an hour or two to spend on each book. The pace will be frenetic. You'll check a book, let the writer know what corrections to make, check another book, receive corrected pages from writers whose books you checked earlier, fill out a collating sheet, check another book, check some print specifications, approve cover mechanicals, and so on.

The next time you come up for air will be Friday morning. Now the real fun begins. The print vendor will call with a question about a book you handed off on Tuesday. There will be at least one last-minute technical change in a book you handed off yesterday. A writer was out sick Wednesday and didn't finish his book in time so you have to squeeze it in today.

When you hand off the last book, go home and get some rest. New projects and adventures await you on Monday.

Appendix B

Sample Style Guides

This appendix contains the tables of contents of three comprehensive and well-organized style guides.

The *Apollo Style Guide* was written for an audience of writers and editors.[1] The writers prepare their own camera-ready copy, using professionally designed templates. This style guide concentrates on writing issues encountered in systems documentation (hardware and software) for workstations.

The *HP Writing Style Guide* has a broad audience: writers, editors, and managers for systems documentation, user documentation, and public relations and marketing literature for a variety of computer and noncomputer products.

The *Publications Standards Manual* for Bull HN Information Systems also addresses a broad audience.[2] Part I is an introduction for all readers. Part II is a guide to planning documentation; its audience is writers, editors, and managers. Part III is a writing style guide, for writers and editors. Part IV contains production specifications for typography, layout, illustration, and printing; its audience includes designers, artists, typesetters, printers, and production editors. These standards cover user and marketing documentation for a varied line of computer hardware and software products.

---

[1] Apollo Computer Inc. merged with Hewlett-Packard Company in 1989.
[2] Reprinted with permission of Bull HN Information Systems Inc.

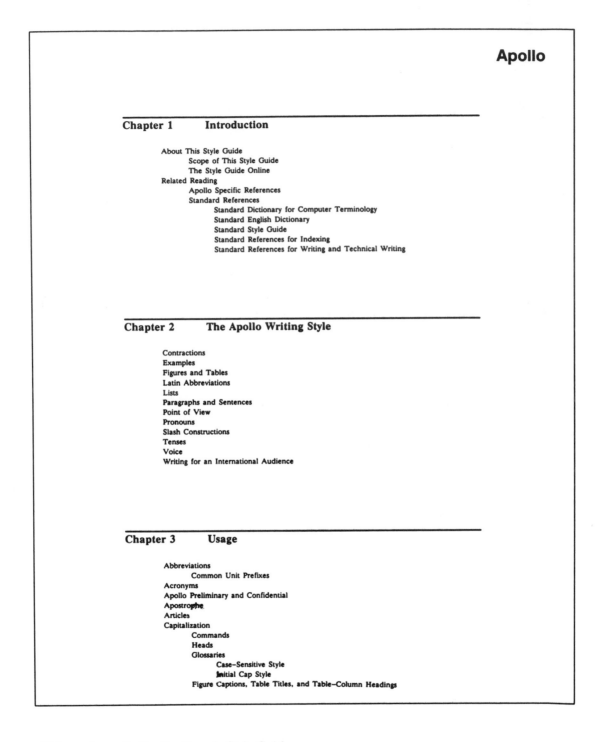

Apollo

Hewlett-Packard

Bull HN

SECTION 1. PUBLICATION PLANNING AND DEVELOPMENT

    Content Standards
    Publications Planning
        Marketing and Publications Coordination
        The Publications Plan
    The Publications Development Cycle
        Writing
        Editing
        Production
        Control
        Local Variations

SECTION 2. EVALUATIVE PUBLICATIONS

    Product Brief
        Objectives
        Availability
        Audience
        Content — Hardware Brief
        Content — Software Brief
        Content — Applications Brief
    Summary Description
        Objectives
        Availability
        Audience
        Content — Hardware Summary Description
        Content — Software Summary Description
        Content — Applications Summary Description
        Content — Comprehensive Summary Description
    Brochure
        Objectives
        Availability
        Audience
        Content — Capabilities Brochure
        Content — Systems Brochure
        Content — Applications Brochure
        Content — Hardware Brochure
        Content — Software Brochure
        Content — Vendor Profile
        Content — User Profile
        Content — Computer Application Profile (CAP)
    Specification Sheet
        Objectives
        Availability
        Audience
        Content

SECTION 3. INSTRUCTIONAL PUBLICATIONS

Self-Instructional/Programmed Texts
    Objectives
    Audience
    Content
  Administrator's Guide
    Objective
    Audience
    Content
  Instructor's Guide
    Objectives
    Audience
    Content
  Student Handbook
    Objectives
    Audience
    Content
  Sales Guide
    Objectives
    Audience
    Content
  Marketing Strategy Guide
    Objectives
    Audience
    Content
  Systems Guide
    Objectives
    Audience
    Content
  Introduction To —
    Objectives
    Audience
    Content
  Guide for New Users
    Objective
    Audience
    Content

SECTION 4. SOFTWARE REFERENCE MANUALS

  The Software Document Set
    Overview Document
    Audience-Specific Documents
    Component-Specific Documents
    Special Purpose Documents
    Compendiums
    Miscellaneous Documents
    Availability
  Concepts and Characteristics
    Objectives
    Audience
    Content
  System Control
    Objectives
    Audience
    Content
  Operator's Guide
    Objectives
    Audience
    Content

Systems Analyst's Guide
    Objectives
    Audience
    Content
System Administrator's Guide
    Objectives
    Audience
    Content
Communications Reference Manual
    Objectives
    Audience
    Content
Programmer's Reference Manual
    Objective
    Audience
    Content
Language Reference Manual
    Objectives
    Audience
    Content — Assembly Language
    Content — COBOL
    Content — FORTRAN
    Content — Report Program Generator (RPG)
    Content — BASIC
    Content — Data Base Languages
Language User's Guide
    Objectives
    Audience
    Content
    Content — Assembler
    Content — COBOL Compiler
    Content — FORTRAN Compiler
    Content — Report Program Generator (RPG)
    Content — BASIC Compiler
    Content — Data Base Subsystem
    Content — Library Maintenance Language
Service and Utility Manual
    Objectives
    Audience
    Content
    Content — Supervisor
    Content — Sort/Merge
    Content — Loader
    Content — Communications
System Generation
    Objective
    Audience
    Content
File Design
    Objectives
    Audience
    Content
Data Management
    Objectives
    Audience
    Content
Program Mode
    Objective
    Audience
    Content

Conversion Planning
  Objectives
  Audience
  Content
Conversion Guidelines
Conversion Guide
  Objectives
  Audience
  Content
  Content — File Conversion Guide
  Content — Language Conversion Guide
Program Logic Manual
  Objectives
  Audience
  Content
System Designers' Notebook
Site Implementation Manual
  Objectives
  Audience
  Content
Compendiums
  Objectives
  Audience
  Content — System Messages
  Content — Control Cards
  Content — System Tables
  Content — System Files
  Content — Master Index
Software Release Bulletin
  Objectives
  Audience
  Content

SECTION 5. HARDWARE REFERENCE MANUALS

Systems Handbook
  Objectives
  Availability
  Audience
  Content
Functional Characteristics
  Objective
  Availability
  Audience
  Content
Peripheral Device Operation
  Objectives
  Availability
  Audience
  Content
Programmer's Reference Manual
  Objectives
  Availability
  Audience
  Content
Site Preparation Manual
  Objectives
  Availability
  Audience
  Content

SECTION 6. APPLICATIONS/SERVICES REFERENCE MANUALS

System Handbook
  Objectives
  Availability
  Audience
  Content
Functional Description
Implementation Guide
Operating Instructions
User's Guide
  Objectives
  Availability
  Audience
  Content
Demonstration Guide
  Objective
  Audience
  Content
Administrator's Guide
  Objectives
  Audience
  Content

SECTION 7. MISCELLANEOUS PUBLICATIONS

Customer Computer Site Organization Manual
(Installation Planning Manual)
  Objectives
  Audience
  Content
General Systems Specification
  Objectives
  Audience
  Content
Pocket Guide
  Objective
  Audience
  Content — Technical Reference Pocket Guide
  Content — Evaluative Pocket Guide
  Content — Salesman's Pocket Guide
Catalog
  Objectives
  Audience
  Content
Quick Reference Guide
  Objective
  Audience
  Content
Reference Cards
  Objective — Programmer's Reference Card
  Audience — Programmer's Reference Card
  Content — Programmer's Reference Card
  Objective — Operator's Card
  Audience — Operator's Card
  Content — Operator's Card

Figures

Tables

SECTION 5. SUMMARY DESCRIPTIONS

General Features
    Fonts
    Margins
    Text Image Area
    Stock
    Artwork
Finishing
    Trimming
    Binding
Front Cover
Inside Front Cover
    Copyright Notice
    File Number
    Special Notices

Table of Contents
    Text
    Section Heads
    Section Hairline
    Layout
    Level Heads
    Body Type
    Listings
    Added Spacing
    "Notes"
    Footnotes
Figures
Tables
    Added Spacing
    Footnotes in Tables
Pagination
Back Cover

SECTION 6. BROCHURES

General Features
    Fonts
    Page Size
    Stock
Finishing
    Trimming and Folding
    Binding
Front Cover
    Honeywell Logo
    Security Notice
Inside Front Cover
    Copyright Notice
    File Number
Text
    Heads
    "Design Models Shown"
    Special Notices
Back Cover

SECTION 7. EDUCATION MANUALS

SECTION 8. QUICK REFERENCE GUIDES

General Features
    Fonts
    Image Area
    Margins
    Text Image Area
    Revision Indicators
    Stock
    Colors
Finishing
    Trimming
    Binding
Front Cover
Title Page
Copyright Page
Table of Contents
    Lists of Figures and Tables
Text
    Splitting Text
    Heads
    Listings
    Added Leading
    Notes
    Footnotes
    Index Slugs
Figures
    Captions
    Added Spacing
Tables
    Added Spacing
    Footnotes in Tables
Pagination
Publications Remarks Form
Back Cover

SECTION 9. REFERENCE CARDS

General Features
   Fonts
   Image Area
   Margins
   Stock
   Colors
Finishing
Front Panel
   Masthead
   Photograph
   Copyright Notice
Text
   Heads
   Listings
   Notes
   Added Leading
Footnotes
Pagination
Back Panel

SECTION 10. SPECIFICATION SHEETS

General Features
   Fonts
   Stock
   Colors
   Trimming
First Page
   Masthead
   Title
   Keylines
   Photograph
   Text
Second Page
   Image Area
   Margins
   Banner
   Text Image Area
   Text
   Heads
   Listings
   Added Leading
   Specifications
   Footnotes
   Special Notices
   "Notes"
   Figures and Tables
   Foot Matter
   Copyright Notice
   Order Number
   File Number

Figures

Appendix C

Answers to Exercises

Exercise 1 Give yourself one point for each correct answer.

Exercise 2 The point of this exercise is to show that you *can't* tell an editor by his or her title. Here are the actual matchups of job descriptions and titles. If you answered correctly, you're either psychic or lucky.

1. Lead editor
2. Senior technical editor
3. Senior editor
4. Senior editor
5. Technical writer/editor
6. Proofreader
7. Senior software editor

Exercise 3 Was the late Armand Hammer reincarnated? (If you thought the problem was in the agreement between *group* and *say,* you may have a point. However, the use of a plural verb and pronoun with a collective noun is OK if the writer is thinking of the individual members acting individually, rather than the group as a whole acting collectively.)

Exercise 4 Winston Churchill was an exceptional leader, but he wasn't American.

Exercise 5 Give the actual count, "33 of the 88 passengers." If the numbers don't pertain to human injury (which is always newsworthy) and are incidental to the story, you could round it off to "about a third." For example, it would be OK to say, "about a third of the passengers were traveling on business."

Exercise 6   Is it McClean Hospital or McLean Hospital? (The latter is correct. The editor should question the inconsistency.)

Exercise 7   Brunch is a blend of *breakfast* and *lunch,* not *lunch* and *dinner.*

Exercise 8   What is the reference to Rhode Island's procedures doing in a Massachusetts telephone directory? A guess is the artwork for the Rhode Island ad was to have been updated for Massachusetts, but somebody didn't read all the fine print. This type of mistake is very common in revisions to technical documents—the writer and reviewers concentrate on the new information and sometimes overlook changes that need to be made in the old "stable" parts. The editor should read *everything,* even the passages that haven't been changed.

Exercise 9   Here's how I'd rank each:

1. Low

2. High (Plan high for all projects with a novice writer. If the writer learns quickly, the effort could be less.)

3. High (Always plan high for novice, even on "easy" projects.)

4. Medium (Effort would be high because of new book, but good rapport with writer decreases level. If the book is a high-visibility, critical project, bump it to high effort. If the book is a low-visibility project, knock it down to low effort.)

5. High (Effort could be medium if writer–editor rapport is good.)

6. High (New book and problem writer.)

Exercise 10   This is one of the finest—and most famous—paragraphs about composition ever written. There is *nothing* wrong with it. This exercise does have a point: to remind you that some text is fine just the way it is—just because you're editing something doesn't mean it has errors. One of the major differences between solving problems in school and solving them for real is that schools test students by giving them contrived problems, often with pat solutions. In the real world, you first have to identify the problem yourself—if there is one—and then search for a solution. Manuscripts don't come prelabeled "there's an error in this line; can you find it?"

Exercise 11   What is Mr. Leighton's first name? The editor wouldn't necessarily be expected to know the answer, but should bring the discrepancy to the writer's attention.

Exercise 12   Milos Forman was the director; Louise Fletcher was best actress. There are no context clues; sometimes editors must rely on their general knowledge.

Exercise 13   *Presidence* for *precedents.* (This really *is* terrible writing, isn't it?)

Exercise 14   The years should increase from left to right. The half-year designation is quite unconventional and unnecessary.

Exercise 15   Check the ASCII values. They're probably listed in an appendix in the same book. Don't assume they're correct. (These are correct, by the way.)

Exercise 16   The abbreviation *lbs.* is less common than *lb* (but a few style guides accept the former). The abbreviation H/W/D is deducible, but should be spelled out, especially if some of your readers aren't native English speakers. AC, for alternating current, is usually lowercase. Why is there no space between the number and the unit with millimeters (86mm), but there is a space in 3.6 kg? (These kinds of details are normally covered in style guides.)

Why is temperature in degrees Fahrenheit given after Celsius, when in all other cases the U.S. Customary measure is given first? This inconsistency may be intentional. After all, the United Kingdom switched to using Celsius rather than Fahrenheit before they switched to the metric system for other measurements. Nevertheless, the editor should ask.

Exercise 17   *Meter* is abbreviated as both M and m in this example. By the way, the period after *in* is intentional, to avoid confusion with the preposition. (Several style guides allow this exception.) The head "PRINTER AND KEYBOARD COMBINATION" is in all caps, yet the other heads are initial caps. "Cord" and "cable" should be capped.

Exercise 18   The difference between the formatted capacity and the unformatted capacity "per surface" seems way out of line, considering the differences in the "per disc" and "per track" specifications. The editor would not be expected to know what the correct specifications are, but should question whether they're correct.

Exercise 19   How to Change a Tire *not* HOW TO CHANGE A TIRE. This exercise is a reminder that *capitalize* does not mean *all caps. Capitalize* means to begin a word with a capital letter. By convention, articles and the *to* in infinitives are not capitalized inside a head. (See a good style guide for more conventions for capitalization.)

Exercise 20   Here is the answer with the guidelines applied.

1.   **mv** *old_file new_file*

2.   **ln –s** //*node*/**domain_examples/pascal_examples/getpas** *dir*/**getpas**
      where *node* is the name of the disk where the examples are stored and *dir* is the name of a directory in your path.

3.   Use the **in** operator to determine if **exp** is an element in **setexp.**

4. Compile a Domain Pascal source code file by entering the following command:
   pas *source_pathname* [*option1...optionN*]
   where:
   source_pathname is the pathname of the source file you want to compile. We recommend that *source_pathname* end with a **.pas** suffix.

5. For example, the following commands compile source code file **circles.pas**:
   pas circles
   pas circles –l
   pas circles –map –exp –cond –cpu 3000

6. The reserved words **begin** and **end** establish the limits of a sequence of Pascal statements. You must use a **begin**/**end** pair to indicate a compound statement.

Exercise 21   The semicolons are in boldface, not italic type. (They don't match the typographic style of the preceding text.) The semicolons in these examples do not represent English-language punctuation; they're literal characters in the computer languages.

Exercise 22   Answers to this exercise are given in figure 12–4.

Exercise 23   The illustration shows an incorrect way to hold a diskette. The fingers are touching the Mylar surface—dirt and oil can ruin the diskette and cause loss of data. This graphical error is not uncommon. Make sure the artwork supports and doesn't contradict the text.

Exercise 24   There is no single correct answer. How do you think *your* users will look up the message? The best answer I can think of is to encourage the engineer to reword the messages to avoid this problem.

Exercise 25   Grade yourself on this exercise.

Exercise 26   The description for **–lf** is missing. The **–rmf** option is missing *n* in the description. Option **–i** is described but not shown in the syntax line. The verb forms in the descriptions (*writes* and *write*) are inconsistent. The **–lm** option is not in bold in the syntax line. In the description, **–m** is incorrectly in italics. The description reads **–out** *path* (instead of *pathname*). The end punctuation is inconsistent.

Glossary

Terms in **boldface** are separate entries in this glossary.

AA *See* **author's alteration.**

Abbreviation a shortened form of a word or phrase, such as *kg* for *kilogram*. *Contrast with* **acronym.**

Accuracy edit a term sometimes applied to an **editorial review** that verifies facts and other technical details in a manuscript. Usually not a separate review.

Acronym a shortened form of a term, created from the initial letter or significant letters of each word, such as ACTH (*adrenocorticotropic hormone*) or UK (United Kingdom). *Contrast with* **abbreviation.**

Active voice in grammar, when the subject performs the action. The active voice contributes to clear, concise, and snappy writing. *Contrast with* **passive voice.**

Addendum (pl. addenda) a supplement to a book. In technical documentation, often a set of pages for the reader to insert into a previously published edition in place of existing pages. *See also* **A page; point page.**

Agreement in grammar, a subject and verb having the same number (singular subject with singular verb or plural subject with plural verb).

Algorithm a set of rules or instructions to solve a problem.

All caps every letter in uppercase (capital) letters. *Contrast with* **initial caps.** *See also* **capitalization.**

Alpha test in the computer industry, the first release of a product still under development for trial use, nearly always to users within the same company. *Contrast with* **beta test.**

Angle brackets   the $<$ and $>$ characters.

Antecedent   in grammar, a word, phrase, or clause to which a pronoun refers. For example, in "Donna's birthday is in December; her sister Paula's birthday is in February," *Donna* is the antecedent of *her*.

Anthropomorphism   the attribution of human characteristics to nonhuman things.

A page   in an **addendum,** a page to be inserted between two existing pages. Its number is based on the page it follows. For example, A page 3–2a follows page 3–2. *See also* **point page.**

Application software   a computer **program** that meets a user's real-world computing needs. For example, spreadsheets, word processors, and games are applications. *Contrast with* **system software.**

Argument   in computers, data that qualifies a command or that is passed to a subroutine. In the writer–editor relationship, a meeting of the minds.

Artwork   *See* **graphics.**

ASCII   in computers, a code for representing alphanumeric data. An acronym of American (National) Standard Code for Information Interchange. Pronounced *asky.*

Assembly   the act of collecting and organizing all the pieces to be handed off to the printer, such as the front matter, chapters, appendixes, back matter, artwork not pasted on the **mechanicals, glossy** prints or slides, **collating sheet,** and instructions to the printer.

Assembly sheet   *See* **collating sheet.**

Audience   the person(s) who will read and use the books you edit or write. *You* represent the audience's interests when you write, review, or edit a book.

Author's alteration   in offset printing, a change made by the client after the print vendor has made the negatives. In typesetting, changes made by the client after the job has been typeset. The cost (over a predetermined amount or percentage) of rework for making author's alterations is billed to the client. Commonly called an **AA.** *See also* **printer's error.**

Back matter   the parts of the book that follow the main body; in **technical writing,** commonly the appendixes, glossary, bibliography, and **index.** Some companies include forms for ordering documentation and/or forms soliciting readers' comments.

Beta test   in the computer industry, the first release of a product under development to selected customer sites for evaluation and testing. *Beta,* as it's sometimes called, typically follows one or more rounds of **alpha testing** within the company. A product may undergo more than one beta test before being released (shipped in volume to all customers who order it). *Contrast with* **alpha test.**

Bindery   the place (usually a department in a full-service print shop) that assembles the parts of the book and fastens them to the cover.

Binding   the process of fastening the cover to the book or, for books without covers, of attaching the parts of the books. The process that makes the difference between a collection of loose pages and a book.

Black box in engineering, something that performs a function, but whose internal mechanism is not visible to the user. For example, a battery can be considered a black box; you can use it without knowing what's inside it or how it generates electricity.

Bleed in printing, any artwork that extends off the page after the pages have been printed and trimmed, as in "These horizontal rules bleed off the page." A *full-page bleed* is artwork that bleeds off all edges.

Bluelines (blues) *See* **salts.**

Blueprints *See* **salts.**

Board(s) *See* **mechanicals.**

Boilerplate standardized text that you reuse in different parts of a publication or in different publications, such as a disclaimer.

Boldface a heavy-faced type such as this.

Boxhead *See* **column head.**

Brace(s) the { } characters.

Bracket(s) the [ ] characters.

Break for color *See* **color break.**

Broadside in page **layout**, the vertical placement of a wide table or illustration. The top of the art is always to the left. See figure 11–3.

Bullet in typography, a **dingbat** that resembles a bullet hole (• a closed bullet; ○ an open bullet). If it's square, ■, it's called a *quad.* A list in which each item is preceded by a bullet is called a *bulleted list.*

Byte the smallest group of binary digits that a computer processes as a unit. (Generally equivalent to one character.)

Callout text that defines or describes something in an illustration and that is located outside the illustration. For examples of callouts, see figure 11–3. *Contrast with* **label.**

Camera-ready copy text or artwork ready to be photographed for reproduction without additional preparation. Copy can be considered camera-ready without actually having been pasted up on **mechanicals**, depending on what your print vendor accepts. (Printers raise their eyebrows when clients promise "camera-ready copy," just as editors do when writers say, "This doesn't need much editing.")

Capitalization the spelling of a word with an initial capital letter. By convention, editors use *capitalize* to mean **initial caps**, rather than **all caps**. To avoid ambiguity, use the terms *initial caps* (or *an initial cap*) and *all caps.*

Caption the title of an illustration. *Contrast with* **legend.**

Case in grammar, a form of a noun, adjective, or pronoun that shows its relationship to the other words in the sentence. The cases in English are nominative, objective, and possessive. In spelling, uppercase or lowercase characters. (In the old days, the printer stored the capital letters in the top box, the upper case.) *See also* **case sensitive.**

Case sensitive in computers, a program that is case sensitive handles or interprets uppercase characters differently from lowercase characters. For example, to a case sensitive program, *go, GO,* and *Go* are three different commands.

Chapter a main division of a book. *Contrast with* **section.**

Cold type in **composition,** type produced without casting metal, such as **photocomposition.** *Contrast with* **hot type.**

Collate in printing, to arrange the folded **signatures** in correct order.

Collating sheet in printing, the form that specifies the desired page sequence, including any blank pages, in the printed and bound book. The collating sheet also contains instructions as to which pages have artwork to be inserted or need photoreduction or other special handling in printing or binding. Figure 6–12 shows a sample collating sheet. In the preparation of **addenda** or insert pages, the collating sheet is the cover letter to readers with instructions for removing and inserting pages. Also called *assembly sheet.*

Color break the point where printing in one color stops and printing in another color begins. Also used for the marked up dummy that indicates to the printer where to make color breaks. Also called *break for color.*

Color dummy a copy of the **camera-ready copy** marked to show what text is to be printed in color.

Color separation a process for dividing the images to be printed into the constituent colors (cyan, magenta, yellow, black) for printing; also, the film negative or positive this process ultimately produces.

Column head the label that tells what information the column contains. Also called *column heading, boxhead,* and *boxheading.*

Command an instruction to the computer. Some ways users can issue commands— depending on the computer—are by typing on a keyboard, selecting from a **menu,** and manipulating an **icon.** *See also* **command line.**

Command line the **command** and its **options** and **arguments** that the user types on a keyboard.

Comment in computer programming, the programmer's annotations in the code, written for herself or himself and other programmers.

Comp abbreviation for **composition** or **compositor.**

Composition the rendering of text in typographic form; includes input of straight text as well as its formatting. *See also* **format; typesetting.**

Compositor the person who performs the **composition** of type, especially **hot type.** *See also* **typesetter.**

Compounding combining words or parts of words (affixes, combination forms) into another word.

Conceptual describes writing that tells about a subject, giving background information, theory, and abstract discussion. *Contrast with* **task-oriented** and **reference.**

Consistency in editing, treatment of like things in like manner, such as in spelling, capitalization, compounding, punctuation, and typographical display.

Content edit an editorial review of the depth, completeness, and order of presentation of the information in a document. Often used synonymously with **developmental edit,** but could also be considered a subset of a complete developmental edit. Also called *organizational edit.*

Conventions standards of publishing practice. *See also* **house style.**

Coordination edit the editorial role in planning and managing the people and processes. Often used synonymously with **developmental edit,** but could also be considered a subset of a complete developmental edit.

Copy *See* **manuscript.**

Copy and literary edit in this book, the **editorial review** that includes a **copy edit,** a **literary edit,** an **accuracy edit,** and a **usability edit.**

Copy edit an **editorial review** of spelling, grammar, punctuation, cross-references, and other mechanical details. *Copyedit* is a more common spelling of *copy edit,* but looks weird alongside open compounds like **developmental edit, production edit,** and **literary edit.** Copy edit is often used synonymously with **substantive edit, screening edit, integrity edit,** and **mechanical style edit,** but these can also be considered discrete reviews or subsets of a thorough copy edit.

Copy editor a person whose primary responsibility is to perform a **copy edit.**

Copyread *See* **copy edit.**

Copyright the exclusive legal right to reproduce, distribute, and sell a published or artistic work.

Crop to trim a photograph or illustration by masking out portions not to be reproduced. *Contrast with* **scale.**

Cross-reference a pointer to another element of a book (chapter, section, figure, table).

Deadline the date something is due; so called because in some companies, if you miss it, you might as well be dead.

Decimal (notation) in mathematics, the representation of a number in base 10.

Decimalization a system for displaying a book's information hierarchy. For example, section 1.1 has subsections 1.1.1, 1.1.2, 1.1.3, etc., and is followed by section 1.2 and its subsections, 1.2.1, 1.2.2, etc. *See also* **double numeration.**

Default what the computer does if not given explicit instructions otherwise.

Deliverable the actual work you hand off on your deadline, such as an edited manuscript, a completed **collating sheet,** a **documentation project plan,** or a presentation to writing managers about the editor's role.

Design the plan for the physical appearance—**typography, layout,** and printing—of a publication.

Desktop publishing the use of computers to produce **camera-ready copy.** *Contrast with* **electronic publishing.**

Developer an engineer who designs and creates a product; mostly used in the computer industry.

Development *See* **product development cycle.**

Developmental edit an **editorial review** during the planning and incipient writing stages of a document. A developmental edit focuses on the content and overall plans and objectives for the book or documentation set. A thorough developmental edit includes a **content edit, coordination edit,** and **policy edit.**

Dialog box in a computer **program** with a graphical **user interface,** a display that gives the user a message, requests information, or asks the user to make a selection. Also called *form* or *stickup.*

Dingbat a typographical symbol or ornamental character, such as ☞ ♀ ♡ ⊞ § ☆. *See also* **bullet.**

Directory in computers, a named group of **files.**

Disclaimer a legal notice that repudiates responsibility for damages, such as "Specifications are subject to change without notice."

Disk in computers, a device for storing information.

Doc abbreviation for document or **documentation.**

Documentation in **technical writing,** technical writing itself. Or the book itself.

Documentation architect a job title sometimes given to writers and editors who plan sets of books.

Documentation project plan (doc plan) a detailed proposal for a set of books that typically describes how the **documentation** fits into the product. A typical doc plan defines the books and other items (**online** documentation, a plastic **template,** stickers) needed to document the product, tells what resources are needed and assigned to meet the plan's objectives, and describes the manufacturing, distribution, and maintenance strategy for the **documentation set.** The doc plan is usually a higher-level view of the documentation; a **doc spec** gives the details for each publication.

Documentation set (doc set) a series of books that documents a single product or product line and that is designed to be used as a set (though not necessarily bound, packaged, or distributed together). The people who plan a documentation set need to ensure that the books in the set collectively cover all the information the user must know or would want to know; that each nugget of information appears in the volumes where users expect to find it; that information is neither omitted nor duplicated without good reason; and that the set has a consistent design, style, and presentation.

Documentation specification (doc spec)   a detailed proposal for an individual book that defines its **audience,** purpose, pace, and other writing strategies, along with production requirements and a schedule. The doc spec also contains a detailed outline of the book's contents.

DOS   an operating system (Disk Operating System) for computers.

Dot leaders   a row of evenly spaced periods, such as from an entry to its page number in a table of contents. For example, How to Edit an Index. 214

Double numeration   a two-level system for numbering pages, figures, and tables, expressed as a compound number. The first number is the chapter number; the second number represents the item's sequence within the chapter. A hyphen, **en dash,** or period separates the two. For example, page 1-1, figure 2–17, or table 3.4. This numbering system is common in technical publications because it enables people to work on different parts of the book concurrently. For example, the writer can make last-minute technical changes to chapters 1 and 3 while the rest of the book is being pasted up; the corrected chapters can be merged with the book down the line. This system also enables a company to revise individual chapters (by means of an **addendum** or **revision**) without repaginating the entire book. *See also* **decimalization.**

Draft   one version of a **manuscript.**

Dylux   *See* **salts.**

Editorial review   any critical reading of a manuscript, at any stage, by an editor (or someone serving as an editor). Also called *editorial pass. Contrast with* **technical review.**

Electronic publishing   the preparation of camera-ready copy on a computer. Many people distinguish between electronic publishing and **desktop publishing:** electronic publishing as the use of powerful computers (workstations and sophisticated publishing systems for newspapers) by professional typographers and desktop publishing as the use of personal computers by writers and editors. Others use the two terms interchangeably.

Em dash   a dash the width of the lowercase letter em in a particular font: —.

En dash   a dash half the width of the lowercase letter em in a particular font: -.

Ergonomics   the science of human factors engineering, or how to make machines, tools, furniture, and so on compatible with the physical limitations of people.

Errata sheet   a page listing the errors and corrections in a previously published document.

Esperanto   a planned international language.

Fences   a shorthand way to refer collectively to parentheses, **braces,** and **brackets,** which enclose text, mathematical expressions, computer **commands,** or programming statements.

File   in computers, a single collection of data stored on a computer system. The data in a file can be text, pictures, a **program,** or a combination of these.

Fill pattern in **desktop** and **electronic publishing**, any of several varieties of shading. For example:

Final edit the last **editorial review** before the publication is handed off to production or printing; the last opportunity for making changes without affecting the production schedule and costs. *See also* **production edit.**

Foldout page a **leaf** that is larger than the book's trim size, and consequently folded to fit in the book.

Folio a page number.

Font the set of characters of a particular **typeface** in a particular size and style, such as 10-pt Helvetica bold. Commonly misused as a synonym for **typeface,** such as Times Roman, particularly among desktop publishers.

Footer in page **layout**, the text at the bottom of the page, outside the **text image area,** usually containing the book, part, chapter, or section title. On this page, the footer contains the word *Glossary* and the **folio.** Often used synonymously with **running foot.**

Foreword an introduction to a book, usually written by someone other than the author. *Contrast with* **preface.**

Form *See* **dialog box.**

Format the physical appearance of the book (such as trim size and colors) and the design (**typography** and **layout**) of its pages.

Format edit in this book, the **editorial review** that ensures that the book's **format** is correct. A subset of a **production edit** or **final edit.** In **typesetting,** the markup of a **manuscript** by a *format editor* or **production editor** to include the format codes for the typesetter. This latter usage is a production, not an editorial function, so it is outside the scope of this book.

Front matter the parts of the book that precede chapter 1, such as the title page, **copyright** page, **preface,** and contents.

Full-page bleed *See* **bleed.**

Functional specification the detailed design plan for the product that the engineers are supposed to produce before the development begins and are supposed to keep up-to-date with design changes. Also called *functional specs*. Sarcastically called *functional speculation.*

Galley proof a proof of typeset copy before it has been pasted up into pages; a galley proof is, therefore, of variable length. Also called *galleys.*

Glitch computer slang for a minor problem.

Glossy a photograph with a shiny finish.

Graphic arts the professions related to creating images with graphics (art) and text to communicate a message. Graphic artists include specialists in **typography**, design, **layout,** and printing technology.

Graphics anything on the page that is not pure text—illustrations, photographs, tables, and other design elements. Also called *visuals.*

Hairline rule a very thin rule, usually the thinnest rule the publishing equipment can produce.

Hairline space a very thin space, generally ½-pt to 1-pt (on some systems, even thinner), depending on the capabilities of the publishing equipment. There's a hairline space between the *a* and the *b*: ab.

Halftone the reproduction of a continuous-tone artwork, such as a photograph, through a screen that converts the image into a series of dots. The dots have uniform spacing, but different sizes; the smaller the dots (or the finer the screen), the sharper the detail in the reproduction.

Hanging indent a style for continuing text onto a second line. For example:

- This is an example of a hanging indent. The text wraps around to align under the word "This" instead of to the left margin.

Hardcopy material printed on paper. *Contrast with* **online.**

Hardware the physical, tangible parts of a computer. The parts of a computer you can kick, drop, or toss. *Contrast with* **software.**

Headhunter an agent for an employment agency.

Heading/Head the words that label the sections or parts of a chapter, usually set apart from the text by spacing and typography. Also called *text head or text heading.*

Heading levels the hierarchy of **headings.** The major subdivisions of a chapter have a first-level head (sometimes called an *A head* or *head 1*); its subsections are introduced with second-level heads (*B head* or *head 2*), followed by third-level and fourth-level heads. Fourth-level (or, gasp, fifth-level) heads may be a symptom of organizational problems in a book.

Help in computers, a **program** that gives users information—usually a screenful of text—about the program they're using, usually only after users ask for help on a topic.

Homophone one of two or more words that sound alike, such as *see, sea*, and *C.*

Hot type in **composition,** casting type from molten metal. Also called *hot metal composition. Contrast with* **cold type.**

House style the preferred usage in a particular company or publishing house. *See also* **conventions; style.**

Human factors engineering *See* **ergonomics.**

Hypertext   a type of computer **program** that lets users "read" **documentation online** in virtually any order. Hypertext documentation consists of bite-sized chunks of information linked to other chunks linked to other chunks. Conceivably, users could each follow a unique path of links, just by selecting the topics that interest them. Some hypertext programs let users create their own links.

Icon   a graphical image (pictogram) that represents a predefined concept. On some computers, users can give **commands** by manipulating icons. For example, on a Macintosh computer a user can discard a document by dragging a picture of the document to a picture of a trashcan.

Image area   the complete page, including the **header** and the **footer**. *Contrast with* **text image area.**

Imposition   in printing, the arrangement of pages on a mechanical form so they will be in the correct order after printing and folding. In **offset printing**, the arrangement of film negatives of the pages on a mechanical form (for the same purpose), and called *stripping.*

Index   an alphabetical list of topics and their page numbers, usually at the end of the book. *Contrast with* **table of contents.**

Index slugs   the headings at the top of the pages in a reference book that tell what topic or topics are covered on that page. In a dictionary, they tell what words start and end the page. *Contrast with* **running head.**

Initial caps   capitalizing the first letter of every major word in a heading, caption, or title. Also called *upper and lowercase,* or *ulc. See also* **case.** (See your company's style guide for what is considered "a major word"; the guidelines vary.) The term *an initial cap* means to capitalize the first letter of the first word only. Example: Here's a Sentence in Initial Caps. Here's a sentence with an initial cap. *Contrast with* **all caps.** *See also* **capitalization.**

Inline comment   in computer programming a **comment** that appears on the same line as code, rather than on a separate line.

Input   the information you give the computer.

Insert pages   *See* **addendum.**

Instructional   describes documentation that teaches, such as a **tutorial**.

Integrity edit   an **editorial review** to ensure that each **cross-reference** to another section is legitimate. Usually a subset of a **copy edit.**

Interface   *See* **user interface.**

Internationalization   the development, manufacturing, sales, or distribution of products in different countries. *Contrast with* **localization.**

Italic(s)   a slanted typeface *such as this.*

Kerning   in typesetting, the adjusting of space between two characters so they fit snugly. For example, the letters "T" and "i" are tightly kerned in *Title.*

Keyword in a book's **index**, a main entry, the term you expect readers to look up to find the page references for the subject. In computers, a term with a predefined meaning. A keyword often cannot be used in a **program** or **command line** in any other way. *See also* **reserved word.**

Label text that identifies something in an illustration; positioned within the illustration. *Contrast with* **callout.**

Language edit *See* **literary edit.**

Layout the arrangement of text and artwork on a page or on **mechanicals.**

Leading the vertical spacing between lines of type, so called from the strip of lead used for this purpose in **hot type composition.** Pronounced *ledding.*

Leaf a piece of paper bound in a book. One leaf equals two pages.

Legend text that describes an illustration or table; positioned outside the illustration or table. *Contrast with* **caption.**

Levels of edit a system by which an editor specifies exactly what tasks are to be performed when editing a particular document.

Literal in computers, a constant value, such as text within quotation marks or a number.

Literary edit an **editorial review** of the writing style, including word usage, transitions, clarity, and smoothness. Also called *language edit* and *style edit.*

Literary editor a job title for a person who primarily performs a **literary edit.**

Localization the tailoring of a product to the language, cultural, and economic needs of a particular geographic region. *Contrast with* **internationalization.**

Logo one or more words, often stylized or combined with a small graphic, used as a symbol for a company or trade name. Colloquially used to refer to the symbol alone. Abbreviation for *logotype.* Most companies have guidelines for displaying their logo which editors should know and enforce.

Managing editor a person responsible for developing and overseeing the editorial process and setting editorial standards. Usually supervises a staff of writers and/or editors.

Manual (man) page reference page for the UNIX operating system.

Manuscript the writer's work-in-progress. Also called *copy. See also* **draft.**

Manuscript preparation an editorial task that ensures that the **manuscript** submitted for **typesetting** meets the physical standards of the **graphic arts** department—for example, that all pages are numbered, that there are no loose inserts, and that the markup is legible.

Mechanicals the pasteup of all the text and artwork for a book, ready for photomechanical reproduction. Also called *boards, reproducible boards, reproducible masters, repro,* or *repros.*

Mechanical style edit *See* **copy edit.**

Menu in computers, a list of available choices (**commands**) a user can make.

Messages in computers, information and warnings given to users.

Metric   a measurement system developed in the eighteenth century, based on the meter and kilogram. The relationship of all units of the same kind (such as length) is decimal (for example, millimeter, centimeter, meter, kilometer). *See also* **SI; U.S. Customary.**

Milestone   in project management, an event, such as a **writing freeze,** the start of a **developmental edit,** or the handoff of a book to printing. *Contrast with* **task.**

Modem   a device that allows two computers to communicate over telephone wires.

Monospace   in typography, a typeface in which all characters are the same width. Also called *fixed-width* or *single-width. Contrast with* **proportional space.**

Navigational tools   aids that the writer, editor, and graphic artist put in a book to make it easy for readers to find information. Examples of navigational tools include a **running head,** the table of contents, and index slugs. Also called *navigational aids.*

Nominalization   the transformation of a good strong verb into a (usually weaker) noun. For example, transforming *decide* to *make a decision* or *evaluate* to *conduct an evaluation.* Also called *smothered verb.*

Noun string   a cluster of nouns, such as database management system operation.

Offset printing   a method of printing that transfers ink from a plate to a cylindrical rubber blanket and then from the blanket to paper. In offset printing, the plate never comes in contact with the paper. Also called *offset lithography.*

Online   able to interact with a computer because the machine is connected and running. Online **documentation** is **technical writing** that you read on the computer screen. *Contrast with* **hardcopy.**

Option   a specifier that modifies a computer **command.**

Organization   the order of information in a publication (and within its divisions, such as chapters, sections) and the transitions from one division to another.

Organizational edit   *See* **content edit.**

Orphan   a single word or line at the bottom of a page or column (such as the first line of a paragraph), to be avoided. Sometimes used to mean a **widow,** which is a single word or line at the top of a page, also to be avoided. *See also* **widow.**

Output   what the computer produces for you.

Packaging   the physical characteristics of the product as distributed to customers. For a book, the packaging includes its trim size, ink and paper colors, covers, slipcase, binders, even the box the documentation is shipped in. (For example, the box itself may have a label that reads, "Documentation enclosed. Open me first!") Packaging also involves the method for shipping aids (rulers, stickers, diskettes, posters, and other goodies) with the rest of the documentation—a plastic sleeve inserted in a binder, a pocket in the front or back of a binder, a separate box, a custom envelope, and similar devices. Packaging also refers to the distribution strategy, according to the contents of each book: which books ship with which product or module; which books go to programmers, which go to end users.

Page layout *See* **layout.**

Parallelism   the expression of parallel ideas in a consistent grammatical form.

Parameter   in computers, and depending on its context, an **option, argument,** or limit.

Pass *See* **editorial review.**

Passive voice   in grammar, when the subject of the sentence is acted upon. *Contrast with* **active voice.** The passive voice makes sentences wordier, clumsier, and dull. The passive voice focuses on the action, not the doer of the action. Use the passive voice sparingly, deliberately, and cautiously, only when it serves your purposes better than the active voice. Use the passive voice when the subject of the sentence is unknown, when you intend to be evasive about who is performing an action (a bureaucratic or political ploy), or when the doer of the action is completely irrelevant.

Pasteup   the act of fastening **typography** and artwork into page **layout** for reproduction.

Pathname   the name of a computer **file** that includes the names of the **directories** above it.

PE   *See* **printer's error.**

Peer edit   a writer's **editorial review** of another writer's **manuscript.**

Photocomposition   typesetting by means of light, as opposed to hot metal or typewriter methods.

Phototypesetter   a machine that composes type by emitting a light through a film matrix of type (a **font**) onto light-sensitive paper or film.

Point page   in an **addendum,** a page to be inserted between two existing pages. Its number is based on the page it follows. For example, point page 3-2.1 follows page 3-2. *See also* **A page.**

Policy edit   an **editorial review** to ensure that the document does not conflict with the company's policies. Used synonymously with **developmental edit,** but could also be considered a subset of a complete developmental edit.

Preface   the author's introduction to the book, which tells about the making of and use of the book itself. The preface does not delve into the subject of the book. *Contrast with* **foreword.**

Preliminary edit   an **editorial review** that takes place early in the writing process. Its purpose is to identify potential problems or to point out style changes that affect the entire document.

Press proof   a sample run of a publication through the printing presses for checking ink (color and other characteristics) and other details. Technological improvements are providing less costly and more efficient proofs.

Printer's error   in **composition,** a typographical error. In printing, a technical error made by the printer, such as an error in **imposition** or **color separation.** Commonly called a **PE.** *See also* **author's alteration.**

Procedure   writing that tells how to do something, usually with no more information about the subject than the user needs to perform the task at hand. *See also* **task-oriented.**

Process guide   a departmental or company handbook that defines how things get done and who does them.

Product development cycle the process through which a company plans, designs, builds, manufactures, maintains, and abandons a product.

Production the part of the bookmaking process that takes place after the writing: **composition, pasteup,** and printing. In **desktop** and **electronic publishing,** many of the traditional production steps occur concurrently with the writing.

Production coordinator a person who serves as the liaison between the people "writing" the book (writer, editor, publications management) and those involved in manufacturing (purchasing, printing, binding, packaging for shipping) and distributing it.

Production edit a **final edit** before the document goes to the print vendor, to ensure that the package is complete and ready. A final edit can be performed before **typesetting** or before printing (or both); a production edit commonly refers to the final check before printing. *See also* **format edit.**

Production editor job title for a person who marks up a manuscript with format codes for **typesetting.** Sometimes used synonymously with **production coordinator.** Sometimes used to describe a person whose editorial responsibilities are limited to **production edits.**

Program a set of instructions to the computer.

Prompt a symbol or text by which a computer tells the user it is ready for more input.

Proofread to compare typed or typeset copy against an original and to mark any discrepancies. Also, to check a **manuscript** for typographical errors.

Proofreader a person who proofreads.

Proofs an impression or test sheet used for checking the book at different stages of production. For example, there is the **galley proof** for checking **composition,** page proof for checking the **page layout, salts** for checking the page **imposition, press proof** for checking the ink colors, color keys for checking color process jobs, Cromalin (a brand name) for checking the **color separation,** and many other types of proofs.

Proportional space in typography, a typeface in which the width of a character depends on its letter form. For example, the letter *l* would be thinner than the letter *m*. Also called *variable-width*. *Contrast with* **monospace.**

Pseudocode the steps of a computer **program** in English, before the programmer translates it into a computer language. Analogous to a flowchart in function, namely, to show the logical flow of a program.

Punctuation use of punctuation marks.

Query a question from an editor to a writer or from a proofreader to the writer and/or editor.

Quick reference a brief, handy summary of information explained in detail elsewhere (in another book or another part of the same book). Quick reference information can be presented in a variety of forms, such as a pocket-size card, a booklet, a plastic **template,** or a poster.

Recto an odd-numbered (right-hand) page. *See also* **verso.**

Reference   describes **documentation** designed for quick, random-access use. Find the page, find the topic, find the answer. *Contrast with* **conceptual** and **task-oriented.**

Reference page   a page that contains **reference** information, usually with **index slugs** or other **navigational tools** to facilitate finding information. A reference page contains a summary of the feature or **command** and tells all the pertinent facts a reader needs or wants, usually without digressing into **task-oriented** and **conceptual** information.

Reproducible boards   *See* **mechanicals**. Also called *reproducible masters, repro*, or *repros*.

Reserved word   in computers, a word that cannot be used in a **program** other than in its predefined meaning. For example, a reserved word cannot be used as a **variable** name.

Review   *See* **editorial review.**

Revise   to amend or update a publication.

Revision   a new edition of a publication, with new or changed information. A straight reprinting of a book to replenish the inventory does not constitute a revision.

Rule   a line used for graphic effect. A rule produced by **typesetting** is measured in points; hand-drawn rules are identified by the size pen (00, 0, 1, etc.) used to draw them. The thickness of a rule is its **weight.**

Running foot   in page **layout,** text at the bottom of every page which identifies the book, part, chapter, or section. *See also* **footer; running head.**

Running head   in page layout, text at the top of every page which identifies the book, part, chapter, or section. *See also* **header; running foot.**

Salts   a printer's prepress, photographic proof showing the **imposition** in offset printing. Also called *blues, bluelines, blueprints, Dylux* (a brand name), and *vandykes* (which are brown instead of blue, but serve the same purpose).

Sans serif   a **typeface** without the short lines at the ends of the main strokes of letters, such as this. *Contrast with* **serif.**

Scale   to determine the reduction or enlargement of material (text, art, photograph) to be reproduced. *Contrast with* **crop.**

Screen   in computers, the only part of the monitor worth looking at. In printing, a process by which a continuous-tone image is converted into a series of uniformly spaced dots.

Screening edit   *See* **copy edit.**

Section   a subdivision of a chapter.

Serif   a **typeface** with short lines at the ends of the main strokes of some letters. *Contrast with* **sans serif.**

A serif typeface:
ABCDEFGHIJKLMNOPQRSTUVWXYZabcdefghijklmnopqrstuvwxyz

A sans serif typeface:
ABCDEFGHIJKLMNOPQRSTUVWXYZabcdefghijklmnopqrstuvwxyz

SI   a system of measurement, formulated by international agreement, in which units are based on natural constants or derived from scientific formulas. The name is an abbreviation of Système International D'Unités (International System of Units). The SI system is not the traditional, eighteenth-century metric system, but is derived from it.

Sidebar   text that accompanies the main story.

Signature   a sheet of a book that has been printed and folded but not yet bound.

Smothered verb   *See* **nominalization.**

Software   a **program** that runs on a computer.

Source code   in computers, a **program** in the form the programmer writes it (a form that humans can read if they know the computer language). Source code is converted (by programs called *compilers* or *assemblers*) into *object code,* the *machine language* that the computer uses (and that people don't).

Spec   as a noun, **specification(s)**. As a verb, to specify, as in *to spec type.*

Specification(s)   a detailed written description of a product.

Standards   the conventions in use in an organization, discipline, or industry. In the context of editorial standards, synonymous with **house style**.

Stickup   *See* **dialog box.**

Stock   in printing, paper (or other material to print on).

String   a collection of letters, numbers, or symbols treated as a single unit, such as *abcd* or *wolf* or *3DogNight* or *w!#34Gx%.*

Stub   the left column of a table, which identifies the topics covered in the table.

Style   the means of expression. *See also* **house style.**

Style edit   *See* **literary edit.**

Style guide   a handbook for making decisions about style or a book that prescribes the **house style.**

Style sheet   an editor's personal, quick reference for making style decisions for a particular document.

Subordination   a writing technique that relegates the less important ideas to an appropriately lesser position in a sentence.

Subsection   a division of a section. A chapter is divided into sections, which are divided into subsections.

Substantive edit   an **editorial review** used to mean a thorough **copy edit,** a **language edit,** or both.

Syntax   in computers, the grammar of a **command** or of the statements in a programming language.

Syntax definition   in computers, a summary of the components of a **command** or programming statement.

System software   the programs that individually and collectively enable the computer itself to work and to run **application software.** End users typically use system software only to access and use applications. *Contrast with* **application software.**

Tab   a divider page, usually printed on heavy index stock.

Table   a matrix of data.

Table of contents   the list of topics, in the order they appear, usually at the beginning of the book. *Contrast with* **index.**

Target audience   the people the writer intends to write for.

Task   in project management, an activity, such as a **copy edit,** that is performed over a period of time. *Contrast with* **milestone.** The copy editing pass is a task, but the deadline for handing the manuscript to the editor and the deadline for the editor to return the manuscript are milestones.

Task-oriented   describes writing that is procedural. *See* **procedure.** *Contrast with* **conceptual** and **reference.**

Technical editing   the job performed by a **technical editor.**

Technical editor   read this book for a complete explanation; chapters 1–5 tell about the technical editor's role, chapters 6–12 tell about the technical editor's job, and chapters 13–16 tell about the technical editor's career.

Technical review   a critique of a document for technical accuracy by technical experts, usually the engineers and scientists who developed the product. For documents written by experts, a review by the author's peers. *Contrast with* **editorial review.**

Technical writing   writing, in an objective style, about technical subjects, for a specific audience, to serve a stated purpose. *See also* **documentation.**

Template   in **desktop** or **electronic publishing,** a set of design elements that can be reused from publication to publication to ensure consistency. In manufacturing, a die-cut overlay, usually made from plastic or a heavy paper stock.

Testing plan   a program for testing the accuracy and **usability** of a product (including the **documentation**).

Text head   *See* **heading/heads.**

Text image area   the portion of the page that prints, excluding the **header** and **footer.** *Contrast with* **image area.**

Text wrap   the continuation of text onto a second line. The text for a bulleted list is often set to wrap as a **hanging indent.**

TOC   acronym for **table of contents.** Usually pronounced *tee-oh-cee,* sometimes *tok.*

Trademark   a name, symbol, word, or group of words that identifies a specific product of a particular company.

Traditional publishing   in this book, bookmaking performed by professional graphic designers, illustrators, layout artists, and **compositors** or **typesetters.** *Contrast with* **desktop publishing.**

Triage   the sorting of and allocation of treatment to patients and esp. battle and disaster victims according to a system of priorities designed to maximize the number of survivors (*Webster's Ninth New Collegiate Dictionary*). Triage means not wasting time on patients who have a negligible chance of surviving or who will survive without treatment. In editing, triage means concentrating on what is important to your customers. Triage also means not wasting time fixing minor nits in a book that needs a major overhaul.

Trim size   the size of the pages after the paper has been trimmed. (The pages are trimmed after printing.)

Turn page   *See* **broadside.**

Tutorial   writing that teaches how to do something, step-by-step.

Tweak   in engineering, to fine-tune.

Typeface   a design of type, with all the letters, numbers, and punctuation marks. Examples of typefaces are Baskerville, Garamond, Goudy, and Helvetica. *Contrast with* **font.**

Typesetter   a machine for setting type or the person who composes type on a **phototypesetter.**

Typesetting   setting copy into type. A method of **composition.**

Typo   a typographical error or misprint.

Typography   the art of designing and using type.

UNIX   an operating system developed by Bell Laboratories which is emerging as a standard for computers in the 1990s. A registered trademark of UNIX System Laboratories Inc.

Update page   an insert page. *See also* **addendum.**

Usability   a goal in product development that the product works as planned, its design reflects its use, and it is easy to learn to use.

Usability edit   an **editorial review** to ensure that the product and **documentation** work together correctly and satisfy the users' informational needs.

Usage   conventional practice; in writing, includes matters such as the difference between *that* and *which*; whether a verb is transitive or intransitive; whether *gas* is slang for *gasoline*; whether the plural of appendix is appendixes or appendices. The conventions that vary from one region to another (British vs. American) or that change (words once considered slang that gain respectability over time).

U.S. Customary   the system of measurement, derived from the British Imperial System, that uses randomly related units, such as feet, inches, and pounds. The measurement system in common use in the United States.

User advocate   a person who actively represents the customer's interests in product development. Good writers and editors are user advocates.

User input   the information the user gives to the computer **program.**

User interface   the part of a computer **program** that the user sees and interacts with.

Value   in computers, a specific number, letter, or **string** that a **variable** or **argument** represents.

Vandykes   *See* **salts.**

Variable   a symbolic representation of a location in the computer's memory; its value changes.

Verso   an even-numbered (left-hand) page. *See also* **recto.**

Visuals   *See* **graphics.**

Voice   in grammar, the distinction between the subject performing the action (**active voice**) and the subject being acted upon (**passive voice**).

W/E   acronym for writer/editor. Used to mark a **query** from a member of the production staff to the writer and/or the editor.

Weight   the thickness of a **rule**. Here are samples of different weight rules:

Weighted decimal system   *See* **decimalization.**

Widow   a single word or line at the top of a page, to be avoided. *See also* **orphan.**

Writer/editor   a title given to writers in companies that don't know what editing is; a title given in companies that pay below-average salaries for writers.

Writing freeze   the date that the writer is supposed to stop writing and hand off the **manuscript,** usually to the editor.

Bibliography

Editing

Boston, Bruce O., ed. *STET! Tricks of the Trade for Writers and Editors.* Alexandria, Virginia: Editorial Experts, Inc., 1986. [A collection of interesting readings from *The Editorial Eye,* a newsletter on publications standards and practices.]

Editorial Experts, Inc. *The Editorial Eye.* [An excellent newsletter. For more information, contact Editorial Experts, Inc., 66 Canal Center Plaza, Suite 200, Alexandria, Virginia 22314–1538.]

Judd, Karen. *Copyediting: A Practical Guide,* 2d ed. Los Altos, California: Crisp Publications, Inc., 1990. [A good overview of what editors should know about grammar, compounding, punctuation, usage, and manuscript preparation.]

Plotnick, Arthur. *The Elements of Editing: A Modern Guide for Editors and Journalists.* New York: Macmillan Publishing Company, 1982. [Worth reading if only for chapter 1, "The Editorial Personality: Good and Bad Compulsiveness."]

Stoughton, Mary. *Substance & Style: Instruction and Practice in Copyediting.* Alexandria, Virginia: Editorial Experts, Inc., 1989. [The best book available for copyediting details—how to mark up a manuscript, review of grammar for editors. Excellent exercises.]

Grammar and Usage

Bernstein, Theodore M. *The Careful Writer: A Modern Guide to English Usage.* New York: Atheneum Publishers, 1965. [Sensible advice on usage. Modern but not permissive. Witty.]

Bernstein, Theodore M. *Miss Thistlebottom's Hobgoblins: The Careful Writer's Guide to the Taboos, Bugbears, and Outmoded Rules of English Usage.* New York: Farrar, Straus & Giroux, 1971. [Exposes the superstitions of supposed purists. Recognizes that language evolves.]

Nicholson, Margaret. *A Practical Style Guide for Authors and Editors.* New York: Holt, Rinehart and Winston, 1967. [A good review of the basics. Out of print, but check your library. Outdated information on copyright law and book production. Worth tracking down for the chapter on "Punctuation Pitfalls," which has excellent examples.]

Schertzer, Margaret. *The Elements of Grammar.* New York: Macmillan Publishing Company, 1986. [An excellent review of grammatical details. Good examples.]

Graphic Arts, Printing, and Bookmaking

Beach, Mark, Steve Shepro, and Ken Russon. *Getting It Printed: How to Work with Printers and Graphic Arts Services to Assure Quality, Stay on Schedule, and Control Costs.* Portland, Oregon: Coast to Coast Books, 1986. [Good insider advice for editors who buy printing.]

Greenfield, Howard. *Books from Writer to Reader.* New York: Crown Publishers, 1976. [If you're new to publishing, read it for a good, nontechnical overview of the bookmaking process. A little out of date, but knowing the "old" ways helps more than hinders.]

International Paper Company. *Pocket Pal,* 12th ed. New York: International Paper Company, 1979. [Everything you ever wanted to know about printing technology, explained in lay terms. Revised every few years.]

Lee, Marshall. *Bookmaking: The Illustrated Guide to Design/Production/Editing,* 2d ed. New York: R.R. Bowker Company, 1979. [Everything you ever wanted to know about publishing, with many examples. Full of useful details and practical advice. A handsome, well-written book for beginners and veterans.]

Lem, Dean Phillip. *Graphics Master 4,* 4th ed. Los Angeles: Dean Lem Associates, 1988. [A tool kit in book form. An assortment of reference material on printing (inks, papers, processes) and typography (including electronic composition and imaging). Planning aids and tools include a pica ruler, proportional scale wheel, samples of halftone screens and styles. A real grab bag of good stuff for editors who have to do pasteup.]

White, Jan V. *Graphic Design for the Electronic Age.* New York: Xerox Press, Watson-Guptill, 1988. [Typography, page design, and book packaging for traditional and desktop publishing. Lists common publishing terms in seven European languages.]

Human Factors and Online Documentation

Horton, William K. *Designing and Writing Online Documentation: Help Files to Hypertext.* New York: John Wiley & Sons, 1990. [The best book on online documentation in print today.]

Laurel, Brenda, ed. *The Art of Human-Computer Interface Design.* Reading, Massachusetts: Addison-Wesley Publishing Company, 1990. [An excellent anthology.]

Norman, Donald A. *The Design of Everyday Things.* New York: Doubleday, 1990. Originally published as *The Psychology of Everyday Things* by Basic Books, 1988. [Read this book. You will never again look at a telephone, a door, or a stove without contemplating its design.]

Rubinstein, Richard, and Harry M. Hersh. *The Human Factor: Designing Computer Systems for People.* Bedford, Massachusetts: Digital Press, 1984. [Written for programmers, but in nontechnical language. Examples show old technology, but the principles are still valid.]

Simpson, Henry, and Steven M. Casey. *Developing Effective User Documentation: A Human Factors Approach.* New York: McGraw-Hill Book Company, 1988. [User documentation from a human factors, not technical writing, perspective. Interesting examples. Better for experienced writers and editors than for beginners.]

Indexing

Borko, H., and C. L. Bernier. *Indexing Concepts and Methods.* New York: Academic Press, 1978. [Comprehensive reference for all details of indexing.]

Cleveland, Donald B., and Ana D. Cleveland. *Introduction to Indexing and Abstracting.* Littleton, Colorado: Libraries Unlimited, 1983. [Covers all kinds of indexes, not just for books.]

Style Guides

Skillin, Marjorie E., Robert M. Gay, and other authorities. *Words into Type,* 3d ed. Englewood Cliffs, New Jersey: Prentice-Hall, 1974. [Full of useful information, especially for typesetting details.]

Strunk, William Jr., and E. B. White. *The Elements of Style,* 3d ed. New York: Macmillan Publishing Company, 1979. [A must own. Read it every year.]

United States Government Printing Office. *Style Manual.* Washington, D.C.: United States Government Printing Office, 1984. [A *must* for government contracts, but if you have a choice, use *The Chicago Manual of Style.*]

The University of Chicago Press. *The Chicago Manual of Style,* 13th ed. Chicago: University of Chicago Press, 1982. [Buy it. Read it. Use it. It will save you hundreds of hours a year. Also has a great index.]

Technical Writing

Brockmann, R. John. *Writing Better Computer User Documentation: From Paper to Online.* New York: John Wiley & Sons, Version 2.0, 1990. [Read this after you've had some experience in technical publishing.]

Brusaw, Charles T., Gerald J. Alred, and Walter C. Oliu. *Handbook of Technical Writing,* 3d ed. New York: St. Martin's Press, 1987. [A good all-around reference book.]

Burnett, Rebecca E. *Technical Communication,* 2d ed. Belmont, California: Wadsworth Publishing Company, 1986. [A good beginner's text.]

Price, Jonathan. *How to Write a Computer Manual: A Handbook of Software Documentation.* Menlo Park, California: Benjamin/Cummings Publishing Company, 1984. [A *must* if you work in the computer industry. The only book about technical writing I've bought with my own money. Well worth owning.]

Writing (Nontechnical) and Communication

Flesch, Rudolf. *How to Write, Speak, and Think More Effectively.* New York: Signet, 1960 (reprint of Harper & Row publication). [Good for getting back to basics.]

Flesch, Rudolf, and A.H. Lass. *A New Guide to Better Writing.* New York: Popular Library, 1963. Originally published as *The Way to Write* by Harper & Brothers, 1947. [Mostly about business writing. I'd recommend any of Flesch's books to engineers who ask for a good review of basic writing skills.]

Vachon, Brian. "What Have You Done to My ~~Verbiage~~ Words?!" and its companion piece, "The Blue Pencil Blues," *Writer's Digest,* July 1982. [Wonderful articles about the editing process from both the writer's and editor's perspectives.]

Watzlawick, Paul. *How Real Is Real?* New York: Vintage Books, Random House, 1977. [Interesting, nontechnical look at communication theory.]

Williams, Joseph M. *Style: Ten Lessons in Clarity and Grace,* 2d ed. Glenview, Illinois: Scott, Foresman and Company, 1981. [Practical advice about writing style. Good exercises.]

Zinsser, William. *On Writing Well: An Informal Guide to Writing Nonfiction,* 4th ed. New York: HarperCollins Publishers, 1990. [A must read. How to write and rewrite.]

Zinsser, William. *Writing to Learn.* New York: Harper & Row, 1988. [Examples in this book prove that good science writing is possible. He gives examples from many disciplines, including geology, biology, and mathematics.]

Other

Editorial Experts, Inc. *The 1991–1992 Directory of Editorial Resources.* Alexandria, Virginia: Editorial Experts, Inc., 1991. [Published every two years. Lists books, periodicals, courses, professional organizations, grammar hotlines, and other resources. Not specific to technical editing, but still useful.]

Fuller, Edmund, ed. *2500 Anecdotes for All Occasions.* New York: Avenel Books, 1980. [When you need a funny story to make a point and you don't have a tale of your own that you dare to tell.]

Kirkman, John. "How 'Friendly' Is Your Writing for Readers Around the World." In *Text, Context, and Hypertext,* edited by Edward Barrett. Cambridge, Massachusetts: The MIT Press, 1988. [Many good examples on writing for an international audience.]

Tidewater Community College Writing Center. *The Grammar Hotline Directory.* [Published annually. For each free copy of the directory, send a stamped (first-class postage), self-addressed business-letter-size envelope to Grammar Hotline Directory, Tidewater Community College Writing Center, 1700 College Crescent, Virginia Beach, VA 23456.]

Tufte, Edward R. *Envisioning Information.* Cheshire, Connecticut: Graphics Press, 1990. [How to use charts, diagrams, graphs, tables, and maps to represent complex data on paper.]

Tufte, Edward R. *The Visual Display of Quantitative Information.* Cheshire, Connecticut: Graphics Press, 1983. [Excellent overview of statistical graphics. Shows how to combine words, pictures, and numbers. Defines excellence and integrity in graphics and tells how to achieve them.]

Van Buren, Robert, and Mary Fran Buehler. *The Levels of Edit,* 2d ed. Arlington, Virginia: Society for Technical Communication, 1991. [For information about membership in the society and its publications, contact the Society for Technical Communication, 901 N. Stuart Street, Suite 304, Arlington, Virginia 22203, (703) 522–4114.]

Index

ethnic slurs, checking at literary edit, 100
examples, 97
   checking at copy and literary edit, 103
   checking at developmental edit, 81
   computer manuals, what users want, 305
   and international audience, 121
   paucity of, 138
   in reference pages, 257
   relevance of, example, 138
   tips, 249–250
exclamation mark, in technical writing, 178
exercises, 12, 13, 32, 33, 108, 129, 131, 136,
     169, 170, 171, 201, 203, 206, 218, 224,
     225, 226, 268, 277, 282, 293, 300, 301, 302, 305
   answers, 407–410
   command reference page, 306
   Pascal programming example, 293–295
     answer, 296
exponent, error, example, 155
expression, 91

F

figure captions, 89, 95, 246
figure of speech, example, 147
figures, 243–249. *See also* illustrations
fill patterns, 243
final draft, and publishing process, 68–70
final edit. *See* production edit
first draft, and publishing process, 68–70
flowchart
   continued onto another page, 247
   for procedure, 230
   and pseudocode, 297
folio
   checking at production edit, 113
   illustrated, 94
   on turn page (broadside), 246
footer
   checking at copy and literary edit, 93
   checking at production edit, 113
   illustrated, 94
   on turn page (broadside), 246
format, 167
   checking at copy and literary edit, 92–94

format edit, JPL, 163. *See also* production edit
format editor, 6
freelance writers, 59
functional specification, 75
function arguments, conventions, 288
function of, 91

G

generalist vs. specialist, 53
gestalt proofreading, 125
glossary, 83, 211, 213, 260–263, 299
   acronyms and abbreviations, 261–262
   alphabetical order, 261
   capitalization, 261
   cross-references, 262–263
   definitions, 262
   and international audience, 120
goals, 340–341, 343–344
Gourmet magazine, 27
grammar, 209–210
   books about, 432
   checking at copy and literary edit, 91
   checking at copy edit, 88
   hotline, 210
   litmus test, 210
   tips, 210
graphic arts, 70, 318
   books about, 432–433
   editor's knowledge of, 215–216, 334
graphic designer, 129
graphics
   errors, examples, 156–157
   statistical, books about, 436
grouping, in computer commands, 286

H

Harte, Bret, 333
header
   checking at copy and literary edit, 93
   illustrated, 94
heads, 268–271
   checking in computer reference pages, 305
help, 309–310

italics
  in computer commands, 284
  for substitutable parameters, examples, 281
  for symbolic values, examples, 282

J

jargon, 175, 177
  checking at literary edit, 100
  in end-user documentation, 304, 305
  and international audience, 120
  software, 276–280
  tips, 211–212
job-hunting, 349–361
job title
  of editors, 5–9, 12–13
  on resume, 350
joystick, 299
JPL (Jet Propulsion Laboratory), types of edit, 162–164

K

keys (computer), example, 140
keyword, 279
  case correct, 180
Kirkman, John, 121
KornShell conventions, examples, 282

L

language
  and culture, 121
  inappropriate, example, 155
  sexist, 155
language edit, JPL, 163. *See also* literary edit
Larousse, 28
lawyers, working with, 77
layout
  checking at copy and literary edit, 92
  checking at production edit, 112–113
  editor's knowledge of, 215–216
legal considerations, 26, 77, 85, 97, 158
levels of edit, 98–99, 161–173
  books about, 436
  exclusions, 164
  informal approach, 165
  JPL (Jet Propulsion Laboratory), 162–164

and schedule for copy edit, 89
  triage, 165–172
  and types of editorial reviews, 87
  uses of, 162
libel, 26, 85, 100, 158
like vs. *as*, example, 142
line breaks, checking at production edit, 112
lists, 216–223
  checking, 216, 220
  consistency of, examples, 219, 220
  fast retrieval of data, 216
  horizontal vs. vertical, 216, 218
  parallelism, 218–223
  punctuation, 222, 223
  and style guide, 196
  tabular, vs. tables, 242
  types of, 217
literals, 279, 286
  caveat, 287
  conventions, examples, 281, 282
literary edit, 7, 87–108
  vs. copy edit, 98–100
  priority of, 344
  and product development process, 71–73
  and publishing process, 68–70
literary editor, 7
logic errors, example, 133
lowercase. *See* case

M

magic, 107, 135
  checking at literary edit, 100
managing
  balancing workload, 360
  describing editing job on interview, 359–360
  editing tests, 357
  evaluating editing samples, 356–358
  hiring editors, 349, 355–360
  retaining editors, 360
manual pages (man pages), 310–311. *See also* reference pages
manuals, updating strategies, 250–253
manuscript
  completeness of at developmental edit, 78–79
  condition of and schedule for copy edit, 89
  desktop vs. traditional, 326–332

noun strings (*continued*)
    example, 143
    and international audience, 121
numbered list, example, 217
numbers
    error, example, 155
    and international audience, 121, 122

O

objective of book, in doc spec, 75
octal, conventions, 288
office, neatness of, 346
offset printing, 127
one (1), confusion with el (l), 297
online documentation, 68, 283, 367
    books about, 433
    color blindness, 308
    copy edit of, 307
    copyright notices, 291
    defined, examples, 307
    demos, 307–309
    and doc spec, 75
    help, 309–310
    manual pages, 310–311
    navigational aids, 308
    and time, 308
    tips, 307–311
    transitions, 308
    tutorials, 307–309
    visual effects, 308
online help, 309–310
options, 277, 278, 281
organization, 24
    checking at copy and literary edit, 92
    checking at developmental edit, 76, 81, 82–83
    of information in lists, 217
    of information in tables, 233–236
        for users with different needs, 234–236
    international audience and, 122
    notes, symptomatic of problems, 82
    poor, example, 138, 139
    techniques, 83
    tips, 212–213
organization edit. *See* developmental edit
outline. *See also* doc spec
    and developmental edit, 74–76

and doc spec, 75
    importance of, 76
output
    conventions, 286–287
    tips, 298

P

page elements, 94
page layout, checking at production edit, 108, 112–113
page numbers, 106, 113
page size, international, 122
pagination
    checking at production edit, 115
    checking in index, 266
    point page, 252–253
    replacement pages, 251–253
paper
    international sizes, 122
    weight, 102
parallelism
    checking at copy and literary edit, 92, 95
    error, example, 139, 140, 150, 151–152
    of lists, 218–223
    of text heads, 268–269
parameters, 279–280, 284
parentheses
    in computer commands, 286, 288
    for function arguments, 288
    in technical writing, 178
part numbers, checking at copy and literary edit, 91
parts list, checking at usability edit, 107
Pascal examples, 282, 293–296
passive voice, 98, 100, 135, 144
pasteup, 108–109, 318
peer editing, 5, 15, 16–18, 34, 43–44
    difficulty of, 98
percent error, example, 153–154
period
    in computer examples, 290
    missing, 148
    in technical writing, 178
perspective, 98

proofreading (*continued*)
   shortcuts, 117, 124–127, 272, 273
   and technology, 124
proportional typeface, vs. monospace, 292
pseudocode, 297–298
publication history, in doc spec, 75
publishing process. *See also* desktop publishing,
    traditional publishing
   conventions, 175–176
   desktop, 320–321
   desktop vs. traditional, 318–324
   editorial reviews, 68–70
   interactions, 325–326
   manuscript preparation, 329–332
   marking manuscript, 326–328
   Murphy's Laws of, 183
   production edit, 108–109
   proofreading, 123–127
   and technology, 321–324
punctuation. *See also names and symbols of*
    individual marks
   checking at copy and literary edit, 91
   checking at copy edit, 88
   and computer commands, 289–290
   in computer manuals, 283–291
   error, example, 148
   inconsistency, example, 157
   of lists, 196
   rules vs. technical accuracy, 177–179

Q

quad, 217
qualifiers, inappropriate, example, 147
quality
   cost of, 38
   and effort, 166
   vs. schedules, 10
questionnaires, for usability testing, 105
questions, dumb, 61
quotation marks, 178
   ambiguity in computer documentation, 181
   and computer commands, 289–290
   computer manuals, 287
   double quotes vs. single quotes, 181
   inappropriate, example, 147
   for literal text, 287
   in technical writing, 178, 179

R

racist language, 98
ratio, writers to editors, 353
readability, checking at literary edit, 100
Red Sox, 119, 124, 335
redundancy, example, 138, 142
reference, as verb, 177
reference manual, 169. *See also* reference pages
   editing quickly, 213
   tips for editing, 214
reference pages, 253–260
   checking at developmental edit, 82
   completeness, 254, 257
   computer manuals, 305–306
   cross-references to, 260
   editing separately, 88–89
   examples, 255–256, 258–260
   manual pages, 310–311
   purpose of, 253
   shortcuts for editing, 214, 254
remember, misuse of, example, 139
replacement pages, 251–253
repro. *See* camera-ready copy
reproducible masters. *See* camera-ready copy
resume, 350–351, 355–356
review. *See* editorial review, technical review
reviewers, and doc spec, 75
revision, 81, 250, 253
revision bars, 250
risks, and doc spec, 75
rules (conventions), 175–184
rules (lines)
   checking at copy and literary edit, 95
   checking at production edit, 113
   example of 1-pt vs. 0.5-pt, 167
running heads
   checking at production edit, 113
   usability testing, 106
run-on sentence, example, 146

S

salts, 127–129
  priority of, 128, 344
  publishing process and, 68–70
schedule, 28, 321–324
  copy and literary edit, 88–90
  developmental edit, 77, 78–79
  and doc spec, 75
  and editorial reviews, 170–172
  estimating, 169
  micromanaging, 345, 346
  and production edit, 110
  vs. quality, 10
screening edit, JPL, 163. *See also* copy edit,
  literary edit
screens, checking at copy and literary edit, 103
semicolon, in technical writing, 178
sentence
  beginning with lowercase term, 180
  construction, checking at literary edit, 100
  run-on, example, 146
  structure
    checking at copy and literary edit, 88
    and international audience, 120–121
sequence
  checking, 92, 103, 112
  editing sequence-critical information, 213
  error, example, 154
  poor, example, 139
serif vs. sans serif, example, 155
sexist language, 98, 100, 155
shortcuts
  for editing reference manual, 214
  proofreading, 117, 124–127, 272
  speed editing, 213–214
  with triage, 165–172
should, example, 146
SI, 223
signatures, 127
sign-offs, checking at production edit, 115
simply, misuse of, example, 139
single-width typeface. *See* monospace
slang, and international audience, 120
slash (/), example, 142
software. *See also* computer manuals
  bugs, 107

indexing, 266–267
and proofreading, 124
publishing, 334–335, 364–366
terms, defined, 276–280
source code, defined, 291
specifications, 75, 158, 223–226
spelling
  checking at copy and literary edit, 88, 91
  of literals, 287
  programming examples, 291
spelling checker, 6, 124, 335, 364–366
staffing, writer-to-editor ratio, 353
standards
  and technical writing, 10
  units of measurement, 224
string, defined, 278
style, 76, 199
  checking at copy edit, 87, 88
  checking at developmental edit, 77, 84
  checklist, 100
  for end-user documentation, 304
  and publishing process, 68–70
  writer's prerogative, 98–99
style guide, 175–176, 182, 185–207
  abbreviations, 196
  Apollo Computer, 393, 394–396
  arbitrary decisions, 200, 203
  Bull HN Information Systems, 393, 398–406
  caveat for production standards, 203
  controversial issues, 195–197, 200
  as cost saver, 187
  decision making, 199–200, 204–205
  and editing portfolio, 358
  enforcement, 88, 92, 205
  errors in, examples, 204
  examples, 201, 393–406, 434
  exceptions to, 195–197, 199, 205
  flexibility, 195–197, 198–199, 204–205
  general-purpose, 186
  Hewlett-Packard, 393, 397
  house, 186–187
  organization of, 201
  process for changing, 205
  vs. process guide, 206
  purpose of, 186–187
  recommendations vs. requirements, 202
  typographical display of information, 196

user interface (*continued*)
  international audience and, 122
  terminology, 299
  tips, 312
users, differences among, 303–304
user vs. *you*, example, 144

V

vagueness, example, 134
value, defined, 278
Van Buren, Robert, 162, 164
variables, 103, 279
verb
  agreement error, example, 151
  error, example, 148
  smothered, example, 146
vertical bars
  to separate options, examples, 281
  to separate parameters, 286
vocabulary
  checking at developmental edit, 77
  inappropriate, example, 155
Vogue magazine, 355
voice, and international audience, 120

W

warnings, 158. *See also* messages
  checking at developmental edit, 77, 85
warranty, 26, 158
weighted decimal system, in text heads, 270
word choice
  example, 143, 144–145
  and international audience, 120, 121
  writer's prerogative, 98–99
wordiness, example, 141–142, 146

wording, checking at literary edit, 100
word usage,
  books about, 432
  checking at copy and literary edit, 91
  tips, 209–210
work-for-hire, 59
work samples
  evaluating, 356–358
  use in job hunt, 351–353
writer, 47–64
  complaints about editors, 57
  as editor, 13, 59
  vs. editor (skills), 14–16
  as editor's adversary, 52
  nonnative speaker of English, 25
  nonprofessional, 62–63, 192
  number, vs. editors, 353
  sensitivity of, 57–61
  technical expertise of, 101
  testing editor, 55–57, 384–387
  tips for working with editors, 60, 61
writer-to-editor ratio, 353
writing. *See also* technical writing
  books about, 435
  collaborative, 339, 367, 380–382
  vs. editing, 14, 29
  inappropriate, 23–24
  process, and editor, 76

Y

you vs. *user*, example, 144

Z

zero (0), confusion with oh (O), 297
Zero-defect, 38